Acclaim for Robert D. Kaplan's

HOG PILOTS, BLUE WATER GRUNTS

ROBERT D. KAPLAN

HOG PILOTS, BLUE WATER GRUNTS

Robert D. Kaplan is a correspondent for *The Atlantic Monthly* and the author of eleven previous books on foreign affairs and travel, which have been translated into many languages. These books include *Imperial Grunts*, *Balkan Ghosts*, *Warrior Politics*, and *The Coming Anarchy*. He is the Class of 1960 Distinguished Visiting Professor in National Security at the United States Naval Academy.

HOG PILOTS, BLUE WATER GRUNTS

THE AMERICAN MILITARY
IN THE AIR, AT SEA,
AND ON THE GROUND

ROBERT D. KAPLAN

VINTAGE DEPARTURES

Vintage Books
A Division of Random House, Inc.
New York

FIRST VINTAGE DEPARTURES EDITION, SEPTEMBER 2008

Copyright © 2007 by Robert D. Kaplan
Maps copyright © 2007 by Mapping Specialists, Ltd.

All rights reserved. Published in the United States by Vintage Books,
a division of Random House, Inc., New York, and simultaneously in Canada
by Random House of Canada Limited, Toronto. Originally published in
hardcover in the United States by Random House, an imprint of
the Random House Publishing Group, Inc., a division
of Random House, Inc., New York, in 2007.

Vintage is a registered trademark and Vintage Departures and
colophon are trademarks of Random House, Inc.

The Cataloging-in-Publication Data is on file at the Library of Congress.

Vintage ISBN: 978-1-4000-3458-1

Author photograph © Jerry Bauer
Book design by Casey Hampton

w w w . v i n t a g e b o o k s . c o m

Printed in the United States of America
10   9   8   7   6   5   4   3   2

To John and Martyna Fox

I could have a well-paying job with a company like DuPont, and be home every night. But life is supposed to have meaning. Whenever I'm ready to collapse on the bridge at 3 a.m., I think of the chiefs' [chief petty officers'] retirement ceremony and the clanging bell that declares, "While others slept, you stood the watch."

—Navy Ensign Zephyr Riendeau of Colebrook, New Hampshire

A sub[marine]'s not a job; it's a way of life. . . . It's easy to mold a sailor into anything you want him to be, because on a sub he can't go anywhere. He's yours.

—Navy Senior Chief Petty Officer Anthony Maestas of Salt Lake City

I was embedded with the 1st Battalion of the 32nd Regiment of the 10th Mountain Division, based out of Fort Drum, New York, and fragged out to the 82nd Airborne Division. That's what I do, that's my identity. I am an Air Force pilot who serves the Army. Providing CAS [close air support] for the 10th Mountain Division was the defining moment of my life. I befriended and loved people, and saw them killed. I was a new captain and there was this very experienced first lieutenant who would never call me anything other than "sir." That does something to you. He had been married for a few weeks and then was killed by an IED [improvised explosive device].

—Air Force Capt. Brandon "Custer" Kelly of Cairo, Georgia

I will fortify the moral high ground. People will attack me with stories about Abu Ghraib and the killing of Filipino civilians a hundred years ago by American troops, actions which I cannot defend. And I will respond that my troops can build a school, or fix a little girl's cleft palate at a MEDCAP [medical civil action program], whereas all the guerrillas of Abu Sayyaf and Jemaah Islamiyah can offer is a suicide vest. I will build my fortress on deeds, because I know that the only force protection I have is the goodwill of civilians. All the guns in the world won't keep an IED from going off.

—Army Col. Jim Linder of Fort Lawn, South Carolina

CONTENTS

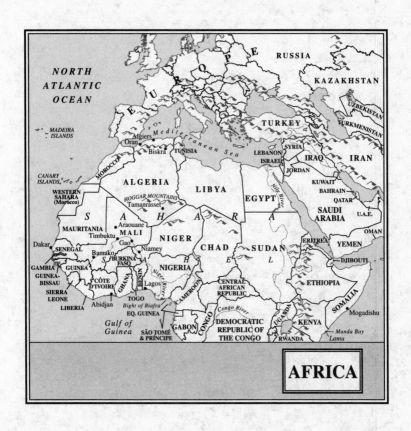

AFRICA

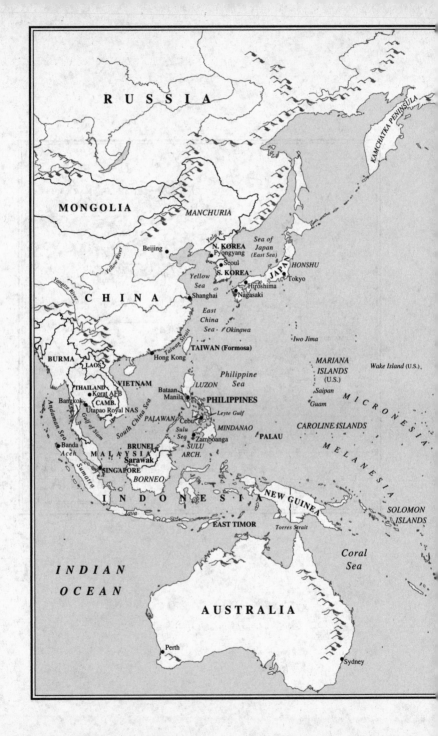

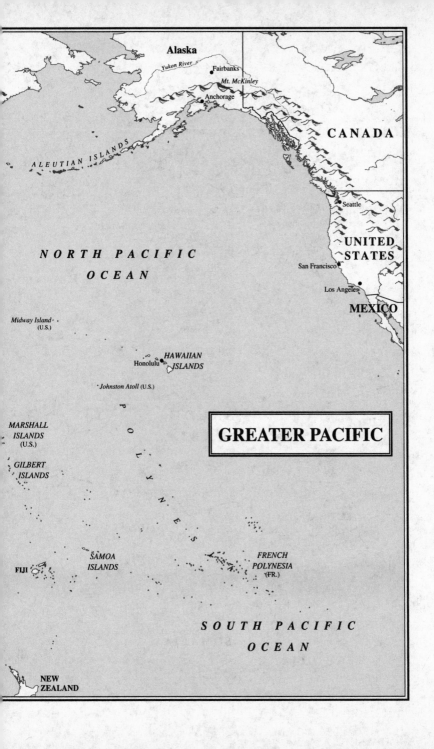

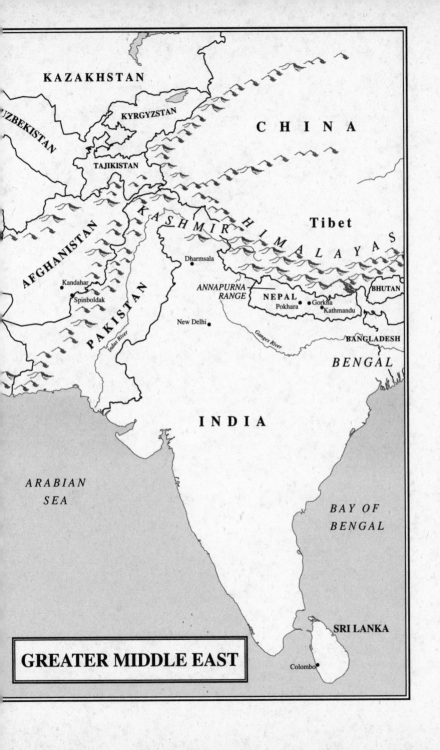

GREATER MIDDLE EAST

HOG PILOTS,
BLUE WATER GRUNTS

THE BETTER THEY FOUGHT, THE BETTER RELIEF WORKERS THEY BECAME

Stage by stage, the USS Benfold, a guided missile destroyer, closed the distance with the USNS Rainier, a fast combat support ship: 9,000 yards, 8,000 yards, until, after fifteen minutes, the $1 billion steel behemoth came alongside a ship of even greater proportions, loaded with fuel and provisions. Only 160 feet of water now separated these two gray armored spirits of the industrial age. There was a deafening holler of wind as a churning funnel of rapids formed between us and the Rainier, the explosions of foam concentrating, it seemed, all the energy of the ocean. One by one, lines were shot across the Benfold's deck from the Rainier and hauled in by "deck apes" and "deck monkeys," the lowest-ranking enlisted sailors, who latched them onto fairleads, pelican hooks, and pulleys. It had begun with a single red string fired by an M-14 rifle, to which a rope was then attached, followed by a cable. Soon gigantic fuel hoses and pallets were sliding from the Rainier across to the Benfold, as deck apes with blue construction helmets and orange vests began a snake dance with the cables that controlled the line tension, so as to carefully "bring in the groceries." A chief petty officer boomed orders over a loudspeaker while another communi-

cated with the Rainier *in whole sentences through signal flags. The world was a roaring black abyss sprinkled with a flurry of glowing yellow lights from the two vessels. It was like a docking in space.*

Few navies in the world could perform an Un-Rep (underway replenishment), which depends less on technology than on sheer seamanship.

Bosun's Mate Chief Andrew Rader of Newark, Ohio, orchestrated the snake dance. "Reconnect the fucking messenger [cable], and stop acting like a fucking girl," he hollered over to a member of his crew, immediately giving a fatherly pat and apology to the female sailor beside him. "I didn't mean that," he told her. He paused for a second only. "Flake the line down, fuckstick. Remove the hook from the ass. Heave!"

was in the Indian Ocean off the coast of Sumatra. It was January 2005 and the *Benfold* had just completed its part in the tsunami relief effort. It was now heading for the Strait of Malacca, to help patrol the world's busiest shipping lane—a choke point crucial to international trade, and hence to globalization itself.

For these sailors, places like Iraq and Afghanistan were at the edge, rather than at the forefront, of their consciousnesses. They and so many others in the U.S. military were busy with the additional responsibilities of a great power—disaster relief, protecting the sea-lanes, training indigenous troops, fighting terrorists on several continents, adapting to the rise of new hegemons, and so on. The two wars in the Middle East might not have been going well, but you would have barely noticed it aboard America's surface warships and submarines, scattered over the world's oceans; or among pilots on deployment from Alaska to Antarctica and many places in between; or among soldiers and marines on small missions across Africa, Asia, and South America. To go from several weeks aboard a submarine in the Pacific with the U.S. Navy to several weeks in the center of the Sahara Desert with the U.S. Army, as I did one time, was normal, given the scope of so many simultaneous operations.

I did not ignore Iraq. But neither was I limited by it.

My travels began in 2002. At first, I had observed counterinsurgency and unconventional war on several continents with Army Special Forces and marines, experiences that formed the basis of an earlier book, *Imperial Grunts.*[1] Back then, I had observed platoon-sized units in South American and Asian jungles, and in Near Eastern deserts. Iraq found me briefly in the thick of urban combat. But for the most part between 2002 and 2004, I observed the bread and butter of imperial maintenance on the ground: the training of indigenous troops, whom U.S. military trainers called "indigs."

Nobody liked the word "imperial." But in terms of the challenges and the frustrations that so many junior officers and enlisted men of the American military faced worldwide, they were in an imperial-like situation, comparable to that of troops of other great powers in centuries past.

My traveling companions mocked and complained, something that soldiers and marines have done since time immemorial. It was unrelated to bad morale: bad morale is only about losing the spirit to fight. They belonged to the combat arms community, a self-selecting elite within the military who fell into two categories: those who were (or had been) deployed to Afghanistan or Iraq, and those who were doing what they could to get there. Rather than fanatics, they were like foreign correspondents whose nightmare was to be left behind at a bureau while a colleague got the nod to cover the latest war or overseas crisis.

When you got to know the world of these infantrymen; got to know, say, the vast differences between an Army major who was a general's aide at a big, rear Burger King–type base and an Army major who was the executive officer (the second-in-command) for an entire battalion at an advanced operating base—a real fighting base, that is; or got to know the differences between a Marine infantry sergeant who commanded twelve men within a platoon and a gunnery sergeant who was the exalted go-to guy (the iron grunt) in a company of 150 men, then from the point of view of any civilian in an age without conscription you were inside a culture as mysterious as any encountered in the far-flung reaches of the globe.

And as I would learn, the Navy and Air Force, owing to the unfamiliar worlds of seamanship and high technology, would turn out to be more exotic still.

You couldn't begin to understand the U.S. military without focusing on noncommissioned officers (NCOs, or noncoms in service lingo)—that is, sergeants and corporals—or chief petty officers in the case of the Navy. It was they who were the repository of the military's culture and traditions, as many a West Pointer or Annapolis graduate would admit. The Prussian baron Friedrich von Steuben, during the 1777–78 winter at Valley Forge, had laid the groundwork for this NCO corps. Thus he provided the bedrock for the American military: the radical decentralization of command, so that the general directive of every officer was broken down into practical steps by sergeants and corporals and petty officers at the farthest edges of the battlefield. Officers gave orders, NCOs got things done.

NCOs were emblematic of American social history. The ever-expanding frontier of western settlement in North America was about doing, not imagining: clearing land, building shelters, obtaining food supplies. Though the family farm was dying across the continent, almost half of the sergeants in a twelve-man Army Special Forces A-team with which I embedded in Algeria had grown up on family farms. That A-team was typical of others I knew.

NCOs were also a product of America's middle-class society. Observing third world armies, I had seen how the gulf between officers and enlisted men was like that between aristocrats and peasants. But such class distinctions did not exist in the United States to nearly the same degree. The consequence was an NCO corps that dealt confidently with its superiors, so lieutenants revered and depended upon their sergeants. This bond was at the core of a military that got the greatest possible traction out of sometimes the worst possible policies.

The importance of noncoms was magnified by the increasing size and emptying out of the battlefield. Instead of large numbers of troops fighting in a confined space—the essence of mass infantry warfare—small clusters of combatants now lay scattered across vast deserts, jungles, and slum cities. It was a world of platoons, squads, and teams: a world of NCOs, who worked at the lowest tactical level, where operational success or failure is determined. In Iraq, noncoms had a 40 percent higher mortality rate than officers. And among officers, the highest mortality rate was among lieutenants who led platoons composed of noncoms and enlisted men.[2]

In an age when field troops were scrutinized under media klieg lights, the actions of individual NCOs carried untold political consequences, for better or for worse. Marine Gen. Charles C. Krulak writes, "The individual Marine will be the most conspicuous symbol of American foreign policy."[3] By "individual Marine," read NCO. Two-thirds of all marines were noncommissioned and in their first four-year enlistment. Nearly 90 percent of Army Special Forces soldiers (Green Berets) were sergeants of one grade or another.

These NCOs had their national identities as Americans engraved in sharp bas-relief. Off duty, they were often tight-lipped, except when I asked them about the technical task at hand. Then they couldn't stop talking. Ask them what they do, not how they feel, I had to constantly remind myself. Only after I got to know them would they tell me how they felt—how deeply they felt—and only if I didn't ask.

———

"Men of action are the unwitting slaves of men of intellect," observes the early-twentieth-century Portuguese poet Fernando Pessoa.[4] Pessoa's categories may be too grand and too neat, but there is a core of truth in his observation. It's certainly true that in regard to Iraq, these soldiers and marines had to deal with the consequences of ideas about liberation, occupation, and democracy that were the product mainly of civilians in Washington with or (usually) without experience on the ground. As someone with experience living with and writing about the military, and who privately and publicly supported the invasion of Iraq from the beginning, I was not innocent in this regard. It has been said that the occupation of Iraq was so grotesquely mismanaged that the war was never given a chance to succeed. But it may also be possible that the occupation would have been cursed with even the best of plans. I backed the invasion, despite my published concerns about anarchy in the event of a flawed strategy, in the expectation that a more liberal regime of some stable sort (not necessarily democratic) would ultimately emerge in Iraq. Given current facts, it was the wrong decision. Though, by increasing the leverage of downtrodden Shiites, and thus disturbing the complacency of calcifying Sunni police states in Egypt and Saudi Arabia—as well as turning al-Qaeda against fellow Arabs—the war has created strategic opportunities still to be exploited.

To say that the U.S. military adapted well to this challenge would be an understatement. The crucible of combat, month after month, in Afghanistan and especially in Iraq, in which American troops some- times went from urban street fighting on one day to trying to get water and electricity hooked up the next, invigorated further the character and quality of the armed services, particularly the Army, despite the damage done to it in other ways by the manpower strain that Iraq imposed. And the better the Americans fought, the better relief workers they became, as the Indian Ocean tsunami of December 2004 would demonstrate. For the logistics of humanitarian assistance were similar to the logistics of war: both demanded fast infiltration and the movement of men and equipment to a zone of activity. It was all about access. The official Ma- rine motto might be "Semper Fidelis," but the unofficial one was "Sem- per Gumby," always flexible.

By igniting a long and bloody struggle that no one in the military wanted to repeat, the overreach in Iraq by civilians in Washington spurred men in uniform to want to increasingly manage the world through quiet alliances on one hand and the use of host-country proxies on the other. That, in turn, required greater emphasis on stealth and small units composed of extraordinary individuals, and on austere dirt outposts rather than on big legacy bases that themselves had become the cause of political friction.

The smaller the American military footprint and the less notice it drew from the outside world, the more effective would be the operation. Get in before a problem began to fester, when you had the leeway to ex- periment and make mistakes without suffering a loss of prestige. It was the military side of crisis prevention. The way to avoid future quagmires was to be engaged in more places, not fewer. Whereas a few hundred Special Forces troops as in Colombia and the Philippines could be ef- fective force multipliers, and 20,000 as in Afghanistan could tread water, 150,000 as in Iraq constituted a mess.

Obviously, Iraq could have used many more troops. Once a decision was made to invade and occupy a country, well, then an overwhelming force was preferable. But small, well-chosen numbers remained a practical approach for train-and-equip and stabilization deployments almost everywhere else, in order to minimize the need for large conventional invasions in the first place.

As one general officer in the Pentagon told me, "After Iraq, we hope not to be invading a big country for a long time, so we'll be reduced to low-profile raiding, which the U.S. military has a very long and venerable tradition of from the nineteenth and early twentieth centuries." It was no accident that throughout my travels, officers and NCOs, who inhabited a tactical universe rather than a strategic one, told me that they found more benefit in studying the nineteenth-century Indian Wars in North America than the two world wars combined, for the former had featured mobile attack sequences, quick strikes, and ambushes and skirmishes where combat was a matter of surprise more than of large-scale maneuver.[5] Small-unit combat, again, a world of junior officers and NCOs.

A military was only as good as the courses taught at its staff schools, and a whole generation of officers and enlistees, again especially from the Army, was returning from combat zones in Afghanistan and Iraq with lessons learned to revitalize curriculums. Through it all, through the course of natural disasters like the tsunami and a badly planned occupation, as well as Special Operations deployments in dozens upon dozens of countries, the all-volunteer U.S. military was producing a caste of long-serving veterans who could govern as well as fight, accustomed to both civilian-style management and urban combat. Before 9/11, this military had enjoyed a relatively comfortable, peacetime lifestyle with only certain units sent to dangerous hellholes.* That period in American military history seemed over.

Leon Uris, a former Marine drill instructor, as well as a radio opera-

---

* Michael Vlahos, "Culture's Mask: War & Change After Iraq," Johns Hopkins University, Applied Physics Laboratory, Laurel, Md., 2004. Albeit to a lesser degree, President Bill Clinton also encouraged an expeditionary spirit by frequently deploying the military. Service in the Balkans, despite strict rules of engagement that severely minimized risk, constituted a morale boost compared to interminable training exercises in Germany.

tor during the World War II landings at Guadalcanal and Tarawa, begins his first novel, *Battle Cry,* with a soliloquy by a salty veteran that, in fact, reveals the mindset of America's expeditionary military a half century after he wrote these lines:

> You can best identify me by the six chevrons, three up and three down, and by that row of hashmarks. Thirty years in the United States Marine Corps.
>
> I've sailed the Cape and the Horn aboard a battlewagon with a sea so choppy the bow was awash half the time under thirty-foot waves. I've stood Legation guard in Paris and London and Prague. I know every damned port of call and call house in the Mediterranean and the world that shines beneath the Southern Cross like the nomenclature of a rifle.
>
> I've sat behind a machine gun poked through the barbed wire that encircled the International Settlement when the world was supposed to have been at peace, and I've called Jap bluffs on the Yangtze Patrol a decade before Pearl Harbor.
>
> I know the beauty of the Northern Lights that cast their eerie glow on Iceland and I know the rivers and the jungles of Central America . . . [and] the palms of a Caribbean hellhole.
>
> Yes, I know the slick brown hills of Korea just as the Marines knew them in 1871. Fighting in Korea is an old story for the Corps.[6]

America's global military footprint, as I've indicated, was made up of not only soldiers and marines, but of sailors and airmen, too. Whereas from 2002 through the middle of 2004, the time frame of *Imperial Grunts,* I concentrated mainly on unconventional land forces, this book includes long interludes with the Navy and the Air Force, as well as with the conventional Army. It wasn't just Humvees that I needed to travel inside of, but also destroyers, nuclear submarines, bomber planes, and Stryker combat vehicles.

And whereas the first two years of my travels with the military were usually clustered around the Greater Middle East and its shadow zones (from the Horn of Africa to Afghanistan), the scene in the course of this volume shifts to the Pacific, over which loomed the challenge of a rising China, as well as of a still-divided Korea. Indeed, it seemed that the ultimate strategic effect of the Iraq war might be to speed up the arrival of the Asian Century not just in economic terms, but in military terms, too. While the American government was distracted by Iraq, and Europe's defense establishments continued to be budget-starved, Asian militaries—China's, Japan's, India's, and so forth—were quietly enlarging and modernizing, even as their economic leaders became more and more integrated among themselves and with the rest of the world. If the development of Asian militaries was anything to go by, the Middle East was *now,* the Pacific *the future.*

But I begin the second part of my travels, from 2004 to 2006, with marines in West Africa. Traveling back and forth between Africa and the Pacific quickly would become a pattern for me.

ONE

AMERICA'S AFRICAN RIFLES

WITH A MARINE PLATOON

African Sahel, Summer 2004

I n the early summer of 2004, just as the United States was disman-
tling the Coalition Provisional Authority in Iraq, sending home its
proconsul, L. Paul Bremer III, U.S. Marines and Army Special
Forces were in various stages of deploying to the southern fringe of the
Sahara Desert, the Sahel, one of the few battlegrounds left in the Global
War on Terror for the U.S. military to enter, as it was already deployed
in so many other parts of the world.

Local alliances and the training of indigenous troops have been a
traditional means of projecting power at minimum risk and fanfare.
This was true of Rome even in regard to adjacent North Africa, to say
nothing of its Near Eastern borderlands; and it was particularly true of
France and Britain, two-thirds of whose expeditions were composed of
troops recruited in the colonies.* As Tacitus writes, "We Romans value
real power but disdain its vanities."[1] Taking Tacitus to heart, I went to

---

* See Sallust's *The Jugurthine War*, composed between 44 and 40 B.C., and Douglas Porch's
introduction to the Bison edition of Col. C. E. Callwell's *Small Wars: Their Principles &
Practice* (1896; Lincoln: University of Nebraska, 1996). These are but two examples of a
vast military literature about how imperial powers used their influence.

the Niger River region of the African Sahel, or "coast," a belt of savannah and scrub on the Sahara's southern edge, to witness a version of
America's reach that was radically different from Iraq, certainly more
modest, and hopefully more successful.

Among the great rivers of Africa, after the Nile and the Congo there is
the Niger, which medieval Arab geographers such as Ibn Battuta called
"the Nile of the Negroes." The Niger rises within 492 feet of the Atlantic Ocean in the jungly, mountainous borderland of Guinea and
Sierra Leone and flows northeast into Mali, past the desert caravan centers of Timbuktu and Gao. Then, arcing southeast through Niger and
along the Benin border, it drops down into Nigeria, breaking up into an
immense delta amid the malarial swamps of the Bight of Biafra. The
curvilinear journey of 2,600 miles from the sea deep into the desert, and
back to the sea again, seems almost contrary to the laws of nature.

Herodotus, in the course of his travels in the fifth century B.C., heard
mention of the river. In the vicinity of eastern Libya he was told about a
group of young and adventurous Nasamonians, who lived in nearby
Syrtis along the Mediterranean coast. These Nasamonians had packed a
good supply of food and water and set off into the interior of Libya.
After traveling for many days southwestward through the desert they
came upon a region of sparse vegetation where they were attacked by
black men "of less than middle height," speaking an unintelligible language. These "dwarfs" carried the Nasamonians through a marshy
country whereupon they sighted a "great river with crocodiles" that
"flowed from west to east."[2]

The Niger was no less remote to twenty-first-century Americans
than it had been to the ancient Greeks. It passed through some of the
poorest and most unstable countries in the world. The Sahara Desert
had effectively cut West Africa off from the traffic of peoples, ideas,
and technology that moved between the Mediterranean and Eurasia
from the classical age onward. Islam itself was weakened in the course
of its arduous journey south. The Tuaregs, for example, a Berber people
who began moving south from the central Sahara to the Niger River
about A.D. 1000, were only nominally Muslim. They built few mosques;
few of them made the *haj* to Mecca. Tuareg men wore veils; not Tuareg

women. The word "Tuareg" itself is Arabic for "the abandoned of God." The flowing robes and headdresses of Tuareg warriors recalled not Muslims but medieval Christian knights.[3]

A Tuareg empire grew up around the caravan city of Agadez, only to be conquered by the empire of Songhai. The empires of Songhai and Mali later overlapped near the middle part of the Niger River, the part with which Ibn Battuta was familiar, and where U.S. Marines had recently ensconced themselves.

These medieval imperiums had raised impressive armies and bureaucracies, with their names enduring through the ethnic identities of the inhabitants. Yet given the sleepy underdevelopment that now defined the region, such mighty kingdoms might as well have been ghosts.

By 1900, the French had conquered much of the Sahara and adjacent Sahel. But as other imperial powers had learned and were still to learn, conquest came easily; remolding a difficult terrain in one's image was another matter. The Tuaregs, as though precursors of modern-day Islamic terrorists, faded into the landscape and waited out the occupiers.[4] A century later it would be the region's political and social failure that raised its stature in the eyes of the American military.

Throughout the Sahel were the ingredients that bred terrorists and their sympathizers: large populations of unemployed young men, growing political disaffection, and increasing Islamic orthodoxy.[5] At each end of the Niger were bustling ports with questionable security, coastlines teeming with pirates, and Arab émigré communities with links to international diamond smugglers and terrorist outfits. Sahelian Africa had the two requirements essential for penetration by al-Qaeda and its offshoots: collapsing institutions and cultural access afforded by an Islamic setting.

The Salafist Group for Preaching and Combat, which boasted links to al-Qaeda, had amassed weapons and vehicles in Mali for use in Algeria. With the help of U.S. Navy surveillance aircraft, it was pushed out of Mali into Niger and Chad, where U.S. Army Special Forces helped Chadian troops kill and capture over forty insurgents.[6] Still, the Salafists were arguably the most dynamic Islamic force in the northern half of Africa. In Algeria they had eclipsed the Armed Islamic Group as the leading threat to the government. Too, they were active along the Libyan-Chadian border. Though founded in 1998 in Algeria, the Salafists traced their ideological roots to the reform movements in nineteenth-century Egypt that had raised the level of political consciousness among Muslims, then mired in antique and decaying colonial systems.[7] This venerable Salafist legacy lent cachet to al-Qaeda extremism.

Big Oil also lured the United States to the region. In 2004 the U.S. was importing 15 percent of its oil from West Africa, a figure expected to rise to 25 percent within a decade.[8] There was, too, the rising specter of the Chinese, who were investing significantly in the Sahel and whose influence the Americans wanted to limit.

Given such circumstances, the U.S. military had dispatched Army Special Forces to Mali and Mauritania, and marines to Chad and Niger. Senegal and other countries would soon be added to the pan-Sahel initiative, designed as a preventive, economy-of-force measure to avert the need for a massive deployment against terrorists as in Afghanistan.

———

I planned to meet up with U.S. marines in Niger, the second poorest country in the world after Sierra Leone. Yet my first impression of Niger was one of august, primordial beauty. The great river did not disappoint: a vast, smoky engraving so wide that it seemed less an actual river than a still life of the sea itself. In the middle, majestically parting the waters, stood long sandbars topped by rich green grass at the beginning of the rainy season. Thickets of coconut palms, neem, and eucalyptus lined the banks, beyond which stretched panels of cultivation that culminated in a series of low mesas. Camels plodded back from the fields at dusk, approaching the bronzed water where gurgling hippos bathed and men in shallow-draft boats fished for perch.

The capital city of Niamey, which unrolled along the river's northern bank, was little more than a sprawling village: absent of tension compared to the teeming African slum cities by the Atlantic Ocean to the south, such as Lagos and Abidjan. Parallel to the river were tranquil streets with stoplights that actually worked, and one-story government buildings with few guards at the entrances. The loose laterite gave the entire townscape a rich orange tint, as though a camera filter had been placed before one's eyes.

There were mud-walled houses and tulip-shaped wattle roofs. Boys stricken with polio went by on makeshift bicycles that they operated with hand pedals. Women in loud robes, buckets atop their heads, appeared almost to float by. There was an affecting, sensual intimacy to these dusty orange lanes. I thought of how the cities of coastal West Africa must have looked decades ago, before massive urban migration had shredded kinship patterns, ignited ethnic strife, and substituted the pageant of earthen colors for the prison hues of iron and concrete. Yet despite a spate of violent crime in parts of town and periodic anti-Christian riots near the Nigerian border, Niger's relatively slow pattern of development had caused it to lack an explosive edge. The traditional class structure of nobles, artisans, and former slaves still survived, leading to unspoken understandings that braced the social mortar.

But Niamey worked better as a city than it did as the administrative center of a country so vast and empty that the Libyan border to the northeast was farther away from the Nigerien capital than the Great Lakes were from the Gulf of Mexico. Seventy-five percent of Niger's twelve million people lived on just a sliver of territory stretching from Niamey eastward, along the Benin and Nigerian borders. Alas, Niger was little more than a demographic spillover of Nigeria, even as Niger's governing class, composed mainly of ethnic Hausas and Songhai-Djermas, had to control a hostile desert extending to Mali, Algeria, Libya, and Chad—a desert where Tuareg bandits were providing sanctuary and logistical support to Islamic terrorists. Niamey was pleasant, even as it was a vacuum surrounded by unstable regional forces.

The U.S. military had the same impossible task here as it had in so many other places where it was deployed: against considerable odds, help make a country that existed only on the map into something real. I stress the military because in weak democracies such as Niger's, politicians came and went, but soldiers and security men remained as silent, behind-the-scenes props—if they hadn't metamorphosed into politicians themselves. Niger's civilian head of state, Tandja Mamadou, was a former army lieutenant colonel. The fact that the State Department constituted the front for security assistance missions like that of the Marines did not mask European Command's importance to Niger. The Pentagon's humanitarian assistance projects, administered at the time by European Command (EUCOM) through a defense attaché at the U.S. Embassy in Niamey, accounted for almost all of the charity relief that the American people provided to the troubled north of Niger. Northern Niger was too insecure for either the Peace Corps or nongovernmental organizations to penetrate. You couldn't establish yourself in the north without the help of the Nigerien military, with whom civilian aid workers had cultivated few, if any, contacts.

—

Beyond Niamey, as I traveled north along the river, dark green scrub and tall millet fields competed with eroding layers of bright orange clay and dust. Niger was losing 7,800 square miles a year to desertification, though for the moment it wasn't apparent because of the seasonal rains.

I was inside a white Toyota pickup driven by Maj. Paul Baker of Drummond, Oklahoma, the commanding officer of a platoon-sized Marine training team, which consisted of twenty-four men, including three Navy corpsmen, drawn from Camp Lejeune, North Carolina, and EUCOM's Stuttgart headquarters. At forty years old, Maj. Baker, with wire-rimmed glasses, a graying-blond high-and-tight, and a frank, uncomplicated expression stamped on his face, was a bit long in the tooth for his rank. But so were some of his lieutenants, he told me, who had started out as enlisted men and later gone to Officer Candidate School at Quantico, Virginia. It would turn out to be a good platoon: the officers had been grunts (combat infantrymen) themselves.

Baker's father had served twenty-eight years in the Army and the National Guard. His oldest brother had joined the Air Force, his middle brother the Navy. "So the only option for me was the Marines," he said in a flat prairie accent. It wasn't so simple. After graduating from Northwestern Oklahoma State University, Baker had tried farming. Then, in the slow burn of a job search during the Texas-Oklahoma oil bust of the 1980s, he called the local Marine recruiter. Months of back-and-forth brought news that he was unqualified to be an officer. So the next day he enlisted and was dispatched to Marine boot camp outside San Diego.

Baker rose to lance corporal and was eventually accepted at Officer Candidate School. This came after serving aboard the aircraft carrier USS *Abraham Lincoln* off Kuwait during the 1991 Gulf War, and evacuating refugees from the eruption of Mount Pinatubo in the Philippines soon afterward. Through a friend in the Navy he met "the wife," a Vietnamese American whose father was a Vietnam veteran and a "Brown & Root type"—a private military contractor, that is. Baker was married at Camp Lejeune five days after returning from a deployment in Norway; his son would be born seventeen hours before he left for Okinawa on another deployment. He had no complaints. "I've been lucky in the Corps, and this," he went on, looking out the truck window at the thorny African scrub, "is a great opportunity for a log officer." For a logistics officer who had not made it to Afghanistan or Iraq, commanding a training mission in two African countries where the U.S. Marines had never been constituted the high point of Maj. Paul Baker's career.

We had entered the Nigerien military base of Tondibiah where the marines had their hootch, or encampment. Even inside the base, there were millet fields and the occasional street urchin. "It's a dramatic improvement over Chad, where whole villages existed within the army bases," Baker noted. Having just finished a two-month training mission in Chad, and a week into one in Niger, Baker was struck by the stark differences between the two countries. On paper, Chad was marginally better off than Niger; moreover, because of three decades of civil war, Chad might have been expected to boast a flinty army. But the Marines had found Chad dirtier, less developed, and with a military in every way inferior to Niger's.

In Niger only two or three men in each platoon required help to write their names; in Chad most did. Whereas the Chadian military manifested little rank structure and recruits often refused orders from their officers, Nigerien officers had real presence among their men, and even the noncommissioned officers showed initiative, which was rare for a third-world military. When the Marines had arrived in Chad, the host-country troops assumed an assault was jumping out of a truck and spraying fire from the hip. Baker was proud that at the end of the course they could execute a movement-to-contact with coordinated machine gun positions.

The Marine hootch was a one-story cement structure with a corrugated roof. It was protected only by concertina wire—the HESCO baskets had yet to be filled with sand. Compared to the high, sandbagged walls and paranoia I had experienced at U.S. Army Special Forces bases in Colombia, where car bombs and makeshift mortar attacks were a daily fact of life, the atmosphere here was laid-back. An American flag waved near a small barbecue grill. Mosquito nets covered the racks and big fat lizards climbed all over the walls and did push-ups in the dirt. I had my own sink, which delivered cold water, a luxury I had never before experienced with the American military. A fan whirred loudly. It was 110 degrees under a bleached iron sky. In the empty, echoing rooms I felt I was at a fleabag hotel. The vast array of weaponry and other military paraphernalia that dominated the Special Forces barracks I had seen in Latin America and Asia were absent. In comparison, the marines traveled stripped down, like backpackers.

They had just begun training three host-country platoons, composed of soldiers who had been individually selected for showing talent and motivation. Nothing fancy here. The initial training cycle consisted of the fundamentals of good soldiery: shooting, land navigation, and basic medicine. Liberty demands authority, for without minimal order there can be no freedom for anybody. If the civilian government was going to survive and protect its borders against transnational terrorists, military professionalization was key. It started with Baker's marines.

———

I spent my first days at Tondibiah on the rifle range.

The instructors were Gunnery Sgt. Eric Coughlin of Shohola, Pennsylvania; Staff Sgt. Stephen Long of Irmo, South Carolina; Staff Sgt. Bobby Rivera of the Bronx, New York; and Sgt. Chris Singley of Milledgeville, Georgia. All were in their thirties except for twenty-five-year-old Sgt. Singley. I had been with marines long enough in Djibouti and Iraq to know that these four had to be an impressive bunch. The noncommissioned ranks were the heart and soul of the Marine Corps to a greater degree than the Army, for the United States Marines were among the most powered-down command structure of any Western military, in which battlefield expertise and leadership depended upon low-ranking sergeants leading even lower-ranking corporals, who in turn led lance corporals and privates. You didn't get to be a sergeant of any kind without advanced training, particularly a staff sergeant who commanded a platoon of two or three dozen men, to say nothing of a gunnery sergeant. To wit, Gunny Eric Coughlin was a specialist in military mountaineering, Sgt. Chris Singley in riverine operations, and Staff Sgt. Steve Long a scout sniper and former PMI (primary marksmanship instructor) at

Marine boot camp in Parris Island. As for Staff Sgt. Bobby Rivera, he was a member of Force Recon—the Marine equivalent of the Navy SEALs and the Army's famed Delta Force. Rivera was on loan from the Special Operations Training Group at Camp Lejeune for this mission.

Because training third-world armies had for decades been an Army Special Forces' affair, this deployment to Chad and Niger constituted a rare opportunity for the Marines to show what they could do. The Corps had sent its best.

It was dark and pouring when we set out for the rifle range at 6 a.m. The pickups halted at the Nigerien barracks to collect the trainees who would ride in the back. Listening to the beautiful singing of the African troops as they stood in formation before their commander, I began my acquaintance with Staff Sgt. Steve Long, a stocky, red-haired thirty-four-year-old with piercing eyes, whom Maj. Baker had tagged for me as one of the brightest marines in the unit. "He's wasting himself doing what he's doing—he should be in a much higher position."

Staff Sgt. Long's father had been a marine, and Long joined the Corps after dropping out of community college in South Carolina and getting his last speeding ticket before losing his license. But after a decade of active duty in various combat-related roles, the next job he was offered just as 9/11 rolled around was as a recruiter. "Fuck that," Long told me. "I'm an infantryman. I wanted to be with the grunts." Long discovered that the best way to return to "the combat arms community" was to leave the Marines: to go off active duty and become a reservist, in which case, the War on Terror necessitated that because of his considerable experience he would immediately be called up and deployed overseas.

"I don't have a family. I just want to do Reserve duty twelve months a year." He got his wish. Since 9/11, Long had been in a uniform the whole time in Europe and Africa, often on training missions. "I just hope GWOT [the Global War on Terrorism] goes on for a long time. I'm still trying to get to Iraq and Afghanistan."

The Nigerien troops jumped into the back of the pickups. I was impressed at how quiet and orderly they were. When we got to the range a few minutes later, they marched out onto the field and began setting up the targets. Then they lined up single file, their field caps in their hands, soon to be filled with bullets, as the rain fell on their heads. After prying open the Chinese-made sardine cans of 7.62mm ammunition for the Nigeriens' AK-47 (Kalashnikov) rifles, Gunny Coughlin and the three other sergeants dumped the rounds into the waiting field caps. "Wait till the end of the day," Long remarked. "They'll actually pick up the brass cartridges on the field without being told to, and not in order to sell them. They bring their own medical equipment to the range. The Chadians weren't like this. The Chadians couldn't even hit the target paper while zeroing their rifles."

The Nigeriens, I also noticed, displayed real muzzle awareness. When not shooting they kept their rifles pointed at the ground, and none of them ever once dropped them in the dirt.

The Nigerien military had participated in messy, violent peace-keeping missions in Côte d'Ivoire, Sierra Leone, Liberia, Burundi, the Congo, and Haiti. This Hausa-dominated military formed its own elite social class, with officers sending their young sons to cadet schools. It was a military that had proved its willingness to die in defense of U.S. interests; on several occasions Nigerien units had followed Salafist extremists in hot pursuit across the border into neighboring countries.

Waiting around, watching the host-country troops quietly load their ammunition into the magazines, I mentioned to Staff Sgt. Long that coups, being a feature of modernization, tended to happen when a military was more institutionally advanced than a civilian authority. Long broke in about the Philippine military and the inefficiency and corruption of successive civilian regimes in the Philippines. His insight was impressive. It turned out he had had a Filipina girlfriend. As Maj. Baker's remarks about Chad and Niger had shown, marines sucked up knowledge wherever they could. Because their personal experience system was so different from that of academics and journalists like myself, their company was invigorating.

Dawn came, revealing sculptural acacias as birds made a racket in the trees and bruise-dark rain clouds raced across the sky. The rain held off the heat momentarily. I inserted my earplugs and walked out on the three-hundred-yard range with the four marines and twenty-three Nigerien soldiers. It was good to be on a rifle range again, where I spent much time in 2003 and early 2004 researching *Imperial Grunts*. Then I had followed a crawl, walk, and run approach with the U.S. military:

observing Army Special Forces train host-country troops in Colombia
and the Philippines before accompanying them on presence patrols and
armed assaults in Afghanistan; then observing marines train and pull
guard duty in Djibouti before accompanying them during urban combat
in Iraq. Continuing this odyssey meant not going forward but backward—back to the basics, just as soldiers and marines themselves never
ceased to do. When Special Forces and Marine battalions returned to
Fort Bragg, North Carolina, and Camp Pendleton, California, from
Afghanistan and Iraq, they returned to the rifle range. The very circular
monotony of military life—going from training to exercises to deployments and back again to training—was fundamental to any experience
of it. With the training of indigenous troops at the heart of power projection, and the rifle range the heart of such training in our era, the range
was truly the center of it all.

"Every time you fire, a bad guy should bleed," Staff Sgt. Bobby
Rivera yelled. "Aim for the high center torso. Any hit is good. Don't
worry about carving up the bull's-eye. This isn't target shooting. It's
about fighting with a gun." Rivera had a loud, grating, intimate Bronx
accent. Because Rivera was a specialist in weaponry and the related
field of close quarters combat, once on the range Gunny Coughlin de-
ferred to the ethnic–Puerto Rican staff sergeant, even though he outranked him.

Maj. Moussa Salaou Barmou translated Rivera's commands into
French and Hausa for his soldiers. Maj. Moussa had trained with the
U.S. Army at Fort Benning, Georgia, and with the Ivorians, Cameroo-
nians, and Pakistanis. "I didn't know what real combat was about until
Fort Benning," he told me. "The Americans have the money to simulate
war in training, unlike most other armies. But I wish the Americans
could see how the rebels settle in our border towns in the desert and
marry local girls so that they become invisible, so that you don't know
who you have to fight." Because Maj. Moussa outranked the American
Marine noncoms, each made sure to address him as "sir."

Rivera went on. The Nigeriens were only fifteen yards out from the
targets—paper silhouettes of soldiers aiming their guns. "You will all
fire a controlled pair followed by a hammer," he explained. "A controlled pair is two slow shots. A hammer is two fast ones. Shooting a

hammer, the rifle will recoil twice. You won't have time to readjust, meaning with a fucked-up body position you will miss the target at least once. And that," he screamed, "is unacceptable."

Rivera demonstrated, repeating and yelling everything, sometimes mixing English with French in his Bronx accent: *"En position. Levez la sécurité. Feu! Avancez."* Meanwhile, Coughlin, Long, and Singley worked quietly with the individual soldiers. Maj. Moussa did his part, shoving his knee behind that of one of his soldiers to ease him into a more correct body position. I remembered a young Philippine lieutenant who constantly had to be told by an American noncom to pay attention to his own troops. That wasn't necessary here.

Rivera now made them repeat the drill from twenty-five yards out, this time while changing magazines. "Don't bend down. Just let the magazine drop. Minimize your movements or you're gonna fucking die." He demonstrated shooting and changing magazines while closing the distance from twenty-five to fifteen yards. As I watched him, the impressive thing was what wasn't there: wasted movements. "Notice," he said, "I'm not fast. I'm just smooth. It's not about speed, but about efficiency."

"Même exercice," said Rivera. Later he taught them how to unjam their AK-47 rifles while also changing magazines and closing the distance with the enemy. "This isn't target practice," he kept stressing at the top of his lungs. "This is about killing people." During the entire morning Rivera checked the targets only once to see how accurately each soldier was shooting. As long as they were hitting the silhouettes or just the paper, he was happy. He wanted them to be comfortable handling a rifle on the move in combat. He knew from assaults on mud-walled compounds in Afghanistan in 2001, during the first weeks of Operation Enduring Freedom there, that survival was less a matter of a perfect shot than of getting a spare magazine quickly out of a side pocket.

Rivera liked the fact that the targets were man-shaped silhouettes rather than concentric circles. "If you're aiming at a bull's-eye, you're being programmed to shoot paper. If you're aiming at a silhouette, you're being programmed to kill motherfuckers.[9]

"Standing is the most unstable platform for firing a rifle," he went on. "That's why fifty yards out is the furthest we will ever shoot standing up. At a hundred yards I'll drop to the prone in two seconds, but then I'll methodically put two in his chest so the motherfucker will die before he can find his iron sights. That way I'll live. And I wanna live because back in America there are a lot of women that love me." The Nigeriens laughed loudly as Maj. Moussa translated into French.

It was almost eleven. We had been on the range for four hours. The cordite had mixed with the rain to form a mist. *"Êtes-vous fatigué comme des demoiselles?"* Rivera shouted in disdain. Laughing hard, the Nigerien troops let out a resounding *"Non."* Training continued another hour until the break for chow.

"There ain't nothing I'd rather do than get shot at. But if I can't shoot or get shot at, just being on the range is heaven," Rivera told me as we broke out MREs (meals ready to eat).

The rain stopped and it was back over 100 degrees. Training resumed for two more hours. Still screaming, Rivera warned: *"Écoutez,* tomorrow we'll do the drills with more magazine changes because you're still fucking up. Remember, you're not learning how to shoot, but how to fight when you're tired and dirty. When you're tired and dirty and hurting I want you to reach down and grab your balls. To find out what you're made of." Everybody laughed. This wasn't about being mature or sensitive. This was about motivating young African soldiers. It was clear from the way that the Nigeriens smiled at Rivera and walked over to shake his hand that he knew how to do that.

While the Nigeriens scoured the range for the brass cartridges, I hung around one of the pickups with the four marines as we broke out more MREs and water bottles. We were swimming in sweat, our faces caked with dust. The marines asked about Fallujah, where I had been the previous spring. They were frustrated that they weren't in Iraq, and each had a bureaucratic strategy for getting deployed there, or at least to Afghanistan.

"A marine," Gunny Coughlin said, "is only happy when he's fighting, humping with his backpack, or on liberty—spending time with his girlfriend or working under his car." Coughlin was an unusual gunnery sergeant: less a leader of men than simply the ultimate grunt, quiet and driven, taut and wiry, a human bullet almost. He just wanted to do his job. He complained about the tan boots issued to marines, which were useless for humping because they were nothing but "laced-up flip-flops without shank support." That led to complaints from the others about the Corps' decision to retain the M-16 rifle and enhance it with a rail system, rather than get the shorter, lighter, easier-to-handle M-4 that the Army used. Thus, the real bitching commenced: about the media, the naïve home front, and the initial hostility of the U.S. Embassy staff in Niger toward the Marines following the friendliness of the embassy folks in Chad. In short, morale was fine. Off the range, they addressed one another by their first names rather than by last ones preceded by rank.

I rode back with the gunny. "I just love this place," Coughlin told me happily, eyeing a line of local women walking through the savannah. "I can train, shoot, drive a Toyota pickup, and look at beautiful women."

The next morning we started again at six. By 7:30 a.m. the sunlight was unbearable, with rotting humidity, no breeze, and no clouds. "Yeah, it's gonna be good today," Rivera shrieked, happily. He was like a kid sometimes, never realizing how tired he got screaming in the hot sun, until he collapsed into a deep sleep in the first chair he saw back at the hootch. He showed the Nigeriens how to handle "*beaucoup* enemy":

"You sweep laterally, two bullets—a hammer—in each motherfucker. You never focus on one man, you keep the rifle moving, the weapon never drops to your side." Twenty-four assault rifles began cracking at once. The Nigerien soldiers spent the day advancing from fifty yards at ten-yard intervals, dropping and replacing their magazines, without taking their eyes off the target. Already they were much better than the day before.

On the third day it rained again. Rivera made them practice jumping flat on their stomachs in the mud to fire in the prone position from three hundred yards. "Set your iron sights at a hundred yards to hit at three hundred yards," Rivera advised, "because when you close the distance with the enemy to a hundred, you may have no time to readjust."

While they were firing, Steve Long pointed to one soldier whose shots, he said, were to the left of the target. "How can you tell?" I asked. The paper silhouettes were specks from this distance. "I can follow the individual bullets downrange. It's a trick your eye picks up after spending eight hours a day at the range for two years at Parris Island." Walking up to inspect the silhouettes later, he turned out to be right.

In the heat of the day, standing for hours just inches behind the line of soldiers firing their rifles, I would get bored and wander to the shade of the ready bench, take out my earplugs, and sit down. Sometimes I talked with 1st Lt. Timothy Dekryger of Mount Pleasant, Michigan, Maj. Baker's executive officer, who came out to inspect the training and enjoy the company of Bobby Rivera's gang. First Lt. Dekryger was an original: tattoos over his body even as he was an addict of classical string quartets. His dad and uncle had been marines, and two weeks after finishing high school with a D average—having majored in "beer, girls, and hunting"—he enlisted. Before he was twenty years old, Dekryger found himself on a fleet deployment in Malaysia, staring at "sharp, tropical mountains falling straight into a blue sea as smooth as glass with vapor rising from it. I wished I could paint," he went on. "That scene gets more intense in my mind as I get older."

Lt. Dekryger left the Corps to study philosophy at Calvin College, a little-known gem of an institution of the Dutch Reformed Church in Grand Rapids, Michigan. Then he went to Officer Candidate School, becoming the commander of a tank platoon in time for Operation Iraqi Freedom. "In Iraq I had to order grunts to do things that were technically difficult and could get them killed. I found myself preparing in advance what I would say to inspire them. I realized how inadequate I was. That's why I love and respect the Riveras of this world," he continued in a low, intense voice. "They're profane as hell, but they know how to motivate. If I had to leave the combat arms community and people like Rivera, I'd leave the Marine Corps."

Dekryger showed me the book he was reading, *Tarawa: The Story of a Battle* by Time-Life correspondent Robert Sherrod. He said that he found the book inspiring. Leafing through it, and reading it carefully at night in the hootch, I discovered that it was like other books popular among marines and soldiers, but which the contemporary media, aside from the military correspondents, were barely aware of. No potboiler, *Tarawa* was just an old-fashioned sort of book, very much in the tradition of great war reporting as defined by Richard Tregaskis in *Guadalcanal Diary,* Bing West in *The Village,* and Harold Moore and Joe Galloway in *We Were Soldiers Once . . . and Young.* These books celebrate the sacrifice and heroism of American troops in World War II and Vietnam not because it had been the authors' intention, but because it was true and happened to be all around them.[10]

The November 1943 Marine assault on Betio Island in the Tarawa Atoll, the most important of the Gilbert Islands in the central Pacific, claimed close to three thousand Marine casualties—including close to a thousand killed—and five thousand Japanese dead in little more than three days of fighting.* The Time-Life correspondent writes of a "husky boy . . . killed ten feet in front of the seawall pillbox which was his objective. He is still hunched forward, his rifle in his right hand. That is the picture of the Marine Corps I shall always carry: charging forward."[†]

Sherrod, like other correspondents of the era, keeps using the words "we" and "our" when referring to the American side, for although a journalist, he was a fellow American living among the troops.[11] Back in Honolulu a week after the battle, he found the naïveté of the home front toward Tarawa "amazing." The public saw the killing of so many troops in so few days as scandalous. There were rumblings in Congress about an intelligence failure, and vows that such a thing must not happen again. But as Sherrod argues, there was no easy way to win many wars (in fact, eight months later, the first day of fighting on Guam would claim nearly seven hundred marines dead, wounded, or missing). Thus, "to deprecate the Tarawa victory was almost to defame the memory of the gallant men who lost their lives achieving it." He concludes that on Tarawa, in 1943, "there was a more realistic approach to war than there was in the United States."[12]

At night, away from the range, Sgts. Rivera, Long, and Singley played poker under the stars amid the lizards, the plague of frogs, and the whining mosquitoes. It was too hot to sleep. Mefloquine, an antimalaria drug that many of the marines were taking, gave some of them insomnia or bad dreams, or both. Those not playing poker read old hunting, weapons, and NASCAR magazines, or watched DVDs. Occa-

---

* Initial estimates of Marine casualties were 1,026 killed and 2,600 wounded, later revised to 685 killed, 169 missing, and 2,100 wounded.
† Robert Sherrod, *Tarawa: The Story of a Battle* (New York: Duell, Sloan and Pearce, 1944), p. 126. For another book with a stirring description of the fighting on Tarawa, see Leon Uris, *Battle Cry* (New York: Putnam, 1953).

sionally there were parties in Niamey where you could drink with the
Peace Corps girls, whose jobs kept them relatively close to the capital.
The educated Nigerien women, dressed to the nines at the one or two
fancy nightclubs in town, wouldn't so much as look at the marines, unlike in Chad, where such women had been all over them. It was another
indication of how Chad, despite the development statistics, was a more
desperate place than Niger.

Some nights a storm would erupt in the wee hours, and those of us
sleeping outside would pull our fold-out cots and mosquito nets back
into the concrete rooms in the pitch-darkness. The nearby river itself,
simply by its beauty, offered relief from the heat and rain. Behind the
hootch was a hill that offered a ten-mile-long panorama of a turn in the
Niger. At sunset, when a clean wind absent of greasy dust would kick
up in your face, the wide pan of water would go from a shimmering aluminum to a deep volcanic red depending upon the sun's angle.

Every evening was story time. Stories would be told sitting on the
hill overlooking the river, or over a local Flag beer behind the hootch, or
riding back from Niamey late at night in the rear of a pickup. For instance, there was Sgt. Nicholas Cervantes, an ethnic Mexican Filipino
from Dallas, a stocky kid in his early twenties with a handsome, square-
shaped face and calm, sleepy manner. He told me about how his grandfather had escaped from the Japanese at Bataan during the time of the
World War II death march, only to die in a convenience store holdup
years later back in America; and how his uncle, a Vietnam veteran, refused to tell him his war stories until after Cervantes had proved himself
by fighting in Iraq.

"I know where heaven is and it's Lithuania," went a story by another
marine who had gone there on holiday. "The women are beautiful,
pagan, with a practical view toward sex. Who says communism was
bad? You're working three levels of advantages: you're a foreign male,
you're a rich, exotic American, and their own men are a bunch of
drunken, criminal slobs. Ukraine's just as good. But it's not gonna last
because of the expansion of the European Union."

First Lt. Michael Aldrich of Lufkin, Texas, also had good stories.
Mike Aldrich was a short, sinewy, Popeye sort of guy who walked with
his shoulders rolled back, confidently swinging an arm as though it had

a billy club attached to it. At thirty-seven he was very old for a lieutenant. Two days after finishing high school he was in Marine boot camp, but left active duty to work as a forklift operator and machinist making parts for oil pumping rigs. Called up as a reservist in 1990, he fought in the Gulf War as a scout sniper. Then he got a job in the Texas state prison system. After the Mexican mafia put a contract out on him for "clocking" one of the inmates (breaking his jaw) in self-defense, he was transferred to another penitentiary for his own safety. Instead, Aldrich joined the Lufkin police department, from which he would eventually be fired. "I was just too aggressive. I didn't want to mark time, I wanted to bust people. But they told me that as long as cars transporting drugs north out of Mexico were not stopping in Lufkin, I should just let 'em pass through. It was so political."

So he went back to the prison system, where he worked on death row. "The death row inmates were easy to deal with—they didn't want to mess up their appeals by attacking a guard. I looked at their case files, though. I'll tell you something: they deserved to die. Texas doesn't bullshit, it executes."

Meanwhile, Aldrich missed the Marine Corps—"the only place in my life where I have been judged completely on my own merits and mistakes." At thirty-four, he reenlisted as a corporal. After years of bad luck, a series of breaks led to the offer of a meritorious commission just before he reached the age limit. Going to school at night to earn a degree from Campbell University in Buies Creek, North Carolina, he was commissioned as a second lieutenant. He became a liaison officer at Bethesda Naval Hospital during the Iraq war, where his job was to assure that wounded marines from Camp Lejeune were getting their convalescent benefits. "It was the most important job of my life. I met the President and the chairman of the Joint Chiefs. I felt that I restarted my life as a Marine officer. You don't know how depressed I was after getting fired from the Lufkin police department. But my wife has stood by me since high school. We can't know our destiny, it's God's plan. I'm headed for Iraq in the spring, finally."

The best storyteller was one of the Navy docs, "Smitty"—his nickname was tattooed in big letters across the top of his back. Hospital Corpsman

2nd Class Brian Smith of St. Louis, with kinky dirty blond hair, was Long's and Rivera's poker buddy. Smitty was crude and nasty. He loved to smoke and drink. He had seen it all. "In a trauma situation, I'd trust Smitty more than any Navy chief or surgeon," Steve Long told me. Smitty had no rhythm, but I often saw him dancing by himself, snapping his fingers as he walked along. He had a distinct southern accent, not unusual given that in some respects St. Louis constituted the northern tip of Dixie.

Smitty joined the Navy out of high school. Seven of his thirteen years in the Navy had been on "the green side"—with the Marines. "Hearing a marine call you 'Doc'—something they've been doing since the dawn of time—well, it's pretty cool. It does something to you," he told me. "Marines won't fight, train, go to the range, or do anything without a corpsman. Technically, the corpsman is a noncombatant, armed with only a nine-mil[limeter Beretta pistol] in self-defense. Bullshit. The life expectancy of corpsmen in the field in Vietnam was among the lowest of Marine units. As long as a corpsman doesn't puss out, marines treat him like their own. That's why I stay on the green side. The blue side [the Navy] just ain't the same."

Smitty's stories about Iraq were likely exaggerated, yet they had a mythic quality about them that was truly impressive. It had much to do with the way he told them. His light green eyes flashed the richest of expressions as he talked. I thought of Faulkner, and the stories that the old men in his narratives told "while chewing tobacco until the suption is out of it."[13] In Operation Iraqi Freedom, Smitty had traveled six hundred miles, for forty-eight days, and saw around a thousand patients while assigned to a forward resuscitative surgical team and a much larger, eighteen-truck surgical company that included its own portable morgue—where the docs would keep their mineral-water bottles cold between the stacks of corpses. "You go inside the truck, ignore the dead guys, and just go about your business."

The first marine who Smitty saw dead had just been pulled off a Black Hawk and "his face was pale, pale, pale. At the beginning of the war," Smitty went on, "they brought in this marine and Iraqi soldier at the same time. They had been found wounded in the same spot, and it seemed from their injuries that they might have tried to shoot each other. Well, when the wounded marine sat up and saw a surgeon treating the Iraqi, he grabbed the doc's nine mil and tried to shoot the Iraqi. From then on, we separated the marine from the Iraqi patients.

"The physicians wanted to treat the worse-off first. That's the civilian mentality, and inside Navy hospitals you might as well be in the civilian world. But in a military surgical unit during a war, you got to understand, the doctors have to treat the minor injuries first, in order to get marines back into the fight. Iraqis should get treated only when the docs are not busy with marines. The surgeons caught on to this only when they started seeing dead marines come in.

"It's the dead you remember more than the ones whose lives you saved," Smitty observed, taking a long drag on a cigarette. "I remember this young lieutenant. Was he a first lieutenant or second lieutenant? I don't know. Anyway, he was young and he had a wedding ring on. Shit, I thought. He probably has a wife who's at the grocery store now, maybe a young kid in school, and I know he's dead and they don't. Stuff like that just does something to you. Over a decade in the Navy and this was the high point."

Once, at a local restaurant with Rivera, Smitty spoke of an Iraqi soldier who was brought in with an entire buttock shot off. "I would'a kept fighting, even with half my ass blown off," Rivera shouted. "No you wouldn't," Smitty cut in, "because the pain and trauma would have forced your blood to the wounded area, and you would have gone into shock and nausea if you hadn't immediately blacked out. These ain't like hunting accidents. Assault rifle bullets are designed to tumble at high velocity through the body."

The most memorable story that Smitty told was about "the gunny who wouldn't die." Everybody in the hootch had heard it. Checking the facts, I learned later that it wasn't a gunnery sergeant at all but a first sergeant: the effect of the story was the same, though.*

"There was this gunny," Smitty would begin, "who came in with his head blasted through with a bullet. But he was still breathing. He just wouldn't die. So we intubated him to help him breathe through all the muck and vomit in his mouth. Then we sent him over to the dental tent

---

* First Sgt. Edward Smith of Chicago.

to die. In a field hospital there was nothing more we could do for him. His eyes were wide open, completely fixed and dilated. He was brain-dead. He was Cheyne-Stoking—taking rapid, shallow, rattling death breaths. All the corpsmen took turns going over to hold his hand. He remained like that for twelve hours before he finally expired."

"He didn't give up because he wanted to fucking get back into the fight," Rivera shouted.

"He was fucking brain-dead," Smitty answered solemnly.

"No, you don't understand," Rivera countered. "He was a Marine grunt, he wanted to get back into the fight." Rivera's expression was notably naïve—he truly believed this.

For three weeks the marines shared the hootch with a twelve-person humanitarian aid mission from the U.S. Air Force Reserves that had been dispatched by European Command. It included three physicians, two dentists, and an optometrist. Every morning, inside the Tondibiah army base, they treated over five hundred people from nearby villages, mainly women with babies hanging on to their backs as though by suction. The Air Force doctors provided relief for worms and other ailments, which would return in a week or two anyway because of the primitive living conditions. "It's less a health program than a health festival," one of the physicians told me cheerfully. "It's kind of an exercise in futility and good intentions that still earns goodwill and gives a technical service like the Air Force the field exposure it needs."

Like the marines, these Reserve doctors were mainly from the South and Midwest, and from working-class areas of the Northeast. They were thrilled to be in Africa, away from the pressures of their daily medical practices, and having a chance to serve their country at the same time. Humanitarian exercises eased the way for bilateral military relations.

The Air Force mission commander was Maj. Melissa Triche of Bucyrus, Ohio. Tall, angular, with a lovely face and sophisticated manner, she was, I was surprised to hear, one of six kids from a family that lacked the money to send her to college. "I enlisted in the Air National Guard for six and a half years. It paid the money for me to attend Kent State. The Guard made me," she said with matter-of-fact gratitude. She was now in the Reserves and divorced, with an eight-year-old son back in central Ohio who was staying with his father, a C-130 navigator, while she was away. Like Staff Sgt. Steve Long, the Reserves had become her livelihood. She figured out how to work the system in order to get activated two hundred days a year. "I'm a Reserve bum. It's been easy to do since 9/11."

The culmination of the two-month training mission was to be platoon-level field operations for 150 host-country troops in a savannah tract two hours north of Niamey. Real-world intelligence about incursions by the Salafist Group for Preaching and Combat would be provided by the Marine advisors to Nigerien commanders, who would then lay out ambushes. The ambush sites would be equipped with dummies to be killed, captured, and searched by Nigerien troops. On the dummies would be documents that the Nigeriens would have to exploit for intelligence purposes. There would be various hostage and prisoner scenarios. One morning we left to do a field survey of the training site.

When you left Niamey on rutted dirt tracks, it was as if the country disappeared on you. There was no police, no sign of authority, nothing. Men with Tuareg headdresses began to appear here and there at roadblocks. The bloody apricot soil thinned out into a bumpy semi-desert, bearded with thorns and punctuated by termite hills. For hundreds of miles, north from the Atlantic Ocean to Niamey, the landscape barely changed. But beyond Niamey, still going north, there began an increasingly dry transition zone that would culminate in utter desert.

Flash floods had left the road washed out in places, with the wheels of gigantic trucks half sunk in mud, the drivers stuck on the side of the road for days. We passed through several villages, the most traditional-looking I had seen in Africa, composed exclusively of wattle and mud brick. There were goat herds and camels loaded down with firewood. Women wrapped in colorful fabrics evocative of exotic birds pounded maize. It was a vision of Africa out of a time capsule, with the stresses of modern development filtered out.

The kids in such places particularly amazed the marines. Steve Long talked about a little boy he had seen in Chad working a field with a primitive implement. When Long had offered him crackers from an

MRE box, the boy collected several other kids from the village, made them line up, and gave each a piece. "That's good-to-go," Long said. "These kids don't need Mommy and Daddy to do things for them, it's like rural America a hundred years ago."

Getting stuck in the mud, we wrapped the winch around a tree. A group of young men helped out by matting the tire area with dried leaves and branches for traction. The marines gave them MREs as gifts, explaining through sign language how to use the heaters. Like the young men I had met in villages near Tondibiah, they were without jobs and complained of nothing to do. These villages would not remain traditional for long, I realized, not with jobless youth, a soaring population, democratization, and the possibility of a small-scale oil bonanza—of the kind that had ruined Nigeria. Something would happen here, good or bad. You could almost feel the ground shifting below your feet.

The training site was an immense, wadi-scarred savannah that featured a series of volcanic plugs: steep hills littered with scree. I accompanied Maj. Baker, 1st Lt. Dekryger, and Staff Sgt. Long to the top of one, from where they surveyed the area. Even at the summit the heat did not abate. The three marines barely noticed. "What an awesome tract," Lt. Dekryger exclaimed. "There's nothing here to impede us." They began picking out wadis and draws where units could be concealed and lay down supporting fire. The two-mile distance between each hill created fire lines for different platoons to operate. They went on about how lucky they were to be here even if, as they told me, it wasn't Afghanistan or Iraq.*

* Months later, I received a message from Sgt. Chris Singley—from Fallujah. Soon after he had left Niger, he got his wish: deployment to Iraq as the senior advisor to a company of the new Iraqi Army, which assisted U.S. marines and soldiers during the fighting in the second battle of Fallujah in November 2004. It was a long e-mail, telling me about the 103 Purple Hearts issued as of Christmas Eve 2004, and of the Americans and their Iraqi allies who died there. The few months he had spent in Iraq were clearly the most meaningful of his life.

TWO

ALASKA TO THAILAND: THE ORGANIZING PRINCIPLE OF THE EARTH'S SURFACE

Pacific Ocean, Autumn 2004

While the American military was building a new system of personalized, bilateral relationships with African armies, in the Pacific it was refitting a constellation of bases that had been the legacy of the Philippine War, World War II, and the Korean conflict. The object in both cases was a global footprint that was deliberately shallower on the ground, even as it was faster on the move. Witnessing its fitful emergence meant traveling from the world's greatest desert to its greatest ocean.

Generally speaking, while Africa represented the unconventional challenges posed by anarchy and weak states, the Pacific represented the more conventional challenges posed by rising powers and rogue states.

———

As suggestive as the Pacific was of the caressing tropics, Alaska represented some of the region's most vital military real estate. I headed there first, arriving in Anchorage at midnight, November 1, 2004. I carried a single backpack stuffed with winter gear for the coming days and summer gear for the rest of the journey. In this trip with the American military, I would be hopping planes from the Arctic Circle to the equator, and from North America to Southeast Asia. Rather than form a personal relationship with a battalion, a platoon, or a lone officer, as in my previous journeys, this time I was after a broad, ground-level view of the world's most developing military theater.

On the Pentagon's map of geographic "area" commands, Alaska appeared as the most interesting place on earth. While every other dryland region was covered in one solid color, denoting which command it fell under, Alaska bore blue and green stripes: blue for NORTHCOM (Northern Command) and green for PACOM (Pacific Command). As part of mainland North America, Alaska belonged to NORTHCOM, whose mission—aligned with that of the newly created Department of Homeland Security—was to protect the continental United States from attack, particularly from incoming missiles. In reality, though, this, the largest of the fifty states, was part of PACOM. Alaska's strategic utility as a boreal lookout and forward base against the Russian Far East, in addition to points along the Pacific Rim, could not be overestimated. Item: Alaska included the Aleutians, a chain of seventy fog-strewn and volcanic islands constituting the northern wall of the Pacific Ocean that stretched across the International Date Line to Russia's Kamchatka Peninsula.

Formally known as "Russian North America," Alaska had been acquired from Czar Alexander II as a result of an 1867 treaty negotiated by William Henry Seward, President Andrew Johnson's secretary of state. Derided as "Seward's Folly," this territorial acquisition would turn out to be anything but that, of course. The U.S. Army opened up Alaska beginning in the last decades of the nineteenth century, putting in the roads and ports and doing the early mapping, as well as policing the territory during the unruly gold rush days. Alaska boomed in the early 1940s, when it became a base for protecting the U.S. mainland against a Japanese attack, as well as the principal node for delivering aircraft to the Soviet Union via Siberia under the Lend-Lease Act, to help Stalin fight Hitler.

The economic and emotional ties between the U.S. military and Alaska never wavered. By the early twenty-first century, one-fifth of Alaska's population was either active-duty soldiers and airmen, mem-

bers of the Reserve and National Guard, veterans who had been stationed in Alaska and decided to retire here for the hunting and fishing,
or civilians who worked for the military. The Department of Defense remained the state's main employer. In the archetypal ideological division
of "red" and "blue" America, Alaska was no less "red" (Republican)
than Massachusetts was "blue" (Democrat).

The Air Force loved Alaska every bit as much as the Army did. Airmen saw the state as one vast training space and make-believe war zone,
featuring great distances and with relatively few low-level noise restrictions. Military pilots could do almost anything they wanted here.

"Welcome to the Banana Belt," said Army Maj. Kirk Gohlke of
Frankenmuth, Michigan, as I stepped into several inches of snow and
fifteen-degree temperature outside Anchorage airport. Maj. Gohlke
wasn't kidding. Because of its proximity to the ocean, Anchorage's climate was mild compared to much of the rest of the state. Because he
had lived farther north in Alaska, Maj. Gohlke saw the state's biggest
city as a bit too temperate climatically and, perhaps, with too many sophisticated airs culturally.

I spent the first night at Fort Richardson, outside Anchorage, named
for Brig. Gen. Wilds Richardson, a native Texan who had commanded
troops on the Yukon River a hundred years earlier. An Army outpost,
Fort Richardson was adjacent to Elmendorf Air Force Base.* This
would be the pattern throughout the Pacific. The Army operated as a
forward presence thanks to the Air Force, which provided the transportation lift.

Fort Richardson was headquarters for USARAK (U.S. Army,
Alaska). USARAK was dominated by the 172nd Separate Infantry
Brigade, which was about to become the Army's third Stryker Brigade
Combat Team. The change in nomenclature carried momentous impli-
cations. Let me explain:

The Stryker was an eight-wheeled light-armored vehicle with an
MK-19 grenade launcher and a .50-caliber machine gun that could transport eleven soldiers—a two-man crew and nine-man assault squad—at

---

* Named after Hugh Merle Elmendorf, born in 1895 in Ithaca, New York. A pioneer in high-
  altitude formation flying, he died while test piloting a Y1P-25 in 1933, near Wright Field in
  Ohio.

60 miles per hour for 330 miles without refueling. Thus, the vehicle represented a lighter and more lethal regular Army suited for an unconventional battlefield, able to send small units great distances over rough terrain in relative comfort. The Stryker was named for Stuart Stryker and Robert Stryker, two unrelated Army noncommissioned officers killed under heroic circumstances: the former in Germany in 1945, the latter in Vietnam in 1967.*

The Stryker's real significance for Alaska was that, for the first time since the end of the Vietnam War, the 172nd—to be the bulk of USARAK—would be a deployable, war-fighting force in fact as well as theory, with rail, port, and pallet facilities soon to be constructed and upgraded, in order to ship men and equipment anywhere around the globe in days and hours instead of months.

The ability to deploy large numbers of troops around the world at a moment's notice had been a Pentagon priority for years. Now that the Air Force was increasingly able to fly large numbers of soldiers over the North Pole, Iraq, Afghanistan, and Kosovo were only five thousand miles away from Alaska, not much farther than Korea and the Philippines. Alaskan military bases were closer to the Middle East than any bases in the lower forty-eight states. The 172nd would be headed to Iraq, where I would link up with it the following year.

"Between the end of the Vietnam War and 9/11 we were basically a hunting and fishing brigade in the far north, it was real demoralizing," one soldier told me. "Post 9/11, the Air Force in Alaska has become a tip of the spear for GWOT [the Global War on Terrorism]. And with the Stryker, we're becoming the spear itself."

Dawn on November 2, 2004—Election Day—did not arrive in Alaska until 9:30 a.m. By four in the afternoon it would be getting dark. But winters this far north were not nearly as depressing as the facts suggested; because sunlight spilled over the pole, it created an ethereal twilight that arrived long before dawn and lingered long after dusk. After sunup I went to the Stryker factory to inspect the vehicle and drive it.

The Stryker looked not much different than other infantry carrier vehicles, but it made a lot less noise, was constructed of metal composites

---

* The Army had two other Stryker brigades, both based out of Fort Lewis, Washington.

that did not give off magnetic signals to lurking mines, and rode as though over a cushion of air. After being rattled around in the dusty interior of a Humvee and in the back of a seven-ton truck in Iraq and Afghanistan, I found the Stryker a pleasure to ride in. The interior, filled with computer screens for remote control of the guns, was like a roomy airplane with its own heating and cooling system. There was an infrared sight for locating enemy troops as far as twenty miles away, and even a microwave for heating MREs. The bottom line: the Stryker could deliver nine well-rested and decently fed grunts a great distance, ready to fight.

To observe the training of Stryker and other units I had to travel farther north. Thus, I went to nearby Elmendorf air base, where an Air National Guard crew flew Maj. Gohlke and me in a small plane to the army post of Fort Wainwright, outside Fairbanks. The flight from southern to central Alaska lasted forty-five minutes. Mount McKinley, the highest peak in North America, lay partially hidden in gunmetal fog, even as a lid of clouds was cracking open to reveal a lava red band on the western horizon. As the sun set in the late afternoon, the moon was already high in the sky.

Directly below, between masses of black spruce, the snow already had a faded February look. The Arctic tundra was a ragged death shroud of vegetation embedded in ice. It was a landscape of abstract brutality. Finally, Fairbanks and nearby Fort Wainwright appeared, meager gridworks in the snowy twilight. Fort Wainwright, where most of the 172nd Stryker Brigade was based, was named for Army Gen. Jonathan Wainwright, a defender of Bataan and Corregidor in the early days of World War II in the Philippines. In an example of the unlimited amount of space available to the U.S. military in Alaska, Fort Wainwright boasted access to no less than 10 percent of all the land controlled by the Army throughout the entire United States.

Maj. Gohlke, who had lived in Fairbanks, adored the area. Normally a quiet, taciturn guy, he lit up while talking about the summer solstice, when the first minor league pitch was thrown at midnight without the need for artificial lighting. "They'll put on a local production of *The Nutcracker,* and people with overalls who arrived in a flatbed truck will be sitting next to people in evening dress. In summer," he continued, "you can practically walk across the rivers on the backs of beavers. The salmon run twelve hundred miles from the ocean to here. They haven't eaten since leaving the salt water and are almost dead, yet they still put up a fight."

Central Alaska near the Yukon River brought to mind, like no other place, the poetry of Robert W. Service and the prose of Jack London, two literary naturals and picaresque balladeers who had rollicking adventures to relate because their education had consisted not of the classroom, but of the school of hard knocks. London's adventure stories, like Service's Kiplingesque poetry, were inspired by the Alaskan gold rush: a last-ditch attempt to forge a new frontier in an increasingly crowded and recently industrialized America.[1] London, an American, and Service, a Canadian, had both come of age in the first years of the twentieth century; thus their writing is unaffected by the literary modernism that came in the wake of World War I. Both had been vagabonds in search of gold in the far north. London wrote a story and Service a poem each entitled "The Call of the Wild." Both were attracted to the brutal mountainscapes and fifty-below, starlit, wolf-howling nights of what Service called the "Great Alone."[2] London was more explicit: "In the Klondike . . . I found myself. There nobody talks."[3]

Truly, Fairbanks was small, very quiet, and more rough-hewn than Anchorage, a Middle American counterpart to the latter's Seattlesque cosmopolitanism. At a restaurant-bar in Fairbanks with a real Klondike feel frequented by locals and off-duty servicemen I learned the results of the 2004 elections between President George W. Bush and Democratic challenger Sen. John Kerry. I was in the midst of a discussion with a lieutenant colonel about the demons of Pentagon bureaucracy when the energy level at the nearby tables suddenly intensified. I looked up at two TV screens whose audio I could not make out, because of the noise around me. On one screen Fox News commentators William Kristol and Fred Barnes were bobbing up and down in their seats with jocular expressions; on the other CBS News anchorman Dan Rather had an ashen, funereal look. The body language alone indicated the result. By the time we left, Bush was one electoral vote short of reelection and smiles and cheers lit up the place. The next morning I was eating breakfast in a local hangout when two young, very hip-looking women started high-fiving each other and shouting, "Bush won, Bush won!" I was a long way from my home in Massachusetts.

Fort Wainwright, around which life in Fairbanks revolved, was an illustration of what Bush's foreign policy meant for infantry line units. Spread out for miles in the surrounding tundra, where the trees only looked dead because of the permafrost, the 172nd Stryker Brigade had turned this part of Alaska into a make-believe Iraq. In a blizzard-strewn forest clearing, I found the 4th Battalion of the 11th Field Artillery of the 172nd bivouacked in heated tents and manning a TCP (traffic control point), set up like so many I had seen the previous spring in Iraq's Sunni Triangle, with oil drums and concertina wire arranged in obstacle-course fashion. The commanding officer had had his men react to eighty-seven theoretical events over the past forty-eight hours—a pregnant woman demanding medical help, a kid hiding plastic explosives, a nervous local police chief ready to flip to the side of the insurgents, an IED (improvised explosive device) that had gone off, and so on.

All these incidents represented exactly what I had experienced with the Marines in Iraq the previous spring. The essential reality of Iraq had been communicated successfully down the chain of command to this battalion in Alaska: a field artillery unit in an unconventional environment faced many challenges that had nothing to do with field artillery.

The Arctic, rather than being unrealistic of Iraq, was good preparation for it. War fighting, particularly in the high-tech twenty-first century, relied on logistics: making sure there were enough MREs, enough battery chargers for intra-squad radios and night-vision goggles, enough ammunition, and so on. The Arctic was an intensification of this burden. In the heat, if you didn't bring enough socks or underwear, you were uncomfortable, but you weren't disabled. In the Arctic, if you didn't pack perfectly you got frostbite, or worse. In the Arctic, every little detail, like zeroing your gunsight, was more difficult because you had to do it with gloves on. In the Arctic, you simply had more things to remember—more clothes to bring, more requirements for protecting your electronic equipment. I remembered what Army Col. Tom Wilhelm, a veteran of the Cold War Arctic infantry, had told me eighteen months earlier in Mongolia: in the Arctic every movement had to be planned minutely since you couldn't afford to break a sweat, because once you stopped sweating you'd turn into a Popsicle.

Since extremely cold weather demanded more planning, it developed leadership. If even one private touched a piece of metal with a bare, frostbitten finger, it could tear some skin off and end the career of his immediate commander. And Iraq, among many other things, was about the effectiveness of platoon-level commanders. Though Green Berets could be very critical of the rest of the Army, they often made an exception for the units in Alaska. There was something about the severe cold, they had told me, that bred good soldiers.

I wandered into the battalion TOC (tactical operations center) and reentered Iraq. There was a beehive of activity under a large canvas tent, with laptops and Blue Force Trackers (satellite-based tracking and communication systems), and separate huddles taking place about the latest incident. The only difference was the vapor-barrier boots that everyone wore against the cold. Elsewhere in the tundra I found a mock Iraqi village with the Islamic prayer call blasting over loudspeakers, and cruddy cement blockhouses, like so many I had seen in Iraq, which, when you entered them, revealed a chaos of cheesy furniture and the Arabic language screams of children coming through hidden speakers.

FROM PACOM TO NORTHCOM

Deploying soldiers to Iraq was a typical task for PACOM, which traditionally supplied many of the troops with which CENTCOM (Central Command) fought its Middle Eastern wars. But to see the NORTH-COM homeland security element of the U.S. military in Alaska, I had to journey for several hours southeast from Fort Wainwright to Fort Greely, past a section of the Alaskan pipeline, through the morbid virginity of ice-curdled streams and unyielding birch forests. Fort Greely, named for Army Maj. Gen. Adolphus Greely, an early-twentieth-century Arctic explorer, was a key component of President Bush's emerging missile defense program. For the nearby town of Delta Junction, which boasted a couple of auto parts stores, one liquor store, and ten churches, the missile base represented the only economic hope.

The missile site was in a quasi-state of activation. Many of the underground silos were filled with interceptor missiles; others waited to be filled. The system was being tested and had yet to be turned on for actual deployment. The key acronym here was FCS (fire control system), insipid bureaucratic dialect for "killing," or intercepting, an incoming missile from a rogue state like North Korea. "It's a surface-to-air system on steroids," explained Army Lt. Col. Greg Bowen of Grand Forks, North Dakota, the local commander. The kill would take place in "mid-course," that is, when the incoming missile was at the highest point of its trajectory a hundred miles above earth, allowing the defender missile time to adjust its own course.

Many serious questions remained about the effectiveness of such a system, designed not to protect against a barrage of incoming missiles from a superpower like the Soviet Union, but against a single projectile fired by a relatively poor and radicalized country. Because such a country could not afford an arms race, this system, however imperfect and untested, might be able, it was claimed, to deter simply because of its existence. As for the threat posed by an emerging superpower, such as China, well, in such a hypothetical situation, other systems would have to be built. Fort Greely was but one "layer" of a growing missile defense network that would soon feature giant, offshore radar plat-forms floating off the most distant of the Aleutian Islands, close to East Asia.

The untested technology did not interest me as much as other things here. Responsibility for the entire facility rested with two hundred Alaskan national guardsmen commanded by Lt. Col. Bowen. Because they lived locally and had been assigned to Fort Greely for a decade al-ready, they had developed an occupational expertise that you rarely en-countered in the regular Army, where everyone was constantly being moved around. They reminded me of the Texas and Florida national guardsmen in Army Special Forces with whom I had been embedded the year before on the Afghanistan-Pakistan border. The Texans and Floridians were cops and state troopers in private life, whose commu-nity policing skills were vital in dealing with teenagers in Afghan border villages. National guardsmen—often a network of "good old boys"—were inching their way toward the front lines for both the exterior War on Terrorism and the interior function of homeland security. The guards-men here interacted fine with the private contractors at the heart of mis-sile defense; it was the active-duty military that was missing, for the missile defense system at Fort Greely was built and maintained by Boeing. The "industrial" part of the "military-industrial complex" had always been private. It was witnessing the tangible reality that made me realize just how inextricable the two parts of that concept were.

Another interesting facet about Greely was that it looked like nothing; it was a bunch of flat-roofed concrete-block facilities, almost Soviet in their ugliness, on a grubby white Arctic desert haunted by caribou, and filled with tractors, forklifts, and shipping containers. The only indication of the actual underground missile site, which included miles of tunnels, was the candy-cane-shaped aluminum air vents sticking out of the ground, reminiscent of any residential septic field. In the distance were granite peaks painted with ice and snow, standing between the Alaska and Brooks ranges.

The biggest social event at Fort Greely was the square dances at the base MWR (Morale, Welfare, and Recreation) facility. It certainly was a bleak landscape, both culturally and geologically. But as missile technology went forward, along with the Air Force's ability to transport troops over the pole, the Arctic was destined to play a large role in America's military future, one that had not gone away with the passing of the Cold War, with its polar trajectories for nuclear missiles and its submarine sorties in the marginal ice.

On the way back to Fort Wainwright, I spotted a moose with her calf in the deep snow. Twenty-four hours later, a series of military and commercial flights brought me from the Arctic Circle to the Tropic of Cancer—to Honolulu, where a tropical rainstorm was in progress.

Honolulu, halfway across the Pacific, was the headquarters of PACOM. Here my Pacific odyssey would start in earnest, as would my introduction to the world of the Navy and Air Force, after two years with Army Special Forces and the Marines. I had stopped at PACOM in the summer of 2003, en route to embedding with the Army's 1st Special Forces Group in the southern Philippines, and I had been back several times since.* It being the weekend, I went to two hallowed sites I had missed on previous visits.

* See Chapter 4 of *Imperial Grunts* for a description of PACOM headquarters overlooking Pearl Harbor, the PACOM area of responsibility, and the Hawaiian island of Oahu's significance to the U.S. military.

The first was the national military cemetery at the Pouwaina ("Hill of Sacrifice"), where the indigenous Hawaiians had sacrificed offenders of certain *kapas* (taboos) to the pagan gods. In Section D, Grave 109, beside a banyan tree, among the other flat markers level with the ground, lay the remains of Ernie Taylor Pyle. An Indiana native, Pyle was killed at the age of forty-four in April 1945 during the Battle of Okinawa. He was a newspaper correspondent who had lived with the troops and wrote from their point of view. Like his fellow World War II correspondents in the Pacific, including Robert Sherrod and Richard Tregaskis, Pyle was sympathetic to his fellow Americans in uniform, demonstrated by the use of "we" and "our" in his narratives. Standing beside his grave, located between two unknowns, I thought of my late editor at *The Atlantic Monthly,* Michael Kelly, killed at a similar age while covering Operation Iraqi Freedom in April 2003. Kelly, like Pyle, manifested an honest, working-class punch in his sympathetic narratives about American soldiers.

The second hallowed spot was the USS *Missouri,* anchored off Ford Island in Pearl Harbor. Christened during World War II by then-senator Harry Truman's daughter, Margaret, the *Missouri* saw action in the last months of the war, at Iwo Jima and Okinawa. It was struck by a kamikaze at the latter battle. Each of its nine main guns weighed as much as the space shuttle: 239,000 pounds. On September 2, 1945, while the *Missouri* lay anchored in Tokyo Bay, the Instrument of Formal Surrender ending World War II was signed on its teakwood deck, next to an American flag brought to Japan in 1853 by Commodore Matthew Perry. Upon the last Japanese signature, 450 propeller-driven Allied aircraft buzzed the battleship. One sailor described it as a sound that shook the world. At a time when China, Japan, and Western Europe lay in ruins, and when the Soviet Union had yet to develop an atomic bomb, that moment aboard this ship represented the climax of American power. The American volunteer military, enjoying the soldiering life for its own sake, and occupied with its train-and-equip missions worldwide, might have been in an imperial-like situation, but it was doubtful that even after the Soviet Union collapsed, at the height of our unipolar power, we dominated the world as much as we did back then.

In the mid-1950s the *Missouri* was decommissioned. In 1984, President Ronald Reagan, against the advice of naval experts, recommissioned the ship out of mothballs, refitted it, and sent it on a world tour, the first time such a thing was done since President Theodore Roosevelt had sent the "Great White Fleet" on a world tour eight decades earlier. Reagan might not have understood naval technology, but he understood national myth.

At the rechristening ceremony, his defense secretary, Caspar Weinberger, charged the assembled sailors: "Listen for the footsteps of those who have gone before you. They speak to you of honor and the importance of duty. They remind you of your own traditions."*

As I had been observing for some years, it was still such traditions adjoined to patriotic myth that constituted a hidden hand impelling the U.S. military forward.

In fact, even under George Bush, a president with a unilateral foreign policy relative to previous presidents, the U.S. military was trying to construct a system of multilateral security relationships, with pivotal political and economic implications. The Pacific was the best place to witness this development. Here PACOM was attempting to tranform itself into a variant of the North Atlantic Treaty Organization in a region that stretched from East Africa to the International Date Line in the central Pacific and constituted more than half of the world's economy. Two of the world's most rapidly modernizing militaries (those of the United States and China) resided within the PACOM area of responsibility. By negotiating bilateral agreements with dozens of countries that had few bilateral security agreements with one another, a regional military alliance of sorts was quietly being formed here at PACOM headquarters.

Otto von Bismarck, the Prussian father of the Second Reich in continental Europe, would have recognized this emerging system. In 2002 the German journalist Josef Joffe argued, in a remarkably perceptive article, that the United States had morphed into Bismarck's Prussia.[4] Just as Britain, Russia, and Austria needed Prussia more than they needed one another—making them "spokes" to Berlin's "hub"—the

---

* The *Missouri* was decommissioned for the last time in 1992, during the administration of President Bill Clinton.

U.S. invasion of Afghanistan, Joffe explained, exposed a world in which America was able to forge different coalitions for each crisis, because the other powers needed America more than they needed one another.

Joffe's insight turned out to be premature, though, because President Bush lacked the nuance and attendant self-restraint of Bismarck, who understood that such a system could endure only so long as one didn't overwhelm it with ever greater goals and challenges. The Bush administration did just that by the clumsy, often insulting way in which it tried to build a coalition for the invasion of Iraq, so France, Germany, Russia, and China, as well as a host of lesser powers such as Turkey, Mexico, and Chile, united against America to bring down this new Bismarckian power arrangement.

It was only in the Pacific that Bismarck's late-nineteenth-century system still survived and prospered for the United States, helped along by the pragmatism of Hawaii-based military officers five time zones removed from the ideological hothouse of Washington, D.C. PACOM represented a purer version of Bismarck's imperial superstructure than anything the Bush administration created prior to invading Iraq. Bismarck forged alliances in all directions from a point of seeming isolation, without the constraints of ideology, writes Henry Kissinger in *Diplomacy*.[5] Bismarck's was an amoral system that brought peace and prosperity to Central Europe, because when power relationships are correctly calibrated, wars tend to be avoided. Such a system could ease China's inevitable reemergence as a great power, without destabilizing world politics. China was now expanding its sphere of influence in the Pacific and beyond, just as the United States had done in the nineteenth century, while carving out a mercantile, seaborne empire of its own, propelled by the economic dynamism that ensued from the industrial North's victory in the Civil War.

China's investment in both diesel- and nuclear-powered submarines meant that in addition to protecting its coastal shelves, it was intent on building a blue water (oceanic) navy that could project power beyond its borders. This was wholly legitimate. China's rulers were not democrats in the literal sense, but they were seeking a liberated first-world lifestyle for many of their 1.3 billion people. That meant protecting sea-lanes for the sake of transporting oil—necessary for the consumption habits of a new middle class. Naturally, China's rulers did not trust the navies of the United States and India to do that for them. Yet as history has demonstrated, big powers all pursuing legitimate interests occasionally come into conflict. Thus, the defining regional struggle of the first half of the twenty-first century might occur within the PACOM area of responsibility (AOR). A war with China was a very remote possibility; more likely was a series of extremely subtle, military and diplomatic standoffs. America's complete dominance over the Pacific was over. China seemed determined to be the master of subtle, peaceful influence, something that, after all, required a military component. It was a reality with which we had to come to terms.

It is worthwhile to note here that military officers had to approach the world in the most cautious, mechanical, and utilitarian way possible, assessing and reassessing regional balances of power while leaving the values side of the political equation to the civilian leadership. This made military officers, of all government professionals, the least likely to be led astray by the raptures of what in the early twenty-first century were labeled "liberal internationalism" and "neoconservative interventionism." The history of World War II shows the importance of this attitude. In the 1930s, the U.S. military, nervous about the growing strength of Germany and Japan, rightly lobbied for building up American forces. But in 1940 and 1941, the military (not unlike the German General Staff a few years earlier) was presciently warning of the dangers of a two-front war; and by late summer of 1944, it should have been thinking less and less about defeating Germany and more and more about containing the Soviet Union.

To wit, Air Force and Navy officers now worried about the dangers of a Taiwanese declaration of independence, because such a move could lead the United States into a war with China that it might not be in our national interest to fight. Or take Indonesia: whatever the human rights failures of the Indonesian military, PACOM assumed that a policy of nonengagement would only have opened the door to Chinese-Indonesian military cooperation in a region that represented the future of world terrorism. Or Korea: a few Pacific-based officers simply took a reunified Korean Peninsula of some sort for granted, and their main concern was whether it would be "Finlandized" by China, or would reside within an American-Japanese sphere of influence.

Certainly, a tendency toward Bismarckian thinking was true of all the area commands. But PACOM was particularly likely to have influence on foreign policy in coming years. PACOM was further removed from Washington and harder to micromanage than, say, CENTCOM. Whereas the CENTCOM headquarters at Tampa was in the eastern time zone, only two hours distant by air from the nation's capital, Honolulu was halfway across the Pacific: farther from Washington than Europe even. PACOM was more unwieldy than CENTCOM. It had more troops under its permanent command, and more complex and numerous political-military relationships to maintain with serious powers like Japan, Australia, and India, whereas the allies of CENTCOM, in the disparaging words of a few military experts, were a bunch of "third-rate Middle Eastern armies."

PACOM hoped to manage a rising China in hub-and-spoke Bismarckian fashion, from a geographic point of comparative isolation—the Hawaiian Islands—with spokes reaching out to major allies such as Japan, South Korea, Thailand, Singapore, Australia, New Zealand, and India. These countries, in turn, formed secondary hubs to help manage the Melanesian, Micronesian, and Polynesian archipelagoes, among other places, and also the Indian Ocean. The point of this arrangement was to dissuade China so subtly that over time the rising behemoth would be drawn into the PACOM alliance system without any military disruptions. Because of the vast economic and trade consequences of misjudging the power balance in East Asia, American business and military interests ran in tandem, toward a classically conservative policy of constraining China, without ever needlessly provoking it.

In the Pacific you couldn't disentangle war fighting from diplomacy, for if the dust ever did settle in the Middle East, the reemergence of China as a great power for the first time in two hundred years loomed as the single greatest military-diplomatic challenge to the United States. China was the world's most populous and culturally dynamic civilization, with an economy that had been growing at 10 percent yearly for over a decade. Pulsing with consumer and martial energy, and boasting a peasantry that unlike others in history was overwhelmingly literate, authoritarian China constituted the principal counterpoint to America's liberal imperium.

China's mixture of authoritarianism and market economics had broad cultural appeal throughout Asia, where it was the biggest trading partner of Thailand, Australia, South Korea, and Japan. Just as stateless terrorists were filling security vacuums, the Chinese were filling economic ones. All over the world, whether it was in the troubled Pacific island states of Oceania, the Panama Canal Zone, or out-of-the-way African nations like Djibouti and Niger, the Chinese, sometimes through émigré communities, were becoming the masters of indirect influence—by establishing business communities and diplomatic outposts, by negotiating construction and trade agreements. China, unlike the former Soviet Union, boasted soft as well as hard power.

Businesspeople adored China; you didn't have to beg them to invest there, as you did in parts of Africa and many other places. Because China's authoritarian regime was improving the material well-being of hundreds of millions of its citizens, the plight of its dissidents did not seem to have the same degree of urgency as did the plight of the Soviet Union's Sakharovs and Sharanskys.

Alas, managing China required far greater subtlety than America's Cold War strategy against the Kremlin. PACOM's goal was to make military bilateral relationships throughout the region so inextricable that even China would become enmeshed in them. Peace had also to be bought by traditional balance-of-power methods. PACOM had become an instrument for improved ties with India and Vietnam—two former U.S. adversaries that remained wary of China. PACOM's numerous unit commanders had all made visits to India as part of a burgeoning military relationship, and the U.S. Air Force was flying training sorties with its Indian counterparts. Meanwhile, the Seventh Fleet was making port calls at Saigon and Da Nang, and Vietnamese special operators were working with their American equivalents.* PACOM's goal was to have similar bilateral arrangements with the Chinese themselves.

In some cases such intermingling existed on the micro as well as the macro level. Lt. Gen. Wallace Gregson, the commander of Marine

---

* Saigon was still the name of the port of Ho Chi Minh City.

Forces, Pacific (MARFORPAC), at the time of my visit, had embedded marines with Philippine Army battalions, and had plans to do likewise with other Asian countries. The goal, he told me, was to have U.S. troops move around permanently from one training deployment with a friendly Asian military to another. By training with the Thais, the Bangladeshis, and "the Sings" (Singaporeans), for instance, interoperability could be forged at the platoon level. The best individual example of this that I would encounter in Honolulu was in the person of Australian Army Lt. Col. Mark Probert, PACOM's commanding officer for homeland defense—homeland defense of the United States, that is.

Nevertheless, military multilateralism in the Pacific was constrained by the technical superiority of U.S. forces; it was difficult to develop bilateral training missions with many Asian militaries that were not making the same investments in high-technology equipment that the Americans were. A classic military lesson was that technological superiority did not always confer the advantages one expected. Getting militarily so far ahead of everyone else in the world created, among other problems, a particular kind of loneliness that not even the best diplomats could alleviate.

The Pacific was a more complicated affair than poverty-wracked sub-Saharan Africa, where the American military could make significant inroads with just a platoon of marines or Green Berets here and there. The North Atlantic Treaty Organization had always been more important to global stability than the United Nations; it kept the Soviet Union at bay, thus keeping the peace in Europe for decades, and boasted a military machine able to intervene anywhere, very competently. That's why PACOM's unstated goal was the creation of the rough equivalent of NATO in the Pacific.

The largest building blocks of such a political-military alliance were America's bilateral relationships with Japan and Australia. The Global War on Terrorism and the military threat posed by North Korea had given the Japanese government the impetus to further remilitarize—a necessary if ironic development for peace in half the globe. Australia owned a vast training space in its northern desert that was to become the tropical equivalent of Alaska for PACOM and its allies. Its political leadership was comfortable with a fighting military that intervened in expeditionary style throughout the terrorist-rich "crescent of instability" from Indonesia to Micronesia, thereby taking some of the burden off the Americans.

PACOM, like any effective peacekeeper, had to transmit to any potential adversary the willingness to fight and kill at a moment's notice. And post-9/11, what was happening in Alaska—converting the U.S. Army there into a fast-deployable combat strike force—was starting to happen throughout the Pacific. Notably, the headquarters of the Army's I Corps was in the process of permanently forward-deploying from Fort Lewis, Washington, to Japan, in order to form the backbone of PACOM's Joint Forces Command—the equivalent of an enlarged Stryker Brigade for fighting on contested littorals.

—

PACOM was, to a significant degree, Big Navy incarnate. It was no accident that many of PACOM's combatant commanders had been Navy admirals. The U.S. Navy was an obvious instrument for the delicate management of growing Chinese power. To a degree not quite true of armies or marines, navies had been instruments of soft state power, and as such were defined less by their war-fighting abilities than was the case with land forces. Peacetime navies suppressed slavery and protected merchant ships, even as they were a traditional means of one state applying discreet pressure on another. Sea power had been a more useful means of realpolitik than land power. It allowed for a substantial military presence in areas geographically remote from the homeland, without the homeland in question appearing belligerent. Navies, combined with air forces, allowed for global access—a need that was constant—whereas the need for army insertions on land was intermittent.[6]

Freedom has had a tendency to follow the shores of the oceans, so a reliance on naval power was more friendly to democracy than a reliance on land power.[7] Navies made port visits, armies invaded. Thus, naval imperialism was not usually recognized as imperialism. Because ships took so long to get somewhere, and were less threatening than actual troops on the ground, naval forces allowed diplomats to ratchet up pressure in a responsible way during a crisis—in a way that was reversible.[8] Navies made one truly aware of the link between military might and diplomatic influence. Take the Cuban Missile Crisis of 1962.

As the British expert H. P. Willmott writes, "The use of naval power by the Americans was the least dangerous option that presented itself, and the slowness with which events unfolded at sea gave time for both sides to conceive and implement a rational response to a highly dangerous situation."*

Submarines have been an exception to this rule. Because of their ability to hide in great oceans and outrun surface warships, plus the fact that their weapons during the Cold War years were often aimed at civilian targets, submarines have been the ultimate stealthy tool of violence. The Battle of the Atlantic, in the middle of World War II, saw the initial relative decline of submarines, though, as their effectiveness decreased with the improved ability to detect them through sonar. But as I would learn at sea in the coming months, sailing both on the surface and below it, submarine warfare was experiencing a resurgence. It wasn't just that the Chinese were investing heavily in subs. In an age of media intrusiveness, submarines were an attractive option. Their ability to operate both literally and figuratively below the surface, completely off the media radar screen, allowed a government to be militarily aggressive, particularly in the field of espionage, without offending the sensibilities of its citizenry. To wit, Sweden's neutrality was a hard-won luxury bought by its own aggressive submarine fleet, so it did not require NATO protection—a fact of life that many idealistic Swedes were incompletely aware of.

Modern navies, in addition to the ability to fight from below the surface, had to fight from above it: through the projection of airpower from carrier decks.[9] The development of the aircraft carrier was gradual. The realization of its use for offensive as well as defensive operations had to wait until fighter planes themselves could increase their speed and range. Another complication was that a carrier had to travel fast—up to thirty-four knots—to create high winds across its deck for the launching and recovering of aircraft.† Because battleships traveled at least ten knots slower than carriers through the 1930s, they could not accompany

---

* H. P. Willmott, *Sea Warfare: Weapons, Tactics and Strategy* (New York: Hippocrene, 1981), pp. 3–4. The following paragraphs draw significantly from this fine, succinct book.

† Anyone who has sailed knows the phenomenon: motoring through the water on a calm day, you may think you have enough wind to sail until you turn off the engine, when you discover that the wind you felt was only that artificially generated by the boat moving through the water under motor.

them. It wasn't until the *Iowa* class of battleships, which included the USS *Missouri,* came on line that fleets and carrier strike groups, as we currently know them, emerged.

The aircraft carrier's apotheosis came at the Battle of the Coral Sea in May 1942, when all the losses were inflicted by carrier-based planes. But the really big news to come out of the Pacific Theater in World War II was less the effectiveness of the carrier than the emergence of the American long-haul navy. As Willmott explains, effective fighting ranges for fleets were assumed to be no more than two thousand miles from their home bases. But the Americans staged landings at Tarawa in the Gilbert Islands and Saipan in the Marianas, which were 2,500 miles and 3,700 miles, respectively, from Pearl Harbor in Hawaii. They were also victorious at the Battle of the Philippine Sea, and off the coast of New Guinea, at distances of 4,500 miles and more. This was due to the immense number of tugs, repair ships, fast oilers, cargo and salvage vessels, and hospital boats the Americans were able to deploy close to their sea battles. "Statistics almost become meaningless in trying to convey the sheer size of the American effort," Willmott writes.[10]

At the end of World War II, the combination of air and sea power allowed the United States to dominate the world's oceans to a degree not seen since the Diamond Jubilee of Queen Victoria in 1897, when the British Royal Navy had three times as many ships as its nearest rival, the French, and boasted ironclads, destroyers, torpedo boats, and other ships with names like *Thunderer, Devastation, Boomerang,* and *Gossamer*— "the names that Kipling loved." As it passed its prime, the Royal Navy considered its job less the fighting of battles than the safeguarding of law and order and of civilization worldwide: by protecting merchant fleets and putting out the fires of onshore rebellions.*

The U.S. Navy at the turn of the twenty-first century now had a similar role, with which I was later to become intimately familiar.

———

The U.S. Navy also had a homeland defense responsibility. To see this firsthand, one morning I drove from my quarters at Hickam Air Force

---

* James (later Jan) Morris, *Pax Britannica: The Climax of an Empire* (New York: Harcourt, Brace,1968), pp. 421, 424, 425. In fact, as Morris mentions, the Royal Navy was already past its prime by then, though few in 1897 had the perspective to notice.

Base* near Pearl Harbor to the Marine air base at Kaneohe Bay, where I boarded a Navy P-3 surveillance plane for the short flight to the Navy's Barking Sands missile range. Hawaiian highways began and ended at these bases. The original Cold War intent of President Dwight Eisenhower's interstate highway system in the 1950s had been to link military bases throughout the mainland United States. That point was lost on the public because the highways linked everything else, too. But here on the island of Oahu, Eisenhower's purpose was visually more tangible.

I was familiar with the P-3 surveillance plane from my visits to Colombia and the southern Philippines in 2003, where it was employed to track movements of narco-terrorists and Abu Sayyaf guerrillas slipping in and out of jungles and small harbors. The P-3 was an old cargo plane packed with the latest electronic surveillance equipment, originally designed to hunt Soviet submarines. Flying in such rattling and austere gray metal crates, which had been converted and reconverted from one purpose to another, and considering other decades-long standbys such as the A-10 and the B-52, I realized that despite the obvious truth about financial waste in the military, another side of the tale was the stingy resourcefulness of the Navy and Air Force, which kept these old planes in the sky.

The missile range was located on the westernmost beach of the westernmost of the populated Hawaiian Islands, Kauai. The International Date Line was relatively close by. There were few other places farther west you could visit. The beach and the area around it were closed to the public. Not surprisingly, a more beautiful beach was hard to imagine, with no footprints on the sand except for those made by turtles.

While the missiles at Fort Greely in Alaska could shoot down incoming projectiles in mid-course, at the edge of outer space, the missiles soon to arrive at Barking Sands represented another layer of protection,

---

* Named after Lt. Col. Horace Meek Hickam, born in Spencer, Indiana, in 1885. A graduate of West Point, Lt. Col. Hickam served in the Philippines and in the expedition against Pancho Villa in Mexico. He became an early advocate of airpower in its own right, not merely as an adjunct to ground forces. He was killed in 1934 when his plane hit an embankment at Fort Crockett in Galveston, Texas.

designed to kill rogue projectiles during ballistic reentry. Fort Greely was an Army base; Barking Sands a Navy base. But the difference meant little. The missiles here would be managed by the Army and civilian contractors from Lockheed. And the oceanic testing area that this Navy base operated—as large as the United States west of the Missouri River—was used often by the Marines and Air Force. "Jointness," as it was called in the military, was slowly breaking down borders between the still-hostile services.

Yet the most interesting people at Barking Sands were civilians: unpretentious locals from sleepy hamlets around the island, who, like the Alaska national guardsmen at Fort Greely, were the ones ultimately responsible for testing President Bush's missile defense program. Take Aubrey Kunihige, Pat Alvarez, and Averiet Soto, three jacks-of-all-trades who served as program managers and technical specialists for the launch sequences. The sons of sugarcane farmers, Kunihige was an ethnic Japanese, Alvarez an ethnic Filipino, and Soto an ethnic Portuguese. All were military veterans, with children currently in the service. They had worked at Barking Sands for decades.

Kunihige and Soto had been on a temporary duty assignment in the naval annex beside the Pentagon on 9/11, and felt the whoosh of the incoming plane. When I asked how it had affected them, they just said that it added "resolve" to their work here. They had nothing more to say. They were quiet, unassuming men, content to work twelve hours daily hammering away at their keyboards in this hectic, anal environment where few people talked, so evocative of the space program. As space itself became militarized—driven, among many other things, by the competition between the United States and China—men like these represented the future of war; or at least the technological aspect of it.

From Hickam Air Force Base in Hawaii, I flew west across the Pacific to Andersen Air Force Base in Guam.* My plane was a KC-135 Stratotanker, a forty-five-year-old all-purpose air-to-air refueler, used

---

* Named after Brig. Gen. James R. Andersen, former chief of staff of the Army Air Forces, Pacific, who was lost at sea in a B-24 crash while returning to Honolulu in 1945.

mainly for B-52s. Flying military air was a crapshoot. Whether in Iraq, Afghanistan, or Hawaii, you were usually delayed not by hours but by days. Two C-5 cargo planes destined for Guam had both developed technical difficulties, and the KC-135 represented my third attempt in twenty-four hours to leave Honolulu. But I wasn't complaining—all the flights were free. They were provided by the Air Mobility Command, a branch of the Air Force that coordinated departures and arrivals of military aircraft between bases all over the world. Because Air Force planes usually had extra space on board for passengers, military families regularly utilized them, trading comfort and reliability for the chance to see loved ones at zero expense.

I took my place alongside smiling adults and small children, as we settled down on hard canvas seats facing inward on the plane's shabby interior, cluttered with exposed pipes and wires. The suffocating heat did not cease until we were airborne. Before boarding, we had all purchased box lunches consisting of processed ham and cheese sandwiches, along with milk and cookies, from Air Force Food Services at $3.30 apiece. It was Veterans Day. Inside the Air Force departure terminal everyone had been watching in rapt silence the official commemorations at Arlington National Cemetery, interspersed with commentary from the latest fighting in Al-Fallujah on Fox News. CNN had been covering the death of Palestinian leader Yasser Arafat. Nobody had wanted to watch that. "Get that communist shit off," one retired sailor had shouted. All this was part of a common experience that separated the military—down to the youngest dependent—from the rest of society.

Because of the noise in the fuselage and the need for earplugs, passengers on military flights never talked. As the plane took off, I contemplated the 3,284 nautical miles to Guam: eight hours of flying over nothing but water, merely to get from the central to the western Pacific. The Pacific Ocean was the central organizing principle of the earth's surface, occupying nearly a third of it, larger than the entire dry land area of the planet. Double the size of the Atlantic, at its widest point, from the coast of Colombia to the Malay Peninsula, it covered half the circumference of the earth. The Pacific's mean depth was over 14,000 feet; and at the Mariana Trench it was much deeper than Mount Everest was high, reaching down 36,201 feet, close to seven miles. The very scale of this hydrosphere suggests the inhuman dimensions of the heavens over-head.

The sea and the sky represented the purest and most abstract land-scapes of war and strategy, in which the peculiarities of culture and terrain played little role. This was especially true when one considered that navies and air forces were primarily transport systems—particularly in a navy's case, because buoyancy has been cheap compared to aero-dynamic lift.* Writes British naval expert Eric Grove: the United States, as a "semi-island continent, must go to sea" to exert military power. Yet sea power was indivisible from airpower, because, as Grove continues, "Seaborne platforms provide some of the most flexible, and least vul-nerable ways of deploying . . . aircraft or missiles."[11]

The watery void below me was deceptive, though, for in the after-math of the Cold War, with dirty little ethnic struggles proliferating across vast Pacific archipelagoes, Navy and Air Force planners had to concentrate on dry-land terrains to an unprecedented degree: 70 percent of the world's population lived in such coastal areas. This would have to translate into a Navy with a larger number of ships that were increas-ingly smaller in size. With an enemy now defined by many small clus-ters of combatants, not just the Army and Marines, but the Navy, too, had to morph down to the unit size of the adversary. Smaller, more nu-merous ships meant an increase in the complexity of the Pacific's battle and maneuver space.

Concomitantly, the Navy and Air Force—whose strategic planning was now inseparable—knew that their services still had to defend im-mense sections of the planet's watery and dry-land surface through old-fashioned, conventional means, thereby allowing Army Special Forces and the Marines to focus on the unconventional edges of the battlefield. So complex were the challenges that when I had mentioned the threat of piracy in the Pacific to a Navy futurist back in Washington, he scoffed and told me piracy was just part of the noise.

The only land directly in our midst during the flight was Wake Island

---

* In all of America's overseas military deployments, sealift has been responsible for the over-whelming percentage of dry cargo and petroleum supplies.

and Johnston Atoll, both U.S. possessions. To the south, sprinkled like fairy dust across the ocean, lay the Gilbert, Marshall, and Caroline islands, among other archipelagoes. The fourteen independent island states that encompassed Melanesia, Polynesia, and Micronesia were symptomatic of the new century's diplomatic and security complexities. While small in population, Oceania constituted a significant voting bloc in the United Nations, and lay claim to immense maritime resources. In particular, Melanesia had become a zone of violent internal conflict and ethnic strife in places such as Tonga, Fiji, East Timor, and the Solomon Islands. Such crumbling states were shadowy conduits for money laundering and weapons smuggling that abetted international terrorism. Their internal weaknesses were providing an opening for the Chinese, who naturally were increasingly active with new embassies in all of these places.[12]

Halfway into the flight we crossed the International Date Line and moved our clocks ahead twenty-three hours, putting Veterans Day behind us. The experience made me think of the days of the Pan Am Clipper service of the mid-twentieth century, fondly recalled to me by Pacific military veterans of a certain age. The Pan Am plane would island hop from Honolulu to Midway, then to Wake and Guam en route to Manila in the Philippines, chasing the sunset all the way.

Eight hours after takeoff, bumpily descending through the tropical rain clouds, for a moment we saw nothing, then, suddenly, the co-pilot exclaimed, "Holy shit, look at that! Land Ho," as a big green monster of an island came into view. Landing at Andersen Air Force Base on Guam's northern tip, bordered on three sides by six-hundred-foot cliffs dropping sheer into the ocean, I beheld long lines of B-52 bombers, C-17 Globemasters, F-18 Hornets, and E-2 Hawkeye surveillance planes, among a plethora of other military aircraft. A crew member pointed to a reinforced-concrete, typhoon-proof hangar under construction for B-1 bombers. "That's for protection against our friends across the Sea of Japan," he said, referring to the North Koreans. I noticed a truck filled with cruise missiles on one of the runways.

In an era of constant jet travel, airports, even military ones, weren't particularly interesting to look at. But if one considered a few facts about Andersen, and where it was located, it was worth several days of awe at least. Andersen was nothing less than the most potent platform anywhere for projecting American military power at great distances, for it was the future that Andersen represented for U.S. strategy in the Pacific that had brought me to Guam. Massive circular tanks held sixty-six million gallons of jet fuel, making it the Air Force's biggest strategic gas-and-go in the world. No other Air Force base in the Pacific stored as much weaponry: 100,000 bombs and missiles at any one time. Its 10,500-foot runways could handle any plane in the Air Force's arsenal, as well as the space shuttle should it need to make an emergency landing in the midst of the Pacific. The runway and taxiway sprawl was so vast that I barely noticed a carrier air wing from the USS *Kitty Hawk,* which was making live practice bombing runs that it could not make from its home port in Japan.

All this was significant because of "location, location, location," Maj. Gen. Dennis Larsen of San Antonio, Texas, the commander of the 13th Air Force at the time of my visit, told me. Whereas the West Coast of the United States was thirteen hours' flying time from North Korea, Guam was four. From Guam, the 13th Air Force—the equivalent of a Marine or Army division—covered almost all of the PACOM area of responsibility. That meant sixteen of the twenty-four time zones, from the strategic Indian Ocean island of Diego Garcia (the departure point for some of the U.S. planes bombing Afghanistan and Iraq) to the coast of Mexico, and including China and Taiwan. In coming months, the headquarters of the 13th Air Force would be relocated to Honolulu, even as the 13th itself would later be disbanded. This was part of a reorganization whose purpose was to centralize control over the Pacific at PACOM headquarters in Honolulu, without diminishing Guam's importance as a forward operating base.

Some of the heaviest bombing runs against North Vietnam, including the "Christmas bombing" of 1972, originated here, when 154 B-52s packed these runways. In April 2001, when the Chinese released the crew members of the Navy EP-3 surveillance plane they had detained, they were flown here.

Maj. Gen. Larsen said, "This is not like Okinawa. This is American soil in the midst of the Pacific. Guam is a U.S. territory. We can do what we want here, and make huge investments without fear of being thrown out." Indeed, what struck me about Andersen, while staring out from the top of the control tower, was how much space there was for expansion to the south and west of the current perimeters, even before reaching the cliffs. Property prices were zooming. Hundreds of millions of dollars of construction funds were being allocated. What Germany, close to the Soviet Union, had been for the U.S. military during the Cold War decades, this little island close to China was on its way to becoming for the early twenty-first century: the spoke in the wheel of a constellation of bases that would move the locus of U.S. power from Europe to Asia.

By making Guam the Hawaii of the western Pacific, the Americans might ironically make it simple for Chinese military planners, by giving them just one problem to solve—how to threaten or intimidate Guam. Therefore, some felt that the way to counter the Chinese was not by concentration, but by dispersion. How might the United States prevent Guam from becoming too big? Well, for one thing, it could build up Palau, an island of twenty thousand inhabitants in the western Pacific, between Mindanao in the Philippines and the Federated States of Micronesia. Palau's financial aid was contingent on a defense arrangement with Washington. In any case, as much as the military adapted to the rise of China, it was clear that keeping the Pacific an American lake—patrolled with impunity by the Seventh Fleet as it had been for decades—was probably not history's final say on the matter.

A house overlooking a golf course, furnished in magnificent Japanese style, with fine carpets and ceramics, constituted my living quarters at Andersen. It was nicer even than the split-level furnished apartment I had had at Hickam Air Force Base in Hawaii. For a traveler, to go from the Marine Corps to the Air Force was like going from a slum to a fancy resort. The Air Force didn't have barracks, it had "dorms," which, even for the enlisted ranks, looked like apartments in a singles' community. In the chow halls, which were comparable to upscale chain restaurants, you left your tray on the table for a waitress to pick up. There were lawn police to ensure that officers maintained the surroundings assigned to them. Hickam, with its art deco buildings, and Andersen, with its manicured, palm-patterned greenery, resembled gated communities and office parks. Inside headquarters buildings, airmen in dull green jumpsuits occupied workplaces as elegant as many in the private sector. Many marines I knew had never experienced such luxury in their whole lives, even on vacation.

There was no scandal in this. Just as spartan conditions were part of the Marine Corps mystique, as well as a psychological tool in maintaining the leathernecks' sheer aggressiveness for house-to-house fighting in places like Al-Fallujah, a comfortable lifestyle accomplished something similar for the Air Force.*

The Air Force, even more so than the Navy, was the technical service of the armed forces—the executive arm of the coming militarization of outer space. Not only pilots and navigators, but much of the ground staff, too, required years of specialized training. And because the air was a zero-defect environment, where the slightest lapse could result in catastrophic consequences, the Air Force required the most competent, fastidious, and driven people—the kind of people who could draw good salaries in the business world. To keep such people in the service, after investing so much money in their training, the Air Force gave them the sort of lifestyle—complete with career-enhancement programs and family services—that the other branches of the military couldn't match. The Marine Corps wanted its ranks filled with young, hungry, high-testosterone men, relatively few of whom were expected to reenlist. The Air Force wanted you for your entire career. The "corporate Air Force" was what they called it, because it was like working for IBM.

Yet, the War on Terrorism was slowly making the Air Force more expeditionary, more like the Marines and other services, taking it back to its roots as a branch of the Signal Corps, which helped the Army chase down Pancho Villa in Mexico prior to America's entry into World War I. The cushy nine-to-five existence for airmen had ended on 9/11; many of them now spent long periods away from home in rough conditions, in places like Iraq and Afghanistan.

The Air Force had always been the only service where the officers—the pilots—took the greatest physical risk. But since 9/11 the expeditionary nature of unconventional warfare was placing greater emphasis

---

* The term "leathernecks" is often used for U.S. marines. It refers to the leather collars that marines wore earlier in their history to protect them against sword slashes. The leather collars, no longer worn, are symbolized by red stripes on the collars of the Marines' dress blues.

on the fighting skills of enlisted men. For example, the Army Special Forces teams that had taken down the Taliban in Afghanistan had Air Force embeds with them for close air support—grid-marking targets for the AC-130s with the 150 pounds of radio equipment that they carried on their backs in the field. Moreover, the quick deployment of the Army's new Stryker brigades gave unprecedented importance to cargo planes like the C-130 and C-17, which could land without lights on short dirt runways—a task requiring the placement of noncommissioned airmen in hellholes throughout the world for ground support.

The Air Force was a branch of the Army called the Army Air Forces until 1947, when it became a separate service. Those Army roots were manifested in how fighter pilots still saw themselves—as the Cavalry coming to the rescue, whether in an AC-130, a B-52 bomber, or a stealthy jet fighter. When I had asked Col. Mark Tapper of Westlake Village, California, a Hickam-based F-16 pilot, about unmanned planes making airmen like himself obsolete, he replied, "It won't happen, because it's not chivalrous. We're the knights—the officers who take personal risk. That's part of our identity."

When you scratched the surface of airmen's emotions, you learned that they, too, like Marine and Army grunts, saw the pre-9/11 period as a bad dream—a time when, even during the air campaigns in the Balkans, risk was not tolerated in the way it was now.

———

I spent part of my time at Andersen hanging out with the B-52 flight crews, on deployment from Barksdale Air Force Base near Shreveport, Louisiana.* The giant, 150-foot-long B-52 was a flying gas tank stuffed with forty-five individual five-hundred-pound bombs. It was the Air Force's hall-of-fame heavy bomber, around since 1954. The B-52s at Andersen had all been built in 1961 and 1962. They were much older than their crews.

You somehow expected B-52 pilots and navigators to be big, strapping guys, but they weren't. They were of average build, and often short, an advantage in the plane's cramped quarters where you couldn't

* Named after Lt. Eugene Hoy Barksdale of Goshen Springs, Mississippi, born in 1897 and a veteran of the Somme, Amiens, and Cambrai offensives in 1918. He died in 1926 test piloting a Douglas O-2 at McCook Field, Dayton, Ohio.

stand upright. The B-52 was like a sub: the ultimate instrument of mass violence. Almost all of its vast space was for fuel and weaponry, with the human beings crouching in a tiny maze filled with flaking old pipes and wires. As one of the last slide-rule-developed aircraft, the B-52 cockpit was a veritable grainy, black-and-white backdrop for a World War II movie. While the image of the Air Force was high-tech, the aesthetic environment in so many of its most commonly used planes harked back to the industrial age. The antediluvian ambience influenced the personalities of the crew members, who were, to a man, self-consciously the cliché image of true blue flyboys, carousing at night in bars just like in the movies.

The B-52s—direct descendants of the B-29s—revived thoughts of World War II. Indeed, like the bases in Germany, those in Guam had been paid for in blood—in Guam's case, the blood of U.S. marines.

For sailors and marines, the fight against Japan in the Pacific was the dominant drama of the Second World War. World War II occupied your thoughts in the Pacific in a way that it simply didn't in Europe, because the sites of sixty-year-old battles were often the only visual expressions of history that these islands had. Yet, because of the region's random configurations of atolls, making narrative sense of World War II here was more difficult than it was in Europe.

The story of the Pacific war became comprehensible only when one realized that the December 7, 1941, attack on Pearl Harbor was merely the start of a broad-based Japanese offensive that also saw the bombardments of the Philippines, Hong Kong, Malaya, and Burma, so by the end of February 1942 the Japanese controlled virtually the entire Pacific Rim from Manchuria in the north to near Australia in the south. Within a few weeks of Pearl Harbor, many islands across the western half of the Pacific Ocean also fell to the Japanese. The effect was a grim and heroic saga of Navy-assisted Marine landings on small islands in Micronesia, which set the stage for the recapture of the Philippines, Burma, and the screen of Japanese-held archipelagoes threatening Australia. The process began with the securing of Midway Island, close to Hawaii, in June 1942, and culminated in 1945 with the taking of Iwo Jima and Okinawa, close to the Japanese mainland. Guam was typical: a nightmarish mass graveyard for marines, characterized by heat, malaria, and hand-to-hand combat. The Omaha Beach scenario of storming ashore under a wall of fire from enemy pillboxes was actually far more common in the Pacific than in Europe. Let me set the historical stage:

Guam's first contact with the West had been the landing in 1521 at Asan Beach of Ferdinand Magellan, the Portuguese mariner who sailed for Spain. The Spanish then killed and converted the native Chamorros, a Filipino people who spoke a related Tagalog language. In 1668, Spanish missionaries rechristened Guam and the other islands in the archipelago the Marianas, in honor of Queen Maria Anna of Spain. The Americans acquired Guam in 1898 as a consequence of the Spanish-American War.

In December 1941, three days after Pearl Harbor, over five thousand Japanese troops forced a few hundred members of the American garrison off this 212-square-mile island. The Marines took back Guam in late July 1944.[13] The Navy had shelled the island for thirteen straight days. Then to the sound of "The Marines' Hymn," played over the ships' loudspeakers, the leathernecks climbed down into the landing crafts. By the time the fighting was over eight days later on July 29, the campaign to retake Guam had cost 1,744 American dead and 6,540 wounded, in addition to thousands of Japanese lives.

From the hillside where Japanese defensive positions had been located, I gazed down at Asan Beach where the Marines (and Magellan) had landed, and imagined the scene in its bloody awfulness. The Japanese had been here for three years waiting for the attack. They had deforested the hillsides to make it impossible for invaders to hide while trudging uphill. Because most of the island was bordered by high cliffs dropping sheer into the sea, there were only a few places to land. Like Asan, the beaches all had long coral tables extending far out into the water; thus an invasion had to come at high tide. Surprise was never an option. No matter what the technological advantage of one side, as another generation of Americans would learn in Iraqi cities, in war some tasks were just tough.

Besides an air base, the Marines bequeathed to their country one of the best deepwater ports between Pearl Harbor and Manila Bay. Apra Harbor, next door to Asan Beach, was home to a forward-deployed submarine squadron—a squadron with which I was to become closely acquainted in the coming months. As at the air base, expansion was imminent here. Capt. David Boone, an intense, dark-haired, and boyish-looking naval officer who had grown up all over the Pacific Rim, told me that while the U.S. military "may have moved beyond the Cold War, its infrastructure still hadn't." During the Cold War, the Navy had a specific infrastructure for a specific threat. Now the threat was multiple and uncertain: from a conventional war against North Korea to an unconventional counterinsurgency against a Chinese-backed rogue island-state. Being more agile, Capt. Boone explained to me, meant leveraging services out to the civilian community on Guam, so that the Navy here could concentrate on military matters only. Concomitantly, he was planning to expand the waterfront, build more bachelor quarters, and harden the electric power system by putting it underground. "The fact that we have lots of space today is meaningless," he went on. "The question is, how would we handle the surge requirement necessitated by a full-scale war?"

Again, I was reminded that while amateurs discussed strategy, professionals discussed logistics. Logistics was the elephantine component of military reality to which civilians were generally blind, like the part of an iceberg below the surface. But only to the uninitiated did logistics seem dull, as I learned off the nearby island of Saipan.

———

Early one morning on Guam, I boarded a Navy MH-60 Knighthawk helicopter—the equivalent of the Army's Black Hawk—and flew to Saipan, in the Northern Marianas chain. The pilots were Lts. Junior Grade Tom Neill, Jr., of Cullman, Alabama, and John Schein of Chama, New Mexico. I would never forget them because of the thrill they allowed me.* They flew five hundred feet off the water during the entire 130-mile journey northeast. Strapped loosely in the seat, I was practically hanging out the open side window, facing eastward on the central Pacific; on the way back, I would watch the sunset over the Philippine

---

* The other members of the crew were Jason West of Hawkinsville, Georgia, and Noah Vogt of East Alton, Illinois. The standby crew was Lts. Ricademus Breitwieser of Susanville, California, and Jason Morton of Eddyville, Kentucky, Crew Chief Michael Bageant of Baltimore and Second Crewman Edmund Hooper of San Bernadino, California.

Sea to the west. In the course of the forty-five-minute flight I was soaked by several rain showers. But the equatorial sun would unfailingly come out, and within minutes I was dry again—that is, until vertical columns of vapor reaching to the top of the sky, like new worlds in creation, would beat up another storm. The sea was an interminable panel of pearly welts through the cloudy sunlight. I could almost smell the rain clouds. The attraction of Navy flying was visceral in these broad ocean reaches, where the water below might as well have been the gaseous void of a distant planet. Eastward to the horizon, the ocean floor quickly descended 36,000 feet to the bottom of the Mariana Trench, a much steeper drop than the Himalayas. The Pacific offered a demonstration of infinity. It was the next best thing to space travel.

A reptilian green planet soon appeared, floating in the watery curvature of the great ocean. Like Guam, Tinian was ringed by massive cliffs against which waves exploded, bearing all the energy built up on their journey south from the Aleutians. Like Guam, Tinian had few beachheads, making it a nightmare for World War II planners and for the marines whom they sent to assault them. Near Tinian's northern tip, I spotted a pair of runways for B-29 Superfortresses, on which the jungle was now infiltrating. Beside the old runways were two pits that had once held the atomic bombs that destroyed Hiroshima and Nagasaki. On August 6, 1945, a lone B-29, the *Enola Gay,* piloted by Army Air Forces Col. Paul Tibbets of Quincy, Illinois, had taken off for Hiroshima from the jungle below me.

Saipan, bigger than Tinian, was another limestone and coral cap peeking out of the sea, another nightmare of cliff walls with few landing spots. On its idyllic beaches, braided with coconut palms and Norfolk pines, the 4th Marine Division came ashore a week after D-day in Europe. In its bloody crawl through sugarcane plantations and raggedy jungle, toward the enemy command center on Mount Tapotchau, 3,500 marines and soldiers died, as well as 28,000 Japanese defenders—more American dead than at Omaha Beach.

Touring the PACOM area of responsibility provided me the privilege of following the course of these island struggles: places, unlike Normandy, where few American tourists got to. Arriving on Saipan, I drove to the U.S. War Memorial that commemorated the battles of

Saipan and the Philippine Sea, the second of which took place days later in nearby waters. (A failed attempt by the Japanese Imperial Navy to reverse the American conquest of the Marianas, the Philippine Sea would turn out to be the last great carrier battle of World War II.)

Battlefields were the most silent places I have ever been, as though to eternally compensate for the mayhem that once transpired on the same soil. At the north of Saipan there was a line of dizzyingly high cliffs bearing a pathetic hodgepodge of memorials: to Japanese civilians—mothers holding their babies—who had jumped hundreds of feet into the cavity of a crashing sea, rather than be taken prisoner by American marines and soldiers who they were convinced were going to torture them.

Like Guam, Saipan was a U.S. territory, and PACOM had been taking advantage of this fact. My guide on Saipan was Navy Capt. Conrad Divis of Bayport, New York. Whereas Army, Air Force, and Marine ranks are vaguely similar to one another, Navy ranks are somewhat different, and thus disorienting at first. A Navy captain is the equivalent of a colonel in the other services; just as a Navy commander is the equivalent of a lieutenant colonel, and a lieutenant commander the equivalent of a major. Because Capt. Divis was the commanding officer of more than one ship, he was referred to by his men as "the commodore," a wonderful operatic title that provided me with my first hint of how the Navy, more than the other services, is the true American heir to the European military tradition of pomp and circumstance.

Capt. Divis was an awkwardly quiet man, and I worried at first how the day would turn out. "You are interested in logistics?" he asked me, after we had seen the World War II sites.

"Yes," I said.

"Fine, I'll show you some things."

At the port, he nudged me aboard a crew boat that bumped out over the waves of the Philippine Sea at eighteen knots, a speed which on a small craft like this one felt like flying. "I command three MPSes [maritime pre-positioning ships]," he told me. "I'm taking you to one of them." I didn't know what he meant by a pre-positioning ship.

About five miles out to sea, we came upon what looked like an oil tanker or civilian cargo ship. There seemed nothing military about it. I was confused. Emblazoned on its hull was the name *Jack Lummus*. Lummus was a Marine first lieutenant from Ennis, Texas, who had died on Iwo Jima, and like the other men for whom MPSes were named, was a Medal of Honor recipient.

The crew boat crept up to the giant stern of the eleven-story-tall ship. In the heaving sea, we jumped onto a ladder and climbed up two levels onto a platform. Because of the sunlight and the white coral and sand at the bottom, the sea had a chemical blue Kool-Aid color. Walking inside the ship I came upon a vast garage space in which about six hundred M1A1 Abrams tanks, Humvees, armored bulldozers, amphibious assault vehicles, Seabee earth movers, seven-ton trucks, and the rest of the rolling stock for an entire MEB (Marine Expeditionary Brigade) of fifteen thousand leathernecks was jammed bumper to bumper. An adjacent part of the cavernous ship held vast stores of ammunition.

The *Jack Lummus* was a floating military base—a larger one than most of those I had seen in Iraq or Afghanistan. If it had to, the *Jack Lummus* had room, fresh water, and food stores to sustain fifteen battalions of marines and sailors for thirty days, yet only about three dozen personnel were required to operate it, half of whom were civilian merchant mariners.

"You should see the handful of eighteen- to-nineteen-year-old Marine NCOs who come aboard to supervise the order of the loading," Capt. Divis remarked, "so that not one inch of space is wasted and no vehicle has to be moved around a second time to make way for another. These marines have organized it all on a computer-generated diagram. They've got this intense combat-ready look as they work."

Navy Capt. Divis was enmeshed in a world of marines and civilian seamen. "As I'm sure you've heard already," he told me, "we're all joint—all purple—these days." He meant that operations usually involved all four services, and private contractors, too.

The fifteen merchant seamen on board were from the Boston area: burly, Irish, and delightful, as they showed me the generators, sewage pumps, steam engines, water purification systems, and myriad other equipment that they maintained and were qualified to repair at a moment's notice. Like Capt. Divis's sailors, they were away from their families for a year at a time. The beauty of civilians was this: had the Navy done the job, the government being the government, and the military being the military, it would have required a hundred men on board, rather than the fifteen that were quite sufficient to do it. As I had seen with Kellogg, Brown & Root at military bases in Afghanistan and Iraq, and with DynCorp in the Philippines and Colombia, both of whose employees were at once physically brave and technically efficient, the privatization of militaries wasn't always the nefarious process that outsiders believed. It might even be the only practical way forward in an age of war when individual expertise and initiative often mattered more than sheer manpower numbers, mass infantry invasions aside.

It was the tugs, hospital boats, and other support ships so far from their home ports, as much as the subs and carriers, that had composed America's victorious long-haul Navy in World War II. Likewise, this civilian-looking ship was key to the force projection required for fighting North Korea, or any insurgency in the South Seas.

"Because we can move around from island to island, we're less vulnerable," Divis explained.

The pre-positioning concept, as I had seen it illustrated on Saipan, grew out of President Jimmy Carter's Rapid Deployment Force, which, in turn, was a consequence of the Iranian hostage crisis. As with many such ideas, it began when one political party was in power and continued under another: the *Jack Lummus* was built by General Dynamics during the Reagan years. Moreover, the ship represented the very epitome of the more light and lethal, Asia-oriented basing footprint that would be a hallmark of the Bush administration's military transformation strategy; a strategy that had originated with civil servants in the Defense Department of President Bill Clinton. America's military was so vast and multi-layered that it was a product of continuity over ideologically diverse administrations.

The pre-positioning ships were one piece of a taut webwork designed to move troops and equipment around forward bases in an oceanic environment defined by what military planners called "the tyranny of distance." I flew to Okinawa, 1,500 miles to the northwest, to see another aspect of that webwork.

At a U.S. port in Okinawa, I went aboard a large car ferry called the *WestPac Express,* built by an Australia-based company. Like the *Jack Lummus,* it had a crew of fifteen American merchant mariners. It was a type of ferry familiar to European holiday makers, who used them regularly to travel within the Mediterranean. For U.S. Marines in the Pacific, it was becoming an icon of expeditionary warfare.

Just a few years before, it had taken seventeen trips on a C-130 or C-17 to move a battalion of marines from one place in the Pacific to another. Because of mechanical and weather-related delays, that meant the better part of a month. This car ferry, essentially a diesel-powered catamaran with water jets that moved at a thundering thirty-three knots, could handle a whole Marine battalion with its equipment, and get them from Okinawa, at the southern tip of Japanese territory, to mainland Japan, South Korea, the Philippines, or Thailand in just a few hours or days. Its cargo hold was as big as twenty C-17s, with lots of space for helicopters. A few *WestPac* ferries made for a seaborne Stryker brigade. With beefed-up communications, you could set up a command-and-control cell for a three-star general aboard.

And it was run by civilians. The civilian captain (a master seaman) ran the ship, on which the marines were the passengers. The Marines or other armed services could never keep someone in a job long enough, or pay him enough, to develop the skills that a master seaman in the Merchant Marine had.

"Who thought up the idea of using car ferries to get marines to a combat zone and then link up with pre-positioning ships?" I asked a Marine chief warrant officer. "No one at the Pentagon. Just a bunch of guys brainstorming here," the chief replied.

Okinawa, 1,400 miles across more ocean from Guam, brought back unsettling memories of Greece and the Balkans, where I had lived and traveled in the 1980s. Like the urban areas of mainland Greece, Okinawa was an ugly, yellowy-white splatter of crummy concrete and squat, functional buildings that smothered all available space on the bumpy landscape in the south of the island. There was no room to breathe. The American military bases rammed up against compressed and crowded civilian areas, so the bases were disliked for environmental, to say nothing of historical, reasons. During the Cold War, Greeks had been humiliated by the presence of American bases, just as they had been dependent upon them; it was the same with Okinawans. The very defacement of the historical landscape by nonstop construction appeared to have intensified the bitterest memories on both the Japanese and American sides.

"Returning to Okinawa," William Manchester wrote in 1978, after having fought here as a marine in 1945, "is like watching a naked priest celebrate mass. . . . The greatest of the island battlefields, more precious than Gettysburg—or at any rate more expensive in American blood—at first glance appears to be covered with used-car lots, junkyards, stereo shops, pinball-machine emporiums, and vendors of McDonald's fast food."[14]

History here, as in some places in the Balkans, was the more overpowering because it no longer had a visual reference. Okinawa was the place where I had the most intense and darkest conversations. It magnified for me just how horrible war had been, and could yet be in Asia.

Nobody was happy. The Americans had built aesthetically pleasing noise barriers against the roar of F-15 Eagles, and had put stringent restrictions on its marines. Yet every time a fighter jet screamed overhead, or every time a local girl was raped, no matter how statistically rare the incident in both absolute and relative terms, it led, as one should expect, to deep and lingering resentment. Kadena Air Force Base, which accounted for 75 percent of the acreage of the American military on the island, was also home to numerous sacred sites of local ancestor worship. The Americans and the Okinawans were literally stuck with each other.

I say "Okinawans" because the island's inhabitants were not strictly Japanese. The moment I had arrived from Guam, I was struck by the racial variety: the faces in the street bore the influences of Taiwan, China, the Philippines, and Malaysia, as well as of Japan. The turtleback ancestor tombs, swathed in creepers inside Kadena Air Base, bore the architectural influence of tombs in Fukien, in China. They were remnants of the intense contact between China and this small island in the southern Ryukus, a distant 350 miles south of the Japanese mainland, and independent for much of its history.

Okinawa was not closed off to the world as Japan had been for long periods. The eclectic influences upon it emanated from as far away as Southeast Asia, though, ultimately, its people were members of the Japanese cultural and ethnic family. Okinawa's equidistance from Japan, Taiwan, China, and the Korean Peninsula made it a nerve center for American military projection in the Pacific. That was partly why the American military had stormed it in the first place.

"Okinawa," writes military historian Victor Davis Hanson, "was the summation of all the macabre elements of a barbarous three years of island fighting. It was not just the last battle of the Pacific war, but the murderous aggregate of all that had gone on before." The Battle of Okinawa lasted from April 1 to July 2, 1945—long after V-E Day. The large-scale use of kamikaze pilots had made Okinawa a veritable "laboratory of suicide" bombers.[15] By the end of the campaign, 12,520 American ground and naval troops had been killed, and another 33,631 were wounded or missing. The Japanese military suffered 110,000 dead. As many as 100,000 civilians might have died, too.

It was the gargantuan cost of taking this one island—sixty-five miles long and only seven miles wide—that, more than any other factor, led to the decision to drop atomic bombs on Hiroshima and Nagasaki. Because of the ferocity with which a cornered Japanese military had fought on Okinawa, American war planners could make only the most dire of predictions regarding the human cost of invading the dense population centers on Honshu and the other mainland islands. Okinawa was the closest thing that World War II offered to the World War I battlefields of Verdun and Passchendaele, Manchester writes, with "two great armies, squatting opposite one another in mud and smoke . . . locked together in unimaginable agony."[16]

As for the Okinawans, they were caught between two imperial powers. The island had been fortified by Tokyo, only so that the Japanese military could sacrifice it in a failed attempt to force the Americans to the negotiating table. The Americans ruled here directly until 1972, making it the last vestige of the occupation of Japan and Germany stemming from World War II. But the departure of an American high commissioner merely changed the goal of local politics from terminating the occupation to terminating the base leases. The issue was aggravated

by the fact of democracy itself. Elsewhere in Japan, the ruling Liberal
Democratic Party completely dominated politics and snuffed out many
debates, whereas in Okinawa, the reformist coalition put unceasing
pressure on the local government to be tough on the American military.

In the mid-1990s, after a much publicized kidnapping and rape of a
twelve-year-old local girl by two marines and a sailor, tens of thousands
of Okinawans demonstrated against the bases and it seemed the bases'
future was in doubt. The incident resulted in the consolidation of some
of the bases, and the decision to move thousands of marines from here
to Guam, compensated for by the building of a $10 billion offshore
American military facility. But because of the ongoing expansion of
Chinese military power (a Chinese nuclear submarine penetrated the
Sea of Japan the week of my visit), as well as a growing threat from
North Korea, a newly hawkish political climate throughout Japan was
emerging. The American bases on Okinawa, of which the immense Air
Force facility at Kadena was but one, might well be here for a long time,
though in a reduced capacity.

The American military, particularly the Marines, who had borne
many of the casualties in the spring of 1945, got just as emotional about
Okinawa as the local population. "The fighting on Okinawa was more
significant than that on Iwo Jima," explained Marine Lt. Col. Phil Ridderhof of Fredericksburg, Virginia, a graduate of the Virginia Military
Academy and the chief planner for the 3rd Marine Expeditionary Force.
"But the battlefield here has been overrun by urbanization, while Iwo
Jima is full of military imagery, especially that stirring photo of the flag
raising. And Iwo Jima is a place where you can make a pilgrimage."

The Marine museum on Okinawa wasn't so much a museum as a
shrine—a humble set of rooms in an office at Camp Albert Kinser.* The
artifacts had been amassed over the decades by Dave Davenport, a retired airman who had moved the stuff all over the world with him in the
course of his deployments, including war-torn Vietnam. In 1992 he
brought the collection here. Recently, his obsession with the Battle of
Okinawa had been passed on to a young protégé, Christopher Majew-

---

* The base was named for a Medal of Honor winner who had jumped on a grenade.

ski, a former marine from southern Nevada. It was Majewski, wearing a purple ball cap over his high-and-tight, who gave me the standard tour.

"This museum is not part of the military museum system—they could break the collection up, and we're not going to let that happen," he told me vehemently, pacing back and forth, working off what he said was a sugar high from a chocolate bar. "The first thing you have to remember is that our intelligence was extremely, extremely poor. We thought there were 45,000 enemy troops on Okinawa. The real number was 116,488.

"The Japanese thought we were weak, and in a way we were," Majewski continued. "The war in Europe was over, and many Americans couldn't understand why we were still taking high casualties in places in the Pacific with names they couldn't pronounce. The system of war rations was getting old, then the media stepped in with photos of dead marines. The Japanese figured that if we couldn't handle just one percent of what it would be like fighting on the mainland, they'd be okay. Remember, for the Japanese, Okinawa didn't matter. The only thing that mattered was a high number of American casualties. Okinawa was Vietnam before its time," he told me, still marching back and forth as if talking to himself, pointing to an old map.

With its bad paintings, faded newspaper clippings, and haversacks and uniforms eaten away by moths and time, all thrown together in corroded glass cabinets, this shrine had an impoverished nature that was painfully and beautifully apparent. There was a Japanese bolt-action rifle so rusted that it looked as if it had been at the bottom of the sea for a hundred years. In one cabinet was a Japanese flag removed from Shuri Castle following its capture. The flag had been taken down by Marine Lt. Don Sinn, the commander of Alpha Company of the 1st Battalion of the 5th Marine Regiment. I told Majewski that in Iraq, the previous spring, I had been with the current commander of Alpha Company of 1/5. He savored that.* He told me that Lt. Sinn did not have an American flag available to fly, but one of the other marines did have a Confederate rebel flag, which they flew for three days before a proper flag arrived.

* Capt. Philip Treglia of Elida, Ohio. See Chapter 8 in *Imperial Grunts*.

Majewski knelt on his knees to demonstrate how Japanese Lt. Gens. Ushijima Mitsuru and Cho Isamu must have committed ritual suicide following the battle: holding knives against their guts and dragging them sideways through their bellies. "Their real bodies were likely never found. They never found their medals." He showed me all the books he had collected about the fighting on Okinawa. This young former marine was determined to preserve the memory of it. Iwo Jima had its memorial. Okinawa made due with this museum.

The other conversations I had in Okinawa were just as intense, even as they were dreary. My interlocutors were full of authentic intellectual passion. The fact that, as the decades bore on in the new century, the Pacific loomed as the principal danger to peace was for them an issue they had to tackle in nuts-and-bolts terms. Marine Lt. Col. Ridderhof told me: "If Korea went off, it could be the most horrific conflict the world has seen since 1945. And by the way, there would be nothing sanitized or futuristic about it. Like in the first Korean War, we'd have to get out of our vehicles and fight." The phrase "first Korean War" was used a lot in Okinawa in reference to the 1950–53 conflict, implying the possibility of a second.

"When you face an Asian foe like the North Koreans," another planner told me, "it won't be like fighting your typical third-rate Middle Eastern army. They're driven, and have been brainwashed for decades. They don't just have dumb infantry troops, they've got SOF [special operations forces] that regularly penetrate South Korean lines. They'd use chemical weapons, and would rain artillery on Seoul," referring to the South Korean capital near the DMZ (demilitarized zone). "Seoul would be soup artillery-wise. I wouldn't even want to be a cockroach there."

The Cold War never really ended here. Okinawa was like West Germany in the dark decades of the 1950s through 1970s. The North Koreans had 170 divisions, 60 of which were near the DMZ. The chance of a mass infantry cataclysm unlike any other was certainly remote. But the consequences were so catastrophic that military thinkers had to forever bear down on the problem.

"And how do you tactically prepare for a major war?" I asked one general.

"Like eating an elephant, one bite at a time." From nine to five in Okinawa, people thought the unthinkable.

Okinawa clarified for me the delicate hierarchy between the Navy and the Air Force. The Pacific was an ocean, and politicians loved oceans because they could use navies to advance right up to the battle-field without being too provocative, while still being able to pull back. It was the oceanic nature of PACOM that made it the most amenable area command from the viewpoint of the State Department. But while 70 percent of PACOM's area of responsibility was ocean, 100 percent was air, and "air can get there faster," as I kept hearing. Even as the world of twenty-first-century combat was increasingly purple (the color of jointness), Air Force blue was becoming increasingly prominent in the American military color scheme.

If any service was going to mitigate the need to saturate the Korean Peninsula and Taiwan with mass infantry, it would be the Air Force: through attacks on command and control centers, enemy computer systems, and so on. Because of air-to-air refueling, the Air Force no longer needed a big footprint. The Air Force required less on the ground to do more in the air. Of all the services, it had the greatest potential to be light and lethal.

—

Thailand was important as an example of how the Pentagon was reconfiguring the pattern of Air Force and Navy bases worldwide. The process had started toward the end of the Cold War. In 1985 the United States had a cluster of large, fully developed bases dubbed "Little Americas" in Europe and the Far East, with 385,000 personnel in Germany and its environs, and 125,000 in the Korean Peninsula. By 9/11, though, sixteen years later, the number of personnel in Europe had dropped to 118,000 and in East Asia to 89,000. Then, in 2004, the Pentagon unveiled plans to bring home an additional 70,000 troops from those fixed-in-place garrisons, even as it planned to expand a network of bare-bones sites in Asia, Africa, and the Middle East to support rotational rather than permanently stationed forces.[17] In short, the future promised no fighting in place. Everything would be expeditionary, in order to handle any eventuality in a chaotic world. Forward operating sites and even more austere "cooperative security locations"—a tucked-away corner of a host country airport, for instance—would be established in obscure and exotic locales such as Bulgaria, Azerbaijan, Uganda, the West African island state of São Tomé and Príncipe, and Honduras.

In Thailand, the Pentagon had its eye on two bases for cooperative security locations, CSLs in the hottest new Defense Department lingo.

I had not been to Bangkok for some years, and walking the streets at night after my arrival I was startled by the driven, buzzing intensity of an Asian mega-city: an anxious cacophony of intricate dynamism that worked at a higher RPM level than urban centers of other cultures. Whereas African cities were victims of globalization, with explosions of crime and social breakdown, Asians had taken advantage of globalization. Because military activity could reflect the sum total of social and economic development, the very frenzy of Bangkok—from its rapid-fire strip-joint transactions to its late-night highway construction—further convinced me that the Pacific Rim would ultimately determine the fate of war and peace in the twenty-first century. This was the most dynamic region of the globe. If geopolitics had a regional pivot, it was here.

Another thing about Bangkok: it was the first place in my Pacific travels where I had to use local currency. Alaska, Hawaii, Guam, and Saipan were all U.S. states or territories, while the U.S. bases on Okinawa were large, self-contained worlds where the dollar rather than the Japanese yen was circulated. Air Mobility Command could get you all over the Pacific, from the American mainland to the Asian rim, albeit with delays and inconvenience. The landings and interventions of the U.S. Navy and Marines in the latter decades of the nineteenth century in search of a mercantile seaborne empire, aided by victory in World War II, had provided America with a sovereign bridge of sorts that extended all the way across the Pacific to Southeast Asia.

Thailand had always been a little-noticed and yet critical military ally of the United States. Cobra Gold, PACOM's biggest annual military exercise (involving twenty thousand armed personnel), took place in Thailand. Army Special Forces and Navy SEALs trained year-round and ran joint maneuvers at the platoon level with their Thai counterparts. An Islamic insurgency had begun in the extreme south of the country, in three former Malay sultanates, in an area by the Gulf of Siam where an American company was drilling for oil. The result was more special operations training missions between U.S. and Thai forces.

But what the Americans truly had their eye on were two bases a few hours by car southeast of Bangkok, Utapao Naval Air Station and the adjacent Sattahip Naval Base. Utapao, like Andersen in Guam, had been a B-52 hub during the Vietnam War. It was remembered fondly by a whole generation of American airmen because of the wall-to-wall strip joints in the nearby town of Pattaya. The Thais shut down U.S. military operations at Utapao in 1975, after reports that the base had been used secretly for military action against Cambodia, in the wake of the Khmer Rouge seizure of the American merchant vessel SS *Mayagüez*. Particularly after 9/11, Utapao was again being used by U.S. airmen. It was all low-key, however.

I drove to Utapao to see what a cooperative security location, or austere forward operating base, actually looked like. It was a concept with which I was familiar from a visit to Kenya ten months earlier. I had been embedded with an Army civil affairs team on the Indian Ocean island of Lamu, deployed on a humanitarian mission to improve America's image in a part of Kenya where the Kenyan military was upgrading the strategically located Manda Bay Naval Air Station, close to the Somali border. The United States wanted it to remain a Kenyan base, from where Kenya could project power. But if the political and diplomatic context was right, the U.S. would have access to its facilities. The humanitarian mission was an element in creating that context.

Utapao, like Manda Bay, was a beautiful setup. It was big, with an 11,500-foot runway—longer than the ones at Guam even—with endless taxi space and lots of green area for expansion. And it was far enough from the town of Pattaya to remain discreet. But the best thing about Utapao, from the standpoint of U.S. interests, was Dan Generette, the chief operating officer of Delta Golf Global. Dan was a private contractor. He could make anything happen on Utapao. "Dan's the man," one American military source told me. "He's the mayor of Utapao. Forget the site survey teams that they send out from PACOM in Honolulu. They don't know nothing. All they know is what Dan tells them."

Dan Generette was an African American from Walterboro, South Carolina, who had grown up in the Brownsville section of Brooklyn, New York. A retired Air Force master sergeant, with twenty-four years experience as a maintenance expert for the Guam-based 13th Air Force, he had been stationed at Utapao as a young man during the bad old Vietnam days (or the good old Vietnam days, depending upon how some looked at it). Dan's sidekick, Roger Coe of Springfield, Ohio, was another retired Air Force master sergeant, also with twenty-four years of military maintenance experience. In fact, all of Dan's efficient little staff, who worked out of a two-room office next to the runway, were—with the exception of the Thai secretaries—American ex-military.

Dan, a tall, imposing man with a jet-black complexion, a tropical shirt, and a soft voice, who lifted his eyelids to make a point didactically, described himself to me as the "buffer" between the American and Thai militaries. "Everything here is transparent," he told me. "I do not work for the Americans or the Thais. I run a for-profit enterprise. I pay rent to the RTN [Royal Thai Navy] and make my income from the fees I charge incoming U.S. military aircraft for the services I provide them. The pilots come with their credit cards ready. They know the drill.

"Look," he went on, "this place ain't Kansas. When a crew of young American airmen arrive, they don't know anything, they can't communicate with the Thais at planeside about their maintenance problems. They don't know where to go for meals, ice, water. They don't know where to find a hotel for the night within their per diem allotment, where to go for fun. My people allay their concerns, immediately. We level with them about what can and can't be done here. I can't tell you how happy they are to see someone like me.

"As for the Thais," he continued, "they'd rather deal with me than with some loud and upset ugly American running around their base, complaining. I know the culture, the language. I'm kind and pleasant."

Because of Dan, the Thais could help the Americans without the political baggage that went with a formal status-of-forces agreement for Utapao. Because of Delta Golf Global, the U.S. military was here, but it was not here. After all, the Thais did no business with the U.S. Air Force. They dealt only with a private contractor.

Dan had retired from the Air Force in 1996 and began working out of his car at the base. He then decided to retire here. Thank heavens that when 9/11 happened, the U.S. had someone like Dan Generette on the ground at Utapao, to take care of the extra jet fuel, mineral water, and all the other mundane paraphernalia without which the U.S. would not have been able to transfer its B-52s from the PACOM area of responsibility to CENTCOM's.

Utapao was a conduit for aircraft headed to Diego Garcia and the Persian Gulf, from where bombing runs were launched on Afghanistan and later Iraq. At the moment, Dan was facilitating the movement of six hundred American military aircraft annually through Utapao: necessary for the forty-three annual exercises between the Royal Thai Navy and the U.S. military, including Cobra Gold, and for troops going to and from the war zones of the Middle East.

Dan's tour of Utapao began in his compound. He had a plush lounge for resting flight crews—complete with male and female shower facilities—a command-and-control room for emergency operations, luxury vans with karaoke machines for transferring flight crews to their hotels, and storage space for pallets and spare parts. We jumped into his car and drove around. The taxiways were endless, with vast grassy fields perfect for drop zones, and long, weedy cul-de-sacs that ended with galvanized metal revetments that had once been used for North Vietnam–bound B-52s. You could hide a lot here, I thought.

"Yeah, nostalgia for the Vietnam days," Dan said. He showed me more Vietnam ghosts: a broken-down PX and bowling alley, an abandoned NCO club, and a line of 1960s-vintage Dodge and Chevys that had still not been taken for scrap metal. An old MWR (Morale, Welfare, and Recreation) facility gave out onto a beach where the pastel blue Bight of Bangkok met the Gulf of Siam. There was, too, the once luxurious, now gone-to-seed Swan Lake Hotel, where American aircrews had once stayed. With a somewhat neglected yet still lovely garden, it was a cliché out of a Graham Greene novel.

JPAC (Joint POW/MIA Accounting Command) missions, which searched for American servicemen's remains in Vietnam, Laos, and Cambodia, often left from Utapao. The supplies for those flights gave the U.S. military a raison d'être for warehouses here. Dan also took me to a state-of-the-art facility hidden in the forest, with an open space for tents, used during Cobra Gold and for any emergency that might crop up.

Dan Generette was a symbol of the ground-level reality that official Washington overlooked. He was out of the official chain of command, but in a crisis he would be more necessary than anyone in the chain of command. He was another demonstration of why the privatization of American military activity could be a good thing. Neither the U.S. nor Thai governments could shoulder Dan's responsibilities as efficiently and unobtrusively as he did, for the essence of an austere forward base was not the facilities, but the human relationships on the ground.

It was the beautiful women and other aesthetic attractions of Asia that, ultimately, were responsible for luring Dan, his staff, and the American military officers I met in Thailand to either retire or do multiple tours here, building up language skills and area expertise in the process. Quite a few had married locally. They constituted proof that you could serve your country best by loving the indigenous culture most. When I mentioned his name to a Special Forces officer a week later at a bar in Manila, the officer replied, with no intended irony, "Dan Generette, a truly great American."

Because of him, what the United States wanted at Utapao it already had: a cooperative security location that belonged to the host country, with no permanent American troops, but in the event of a crisis could be used by American troops. Indeed, Utapao, a few weeks after my visit, would become a U.S. military hub for tsunami relief in Indonesia—something that never could have happened as efficiently as it did without a private contractor like Dan.

The same low-key arrangement also held at nearby Sattahip, where American frigates and destroyers stopped en route to the Persian Gulf, and where American and Thai SEALs trained together in a shoot house built by the Americans. The worst thing that the Pentagon could do, I thought, was to officialize and otherwise make a big, public deal about such austere bases, for the brilliance of the concept relied on its quiet informality.

The American-Thai military relationship was so multifaceted that it necessitated a bureaucratic entity of its own, the kind of which existed in only a few places in the world. It was called by its acronym, "JUS-MAG" (the Joint United States Military Assistance Group). JUSMAG was definitely not part of the United States Embassy in Thailand. Whereas the embassy was a marble and stone palace where people walked around in suits and ties as in Washington, JUSMAG, located on Thai military property, was a series of dilapidated offices with low ceilings and fluorescent lights that gave onto a dusty garden of palms and banana leaves. The fifty American officers here wore polo or short-sleeve shirts to work. JUSMAG felt like the real Thailand. It even had a bar with wicker-backed chairs. Some at JUSMAG had been in-country for two decades, on and off. The compound was said to be haunted by ghosts from the Vietnam era, when body bags had been among the items stored here in large numbers.

The head of JUSMAG-Thailand was Army Col. Jack Dibrell, a descendant of the Confederate cavalryman Nathan Bedford Forrest. Colonel Dibrell was born at Fort Hood, Texas; grew up in Japan, where his dad had served in Gen. Douglas MacArthur's occupation force; and was soon to retire to Savannah, Georgia. He had a passion for military history and collected World War II–era motorcycles: MMTs, he called them, Male Menopause Toys. One day he and his assistant, Army Maj. Tom Weaver of Rockport, Texas, drove me to the Thai-Burmese border to see the remains of a World War II railway built by British, Australian, Dutch, and American prisoners of war of the Japanese.

It was a two-hour drive in which I listened to the two men's stories. Both Dibrell's and Weaver's dads had served in Vietnam: Maj. Weaver's was killed there in 1969. Both men had roots in the South. "I went to the University of Alabama and Tom went to the University of Mississippi, and between the two of us maybe we have one college education," Dibrell joked. As I had learned over and over again, it was no use denying the strong role played by the Confederate military tradition in the esprit de corps of the twenty-first-century American military. If you frowned on it, or you denied it, you missed a significant element of what accounted for the fighting tradition of this all-volunteer force. With the end of the draft, the influence of the Old South had gained ground in military circles, if only because of the geographical origins of so many who had joined.*

The subject was relevant to our destination. An obscure theater of World War II for Americans, for the Australians the POW experience in the Thai-Burmese border area was central to their national patriotic myth. The fact that Australia and America had become inseparable military allies was partly the result of how dormant military traditions in both countries had, against some odds, resurfaced at the turn of the twenty-first century.

Laterite soil, tapioca fields, and dusty limestone hills protruding out of the earth like sword points marked the border region of western Thailand. The scenery got Col. Dibrell going about U.S. servicemen still missing in action in Burma from World War II. Some casualties were Army airmen lost "flying the hump" over the Himalayas, from the British-held Asian subcontinent to areas held by the anti-Japanese resistance in China. Because the military regime in Burma had kept that country in a lockdown for decades, Dibrell explained that the sites of possible POW remains there had not been pillaged to the extent that they had been in Laos and Vietnam. The search for remains might offer a humanitarian approach to opening up links between the American and Burmese militaries, he thought. "Hey, they've been in power since 1962. Rather than bash them to no avail as Madeleine Albright did in the mid-1990s, shouldn't we quietly infiltrate them to find out what makes them tick? What better way to have influence."

Dibrell, a former member of Delta Force (the elite outfit of Special Operations Command), had lived in Asia for much of his life. He was particularly knowledgeable about Burma because Army Special Forces had some of its roots there, helping Kachin tribesmen against the Japanese. Dibrell was just as much the area specialist as any diplomat or academic, in love with the regional culture and geography. And like many area specialists, he was supremely practical about what could and could not be achieved.

---

* The South accounts for 40 percent of all Army officers: Greg Jaffe, "A Retreat from Major Cities Hurts ROTC Recruiting," *The Wall Street Journal,* February 22, 2007.

Dibrell's love of local and military history came together with the Railway of Death, which the Japanese had built with the slave labor of POWs. The railway went from a Burmese port on the Andaman Sea, southeast through mountains and thick jungle, to a point in Thailand near the Gulf of Siam. With their sea-lanes vulnerable to Allied attacks, the Japanese needed the railway to supply their forces fighting the British in the Indian subcontinent. Of the 60,000 Allied POWs who worked on the railway, 12,399, or 20 percent, died, in addition to 80,000 civilian laborers. This saga in World War II history was the subject of the 1957 movie *The Bridge on the River Kwai.*

On ANZAC Day, April 25, 1998, the Australian government opened a memorial museum on the site of Hellfire Pass, a limestone and granite formation through which POWs cut with picks and shovels, creating an entire canyon in twelve weeks during the summer monsoon of 1943. The Japanese guards had forced the prisoners to work eighteen-hour shifts. Sixty men were beaten to death for not keeping pace. The POWs had no clothes except for scanty loincloths called "Jap happys." The name "Hellfire Pass" came from the way it was lit with torches during the nighttime toil. In the words of Australian Prime Minister John Howard, who spoke at the dawn prayer service for the museum's opening, the survivors owed their lives to their "mateship" with one another, and to the doctors and medics among them, particularly Edward "Weary" Dunlop, whose ashes would later be scattered at the site.*

The museum and the pass below was a site of great beauty and sadness, as if the spirits of the men who had died here hovered about still, in order to have their story told. Col. Dibrell, Maj. Weaver, and I went for a hike around the pass with Bill Slape, the museum manager, a retired warrant officer in the Australian Army. Slape showed us a fine prospect of the Kwai River valley with the burnt, gray-brown ridgelines of Burma in the background, matted with taro trees. Slape worked daily to build culverts and propagate bamboo on the ridges atop Hellfire Pass, in order to anchor the rocks in the monsoon and thus preserve the

* For an epic documentation of the sufferings of Australian prisoners of war, including on the Burma-Siam railway, read Ray Parkin's wartime trilogy: *Out of the Smoke, Into the Smother,* and *The Sword and the Blossom* (London: Hogarth, 1960, 1963, 1968).

landscape as the POWs had experienced it. "See that clearing?" He pointed. "That's where the prisoners walked to work."* We walked beside the original "sleepers" (wooden rails) that jutted out through the dirt, as though in the early stages of transformation to fossils. Observing the chemistry between Slape and the two American Army officers, I thought of the similar road that Australian and American societies had traveled in the latter part of the twentieth century.

It was the fighting on the Gallipoli Peninsula on the western edge of Asia Minor in World War I, with its horrific casualties suffered by soldiers of the Australian and New Zealand Army Corps (ANZACs), that established the grand narrative of Australia as a warrior, expeditionary nation. The death railway, with its theme of mateship, became incorporated into that narrative. Because Vietnam was the first war in which Australia had sent conscripts chosen by lottery to fight overseas, it was highly unpopular in Australia, and thus ANZAC Day took a battering in the process. Yet the end of the Cold War, because it occurred at the same time as the deaths of the last Gallipoli survivors and the bicentennial of Australia's founding as a nation, brought about a return of historical memory that would correct the amnesia of the 1960s' youth rebellion in Australia. The reaffirmation of the ANZAC tradition, in the words of Australian historian Joan Beaumont, was fortified further by the need for "some kind of spirituality in an increasingly secular society."† It was certainly an element in the string of Conservative governments at the turn of the twenty-first century led by John Howard, who forged an alliance with George Bush that brought the two countries' militaries closer together.

Next we went to the war cemetery at nearby Kanchanaburi, the site of thousands of Commonwealth and Dutch graves. In third-world Southeast Asia and the Pacific, with its ancient Buddhist temples and soulless modernity—where, unlike in Europe, Western visitors found no architectural accumulation of history that they could call their own— the memory of World War II achieved a particular poignancy. It was the

---

* The hiking trail itself was built by Rodney William Beattie, another Australian.
† I spoke with Professor Beaumont, of Deakin University, who was working at the Thai-Burma Railway Centre at the time of my visit to western Thailand. Much of this paragraph reflects her insights, even though her opinion of Prime Minister Howard is less benign than my own.

exotic nightmare that old Asia hands in the American military grasped
on to, in order to link themselves with their Australian brothers, and to
fortify morale for what might lie ahead in these parts.

———

In a few days I was looking down another massive, two-mile-long runway that could handle any aircraft in any military arsenal, with unlimited MOG (maximum on ground) space hidden away in the weeds of an
immense, mountain-ringed plain. You could fit the whole Pacific Air
Force in this place. I was at Clark Field, on the island of Luzon in the
Philippines, the very base whose loss in 1991 had helped the Department of Defense to embrace the concept of cooperative security locations in the first place.*

In the wake of the Gulf War of 1991, with Saudi Arabia extremely
uneasy about American servicemen on its soil, the United States saw
how even after victory there were basing problems with the very country it had defended. But it was the forcible closure by the Philippine
government of Clark Air Force Base and nearby Subic Bay Naval Station that truly rattled the American military brass. Clark and Subic were
heirlooms of the Philippine War of the turn of the twentieth century.
They had been occupied by the Japanese in World War II, and subsequently liberated with significant loss of life. They were the massive,
storied Air Force and Navy equivalents of the Army bases in western
Germany; here airmen and sailors had married local girls and retired in
numbers unrivaled by soldiers in Europe. Then it all ended. The upshot
was a period of introspection by defense officials that led, in turn, to the
realization that U.S. bases almost anywhere outside U.S. territory were
a risky investment. One solution was to have access to foreign bases
through well-developed personal relationships.

That was already happening. In one part of Clark, amid villas with
collapsed roofs and lawns reclaimed by the jungle (where American Air
Force officers and their families had once lived), I found Charlie 1-1,
the elite combat unit of the 1st Battalion of the Army's 1st Special
Forces Group. It was here training a Philippine light reaction company

---

* Named after Maj. Harold M. Clark, born in Minnesota and reared in the Philippines, who
was the first U.S. airman to fly in Hawaii. He died in a seaplane crash in the Panama Canal
Zone in 1919.

in urban warfare. "Where did you go for Thanksgiving?" I asked the warrant officer in charge of the training. He told me that the team had paid a restaurant owner in nearby Angeles City to prepare a turkey dinner for them.

Angeles City boasted miles of the world's most outrageous restaurants, bars, and nightclubs ("A Beer and a Blow-job for $9"), which had grown up around the American air base in the post–World War II decades. Counter to expectations, they were still thriving thirteen years after the last permanently stationed U.S. troops had left. Waitresses wore laminated hygiene cards indicating the date of their last blood test for sexually transmitted diseases. Business nowadays came from elderly Australian and American "sexpatriots," some looking as old as George Burns and in motorized wheelchairs, led around by slinky young Filipinas. The notorious KSM—Khalid Shaikh Mohammed, 9/11 mastermind and number three in al-Qaeda—had caroused in places like this, using bar girls to help him set up a business network in the Philippines.* "Everyone thought it was the Americans who brought the mosquitoes," explained one American Army officer, referring to the prostitutes who buzzed around. "It wasn't," he went on. "It was poverty and a particularly aggressive service mentality" applied to the bodily function of sex—another cultural indicator of Asian economic dynamism.

Pentagon officials were also keen on an airport on the small island of Mactan, in the central Philippines, for a cooperative security location. I went there the next day. I was met by Larry Johansen, a crusty, retired Air Force staff sergeant from Dallas, with reddish blond hair and a wry expression. If Larry didn't have a cigarette in his mouth, he looked as if he should have. Larry had married a Filipina, spoke fluent Tagalog, and was the rough equivalent of Dan Generette at Utapao.

Larry had served at Clark as an eighteen-year-old in the 1970s, when Angeles City was especially wild. In 1986, when the Air Force offered him a position in Little Rock, Arkansas, he said the proverbial *fuck that,* and did not reenlist. Instead, he went to work for Lockheed and then

---

* For an excellent briefing on the connection between al-Qaeda and the Philippines, see Maria A. Ressa's *Seeds of Terror: An Eyewitness Account of Al-Qaeda's Newest Center of Operations in Southeast Asia* (New York: Free Press, 2003).

Boeing, which got him to Riyadh, Saudi Arabia, for eleven straight years: a great deal, because he got sixty days' paid vacation annually, which he spent in Thailand and the Philippines. "Let's go have breakfast," he said. "There's this French-type place. It's got, I don't know, French shit."

Larry was the ultimate mechanic-trainer. He oversaw logistics and maintenance for the Philippine Air Force at Mactan. He was the U.S. military's eyes and ears here. But he was a private contractor. He explained that his salary was paid by TeKontrol, a Florida-based firm hired by the Security Assistance Technical Management Office at Fort Bragg, North Carolina, at the behest of JUSMAG-Philippines. And because JUSMAG-Philippines, like JUSMAG-Thailand, came under the umbrella of security assistance provided by one government to another, Larry's chain of command ultimately ended with the diplomats at the State Department. There were plans for more Larrys at Mactan.

Larry, who was in his mid-forties and looked a decade older—the result of hard, fun living—had an office that was the nerve center for C-130 and other fixed-wing and helicopter maintenance, with neat flowcharts on the walls showing the status of each aircraft. The reality indicated by the charts was grim. When the U.S. military had Clark and Subic, it took care of maintenance for the Philippine Air Force—not officially, but that's how the dependent, colonial-style relationship worked. When the Filipinos asserted sovereignty, aircraft maintenance went into a death spiral.

If a U.S. Air Force plane needed a spare part that had to be taken from another plane, a requisition order had to be filed to guarantee that the second plane would have its part replaced immediately. This was known as controlled cannibalization. The Philippine Air Force practiced uncontrolled cannibalization, so that once-operable C-130s were stripped like old cars. Maintenance was the traditional responsibility of noncommissioned officers, and the Philippine military, like almost all those in the third world, had a weak NCO corps.

A half-dozen C-130s sat on the ground at Mactan, rusting and ready for the scrap heap. Of the other half dozen, one was operational. Larry's goal was to have four operational. He couldn't just reintroduce controlled cannibalization, for that meant other reforms, such as bringing back a tool-control program from the pre-1992 era, so that missing tools would not hamper repairs. It was a cultural challenge as much as a logistical one, meaning it was a seven-day-a-week job. Every time a plane landed with a problem, Larry was there instructing, mentoring.

Larry took me everywhere on Mactan, an interminable rash of corrugated shacks and sagging clotheslines that met the dappled, turquoise mirror of the Camotes Sea. On a cruddy Mactan inlet filled with beggars stood a weather-stained monument with weeds growing from its crevices. It was erected in 1866 by the Spanish occupiers to honor the navigator Ferdinand Magellan, cut down on this beach as he and his men came ashore on April 27, 1521, and were attacked by indigenous natives led by the petty chieftain Lapulapu. Magellan's arrival in the Philippines, after the discovery of a strait near Cape Horn that forever bears his name, followed by a nightmarish 12,600-mile journey across the Pacific, brought Europeans to Asia for the first time via a western route, thereby establishing in fact what had been known in theory: that the earth was a sphere. Thus ended the medieval ages.

Yet the earth was still vast, vaster than many in Washington supposed. And Larry Johansen knew this wild and strategic corner of it better than anyone else. On the nearby island of Cebu, where guerrillas of the New People's Army lurked in the mountains, he knew which nightclubs were safe and which weren't, whom to go to in order to get something built or to get something through customs. Larry wasn't a saint. But he was—boiled down to an individual—the shallow footprint that the Pentagon needed, whether it knew it or not.

Nor did he want to leave. As Larry's friend, another American military contractor, put it to me over lunch, "I don't want to die warehoused in some senior citizens home in the States, surrounded by other old people smelling like vitamins. I'd rather retire here, or in Thailand, taken care of in a village by my wife's relatives." Such motives were crucial if the U.S. was going to project power subtly by, through, and with host-country militaries in Asia.

The Philippines constituted the ultimate litmus test for the competition between the United States and China in the Pacific.[18] The Philippines was where ungovernability met great power conflict. If, despite a century of American economic aid and American blood, China would ultimately emerge on these islands as the most influential power, that indicated a dire prospect for the U.S. in the Pacific.

Everywhere I had been in the PACOM area of responsibility, people were concerned that all the money was going down the shit hole of P. I.—the acronym used by the American military for the Philippine Islands. "Is P. I. a black hole or an important historical legacy?" one of my dinner hosts at Thanksgiving asked rhetorically. "The answer is both." Said another at the table: "P. I. is like an old house. Whenever you peek inside the walls or under the floor to inspect a problem, you find so many others."

Because this time I had arrived from Thailand, another developing country, the dysfunctional nature of the Philippines was more apparent than it had been in 2003, when I had come from Hawaii and saw merely a poor and populous country lacking any measure of comparison with the United States. Now I gasped at how dicier, rattier, and more perverse Manila was in relation to Bangkok, and how much starker the slums and wealth disparities were. In 2003, I had learned how Army Special Forces had helped the Filipinos clear Islamic terrorists from parts of Mindanao and the Sulu Archipelago. But as Philippine troops relocated to the south of the country to consolidate those gains, fresh pockets of ungovernability emerged in the north, as other insurgent groups swarmed out of the forest woodwork in remote parts of Luzon.

The U.S. had been in Iraq only a few years, and it was questionable if an appetite existed for a long-term presence. But the U.S. had invaded the Philippines at the end of the nineteenth century, fought a costly war here that descended into an interminable struggle against insurgents, then built the country's entire infrastructure only to see it occupied by the Japanese. After liberation in 1945, the U.S. maintained, right up through the present, a deep and abiding involvement with the Filipino political-military establishment, buttressed by massive aid packages.

But with China investing heavily here and signing economic and military agreements, Manila might provide a surer vantage point than Baghdad for espying the ultimate destiny of American power.

For example, in late July 2004 the Philippine government pulled its troops out of Iraq with great fanfare, one month before the deployment was due to expire anyway, in order to obtain the release of a Filipino truck driver kidnapped by Iraqi insurgents. The Chinese, sensing an opening, offered the Philippine government a defense pact that featured an intelligence-sharing agreement. That elicited a U.S. threat to cut military assistance across the board.

The intelligence agreement went unsigned, and now the U.S. was embarking on a $30 million program to reform the Philippine military from the ground up, using a model employed by NATO for reforming the militaries of Eastern Europe. Angry as it was at Manila, Washington knew that with China rising and this unruly archipelago-nation so close to Taiwan, after a hundred years of effort it still had no choice than to mount yet another rescue attempt of this imperial legacy.

One night in the Philippines, I ate dinner with nine American military personnel, including six Navy SEALs here on a training mission. We occupied a table on a steamy, humid street. The food was great and two bottles of Jack Daniels were ordered. The conversation flew from subject to subject. The SEAL next to me talked about his time in Iraq when he had done nodal analysis of terrorist ratlines coming through the western desert from Syria. "All roads led to Fallujah," he declared. Across the table sat a ruddy-complexioned Army officer in a tropical shirt, who had grown up in Georgia and Alaska as a military brat, and had a lifetime of experience in Asia. "Here's the difference between Thailand and P. I.," he told me. "If you go to a driving range in Thailand, there are automated ball dispensers, good food, bar girls, and massages. If you go to a driving range here, there is just one guy clumping up mud in his hands for ball mounds. Thais have no principles, but they never compromise, so they have high standards of efficiency."

I thought of Colombia.

"Thai mafias are disciplined," he went on. "They provide some order and useful intelligence. In the Philippines, the government *is* the mafia, a poorly run one." The corruption here, they all agreed, was a perfect fit with China's, whose own criminal networks couldn't wait to extract Filipino girls for prostitution and set up local methamphetamine rings.

Still, this Army officer was full of cautious optimism. He outlined for me how JUSMAG was going to reform the Philippine military, by creating new bureaucratic structures that squeezed out opportunities for corruption and cronyism. Duty tours would end in three years, so that people wouldn't be able to entrench themselves. Tours would be staggered so that generals wouldn't take their whole entourages with them on each assignment. That way the careers of others did not rise and fall with that of the general, thereby busting up patriarchal systems. There would be retirement incentives so that an "up and out" system could take root. If you weren't promoted, you left the service, as in the U.S.

"We're bringing in a Marine sergeant-major to work NCO development," he told me: the kind of bullying noncommissioned officer that, as I knew from my own experience with marines, was like a Chihuahua on crack, full of energy and aggression. "There's no better time to attempt this," he said in a dogged, gravelly voice. "We can't fail here."

A week later, at the end of November 2004, following a typhoon, U.S. marines from Okinawa landed in the Philippines to provide humanitarian relief.

THREE

A CIVILIZATION UNTO ITSELF, SWISHING THROUGH THE CRUSHING VOID

ON A NAVY DESTROYER

Indian Ocean and Andaman Sea, Winter 2005

I n late December 2004, not long after the Okinawa-based Marines had completed their humanitarian mission in the typhoon-lashed Philippines, an earthquake and subsequent tsunami devastated Indonesia, Thailand, and Sri Lanka. The USS *Abraham Lincoln*'s Carrier Strike Group, in port at Hong Kong, immediately changed its mission from keeping the commercial sea-lanes open to disaster relief. What had been a pulse (a planned deployment) became a surge (an emergency one). The *Nimitz*-class carrier fired up its twin nuclear reactors and proceeded to Indonesia at best speed (up to thirty knots).* It was followed by the USS *Bonhomme Richard* Expeditionary Strike Group, located just south of Guam at the time. Thus began Operation Unified Assistance.

---

* W. Thomas Smith, Jr., "Angels with Rotary Wings," *National Review Online,* Jan. 7, 2005. Smith, a former U.S. Marine infantry commander, wrote perhaps the best concise summary of the U.S. military's relief effort, on which my account is mostly based.

The carrier *Abraham Lincoln* and the amphibious assault ship *Bonhomme Richard* (named after John Paul Jones's frigate in the American Revolution) functioned as the two command posts. Nearly a hundred Navy and Marine helicopters began a ship-to-shore circuit, delivering supplies and evacuating the most gravely ill and wounded. This was in addition to assistance provided by Navy engineers, rescue swimmers, doctors, and medical corpsmen. The *Abraham Lincoln* had a long record of disaster relief, including the 1991 Mount Pinatubo eruption in the Philippines and the annual flooding in Bangladesh.

In fact, there was no more suitable organization in the world for emergency assistance than the U.S. military, with its air and sealift capacity, and the ability of its nuclear carriers to reprocess seawater into hundreds of thousands of gallons of fresh drinking water. After the tsunami, sailors aboard the *Lincoln* stopped taking showers in order to provide as much water as possible to the victims.

The tsunami relief effort demonstrated a navy's soft power. To wit, a carrier strike group offered an impact on land that was out of proportion to its small, nonthreatening footprint, located as it was some miles offshore.

Though the world (and Muslim Indonesians, in particular) was taken aback by the Navy and Marine effort, it was something the military did all the time as part of its normal battle rhythm. Every time a U.S. warship stopped at a port in the developing world, part of its crew conducted a humanitarian Comrel (community relations exercise). In the Horn of Africa, I had reported on covert operations to kill al-Qaeda terrorists, even as I embedded with an Army civil affairs team engaged in relief projects in the same area. Multiple tasking—acting sequentially as warriors, local governors, and relief workers—constituted the very definition of an imperial-like, expeditionary military.

If anything, the Global War on Terrorism, by forcing the U.S. military to embrace the concept of flexible response, made it easier for a carrier strike group to help in a humanitarian emergency. For example, though the strike group's navigators planned for a deployment in the vicinity of China and the Korean Peninsula, they carried sailing charts for all of Asia, including Indonesia—something they would not have done before 9/11.

While the USS *Abraham Lincoln* was still off the northwest tip of
the Indonesian island of Sumatra, engaged in humanitarian assistance, I
headed to Singapore to link up with the strike group. My plan was to
take a Navy plane from Singapore to the *Abe* (as the *Abraham Lincoln*
was fondly called by sailors), and from the carrier hop a helicopter to a
guided missile destroyer, where I would spend a few weeks among blue
water grunts.

SINGAPORE

Singapore stunned me with its manic cleanliness and efficiency. Arriving at the airport was like being slotted onto a fast-moving conveyor
belt, with worker bees at designated stops where my passport was
stamped, my money changed, and my checked luggage delivered within
ten minutes of deplaning. A metered cab smelling of freshener awaited
me at the end of the process. The geodesic architecture and rows of
stone pyramids atop a shopping complex created an aura of sterility,
central control, and placelessness that reminded me slightly of Dubai.
The taxi flew down and around sleek highways and rotaries landscaped
with young trees and clipped hedgerows to my hotel, located amid a
forest of other skyscrapers that resembled computer memory sticks.

In three decades, Singapore had gone from a dirty, malarial hellhole
of overpowering smells and polluted, life-threatening monsoon drains
to a global economic dynamo that topped businessmen's lists for efficiency and quality of life. Singapore was so easy to negotiate that I
thought of it as beginner's Asia. In the early 1960s, it was as poor as
many countries in sub-Saharan Africa; by the 1990s, this city-state,
one-fifth the size of Rhode Island, had a standard of living higher than
Australia. Credit for the miracle went to one man: an English-educated
ethnic-Chinese barrister, Harry Lee.

Harry Lee is worth a few words. While he might at times have vio-
lated some of the democratic principles for which America stood, for
the U.S. military in Southeast Asia he was a godsend.

In the best short analysis of Lee's career, the Australian editor and
intellectual Owen Harries writes that Lee's political philosophy was the
upshot of his experiences in the 1940s, which served him better than

any standard university education could have.[1] In the first half of that decade, Lee observed up close a society thrown into chaos, followed by the ruthless brutality of Japanese occupation. Japanese rule in Singapore taught Lee all he needed to know about human weakness—specifically, that the fear of physical punishment dramatically altered behavior. But in the second half of the decade he went to study at Cambridge, and was stunned by the civility of a society established on the rule of law.

When Harry Lee returned to Singapore, roiling cultural and political forces in the region made it hard to be an optimist. The feudal Chinese majority was divided by clan and dialect, with the exception of a small group of English speakers to which Lee's family belonged. Within the Chinese community, the dominant political force was the local Communist Party. Then there were the Indian and Malay minorities, the latter particularly important as Singapore was immersed in a Malay area. (Singapore, or *Singapura,* is Malay for "city of the lion.") Malay culture, Harries explains, was "hierarchical, deferential, and characterized by an easygoing cronyism that shaded into corruption." Then there was Indonesia, adjacent to Singapore and the Malay Peninsula, where Sukarno, the most anti-Western leader in the third world, was about to run amok through the manipulation of the largest Communist Party outside of the Warsaw Pact.

It was this social and political reality that Harry Lee had no choice but to engage. Upon entering politics, he changed his name back to the traditional Lee Kuan Yew. As a defense against Sukarno's Indonesia, he supported a merger between Singapore and Malaya that was consummated in 1963, with the creation of Malaysia. Two years later, he split from Malaysia, creating an independent city-state that would forge a first-world military and education system.

The virtual dictator of Singapore, he organized a meritocracy that would become the envy of the world. Lee himself remained uncorrupt; despite his immense power he killed no one and was careful to observe legal limits, even as he governed in the spirit of an enlightened despot rather than as a democrat. Through Machiavellian tactics that combined Oriental toughness, inspired by the Japanese fascists, with an almost anal-retentive Western legal code, inspired by English constitutionalism, he single-handedly built an Asian replica of ancient Athens despite being surrounded by chaotic third-world regimes. Trash cans were filled with cigarette butts because no one dared to throw them on the sidewalks, for fear of a hefty fine. The city was full of leafy parks, even as walls and offices were empty of the photo of the man who had created it all. Singapore was, allowing for size, America's most prosperous and dependable ally in the Pacific, practically a home port for the U.S. Seventh Fleet.

The city-state's multi-ethnic military meritocracy, its nurturing concern for the welfare of its officers and enlisted men alike, and its jungle warfare school in Brunei were second to none. Singapore offered the only non-American base in the Pacific—Japan far to the north excepted—where U.S. nuclear carriers could be serviced. "The Sings, well, they're just awesome," a Navy analyst in Washington had told me. Singapore's intelligence tips and other help in hunting down Islamic terrorists in the Indonesian archipelago had been of a standard equal or superior to that of America's most dependable Western allies. CNN Jakarta bureau chief Maria A. Ressa writes in *Seeds of Terror* that Singapore "has been the only nation in the world to be completely transparent about its terrorism investigations, releasing pictures and biographies of everyone arrested under its Internal Security Act."[2]

Whenever I sat with influential figures of the Arab and ex-communist worlds and posed the question, Who was the greatest minor man of the twentieth century, not someone on par with Churchill or Roosevelt, but a tier below: the kind of man your country needs at the moment? the answer was never Nelson Mandela or Vaclav Havel, but invariably Lee Kuan Yew. Some journalists and intellectuals who had never wielded bureaucratic responsibility, and who preached moral absolutes from the sidelines, disliked him. But Western leaders—Gerald Ford, George H.W. Bush, and Margaret Thatcher, to name a few, each of whom understood the need for moral compromise in the face of implacable, violent forces—rightly held him in awe. Lady Thatcher observes: "In office, I read and analyzed every speech of Harry's. He had a way of penetrating the fog of propaganda. . . . He was never wrong."[3]

Surrounded by this glittering, orderly prosperity that lay just a few miles across the Strait of Malacca from the feudal, ethnic violence of Indonesia, and reading in the newspaper my first morning in Singapore about terrorist bombings in Baghdad, I couldn't help believing that the situation in Iraq would have turned out better (and more amenable to the West) had President George W. Bush read Lee Kuan Yew's tragic-realistic book about how he had created contemporary Singapore, rather than the idealistic work of former Soviet dissident Natan Sharansky about bringing democracy to the world—the book that, as it happened, the President was handing visitors to the Oval Office.

———

Lee's transformation of Singapore from an exotic hellhole to a post-industrial trading tiger was so complete that the old Singapore appeared at first glance to have vanished. But it was the old Singapore that I wanted a glimpse of, for the sake of another great name with which this city-state is associated: Joseph Conrad. You couldn't go to sea, as I intended, without thinking of him.

Conrad, a turn-of-the-twentieth-century English writer of Polish origin, might have been history's greatest foreign correspondent, on par with Herodotus, for in the guise of fiction a writer can tell the truth more easily.*

On almost every page of his most richly developed works, Conrad re-creates the overwhelming compactedness of what journalists experience when they are alone in far-off places: the sorts of vivid and searing memories that burden reporters till the end of their days, because they don't fit within the strictures of news as defined by their editors. But while journalists have a tendency to go weepy whenever covering the weaker side in a conflict, Conrad, in his rationalism and analytical compass, never gives way to his emotions.[4] Because he knows that the record of human experience indicates just how many problems simply have no solutions, his fictional correspondences from the tropic seaboards evince a majestic, god-like objectivity in which humankind is at once loved and deeply pitied.

Conrad's Singapore was all that was available to me. My Navy friends had counseled only hiking gear for my time on ship, and thus I lacked the formal clothes for any appointments with political and busi-

* This section on Conrad borrows from my Introduction to *Lord Jim and Nostromo* (New York: Modern Library, 1999).

ness leaders. The short time that I had here I spent on foot, walking from one landmark of late-nineteenth-century British Singapore to another: from Raffles Hotel, with its tiled roof, wicker furniture, and palm- and banana-fringed white arcades; to the Anglican glory of St. Andrews, with its lazy overhead fans; to the Central Fire Station, which, with its striped russet and white stonework, was reminiscent of Mamluk mosques in Egypt; and finally to the classical pile of the Hill Street Police Barracks by the Singapore River, where the boats of Conrad's day took refuge from storms.

In Conrad's sea stories, individuals are thrown back upon their own failings by the isolation of an unfamiliar and inhospitable setting, so Singapore and its world of the Eastern Seas, rather than mere exotic bric-a-brac, become a laboratory for the dissection of the human character.

That dissection is never more intense than aboard a ship, where individuals are crammed together and cut off from land-based entanglements. In such a minute universe, under the most ascetic of conditions, reputations are made that are the opposite of fame, because outside the narrow world of seamen, no one will ever hear of them. To Conrad, a ship is nothing less than a planet sailing alone through black eternity.

To such a planet I was headed. After a few days in Singapore, I left the pampered environment of the global business world and reentered the aesthetically impoverished, gray-riveted monastery of the U.S. military, without which, for want of security of the sea-lanes, that business community might not have existed.

———

A U.S. Navy lieutenant in khakis met me in the luxurious lobby of my hotel and drove me to Singapore's Paya Lebar Air Base, where several U.S. Navy C-2 Greyhounds shuttled sailors, journalists, and officials from various Washington agencies to the *Abraham Lincoln* on a daily basis. With 5,500 sailors aboard at any one time, the *Abe* was less a boat than a small city, requiring an entire section of this foreign military base just to fly people on and off it. On my flight would also be eleven sailors, two Turkish journalists, and an interagency team from the Department of Defense and U.S. Agency for International Development, which was developing a plan to permanently embed civilian relief workers on Navy hospital ships in future emergencies.

The C-2, a miniature version of the C-130, was the most uncomfortable plane I ever flew on. I faced backward in a windowless fuselage, wearing a tight helmet with ear pads, strangled inside a four-way harness and a life vest. For two and a quarter hours we vibrated violently in the disorienting blackness before beginning a steep descent. Landing on a carrier facing backward with no visual warning was like being in a car crash. All of a sudden I was smashed against the seat as though against a cement wall. Then the hatch opened to reveal a stunning line of F-18 Hornets on a tarmac. As I stepped onto the vast flight deck, it was only the water swiftly running beside me that indicated where I was, for a carrier is so big that one has no physical sensation of moving through an ocean, let alone at thirty knots.

On the flight deck the passengers were yelled at by an air transport officer, who marched us down ladders and through a bewildering series of narrow passageways into a tiny room, where we handed in our helmets and life vests, and signed a logbook. I was then hustled into another room where I learned that the helicopter that would take me to the destroyer would leave in an hour. In the meantime, I got a nickel tour of the carrier—the ultimate articulation of the industrial age and the urbanized anonymity that accompanies it, in which each door and hatchway led to a different neighborhood, and every function was so compartmentalized that the fighter pilots, the combat operations team, the nuclear reactor technicians, the fire brigades, the bridge controllers, and so on had little to do with one another, and knew or cared less about the others' jobs. One of the few common intimacies for onboard sailors was renting fishing rods, in order to try their luck at the edge of the deck whenever the carrier slowed its engines.

The heart of an aircraft carrier is the hangar, many hundreds of feet long with a four-story-high ceiling, and jam-packed with F-18s and E-2 Hawkeye surveillance planes, which are moved up to the flight deck on massive elevators. These were not the happiest times for the F-18 pilots, normally the studs on board. Because of the tsunami emergency, most of their training runs had been canceled and it was the helicopter pilots who were suddenly in their glory. Nevertheless, the fighter pilots bucked up their morale by going ashore to assist in the relief work.

I almost lost my guide amid the crowds of Navy maintenance crews and civilian contractors. In the hangar, more than on the flight deck, you got a sense of the "boat's" gargantuan size. Carriers and submarines are "boats," while cruisers, destroyers, and frigates are "ships."

In the middle of the tour I got yanked away and told my helicopter was leaving early. Again I was barked at and rushed up to the flight deck. More fiddling with strange harnesses and life vests. Then, as though lifted high above the deck on puppet strings, with the windows of the SH-60 Seahawk open and the wind's muffled roar pouring into my ears, I skidded along the Indian Ocean through low-hanging tropical rain clouds off the coast of Sumatra and headed for the USS *Benfold*. I was glad to be on my own again, the only civilian passenger on the helicopter, away from the world of Washington that the *Abe Lincoln,* in the midst of a front-page emergency, had come to represent. Congressional delegations and television crews visited carriers; few went to destroyers.

—

Approaching the USS *Benfold*'s starboard quarter, the Seahawk hovered to one side of the fantail, which also functioned as the flight deck, and then executed a sharp sideways jink at the proper moment, after the pilot had assessed the up-and-down movement of the ship. As wind exploded on the flight deck and safety nets were drawn down along its sides, swarms of men and women in vests and helmets encircled the helicopter. In white vests was the medical team; in green the "comms" element for communicating to the bridge; in red the fire brigade; and in blue the chalk-and-chain detail, which anchored the chopper onto the flight deck so that it would not be tipped over, or be blown off by the wind. It was all just one facet of "helicopter ops" on a surface warship.

As I ran off the chopper, my back bent over by the wind, the crowd of seamen in their assorted vests cleared a path. I climbed a ladder onto the aft missile deck, at the rear of the two smokestacks, where an officer in pressed khakis, alone among sailors in blue coveralls, greeted me. He then led me inside to "officers' country." In a moment I was in the captain's stateroom, where a coffee and tea service had been prepared with fresh fruit.

I had arrived at my destination—the front line of a fighting oceanic ("blue water") navy. Because it *was* the Navy, everything from the terminology to the rank structure to the array of different uniforms was bewildering. I was aboard the USS *Benfold,* or DDG 65 (Hull number 65), an *Arleigh Burke*–class guided-missile destroyer that packed ninety launch cells in its two vertical launch systems (VLSes) with Tomahawk missiles for striking land targets, SM-2s (standard missile-2s) for shooting down aircraft and missiles, Harpoon missiles for hitting other warships, and anti-submarine rockets. The Navy had fifty-five such destroyers, as well as four *Spruance*-class ones. But the *Spruance*-class destroyers lacked the SPY-1 Radar and Combat System Integrator, which provided three-dimensional vision far over the horizon. *Arleigh Burke* destroyers could see and kill anything before anything could see and kill them. Well, not quite: another *Arleigh Burke*–class destroyer was the USS *Cole,* attacked in 2000 by suicide bombers in a fast boat, who pulled up to the warship and exploded themselves while the *Cole* was in a Yemeni port to take on fuel.* Seventeen sailors were killed.

Incidentally, Arleigh Burke, Spruance, Benfold, and Cole were all names of naval heroes, often Medal of Honor winners. The connection between these names and the ships' crews was often quite personal, as I would learn.

The destroyer, as the name suggested, was the ultimate surface warship.† It was the original submarine hunter and frontline defender for an aircraft carrier. Its crew of thirty-two officers and 330 enlisted sailors embodied the oceanic naval equivalent of infantry grunts. "We suck up all the punishment in order to protect the big deck [the carrier]," explained Lt. Comdr. David Dunn of Roswell, New Mexico, the ship's executive officer (XO), who had greeted me on the missile deck.

As a lieutenant commander, Dave Dunn was the Navy equivalent of a major in the other services. He was one of four crew members in the captain's blue-carpeted stateroom with me. There was the ship's captain, Comdr. Donald Hornbeck of Indianapolis, the equivalent of a lieutenant colonel. Aboard ship, function took precedence over rank, so he was referred to as "Capt. Hornbeck" rather than "Comdr. Hornbeck,"

---

* The *Cole* was the next *Arleigh Burke* destroyer built at Pascagoula, Mississippi, after the *Benfold.*
† The original name was "torpedo boat destroyer."

even though he had not yet reached the higher rank of a naval captain. Whereas Capt. Hornbeck—a former civilian geophysicist and planner on the Joint Staff at the Pentagon—was dry and cerebral, with a stony expression, the XO, Lt. Comdr. Dunn, was chatty. There was, too, Master Chief Petty Officer Terry Craddock of Eufaula, Alabama: the senior enlisted man on the USS *Benfold,* the equivalent of a Marine or Army sergeant major. A big and soft-spoken African American, Master Chief Craddock was the lord-god-protector and enforcer of the enlisted ranks, which accounted for 90 percent of the ship's crew. The fourth crew member in the stateroom was Ensign Mitch McGuffie of Goliad, Texas, the equivalent of a second lieutenant. A graduate of Annapolis who had worked on John Kerry's senatorial staff, Ensign McGuffie, a tall and intellectually serious young officer, would be my guide during my first days on the *Benfold.*

I was told that I would have "free roam" of the ship. I could go anywhere I wanted, except for the cryptology room, and walk in on almost any meeting. Yet, even as I was welcomed by the ship's command, I knew that I would have to escape officers' country and make my way among the enlisted ranks. It was the enlisted sailors of a destroyer who were at the heart of naval warfare. Given the rise of the Chinese Navy, they might be just as important in future years and decades as marines and Army Special Forces had been in Iraq and Afghanistan.

After the welcome session, Ensign McGuffie showed me my "stateroom." Though the term conjures up something spacious and elegant, in fact it was a cubicle, with three coffin-like racks for two officers and me. Still, such accommodations constituted the top of the social hierarchy compared to the "berthings" in the bowels of the hull, where enlisted sailors slept as many as forty to a room. The overwhelming reality of all ships, especially military ones, is the premium on space. It is a claustrophobic existence amid the hostile sea. Unlike land, there is no place to go AWOL. People were inches away from one another at meetings. Thus, strengths and flaws of character were magnified and noticed quickly.

"Staterooms," "berthings," "ropeyarns" (running errands), "bosun" (deck crew chief), and other words flew at me, either unfamiliar or meaning something very different than they would have on land. Nautical English, because of its reliquary strangeness, awards a special camaraderie to those who use it, something I had observed with marines, another naval force, in the Iraqi and West African deserts. Floors were "decks," stairs "ladders," and walls "bulkheads." "Doors" went through bulkheads, while "hatchways" went through decks. Bathrooms were "heads," because in the days when ships could only sail with the wind at their backs, the toilet was placed at the "head" (front) of the ship, so that the wind could carry away the smell quickly. The front of the ship was the "bow," the rear the "stern." "Starboard" indicated the right side facing forward, "port" the left. The deck near the bow of the ship was never the front deck, but the "forecastle," the rear deck the "fantail." Making it stranger, forecastle was pronounced "focsle." Enlisted sailors from small towns, some with barely a high school education, could rattle off these words in the course of normal conversation. This was in addition to the scientific and military terms they employed. Many a sailor would tell me, "When I call my folks at home and talk about what I'm doing here, they barely understand what I'm saying."

Dinner commenced soon after I had arrived aboard. In officers' country meals were served in the wardroom, decorated with blue carpets and tablecloths, and graced with a picture of Hospitalman Third Class Edward C. Benfold of Audubon, New Jersey, a Navy corpsman killed at the age of twenty-one in the Korean War. He was awarded the Medal of Honor posthumously for his bravery. Every officer on board knew the story of how Eddie Benfold had moved from position to position in the face of intense artillery fire, treating the wounded. When two grenades were hurled at a group of wounded marines, he picked up the grenades and threw himself against onrushing enemy soldiers, killing them and himself in the process. The story did not go with the face, that of a smiling, angelic boy who appeared to be in his late teens at most.

Looking at Eddie's face, I thought of Smitty, the soulful Navy corpsman with the Marines in Niger, who had previously served in Iraq, and who, it seemed to me, might actually have had the heart for such an act.

At dinner I was confused by the exotic uniforms. Soldiers and marines had two or three kinds at the most. In the Navy, there were nine uniforms for enlisted men alone. For example, there were dress blues for formal occasions in wintry climates and dress whites for such occa sions in the tropics. Then there were the even more formal dinner dress blues and whites with cummerbunds. On ship, officers and senior enlisted sailors wore pressed khakis, while the lower ranks wore pressed blue utilities when standing bridge watch. Yet almost every officer and sailor could also wear blue coveralls. It depended upon where in the ship they would be working that day.

There were also women present in the wardroom. Because I had spent the bulk of my time covering frontline field units, the presence of women in the armed forces had remained an abstraction to me until I arrived at the *Benfold,* which had about fifty of them. As I would see, more than refining or softening the American military, they completed its internalization as a separate caste.[5]

Here on a destroyer women served in frontline positions, and men had slightly longer hair and more ordinary physiques compared to the marines and Army Special Forces troops I had known. Whereas the Marines were a cult, the Navy was a calling—a way of life. Esprit de Corps came from a ship's isolation, the multiple levels of nautical and military jargon that only those on board could understand, and the way each officer and sailor addressed the other: employing the honorifics of "Mister" and "Miss." Marine grunts in Iraq and Djibouti had complained to me that on Navy ships they were treated as second-class citizens. They didn't realize that because of the hostile environment of the high seas, and the number of young people jammed together on board, iron discipline was a life-giving necessity, enforced through an unquestioned and minutely stratified hierarchy.

Following dinner, Ensign McGuffie—Mr. McGuffie to his subordinates—gave me a tour of the intestinal passageways (p-ways), with which I would have to become familiar to get around on my own. It was so confusing that the first days I used the map-numbering system: if a door had 1-222-1 on it, that meant I was at the waterline, 222 feet to the rear of the bow, and starboard from the center of the beam.*

———

It happened that my first night aboard there was an Un-Rep (underway replenishment), the naval equivalent of an air-to-air refueling.

* An even number would indicate to port of the centerline.

The object of this Un-Rep was to transfer 200,000 gallons of diesel fuel and twenty pallets of food and equipment from a fast combat support ship, the USNS *Rainier,* to the *Benfold.** It was an overcast night, and the sky and ocean were black. To catch up with the *Rainier,* the *Benfold* accelerated from "one-third" engine speed of four knots to a "full" speed of twenty-five knots.† The wind hissed and the rooster tail of white water behind the propellers rose several stories in the air, leaving a wide wake of phosphorescent white against the black void.

Stage by stage, the *Benfold* closed the distance: 9,000 yards, 8,000 yards, until after fifteen minutes, the $1-billion steel behemoths, weighing 8,300 tons and longer than one and a half football fields, came alongside a ship of even greater proportions, weighing 40,000 tons because of the fuel it carried. Now only 160 feet separated these two wonderfully ancient-looking ships, gray armored spirits of the industrial age.

There was a deafening holler of wind as a churning funnel of whitewater rapids formed between them, the explosions of foam concentrating, it seemed, all the power and energy of the ocean. One by one, lines were shot across the *Benfold*'s deck from the *Rainier* and hauled in by "deck apes" and "deck monkeys" (the lowest-ranking enlisted sailors), who latched them onto fairleads, pelican hooks, and pulleys. It had begun with a single red string fired by an M-14 rifle, to which a rope was then attached, followed by a cable. Soon gigantic fuel hoses and pallets were sliding from the *Rainier* across to the *Benfold,* as deck apes with blue construction helmets and orange vests began a snake dance with the cables that controlled the line tension, so as to carefully "bring in the groceries." A chief petty officer boomed orders over a loudspeaker, even as another communicated with the *Rainier* in whole sentences through signal flags. The world was a roaring black abyss sprinkled with white water and a flurry of yellow lights from the two vessels. It was like a docking in space.

Sometimes the aircraft carrier itself would refuel the *Benfold.* But the *Benfold* crew was not crazy about this type of maneuver. Not only

---

* USNS was a designation for Navy ships with mixed crews, of both sailors and civilian merchant seamen.

† Beyond "full" was "flank" speed of over thirty knots.

did the carrier tower above the destroyer only 160 feet away, but because carrier crews did not do Un-Reps very often, there was a lot of fumbling around. "It's like having sex for the first time with a girl," one sailor remarked.

Very few navies in the world could perform an Un-Rep, which depended less on technology than on sheer seamanship. I wondered how many people in the Pentagon knew about this maneuver or, more to the point, could appreciate it. Watching the whole extravaganza, a chief petty officer told me, "It's how we won World War II" in the Pacific, for it was a long-haul navy's ability to resupply warships thousands of miles from friendly ports that had provided a pivotal advantage over the Japanese.*

World War II had a meaning on the *Benfold* that it lacked elsewhere I had been with the military. Marines and Army Special Forces had many proud moments in Korea, Vietnam, Panama, Iraq, and so on; for them the Second World War had receded into antiquity almost. But for destroyer crews, World War II marked the last time that surface warships had been engaged in sustained, close-quarters combat.

The captain, Comdr. Hornbeck, sat in a high blue chair on the starboard bridge wing, silently observing the Un-Rep. He spoke only if there was a problem, and this time there wasn't. Navigating the ship during the Un-Rep was the responsibility of the conning officer, who kept the ships from colliding by minute attention to compass direction and continuous adjustment of speed and rudder angle. Overseeing the conning officer was the officer of the deck. Standing next to the captain, binoculars around their necks, these two officers ran the Un-Rep by means of mathematical calculations and an instinctual reading of the sea and its biblical swells, for it was common to do an Un-Rep in the midst of a storm.

Both the conning officer and the officer of the deck were shy and diminutive female ensigns in their early twenties: Michelle Mecklenburg of San Diego, a graduate of the ROTC program at the University of California, Berkeley; and Lori Boles, an Army brat from Augusta,

---

* Indeed, not even Britain's Royal Navy could refuel at sea until 1943, and almost had to let the *Bismarck* go as a result.

Georgia. Mecklenburg was of Peruvian descent, Boles an African American.

Lori Boles, the officer of the deck, told me about a previous Un-Rep she had directed in these waters immediately after the tsunami, when the bodies of dozens of adults and children were swept into the white water between the ships. "It was a floating cemetery," she said. "Because we also saw shoes and clothes and the insides of houses, it was like whole lives were passing by us."

The tsunami was real and traumatic, marking the first time many of the *Benfold*'s sailors had seen dead bodies. In the spring of 2003, they had fired Tomahawks into Iraq from another destroyer, and then run over to a television to learn from CNN what they had hit. For them, Iraq had been an abstraction, a video game almost. But going ashore by helicopter to help in the relief effort at Banda Aceh in Sumatra, they had observed trees, bridges, and houses laid down in an inland direction, as if by high-pressure fire hoses. In less than a month, there had been 117 helicopter landings on the *Benfold,* breaking a record. It was a natural disaster, not a war, that had toughened these sailors, turning more than a few into salty veterans.

I drew the curtains on my rack. I had just a few inches of extra room to sleep on my side without my hip hitting the rack above me; it was still more space than marines transiting the Pacific in World War II had had.* At first, my stateroom felt like a closet, though as I began to organize myself in coming days, it would seem to grow in size. Sleeping like this was merely one aspect of the strange world of a surface warship. You were constantly oppressed by valves and pipes and low ceilings ("overheads") that further narrowed the p-ways, and by steep, narrow ladders that barely felt wide enough for squirrels. There was also the loud, vibrating hum of air conditioners, and the constant announcements and clanging alarms that 24/7 invaded racks and toilets even.

The only escape was the deck. Every time you went outside you passed through an airlock created by two watertight doors that you opened and closed by swinging heavy iron latches, which caused your

* For a heartfelt evocation of conditions on troopships during World War II, see Leon Uris, *Battle Cry* (New York: Putnam, 1953).

ears to pop violently. This allowed for a pressurized environment inside that was a defense against chemical weapons. It was one discomfort after another. Sailors only looked normal; they were often chubby or gangly, as well as unshaven during much of a voyage.* Yet in ways that were subtle and, therefore, took time to appreciate, they could be just as tough as marines and Special Forces soldiers.

——

Breakfast in the wardroom was at six, and officers' call at 7:10 a.m. The latter took place on the port side of the aft missile deck, pouring rain or shine. As an inhabitant of officers' country, I was required to go. In attendance were not only the officers but all "khakis," meaning the senior chief petty officers who, because of their high noncommissioned rank, were entitled to wear pressed khaki uniforms or, depending upon their task that day, khaki belts over their blue coveralls. Throughout my odyssey with the American military, I had always been impressed by the authority wielded by the enlisted ranks, a testimony to the country's mass democracy, which kept in check the power of the elites. But the Navy went one better than the Army and Marines in this regard, by giving senior enlisted men and women sartorial equivalence with officers.†️ It was a symbol of something I would get to know more about: the aura of "the chiefs."

Officer's call, conducted by the XO, Lt. Comdr. Dunn, and the ship's senior noncom, Master Chief Craddock, lasted only a few minutes, with each man making a series of terse announcements followed by orders. Immediately following, each of the officers and chiefs met with their own divisions, so the aft missile deck and the adjacent fantail were filled with sailors meeting in separate semicircles. Following that, everyone on deck went below to brief his or her own department. By 7:45 a.m., every sailor on board knew what the XO and master chief expected of him, translated into specifics by his or her immediate superior. As a service

---

* Going unshaven was a privilege that required the individual sailor to make a donation to the ship's Morale, Welfare, and Recreation (MWR) fund. Also, beard growth had to be trimmed to allow a gas mask to seal onto the face.

† In other ways, though, the Navy had a rigid hierarchy. The gulf between a common seaman and an admiral was much greater than that between a grunt and a general in the other services. Moreover, senior noncoms in the Navy were not encouraged to go to Officer Candidate School to the degree that they were in the Army and Marines.

forged in loud seas and reeling ships before the invention of bullhorns, repeating commands verbatim down the chain, followed by salutes and other decorum—even if the distance from one verbal link to the next was only a few feet—was the only way to assure accurate communication.

The first morning I surveyed the deck. The inky blue water was relatively calm: a level three sea on the Beaufort scale of wind force, which goes from one through twelve. The dense mountains of Sumatra were close enough to form a rugged pattern, yet still far enough to remain unknown. The term "landscape" entails a personality, an intimacy; and Indonesia at this ten-mile distance, even though I was inside its coastal waters, did not quite have one. I stared at shadows only. On the other hand, I was already developing an intimacy with the USS *Benfold*. John Steinbeck had written that in her "beautiful clean lines," a destroyer is "completely a ship, in the old sense."[6] But it was also the modern version of a Civil War ironclad, a linear descendant of the *Monitor* and *Merrimack:* an instrument of orchestrated violence and deception. Even the handrails were crooked because right angles meant a stronger radar signature.

The next generation of destroyer on the drawing boards looked like a combination of stealth bomber and submarine that rode on the surface. The bridge was completely enclosed and the sloping deck was there for weapons and electronic surveillance, not for human beings. I felt privileged to experience a destroyer while it was still a ship.

Gunner's Mate 2nd Class Steven Breakhall of Richmond, Virginia, a kid with a shock of blond hair who had volunteered for the SEALs after 9/11 and did not quite survive Hell Week, gave me a tour of the *Benfold*'s deck plate, from the forecastle to the fantail. What gave the forecastle of a destroyer its familiar look, especially to boys who built model ships, was the 5-inch gun sticking out of a squat, revolving mount. You didn't have to see it fire to understand its violence. All you had to do was climb several stories down a ladder into its deep magazine smelling of oil and metal, and hold your ears against the whining siren of its loader assembly, and observe the belligerent speed with which the hydraulic cradle loaded the projectiles. In heaving seas during World War II, the gunner had to be careful to fire on the up-roll; nowadays a computer gyroscope made the adjustment.

Behind the 5-inch gun came something that was missing from the model toys of World War II: twenty-nine vertical launch cells, distinguished only by a series of hatches barely rising over the deck plate. Each self-contained cell held either a Tomahawk, an SM-2, or an anti-submarine rocket, the last of which fired 12,000 yards over the sea where a parachute opened, allowing it to fall into the water to attack a sub under its own guidance system. Behind the VLS cells was the tapering superstructure, which culminated with the mast and yardarms. But except for the shrouds, there was nothing here that resembled a sailing vessel. Everything was made of steel. There was a robotic device with a 20mm gun sticking out of it that sailors referred to as "R2D2 with a hard-on."* When it fired, it sounded as if all the machines in the world were grinding in unison to a halt, sending a shudder throughout your body—earplugs were little help. Behind R2D2 were clusters of giant steel radar bubbles, dishes, and antennae, providing vision from the surface to 90,000 feet up and dozens of miles in any direction.

Walking behind the bridge and along the two stacks, Gunner's Mate Breakhall pointed out the electronic-warfare equipment, the various machine guns for obliterating small boats, and the cluster of chaff launchers for dispersing aluminum debris into the air to serve as radar decoys. Dropping down to the aft missile deck, he noted sixty-one more VLS cells, four giant Harpoon launchers for use against enemy warships, and six tubes for shooting anti-submarine torpedoes into the water. The last were for subs nearby, while the ones fired out of the VLS cells were for subs farther out. All the weaponry was orchestrated by the Aegis system, which informed the crew what weapons and defensive electronic devices to use and when.

Steve Breakhall thought it was all just neat, decent compensation for not making it into the SEALs. To note that such an array of weaponry might never be used was to miss the point, for by monopolizing the use of force over a large oceanic space, destroyers like the *Benfold*—along with the rest of a carrier strike group—were able to ensure satisfactorily

---

* The weapon is actually a CIWS (pronounced "seawhizz"), which stands for Close-In Weapons System; it has a gyroscope and its own radar apparatus for identifying a target. It is a last line of defense against sea-skimming missiles like the Exocet.

safe and predictable commercial sea-lanes. In such a fashion, commerce and subsequent globalization could occur. Lee Kuan Yew's Singapore certainly would not have prospered to the extent that it had
without all this neat stuff.

"Don't be too impressed," one deck ape warned me. "Sometimes the
multi-million-dollar radar sucks, and we have to man visual lookouts
for a large piece of plastic or dead animal near the ship that might be a
mine." True, but for all the headlines it garnered, terrorism was still
more of an irritant to a blue water navy than a strategic threat.

Of course, that might change. For a better sense of where sea warfare was going, I needed to talk to the sailors. After all, if there was one
thing I could count on with the military, it was that the people were
more interesting than the equipment. In particular, I gravitated toward
sailors and officers who had earned a certain reputation among their fellow seamen.

———

Among the first enlisted men I met was Petty Officer 2nd Class Robert
Contreras, twenty-two, of San Fernando, California, the tactical information coordinator in the CIC (combat information center), a freezing
and cavernous region of blinking green computer terminals where the
quieter it was, the more that was going on. Contreras spoke in a slightly
hesitating manner, as though his words were trying to keep up with the
speed of his mind, as registered in his eyes. He had dark hair, a pale and
clammy face, and the concentrated expression of the kid who had won
the science fair at high school, but had yet to go out on a date. Had Contreras grown up in a secure and prosperous suburban environment,
that's probably what would have happened to him, and it would have
been his country's loss.

Instead, he was the oldest of six children of divorced parents, who
had to hold down a job as a store clerk to help pay the family's bills. To
make matters worse, he was a screwup in high school. He could have
gone to the local community college, but figured he would have fallen
into the same bad habits. He learned that the Navy would pay for him to
go to college somewhere far from his home. Moreover, one of his
grandparents had been a corpsman, so he enlisted. The Navy straightened him out, making him the geek that he was always meant to be.

Contreras's ability to cold-crunch probabilities at a nearly inhuman speed was so legendary in his department that when I mentioned his name to Capt. Hornbeck, the latter's eyes lit up. He, too, held Contreras in awe.

Petty Officer Contreras worked with the radar and electronic-warfare supervisors to run and design the war games in the CIC. "Our surface radar can see twenty-five miles, but through a data link with another ship I can see sixty miles," he explained, after I pleaded with him to cut out the math jargon and acronyms. "I'm also the air controller. I can see further than the fighter pilots because I've got access to the whole strike group network. During OIF [Operation Iraqi Freedom], the network was so vast I could see all the screen activity from the Mediterranean to the Strait of Hormuz."

After every air attack into Iraq, Contreras had to make sure that only friendly air was returning to the carrier group. But it wasn't always clear on the screen if a signal was a "friendly" or not. A plane might cut corners on a pre-designated flight path because the pilot really knew what he was doing, not because he was an infiltrator. Thus, sometimes you had to decide on instinct. In OIF, Contreras's judgments were nearly perfect. "He's a goddamn second-class petty officer," one of his commanding officers told me later, "yet when we were having trouble early in the war, getting the radar and weapons systems to electronically shake hands with each other, he figured out how to do it on a higher frequency." Contreras was too modest to tell me the things I heard from others.

During OIF, Contreras's destroyer, the *Arleigh Burke*–class USS *Higgins,* was the closest American warship to the Iraqi coast, coming as close to shore as its draft would allow. His department constituted the Navy's main unit for theater ballistic-missile defense—meaning he and about fifteen other operators were the front line for warning Patriot missile batteries about incoming Scuds. Of twelve missiles fired by Saddam Hussein, the operators detected eleven by noticing oddities of speed and altitude, amid the clutter caused by the U.S. military's own activities. (The one they missed landed in a Kuwait City shopping mall in the middle of the night, causing relatively little damage.)

Just as the expeditionary American military boasted iron majors,

Contreras represented something newer still, the "strategic corporal"—someone barely out of his teens, who with one keyboard tap can affect the lives of thousands, as well as the foreign policy of a great nation.*

So I asked him, given his experience and all the technical magazines he read, what worried him the most about the *Benfold*.

"Sub-surface threats," he responded. "This ship is much less vulnerable to air attacks. But we can only hunt subs to the degree that we need to by calling greater radar attention to ourselves. We need a remote mine-hunting capability and a hangar to support helicopters for tracking what's underwater."† In other words, Contreras was worried about the future: about China.

Then there was Sonar Technician Guns 2nd Class Kate Szlamas of Falmouth, Maine, also in her early twenties, with blond hair and a frank, eager expression that told you the *Benfold* was where she was meant to be. Her dad had been in the Navy, and she didn't want to go to college like everyone else she knew. After four years in blue coveralls, she was looking forward to reenlisting for another four years. "Unlike my friends who went to college, I now have a marketable skill." The Navy had thrown courses in oceanography, digital electronics, and acoustics at her, and consequently she lectured me about the electronic signatures of Indian, Pakistani, and Russian submarines. Like Contreras, hers was a world of blinking green lights where she played chess blindfolded, by figuring out how to position the ship in the event of an approaching sub, which she knew was there because of the sound pulses she heard. Like Contreras, I had to frequently slow her down and get her to explain things in nonscientific English. It might be telling that the first time she played No Limit Texas Hold'em in a mess hall full of enlisted sailors, she beat everyone at the poker game except for one other sailor.

Too, like Contreras, Szlamas had been in OIF aboard the USS *Hig-*

---

* The term was initially coined by Marine Gen. and Commandant Charles Krulak in 1999.

† Contreras's point about a hangar for two helicopters deserves expansion. Choppers were perfect for anti-submarine work. In the air, the noise of the ship did not interfere with their dipping sonar when it was in passive mode, and when it was in active mode the chopper did not give away the position of the ship to the enemy because it was flying some distance from it. Moreover, two choppers flying about with dipping sonar covered a much wider range of territory than would a ship by itself.

gins, a destroyer with which every member of its crew felt an intense affinity. The hero for which the *Higgins* was named, Marine Col. William R. Higgins of Danville, Kentucky, had been killed in Lebanon shortly after he was kidnapped by pro-Iranian terrorists in 1988, while he was working for the United Nations. Col. Higgins had refused the advice of U.N. colleagues to remove the U.S. flag on his U.N. uniform, even though it put him in especial danger. The fact that his was a recent story—one that did not hearken back to a half-century-old war—helped give young sailors like Szlamas a particular identification with him.

A large portion of the *Higgins*'s crew had been transferred to the *Benfold* as part of a "sea swap," which allowed a ship to remain at sea without having to return to port in order to give its crew a rest. The Big Navy liked the idea because it was efficient; the sailors I met hated it, because their esprit de corps, they said, was closely related to an emotional bond with a particular ship.

At the same time, Petty Officer Szlamas liked the fact that the Navy was no longer in a scheduled existence, and deployments got changed or extended because of events like wars and tsunamis. She had gone ashore at Banda Aceh to do disaster relief and encountered the world media for the first time, for which she and the sonar girl who sat next to her didn't much care. "They were like a mob, in your face, getting in the way of what we were doing."

"Come, let's go," they told me, "we've got to run checks on the fishes," referring to the torpedoes.

I just wandered around every day for four weeks, meeting people. It was sort of like an academic conference where the conversations you had in the hallways were more worthwhile than the panel discussions. Quarters were so close on a destroyer that the head was no less common a place for a long conversation than a stateroom or, for that matter, the entrance to the sonar bubble in the narrowing hull at the bottom of the ship. In a head down in berthing, I met Petty Officer 2nd Class John Strange of Albuquerque, New Mexico, who asked me about the different translations of Dostoevsky's novels, which he was reading on ship. "I've been to the Seychelles, Hong Kong, Singapore. The kids I went to high school with have gone nowhere. I bank $36,000 yearly after taxes. That's a lot of money in Albuquerque."

Then there was a nineteen-year-old deckhand from the Deep South who had joined the Navy partly to escape the alcoholism in his extended family. He told me he had been saved by Jesus, with whom he spoke every night.

In the sweaty, loud commotion of the engine room—down several stories on a ladder to the ship's bowels—amid an intestinal, Dickensian maze of pipes and catwalks, and a temperature of 105 degrees, I had a long conversation with Petty Officer 1st Class Robert Wynot of Weston, Massachusetts. Petty Officer Wynot had joined the Navy thirteen years before, because he needed discipline and didn't have money for a proper college education. He did exceptionally well on his aptitude tests, so the Navy sent him to study nuclear propulsion ("nuke school"); he mastered college-level physics, trigonometry, and thermodynamic theory. "But being the kids that we were"—Wynot always spoke finely, in the way of a wise and calm old man—"we had a fight. I spit on another seaman's locker and was thrown out. I was busted from seaman to seaman recruit," the equivalent of a private.

Next, he was ordered to work twelve- to fourteen-hour days in the engine room of a frigate for a year. The humiliation of being thrown out of nuke school and having to work his way up from the bottom of the hierarchy affected Wynot deeply. It made him an adult. In the intervening year he won seven Navy achievement awards, and was recently ship and squadron sailor of the year.* He had been at sea for most of the past five years, but was happy to be going home for the birth of his second boy. Like many others I met, he had a forgettable face that I'll never forget.

I went down another long ladder to a catwalk, at the base of the vertical launch cells: here I encountered Gunner's Mate 1st Class James Vigliotti of Suffolk County, New York, who maintained the missile unit. Before coming to the *Benfold,* Vigliotti had been a trainer for the new Iraqi Army. It took several meetings to get out of him the fact that he had been awarded a Bronze Star in Iraq, and was a leader of an operation that captured number seven in the notorious deck of cards, the fifty-five most wanted figures from the Saddam Hussein regime.† I was used

---

* He was subsequently named Sailor of the Year for all surface ships in the Pacific Fleet, and was promoted to chief petty officer in 2005.

† Number seven was Ayad Futayyih Khalifa Al-Rawi, Quds Forces chief of staff.

to such modesty. When I asked Vigliotti whether he had any doubts about the way the Iraqi Army was being formed—picking people from scratch to be colonels, corporals, and so on—he replied: "The Continental Army was stood up in the same way. For me," he continued, "the only depressing thing I encountered in Iraq was the negative shit on the news each night." This was early 2005, remember, a year before the Samarra mosque bombing.

I never argued with people. I wanted only to experience their lives and points of view. The *Benfold* was a civilization unto itself, swishing through the crushing void. As opposed to a carrier, a destroyer is a "small boy," where after two weeks or so you became quite familiar with the crew and its routine. There was the boredom of smoking on the flight deck under leaden tropical rain, and the exhilaration of a steel beach picnic, when the chief petty officers barbecued burgers and hot dogs topside for the officers and junior enlisted sailors. At night, there was the release offered by Eddie's, the mess deck for the junior enlisted ranks, named after Eddie Benfold. Here, on long tables with plastic swivel chairs under oppressive fluorescent lights, young sailors, their tattoos showing on their forearms, played No Limit Texas Hold'em while listening to patriotic country music singer Toby Keith's "American Soldier."

There were also "ice cream socials." As corny as that might sound, keep in mind that alcohol was forbidden, and the officers and senior noncoms constantly had to contrive events to break the tedium of a long sea deployment. African-American History Month was a particularly welcome diversion, whose celebration with lectures and songs at Eddie's was attended by blacks and whites alike. After all, we all knew one another.

Things happened, and were anticipated. An enlisted sailor made a gesture of committing suicide by hanging himself in the windlass complex, in view of other sailors. Capt. Hornbeck called an all-hands-on-deck meeting to discuss it. "I want to look you all in the eyes," he said, "not send out an internal e-mail." Actually, the crew's reaction was severe. Nobody felt sorry for the badly injured sailor. The feeling was, if he really wanted to kill himself he could have; a stunt like this only makes him a coward.

A few days later, before docking at the next port, I heard some deck monkeys discuss the low HIV rate there, which they had researched on the Internet. One declared: "I don't want to fuck a virgin. I want someone who knows what she's doing. A virgin's no better than using your own hand."

———

The officers ran the ship, but the chiefs made it happen. The very word "chief" defined a senior noncommissioned officer in a way that "sergeant major" did not in the other services. The chiefs taught the ropes to the young officers, who were often straight out of the Naval Academy. The chiefs were the fathers-mothers-priests-dictators for the grunt sailors. Some of them had whored their way for years around the Pacific. They smoked. Burly and *über*–working class in a prosperous, old-fashioned 1950s sense, the chiefs just oozed authority without trying to.

When I asked the chief of chiefs on the *Benfold,* Master Chief Craddock, what was the most important thing he did, he replied, his face a few inches from mine: "I don't put up with any *stuff.* Anyone gives me *stuff,* they'll be sorry." Indeed, the very intensity of human contact among hundreds of sailors in a dangerous and claustrophobic environment meant that not one, but many lines in the sand had to be drawn.

Helping to draw those lines was Chief Master-at-Arms Darrell McWilliams, a massively built African American from Detroit, who had spent years in the Persian Gulf, forcibly boarding ships suspected of breaking the sanctions regime against Iraq. "One time," he told me in his soft, pleasant, well-enunciated voice, "a captain would not slow his ship down for an inspection, so I had to physically lift him up and carry him away from the bridge. I just love law enforcement."

He went on: "I'm an outsider here. I can't get too close to people, because I may have to bring charges against them. I can bring charges against anyone except the captain. My authority is directly from him."

The holiest, most laid-back place on the *Benfold* was the chiefs' mess. A chief petty officer could walk into the officers' wardroom, but no officer, not even Capt. Hornbeck, would enter the chiefs' mess uninvited. Whereas the wardroom served meals at appointed hours, the chiefs' mess offered hot food, coffee, and a movie 24/7. "Instead of grog, we now have coffee, filtered through a sweat sock," someone re-marked. "That's why for Western navies it's been downhill the last hun-dred years." The wardroom was a dining room, the chiefs' mess an after-hours lounge that never closed. By tradition, there is no shoptalk when Navy officers dine in a wardroom, while the chiefs' mess is where much of the work of a ship gets done. "If you're thin-skinned, you can't come in," I was told the first time I crossed the threshold into the chiefs' domain.

"What do you do?" I asked one chief. "As little as possible," came the rude reply. "Who am I?" he went on. "The biggest asshole on the ship." I ate about half my meals in the chiefs' mess, where I learned my way around the *Benfold*.

Bosun's Mate Chief Andrew Rader of Newark, Ohio, whose low stocky frame moved like a tumbling boulder on deck, was described to me by his fellow chiefs as "good-to-go," the highest accolade in the noncommissioned officer lexicon. Bosun Chief Rader hung out a lot in the chiefs' mess, appearing to do nothing except watch movies with a droopy look, extenuated by a mustache that he had grown between port visits and that curved down to his chin. In fact, he knew everything that was going on among the deck apes whom he commanded.

During Un-Reps, Chief Rader's profanities were peppered with a deadpan sarcasm. "You," he said, referring to one sailor, "taught me something new today, [that] if you put the hook upside down in the wrong position, it won't work." Not waiting for a reply: "Roger that, fucking retard . . ." He then turned to me with his hands held out, plead-ing, "It's all about safety." He wasn't kidding. The smallest change in the relative position of the ships could put tremendous tension on any one of the lines, so if they were not secured well, they could whip back like an elastic band and literally take a few heads off.

"I have a philosophy," Chief Rader explained to me afterward. "I hate you all equally. Look, I can't be their friend. But at times, I have to be their father or mother." The sailors understood. One quiet and sensi-tive female confided to me: "Chief Rader's awesome, he really looks out for us." Rader was the ultimate salt, a twenty-year veteran who had joined the Navy out of high school and spent thirteen of those years at sea on destroyers, destroyer tenders, fast-attack oilers, and frigates, always working topside. He had the memorable experience of spending his first Christmas in the Navy as an eighteen-year-old male in the Philippines. He was in Desert Storm and Operation Iraqi Freedom. Most importantly, he understood the young seamen under him.

"I get people from Puerto Rico to Samoa, from Maine to Texas, from all over the United States and its territories, men and women, and I have to treat each one slightly differently. Whenever a new sailor arrives," he went on, "I talk to him alone for twenty minutes. I ask pointed questions: Are your parents divorced? Were you the nerd or the jock in high school? I need to know fast what makes them tick." Rader was worried about a new generation of enlistees, what he called the "video game kids," who never worked with their hands and didn't know the difference between a Phillips and a flat-head screwdriver. With a what's-this-world-coming-to expression, he exclaimed, "I mean, I ask for a mallet and they don't know what it is."

The bosun, or boatswain, was—along with the officer of the deck, the conning officer, and the quartermaster—the last real seaman in a post-modern navy. His job, and especially the related one of beachmaster, had a heroic function in the World War II landings at Normandy and various Pacific atolls. It was the deck chiefs who had directed Army and Marine assault units from the five-fathom point to the high-tide mark on the beachhead.

While Chief Rader made it happen on deck, where old-fashioned seamanship was required, Chief Charles Benoit of Yakima, Washington, another old salt with nearly seventeen years in the Navy, made it happen when it came to surface warfare. "Sinking a U.S. ship would make a pretty big statement," he coached me in the chiefs' mess. "The last people who did that were the Germans and the Japanese." In the coming weeks, Chief Benoit, who lacked a college degree, would connect some of the dots concerning the theories about the future of sea warfare I had heard at PACOM and at the Pentagon. It was Benoit who tutored the officers, Annapolis graduates among them, about the ins and outs of fighting enemy submarines from the *Benfold*.

From Chief Benoit I learned that submarines tended to operate in the "layer depth" several hundred feet below the surface, where cooler temperatures and greater water pressure optimized the movement of sound

waves; but that Chinese diesel subs could hide in the upper surface layers, amid diesel-powered fishing fleets, the same way someone in green
camouflage could hide in a jungle. The United States had been late
coming to the challenge of a growing Chinese submarine fleet, Benoit
told me. He noted that pre-programmed data identifying Soviet subs
had been installed in the Navy's sonar-triggered combat systems toward
the end of the Cold War. But rather than install data about subs from
other navies like those of the Chinese and the Iranians into our systems
in the 1990s, the Navy had let the technology wither until recently.
Chief Benoit was always thinking. For him, the ferrying of rice and
water to Banda Aceh by small boats and helicopters during the tsunami
emergency had shown him how, using similar tactics, a carrier strike
group could insert "guys with guns."

Quartermaster Chief Paul Bischoff of Milwaukee had a peering-
into-the-distance gaze that recalled the photos of Charles Lindbergh
just before he had crossed the Atlantic. Chief Bischoff's grandfather
had been a bosun's master chief, and when Bischoff attended his second
cousin's Navy boot camp graduation ceremony at Great Lakes, Illinois,
he knew that's what he wanted to do. He enlisted before finishing high
school. His first deployment was aboard the USS *Savannah,* an oiler
that was among the oldest, homeliest ships in the Navy. Right after he
left it, the *Savannah* was decommissioned and chopped up into razor
blades. "But for me she was beautiful," Bischoff said while we sat atop
the vertical missile launchers one sunny day. "When I first saw that
monstrous steel hulk against the blue, I said, 'That's it, she's mine.'

"Being at sea is fun," he went on. "You get to make it up because nobody knows what happened there, that's why there are all these great
sea stories." As a quartermaster, Bischoff plotted the *Benfold*'s course
on the paper charts with a pencil, eraser, parallel ruler, and compass.
That skill, along with the bottom-contour charts of the ocean that
evoked old etchings, would soon be gone, as the Navy increasingly
veered toward electronic navigation on computer screens. "Now it's all
about being as gray as we possibly can," he said. "The only teakwood
left on a surface warship are the handrails on the bridge wings. The U.S.
Navy preserves traditions as artifacts, but not as living things."

Yet there was still romance left, especially at dusk on the bridge wings, after the dying sun had painted a bar of gold leaf over the water. There was something about being at the highest point on deck after the sun dropped down and the stars came out and the wind hit you in the face that encouraged conversation. This was especially true of a warship, where sunset meant "darkened ship"; all the lights went out so the starscape appeared even more brilliant, and the bow cut a majestic phosphorescent trail of white water on account of the twenty-five-knot speed.

It was while arcing around the northern tip of Sumatra, from the Indian Ocean to the calmer Andaman Sea, that I got to know the women aboard better. The women I met either loved the Navy or hated it: either they couldn't wait to reenlist or couldn't wait to get out. Unlike the men, there was no in-between for them. The female officers were as petite and feminine as some of the female noncoms were manly. Of course, there were exceptions, like one attractive deck ape I met on the port-side bridge wing who delivered a monologue about how her brothers and cousins had all joined the Navy and Marines, and thus she enlisted after high school without thinking about it. But a few months into her enlistment, with close to four years still to go, she realized that it was not for her.

"In berthing the guys mainly read porno," she said. "There are too many fat girls, too many dykes, there's no possibility of a bath, I give myself a pedicure once a week to remember what I am. I got punished for kissing another deck ape in Hawaii—he was just a good friend." (In fact, the chief master-at-arms had caught several couples alone together in a fashion that forced him to break it up and bring reprimands. He felt bad about it, but as he told me, "After all, this *is* a U.S. Navy warship, and these people knew what they were signing on to.")

On the other hand, there was Ensign Melissa Jolley of Salt Lake City, also from a service family. Both she and her brother were graduates of the U.S. Naval Academy. She loved being on ship. Looking out over the blackness of the Andaman Sea, she told me about the first time she got seasick, something that occurred to even the most hardened sailors under certain conditions. "It was on a family fishing trip off the Oregon coast. We got caught in a storm. I was so miserable that I crawled up into a fetal position and didn't move for hours. But now I've got my sea legs." I had to remind myself that these women were frontline troops, and would be tested as such if a new cold war of the seas ever ensued.

Like her, the other officers aboard, whether Naval Academy graduates or not, were transparently brainy and middle class in a way I had not encountered in the Marines and Army Special Forces. They had not come to the Navy the way quite a few Army and Marine officers had to their service branches: as a way to rise out of social and economic difficulties. Rather, many of the officers aboard the *Benfold* had come here by happenstance. Often there had been a single individual—a mentor—whom they encountered briefly at church or in high school, who had pointed them in a direction different from the rest of their peers. Then there was that indefinable factor—some people just had a calling to go to sea, like one officer from the beautiful sand hills of north-central Nebraska who, whenever he stared out at the water, missed home, yet at home as a boy always longed for the sea.

Among the exceptions was Ensign Michelle Mecklenburg, the conning officer for the Un-Rep. She had gone to Berkeley on a Navy ROTC scholarship because it was the only way she could afford school. Being in ROTC at a campus with a radical reputation wasn't that bad, she said. A lot of students from places like Orange County quietly came up to her to say they approved of what she was doing. There were actually a few Berkeley graduates among the officers. They drew a portrait of a school where the student body was increasingly more conservative than either the faculty or the area residents.

Whereas the Marines were a working-class warrior cult and Army Special Forces had a southern, Confederate edge, coupled with an exotic Latino component, their Navy officer brethren were the math-science whizzes who, without necessarily being musclemen, nevertheless liked the athleticism of the outdoors. They were conservative only in the same moderate, nonideological way that business, science, and engineering graduates often were.

It was all in the element. Marines and Special Forces occupied ground, they fought physically and got dirty. The job of Navy officers was to remain undetected and then kill from over the horizon. It was a different sort of aggression, in which everything was reduced to math equations. There was so much technical knowledge to absorb that one-third of the time spent in Navy boot camp was in the classroom. Even on ship, nearly every officer was studying for one oral examination or another—in basic engineering, surface warfare, small-boat operations, helm safety, etc.—to help him or her advance in rank or function.

Looking at the nameplates on the doors of the officers' staterooms told you just how much specialized training was involved: electronic warfare officer, main propulsion officer, missile strike officer, combat systems officer, signals intelligence warfare officer, navigator, gunno . . . Officers and chiefs usually addressed one another by acronyms that described their function. "How are you doing today, MA1?" "Very well, CSO." MA1 was the first-class chief master-at-arms; CSO the combat systems officer. Chief Rader was called BMC, bosun's mate chief; Paul Bischoff was addressed as QMC, or quartermaster chief. And so it went.

Just as every marine was a rifleman, every officer and sailor was a firefighter, because every combat situation aboard a warship was also a fire or flood situation, or both. Several times a week there were extensive fire drills where whole sections of the ship were sealed off from one another, and all the hatches and scuttles closed, as many a sailor lumbered around with a mask, fire helmet, and compressed air tank.

—

The *Benfold* loitered for many days around the Indian Ocean and Andaman Sea, doing "plane guard" for the *Abe:* the destroyer's lights served as a point of reference for the carrier's F-18 pilots on their maneuvers, even as the *Benfold*'s swimmers and small-boat units were ready to rescue a downed pilot. The *Abe*'s F-18 pilots were finally getting the training hours denied them during the tsunami aid effort.

Following the last air drill, the crew of the *Benfold* prepared to enter the Strait of Malacca, to help police that vital waterway, and to begin the voyage across the Pacific back to the ship's home port of San Diego. First there was an all-hands-on-deck wash-down to the tune of rap and country-rock songs blasting over the loudspeaker. Chief Rader was everywhere cursing, and scrubbing with a small sponge obscure corners of the non-skid deck himself. "We're not going to look like some rust-bucket Russian ship when we pull into Singapore," one of his fellow chiefs declared. "We want the *Benfold* to look like a young, strong, virile lady, in order to intimidate the enemy."

The fifteen-hour passage down the Strait of Malacca to the pier at Singapore, where we would tie up for two days before continuing onward, began at 10 p.m. The narrow channel was the busiest shipping lane in the world, with easy-to-miss shoals and eddies everywhere. Capt. Hornbeck stationed himself on the bridge all night and the next day, until the *Benfold* docked.

On warships the bridge was traditionally a very formal place, where dress whites or khakis were worn and nobody was permitted without permission. In recent decades standards had gone down, with ship's ball caps and coveralls becoming commonplace. Now tradition was coming back. Capt. Hornbeck required khakis and, in place of ball caps, combination hats: the formal service hats with visors and interchangeable white and khaki tops. Though Don Hornbeck was hard to get to know on account of a quiet and serious manner, I gradually learned that his crew genuinely liked him and his decisions. Said one warrant officer: "He's one of the few captains who calls me by my name, rather than by 'you fucking idiot or asshole.' " "He's very calm, he doesn't get angry," another noncom said. On the bridge, he sat in the raised captain's chair, from where he let the ensigns work out one navigational challenge after the other, inserting himself only when he saw they were close to panicking. Then he would say something like, "Come right rudder five degrees," allowing them to move on to the next issue. "I remember when I was an ensign," he whispered to me, "I'd get intimidated every time a big ship came within five miles."

Lt. Comdr. Dunn, the executive officer, was less popular, but as he told me, it was his job to be so. As second-in-command, he handled the thankless administrative minutiae that permitted the captain to remain within big-think territory. The XO wrote the evaluations, inquired into infractions, checked the cleanliness of the berthings, wrote the plan of the day, and so forth.* He took all the hits so that the crew could revere

---

* Only the commanding officer was allowed to punish, done through nonjudicial punishment ("captain's mast").

their commander. The same division of labor existed within Army and Marine battalions.

To ride with a carrier strike group through a major international waterway was an unforgettable experience. There was a certain mystique about driving a ship through constrained waters with a high landmass on either side. As dusk fell the armada formed up in single file, each vessel about 4,500 yards distant from the other. First came the USS *Shiloh,* a *Ticonderoga*-class cruiser, bigger than a destroyer with a slightly larger crew; then the *Abe* itself, followed by the USS *Shoup,* another *Arleigh Burke*–class destroyer. After the *Shoup* came the *Rainier,* the support ship that had given us diesel fuel a few days earlier, with the *Benfold* guarding the rear. Somewhere lurking in the mouth of the strait or the nearby seas might also have been the USS *Louisville,* a *Los Angeles*–class, fast-attack nuclear submarine. Only a few people on the ship, including the captain and the signals intelligence shop, knew exactly where it was.

Even before we entered the strait proper, cargo ships, fishing boats, tugs that were hauling barges, and tankers bringing oil to the demographic and economic fleshpots of Asia were all over the rippling blue, lacquered surface of a level-one sea. The conning officer was clad in blue utilities, for Capt. Hornbeck had decreed that noncoms could navigate the ship just like the officers. "Steady on course 145 degrees," said the helmsman, another noncom. "Very well," the conning officer replied.

With darkness, the bridge took on the quiet, pulsing tension of an operating room, with twenty officers and noncoms peering out through binoculars and hovering around computer screens that displayed everything from rudder angles and shaft revolutions per minute to the minutes and seconds of latitude and longitude. One quartermaster, checking the depth meter and looking at a chart, remarked that a nearby shoal had the "shape of Shrek's head." A sprinkling of lights were always closing in on us from the blackened sea, only to pass to the sides of the *Benfold* as we overtook one tanker and fishing vessel after the other. Odd lights that didn't make any sense at all had to be quickly resolved into a pattern. It was like a fast slalom run with dry thunder and stars overhead. The strike group constituted the big rigs of the road, barreling at ninety

miles an hour down an interstate, overtaking passenger cars going at
fifty. All night long, sailors in helmets and Kevlar vests manned .50-
caliber light machine guns with night-vision goggles, prepared to shoot
at any boat with hostile intentions. But the captain and executive officer
had informed the crew that the strait was the workplace for many a poor
fisherman. Therefore, small boats "would have to work hard to con-
vince us of hostile intentions."

A flaming sun rose over what Joseph Conrad called "the great thor-
oughfare of the East," as the suggestive outlines of the Malay Peninsula
and Sumatra appeared on the port and starboard sides, respectively. Little by little, officers and sailors began filtering up to the bridge for the
morning watch, cleanly shaven for the first time in weeks and wearing
their dress whites, which tradition demanded for entry into a port. By
mid-morning, the khakis and blue coveralls and utilities had disappeared, and everyone was in white with battle and campaign ribbons on
their chests. From a crew of grubby individualistic sailors, the *Benfold*
became a dazzling movie set. Even the sailors behind the machine guns
now wore whites under their green flak vests.

The *Abe* and the other ships soon began their sequential entry into the
harbor, studded with tankers and buoys, as the skyline of Singapore appeared and the blue water turned to green.

The anchor crew was mustered by Chief Rader, while an officious
ethnic Indian came on board from a pilot boat to guide the *Benfold* in.
"All hands man the rails," boomed the order over the loudspeakers, as
the deck became braided with sailors standing at ease in their whites.*
Thus began the sacred and timeless formality of an arrival by sea, as
moving to the soul as my airport arrival into Singapore two weeks earlier had been soulless.

Tugs pulled and pushed the *Benfold* against the USS *Shoup,* which
had arrived before us, the two destroyers separated from each other by
giant rubber fenders known as "Yokohamas." Rigidly controlled Singapore was not Yemen, where the USS *Cole* had been attacked. Moreover,
the U.S. Navy was taking precautions it hadn't always done before that

---

* The origin of "manning the side" when on a friendly port visit was to demonstrate that the
crew was not down below manning the guns.

incident. Bomb and mine squads swept the pier prior to the *Benfold*'s arrival. Singapore Navy corvettes were maintaining a small-boat exclusion zone, and Singapore Navy divers were inspecting nearby ferries and barges.

As the *Benfold* tied up, sailors raised the "first ensign" on its jack staff. Brought back into use after 9/11, the first ensign featured red-and-white stripes and a yellow rattlesnake emblazoned with the words "Don't Tread on Me." The pennant had been a symbol of resistance to the British during the Revolutionary War era. With the solemn ceremony complete, all the sailors not on watch changed into civilian clothes, streamed off the gangplank into waiting liberty buses for the journey downtown, and promptly got plastered.

It was the first time they had been off-ship for six weeks, when in late December they had gotten the word to steam out of Hong Kong toward tsunami-devastated Indonesia. It's hard to explain, but there was something about being confined in tight quarters on a ship that made you want to start drinking the moment you were on shore. Just as when I had arrived in Dubai after weeks embedded with marines in Iraq, the first thing I noticed was the smell of expensive women's perfume.

Though a sprawling city-state of 3.5 million, we all wound up at the same bars along the Singapore River—the very same riverfront where in Conrad's day sailors caroused, swapped sea stories, and were ripped off by locals. Little had changed, despite the global Disneyland ambience of the high-priced restaurants and breweries. As drunk as everyone got, sailors were careful to address those of a higher rank with the prefix of "Mr." I noticed a group of tourists aghast at the behavior of some of the chiefs, wrestling on a restaurant floor. They'd never imagine, I thought, that these clowns without social skills could, when sober, deliver a briefing on future threats in the Pacific more incisive than many an academic.

After two more days of bacchanalia we departed, en route across the Pacific to Pearl Harbor in Hawaii, and then to San Diego. Free from the pier, the *Benfold* steamed southeast out of the Strait of Malacca, then turned northeast into the South China Sea, between Vietnam and Malaysian Sarawak on the island of Borneo.

Officers' Call at 7:10 a.m. the next morning, February 8, 2005, found us in the heart of the South China Sea. Tropical rain clouds, a darker steel gray than the ship, slid across the beam as rain sprayed lightly on the deck and we all stumbled a bit to keep our balance. Quartermaster Chief Paul Bischoff had arrived a few minutes early to smoke a cigarette with the other chiefs and savor the view. He was smiling. "Finally I feel like I'm on an ocean," he told me. There was no serious weather, just the normal rocking generated by a jagged, foam-encrusted sea, now that the *Benfold* was a reasonable distance from land. The pleasure cruise was over, as were the hangovers from Singapore. The tilting of the ship intensified, and taking a shower became an acrobatic feat. Chairs and other objects had to be secured with bungee cords. A quiet, lugubrious mood set in, as sailors went about their work and chores: sub-surface warfare, air defense, and communications drills; urinalysis tests; course corrections for the route out of the South China Sea and through the Philippines. The list went on. The pressure on people never ceased.

Late afternoon of the following day saw us exit the South China Sea into the Balabac Strait, between the northern tip of Borneo and the Philippine island of Palawan. But before entering the strait there was another Un-Rep, to take on 200,000 gallons of fuel. The *Shiloh,* the *Shoup,* and the *Abe* also took on fuel, the *Abe* a whopping 800,000 gallons for its fighter jets and surveillance planes. The great big gas station in the South China Sea was the USNS *Tippecanoe,* a six-hundred-foot-long oiler. It was quite a pageant: the cruiser *Shiloh* and the destroyer *Benfold* on either side of the *Tippecanoe,* with their fuel lines attached in the heaving sea, and the destroyer *Shoup* and the carrier *Lincoln* close behind, waiting their turn at the pump.

The Balabac Strait brought us into the Sulu Sea, amid the various island groups of the Philippines: Palawan to the northwest, the central Philippine islands to the northeast, and Mindanao and the Sulu Archipelago to the east and southeast, where I had been eighteen months earlier with Army Special Forces. Light machine guns were manned topside, for this was the lair of the Abu Sayyaf and Jemaah Islamiyah terrorist groups. The USS *Cole* incident was never far from people's minds, though, as one petty officer with counterterrorism experience remarked, "All I'd need to do is spray bullets from an assault rifle at our radar array, and I would do enough damage to mess up the entire combat system for a while." Truly, the exposed architecture of these destroyers was not suited for an age of unconventional attacks. The *Benfold* was like a clunky old software program with too many upgrades on it.

In fact, the U.S. Navy was at a fork in the road, and it had to take both directions at once. On the one hand, a street-fighting, green water Navy was required for littoral combat along terrorist-infested coastlines, such as the southern Philippines and the Indonesian archipelago. A new class of fast, small ships was being built for that purpose. Contrarily, the rise of the Chinese Navy, coupled with tensions in the Taiwan Strait and the Korean Peninsula, meant that a World War II–type sea battle, made faster and more furious by the latest missile and electronic technology, was also a possibility in the worst-case-scenario world of the military. Thus, as soon as the *Benfold* was out of the tsunami disaster zone, both officers and sailors busied themselves with war games.

The war game conducted the day we entered the Balabac Strait was typical. Political tensions inside China (Country Orange) over Taiwan (Country Blue) had led to an exchange of fire just south of the Taiwan Strait, between the Chinese and Taiwanese navies and air forces. The nearby *Abe* strike group, including the *Benfold,* could not help being drawn in. Confusion, as much as anything, ramped up the violence, for it was hard to know, as one officer remarked, "who's who in the zoo." The Chinese had fired a missile barrage at Taiwanese ships that were also vaguely in the direction of the U.S. strike group, causing an American plane to take out a Chinese one, leading, in turn, to an attack on the *Benfold.*

The drama played out in the CIC, or combat information center, where the TAO, or tactical actions officer, led the response. Though it all happened via headphones and computer keyboards, the stress level was acute because a wrong decision would lead to a catastrophic missile strike on the ship. Programmers in the CIC wore flash gear— semi-fire-retardant hoods and gloves—in case their screens exploded. Imagine the anxiety in a cockpit when a plane was facing serious mechanical difficulties and the pilot was trying to calmly work through the problem with his co-pilot. It might have been a game, yet it felt real. As one of the chiefs said later, "The pucker factor was strong," a reference to the tight assholes in the CIC.

Everything was spoken in code and acronyms, in order to communicate as much information as possible with as few words as possible. Naval warfare was divided into five areas: air, surface, sub-surface, strike, and electronic. Each of those areas had its own commander (or "watchstander") in the CIC, who spoke to the TAO to convey important news; or to request a judgment from him that the commanders or their pre-programmed computer systems could not make. While the TAO was being fed information vertically from the five watchstanders, he also had to communicate horizontally with the other ships in the strike group, and with watchstanders elsewhere on the *Benfold* regarding damage on board. He had seconds, not minutes, to make decisions. Being a TAO was a perishable skill, like speaking a foreign language. The TAO was usually a middle-level officer in his late twenties or early thirties.

The TAO's job was further complicated because American naval ROEs, or rules of engagement, manifested the subtlety of a new cold war. There were legal issues regarding when the TAO could and could not fire. Thus, he had to refer some decisions to Capt. Hornbeck, something unnecessary in an all-out, World War II–style struggle. It was like conducting an orchestra that every few seconds had to play different music. The object was more deception than aggression: getting the other side to shoot first so as to gain the political advantage, without having to absorb the hit.

The TAO that day was Lt. Scott Wilbur, an Annapolis graduate from Wellfleet, Massachusetts.* After the drill, he told me, "Sometimes I was not getting enough information from the watchstanders, other times I was getting too much. It's all about proper communication. Identifying the threat and applying the restrictive ROEs were the hardest parts, since once you decide you can kill someone, it's easy."

---

* A Navy lieutenant is the equivalent of a captain in the other services.

"If we don't communicate well, we die. It's that simple," another lieutenant emphasized.

Early the next day we reached the other side of the Sulu Sea and entered the heart of the Philippines, between Mindanao and the smaller island of Negros. The calm sea was like milky satin as dolphins played on the starboard side of the ship. Later, in the Bohol Sea, we were enveloped by a fog that continued to strengthen as the strike group entered the Surigao Strait, which, in turn, led into Leyte Gulf. The steep mountains of Leyte peeked through the mist: watercolor brushstrokes only. I strained for a glimpse, as though looking into the past. Everybody on the bridge knew the significance of where we were; the captain had already explained it over the loudspeakers.

Leyte Gulf was where Army Gen. Douglas MacArthur made his promised "return" to the Philippines on October 20, 1944, after being forced to withdraw from Corregidor two and a half years earlier. Gen. MacArthur had walked onto the beach at Leyte from an offshore landing boat, almost knee-deep in water. It might have been the most famous staged photo op of World War II. The campaign at Leyte and the Surigao Strait would mark the first real breach of the inner defensive line of the Japanese Empire: a line that, besides the Philippines, included Formosa, Okinawa, and the home islands of Japan. Close-quarters combat ensued in Leyte Gulf and the area around it from October 1944 through December: at sea, on the beaches, and in the jungly hills. The cost was 15,584 American casualties, including 3,504 killed, and the death of 49,000 Japanese troops.[7] From Leyte, the Americans had gone on to capture the main Philippine island of Luzon.

The *Abraham Lincoln* strike group was now driving through a graveyard of American and Japanese sailors. In the last fierce naval engagement of World War II, six American ships and twenty-six Japanese ones were sunk in the Surigao Strait and adjacent waters. Never again would the old "tin can" warships play such a role in war.[8] With the majestic gray silhouettes of the *Shiloh* and the *Abe* a few miles ahead of us, it was as though the strike group were an honor guard in silent procession through these ghostly waters.

The *Benfold* began to roll and plunge as the Philippines receded behind us, and we entered the vast Pacific, which between here and the Marianas island chain was called the Philippine Sea. Soon we were in waters 20,000 feet deep, with the surface resembling a granite and white-capped mountain range of steep cliffs and dizzying canyons, in the perpetual motion of a level-seven sea. You felt every movement of the ship. Still, the Pacific, as the name suggested, was less unruly than the Atlantic, where sailors had memories of empty mess halls because so many of the crew could not get up from their racks, except to vomit.

Beyond the Marianas, the Pacific was a thundering, faceless, hard-to-pin-down immensity, empty of human habitation with the exception of scattered islands. Unlike the Philippine Sea, here it had no name. Between the Marianas and Hawaii, a stretch of over three thousand miles, it was simply the Pacific, identified by the Mid-Pacific Mountains that sat on the ocean floor. It was a landscape you could imagine only with a depth meter, as when the *Benfold* passed over the Mariana Trench and the instruments revealed that the seafloor lay more than seven miles below.

Standing watch on the bridge one especially turbulent night—when waves crashed in spiraling formations on the forecastle, and granules of salt lay in your hair and everywhere topside—was Ensign Zephyr Riendeau of Colebrook, New Hampshire, with whom I shared a stateroom. Zeph was a dark-complexioned and intense young officer, with an engineering degree from Drexel University in Philadelphia. I had watched him stumble into the stateroom before dawn for two nights running. He had had bridge watch throughout those nights, despite a grueling daytime drill schedule that included several "murder boards"—when fellow officers fired technical questions at you, to prepare you for exams. Truly, the Navy officer corps was a world where a lot of high achievers put tremendous pressure on themselves, and on one another: the Ivy League with uniforms and a strong NASCAR following. Ensign Riendeau had barely slept in days.

"Why do you do it?" I asked.

"I could have a well-paying job with a company like DuPont, and be home every night. But life is supposed to have meaning," he said simply. "Whenever I'm ready to collapse on the bridge at three a.m., I think of the chiefs' retirement ceremony and the clanging bell that declares, 'While others slept, you stood the watch.' "

Officers have a similar ceremony when they retire, but for some reason it is that of a senior chief, with decades in the service, that really hits home. After all, officers know many honors and compensations. But a chief has only the honor bestowed upon him by the brotherhood of seamen, the kind of honor of which Conrad writes.

The retiring chief will walk between two lines of side boys (enlisted seamen like himself) while a bell is rung. A folded American flag will then be passed from one side boy to another until it is handed to the chief, as his wife and children look on. Then a poem about "Old Glory" is recited:

> *I have been soiled, burned, torn and trampled on the streets of*
> *countries that I have helped to set free.*
> *It does not hurt for I am invincible . . .*

Short speeches follow. At the end, there is the reading of "The Watch":

> *For twenty years*
> *This sailor stood the watch.*
>
> *While some of us were in our bunks at night*
> *This sailor stood the watch . . .*
>
> *He stood the watch for twenty years*
> *He stood the watch so that we, our families and*
> *Our fellow countrymen could sleep soundly in safety,*
> *Each and every night*
> *Knowing that a sailor stood the watch. . . .*

Then the bell rings one final time, just as it has rung for high-ranking officers and dignitaries coming aboard a ship or going onshore since the 1500s, since the days of the great Spanish, Dutch, French, and British navies. That last ring signals that the retiring chief can now, too, be thus honored, and that he finally stands relieved of watch duty. It is the only time that sailors will see a chief cry.

The sea journey from the Marianas to the Pearl Harbor Naval Station in Hawaii, where I would leave the ship before it continued on to San Diego, took ten days. Yet, it seemed longer as Sunday, February 20, lasted for a full two days, because of crossing the International Date Line late one night and having to set the clock back twenty-three hours. For those on the bridge, one break in the monotony was the appearance of gulls when we passed within twenty miles of Wake Island. Otherwise, it was more Un-Reps, oral examinations, and fire and engineering drills that went on unabated from dawn till dusk. I overheard one deck seaman complain to his chief, "I've only slept two hours in the last three days." One of the exercises concerned an imaginary fuel leak in the Dantesque horror of the engine room, when the electricity was deliberately switched off and we stumbled around on catwalks in the dark in 105-degree temperature. With us were test evaluators from the carrier, who had come aboard by helicopter to judge the performance of the *Benfold*'s own evaluators. "If you think we're being anal about this, you'd be right," one evaluator from the carrier told me. By now channel fever had set in: no one could sleep because of the anticipation of seeing spouses, girlfriends, boyfriends, and so on for the first time after a five-month sea voyage.

Yet the Pacific would not end. For many days there was nothing to look at but foaming water with eight-foot swells. Your mattress during this period functioned more like a trampoline than a bed, as the bow kept dipping to the waterline only to fly back up one or two stories above it. To know that most of the planet was undulating ocean was one thing; to tangibly experience it another. Usually the ship was traveling at twenty-five knots directly into the wind, making the relative wind speed on the bridge wings around forty knots. It was painful to go outside, despite the magnificence of the sunrises and the sight of the Southern Cross crawling over the horizon around two in the morning.

Along the way to Hawaii we passed the strike group of another *Nimitz*-class aircraft carrier, the *Carl Vinson,* going in the opposite direction to relieve us.* A day did not go by without a big American naval presence in the Pacific Rim.†

---

* Carl Vinson of Georgia was a member of the House of Representatives for over fifty years, and played a substantial role in getting the funds for a two-ocean navy.

† Because I departed the *Benfold* in Honolulu, I was not there to experience the arrival at its home port in San Diego, where helicopters flew overhead in formation to celebrate its return, and the crew lined the rails with roses in hand for their loved ones.

FOUR

GEEKS WITH TATTOOS: THE MOST DRIVEN MEN I HAVE EVER KNOWN

ON A NUCLEAR SUBMARINE

North Pacific Ocean, Spring 2005

now planned to travel back across the Pacific Ocean on a fast-attack nuclear submarine.

It might seem that I was on a very different path than the one I had staked out the previous spring in Iraq.[1] But I wasn't. As long as men walked the earth, war would be a permanent feature of human history. Thus, it was merely a question of what kind of wars we would have. During the fighting in Al-Fallujah the year before, I had seen how the future of war was *the past.* Despite technological advances, the grubby work of infantry was still relevant and at times necessary, a drama of corporals proceeding house to house with guns and bayonets. But the future of war was also *the future,* in which conflict would be reduced to blind mathematical abstractions, without even the sky or the surface of the earth to keep one's bearings, where nothing could be seen, but only intuited through electronic transmissions.

Nor was there anything contradictory about the growing relevance of both urban combat and submarine deployments: of both *the past* and *the future.* Their dual importance was explained by the emptying out of the twenty-first-century battlefield. Rather than large concentrations of infantry or surface warships in a confined geographical space—the stuff of conventional, industrial-age land and sea battles—there were now small clusters of combatants hiding out in cities, jungles, and deserts, as well as beneath coastal shelves and great oceans. The entire earth was now a battlespace. Killing the enemy was easy; it was finding him that was difficult, whether he was concealed amidst civilians on a crowded bazaar street, or lurking in oceanic layers where sound waves traveled and refracted at unpredictable speeds and angles.

This meant a premium on intelligence gathering. In an age when rogue states and transnational terrorists might avoid satellite surveillance by anticipating their patterns across the sky, no instrument of warfare was as integral to espionage as the submarine, able to pull down onshore cellphone conversations by dipping an antenna above water.[2] During the Cold War, submarines were a principal means of spying, through the collection of electronic data close to the Soviet coastline. By placing taps on underwater telephone cables, subs snooped on enemy phone conversations more effectively than did satellites overhead. Facilitating this was the development of nuclear-powered submarines, which, with virtually endless stores of energy, could remain obscured underwater for months at a time. With the advent of nuclear reactors, the only limiting factor in a submarine deployment was the amount of food that could be taken on board.

By the end of the Cold War, American nuclear attack submarines had carried out over two thousand spying missions against the Soviet Union and its allies. Of these activities, the most important was tracking the "boomers," Soviet subs over three hundred feet in length that packed up to twenty ballistic missiles, with ten nuclear warheads each. While President Dwight D. Eisenhower had "only hesitantly approved" U-2 spy flights over the Soviet Union, for fear of aggravating Nikita Khrushchev, American submarine captains "believed it was their job—and forget the niceties of international law—to drive straight into Soviet waters," write Sherry Sontag and Christopher Drew in *Blind Man's Bluff: The Untold Story of American Submarine Espionage.* Few of these men suffered moral or political doubts. "As far as they were concerned, détente and diplomacy were public shows put on by both sides to hide true inten-tions."[3] Nowhere was the Cold War hotter than under the sea.

After the Cold War, submarines snooped around likely battlefields in Iran and North Korea. They helped enforce the economic embargo against Iraq, and seal off Bosnia and Haiti from arms shipments. They launched cruise missiles against Iraq during the first Gulf War and again in 1997 and 1998, and against Serb targets in Bosnia in 1995. Subs fired 25 percent of the Tomahawks in the Kosovo war of 1999, and a third of them in Operation Iraqi Freedom (OIF) in 2003. The first shot of OIF was fired from the USS *Cheyenne,* a Pearl Harbor–based sub.* The mis-sile strikes against suspected chemical weapons facilities in Sudan and terrorist camps in Afghanistan in 1998 also came from submarines.[4]

Now the Chinese Navy was preparing to push out into the Pacific, where it would encounter a U.S. Navy and Air Force unwilling to budge from the coastal shelf of the Asian mainland. There was no better indi-cation of China's blue water ambition than its investment in both diesel-*and* nuclear-powered submarines. China was attempting to achieve a sort of parity with the U.S. Navy through an emphasis on missiles and submarines, rather than by a proportional, across-the-board buildup of conventional assets like carriers and other surface warships. In terms of raw numbers, if not in quality, China's submarine fleet could at some point become larger than that of the United States. Most of China's sev-enty submarines were past-their-prime diesels of Russian design; but these vessels could be used as the equivalent of mobile minefields in the South China, East China, and Yellow seas, where "uneven depths, high levels of background noise, strong currents and shifting thermal layers" would make detecting them extremely difficult.[5] Add to that seventeen new stealthy diesel subs and three nuclear-powered ones that the Chi-nese Navy was planning to deploy by 2010, and one might envisage a Chinese Navy with the ability to launch an embarrassing strike, or stunt, against the United States or one of its allies.

To compensate for the increasing demand for American subs in the Pacific, tied to the military rise of China, East Coast–based subs were transiting to Pacific locations via the North Pole and the Panama Canal.

---

* The Tomahawk was designed originally as a submarine-launched weapon.

"The Cold War was about finding and being able to sink Soviet subs in the deep and open oceans," explained Rear Adm. Paul F. Sullivan, the departing commander of the Pacific Fleet's submarine force. "Today, there is a shift in focus from the Atlantic to the Pacific, due to the proliferation of subs among certain nations [like China, though he didn't say it], that tremendously complicates" American security. "Instead of one mission in the deep ocean," he went on, "there are now multiple missions in shallow waters, crowded with fishing fleets."

Sullivan, a Naval Academy graduate from Massachusetts, was delivering his farewell address during a change-of-command ceremony at Pearl Harbor, where he was being replaced by Rear Adm. Jeffrey B. Cassias, a graduate of the University of Texas at El Paso.* Such ceremonies, though practically a daily occurrence in the U.S. military, were nevertheless stirring, particularly this one, which I attended my first day back in Hawaii.

Consider the scene: a makeshift wooden platform with red, white, and blue bunting atop the fast-attack nuclear submarine USS *Pasadena,* which looked out onto a crowd of submariners in full-dress and summer whites, here with wives and retired officers and sailors in colorful Hawaiian shirts, all huddled under a tent at the Sierra Nine pier. Behind us was the USS *Cheyenne,* and near it the USS *Alabama,* a ballistic missile nuke. In the middle distance, across two hundred yards of shimmering milky turquoise water, were four *Arleigh Burke*–class destroyers. Bells pealed. A Navy band played "Ruffles and Flourishes." Guns fired from the USS *Frank Cable,* a submarine tender, also decorated with bunting for the occasion.† Sullivan and other speakers reminisced about submarine "warriors" who spanned the decades, from the Vietnam era of "student protests against authority in general" to the current season of "bringing democracy to Afghanistan and Iraq."

---

* Both were two-star admirals, or rear admirals upper-half.

† Submarine tenders are massive surface ships that service almost every aspect of a submarine. Their size is necessitated by their Tomahawk and torpedo magazines, and the numerous machine shops that repair and manufacture everything from engines to lockers. Women constitute around half of a tender's crew. It was Frank Cable, at the turn of the twentieth century, who commanded the sea trials of some of the earliest American submarines.

The ceremony, which ended with a chaplain's blessing and the decking of flower leis on the two admirals and their wives, was a gathering of an extended family. Much of the crowd knew one another. The wives had the weathered expression of hard-faced, good-looking women accustomed to weeks and months alone at a time, while their men were on deployments that could not be spoken about. During the Cold War, a wife would get a phone call the day before her husband's arrival at the pier—the only advance notice she would get. It was a culture different from that of the surface Navy.

———

The next day I left on my journey aboard the USS *Houston,* or SSN 713 (sub-surface nuclear-713). The *Houston* was one of fifty-four *Los Angeles*–class, fast-attack nuclear submarines, to be distinguished from the larger SSBNs (sub-surface ballistic nuclear boats). Able to gather all sorts of intelligence, hunt old adversaries like the Russians and potential new ones like the Chinese, escort carrier strike groups, insert Special Operations forces, and project power by their ability to fire long-range missiles, SSNs were among the country's most critical national security assets.* In all but a few cases, they were named after American cities.

The *Houston* had been commissioned in 1982. Its namesakes included two surface warships: the cruiser USS *Houston,* which had carried President Franklin D. Roosevelt on four official cruises and was later sunk by the Japanese during the February 1942 Battle of Java Sea, and the light cruiser USS *Houston,* which was commissioned in 1943 and distinguished itself in the Battle of the Philippine Sea in June 1944.

This *Houston,* the first submarine to carry the name, carried a price tag of well over $1 billion, had a best speed of greater than 25 knots (28.8 miles per hour), and could go to depths below 800 feet. Its claim to fame was executing an emergency blow near the climax of the film *The Hunt for Red October,* when, in the fictional role of the USS *Dallas,* the *Houston* shot high out of the surface at a thirty-degree angle by

———

* For Navy SEALs, the sub was the preferred method of insertion and extraction in 90 percent of their missions.

flooding its ballast tanks with pressurized air, thus quickly emptying them of water.

The *Houston* was 33 feet wide and 360 feet long, though it would seem a lot smaller as I would be restricted to the forward half of the boat; in the aft section was located the nuclear reactor and propulsion system, which I lacked the security clearance to access. The crew during the time of my travels numbered 17 officers and 130 enlisted men. This was about half the size of the crew of the *Benfold*, in dramatically less than half the space. The age of the average crewman was twenty-six. There were no women, unlike in the surface Navy. The men often had higher test scores on their résumés than those of a destroyer crew.

Once I boarded, the *Houston* would spend two days firing torpedoes off the western Hawaiian Islands. Then it would sail underwater to Guam, almost four thousand miles westward across the central Pacific, the boat's home port. Guam was also home to the forward-deployed Submarine Squadron 15, which, in addition to the *Houston*, included two other fast-attack subs, the USS *City of Corpus Christi* and the USS *San Francisco*. The *San Francisco* had recently suffered a near-catastrophic underwater collision with an uncharted seamount southeast of Guam, which had resulted in the death of one crew member and injuries to twenty-three others. On the *Houston*, I would meet several crew members of the *San Francisco* who had experienced the crash.

Though the journey would take me from one tropical archipelago to another across the central Pacific—over the Central Pacific Basin and the Mid-Pacific Mountains, rearing up 9,500 feet off the ocean floor—the Navy called this part of the ocean the "North Pacific," because both Guam and Hawaii were located north of the equator. In all, I would spend two weeks below the surface.

During the first few hours, the experience was similar to my previous embeds—a bewildering new environment coupled with a bewildering sameness of faces and uniforms that I would quickly have to separate out into individual personalities. At the same time, everything was different. The Marine infantry unit with which I had been implanted in

Iraq represented one end of a cultural spectrum; the crew of a fast-attack nuclear submarine another. Yet I found them similar: both were manned by a certain brand of extremist, men who enjoyed a deserved superiority complex because of their willingness to incur extreme sensory deprivation.

Like marines, submariners had a very personal relationship with their service's history. The first submarine in the U.S. Navy was commissioned in April 1900 as the USS *Holland,* named after its designer, John P. Holland, who sold it to the Navy for $160,000 after sea trials off Mount Vernon, Virginia. Just as marines celebrated the birth date of their service with a ball in November, so did submariners in April, when they remembered those who had fallen and were thus "on eternal patrol."*

Still, as I said, this journey was radically different from my previous ones. The pier at Pearl Harbor had looked empty at first, until I got closer and noticed the *Houston*'s sail and top third of its steel hull sticking out of the water—coated in blackish-gray, hard rubber tiles.† Unlike at a destroyer pier, only a few people were milling about. This was mainly because of the higher level of secrecy surrounding submarine deployments. I was greeted by the boat's captain, Comdr. John Zavadil of Grosse Ile, Michigan, and the executive officer (or XO as he was better known), Lt. Comdr. Brian Davies of Newark, Delaware.‡

Though the rank structure was exactly like that of the *Benfold,* the personalities were not. I noticed immediately that Capt. Zavadil was more communicative than Capt. Don Hornbeck of the *Benfold,* with a lively, boyish look and shock of bright red hair; whereas the XO, Brian Davies, was not domineering in the manner of the *Benfold*'s executive officer, Dave Dunn. A submarine, with a smaller crew and quarters, constituted a less formal environment than a surface warship. And be-

---

* In World War II, submarine casualty rates were six times as high as other American naval forces: 52 submarines and 3,500 submariners lost.

† Officially, the color of U.S. submarines was "dark gray," and that of surface warships the much lighter "haze gray."

‡ As on a destroyer, the captain of the boat holds the rank of commander, or lieutenant colonel in the other services. But since function takes precedence over rank, he is referred to as "captain." Similarly, aboard a submarine, the various lieutenants are not addressed as such, but as "nav" for the lieutenant in charge of navigation, "weaps" for the one in charge of the weapons systems, "eng" (soft *g*) for the reactor engineer, "chop" for the supply officer, and so on.

cause there was no night and day—only the smell of frying bacon to tell you that it was morning—there was no reveille, so everyone, including the boat's commanders, wore what Capt. Zavadil called "warrior blue coveralls."*

Except for the khaki belts of the officers and chiefs, I never saw khakis, let alone dress whites, on the *Houston,* even when we entered a port. The pomp and circumstance had ended the day before at the change-of-command ceremony. The distance between the rulers of the *Houston* and their men was less daunting than on the *Benfold.* It had to be, for as soon as I descended the ladder with my backpack into the bowels of the boat, I realized that while a destroyer was a civilization unto itself, comprised of both men and women, a fast-attack sub was a single organism—as though one human being had replicated himself over and over again.

Such togetherness was borne not only of proximity, but of psychological isolation from the outside world as well: e-mail connections were worse than on a surface ship, and there was much that occurred on a sub that the crew could not talk about with family and friends, because of the classified nature of their operations.

It was as if the world of the destroyer had been exponentially shrunken. The *Benfold*'s staterooms and p-ways, whose reduced size and low-hanging pipes had made me gasp upon first exposure, now seemed immense by comparison. I was put in Lt. Comdr. Davies's stateroom, the second largest on the boat. Yet it was half the size of the one I had shared with an ensign on the *Benfold,* and only about a quarter the size of the XO's stateroom there. Both the sink and the desk folded out from the wall. The plastic garbage can was cut to a width of two inches. The blue carpeted floor was partially concealed under neatly stacked notebooks for all of the XO's paperwork. The lone chair was used to stack more notebooks. There was dramatically less space than in a college dorm room, yet with dramatically more work expected. Whereas most bright and privileged students look forward to more privacy in living conditions upon college graduation, these men willingly chose less.

---

* Only on Saturday, Field Day—when everyone cleaned the boat—was there reveille.

And this was luxury. Other officers were packed together in a single stateroom, with racks stacked vertically a foot or two apart from the other. The dirty laundry was in canvas slips attached to the wall against their bodies. The enlisted berthings were more crowded still, with ninety-six racks for 130 sailors, so many "hot racked" (shared the same bed). On account of rolling eighteen-hour shifts, this was not a problem. When one sailor was ready for his six hours of sleep, the other was on duty. Some slept in the torpedo room, where the lights were never turned off, and where racks were interspersed with the weapons on sliding stows.

Prior to departure, lunch was served in the officers' wardroom—a replica of the *Benfold*'s, though so much smaller that the Formica-covered walls seemed almost to breathe. Instead of a picture of Eddie Benfold, there was the *Houston*'s insignia, featuring the American and Texan flags, along with the Latin words for "Always Vigilant." The officers sat jammed together, making light fun of a Virginia Military Institute graduate at the end of the table, Ensign David Bartles of Falling Waters, West Virginia, who, they told me, could never stop talking about how superior VMI was to the Naval Academy and every other institution of higher learning.

There was the usual military formality that for a civilian in the early twenty-first century was impressive to behold. In an age when both young waitresses and elderly corporation presidents insisted on calling strangers by their first names—in a manner that was often completely insincere—in the *Houston*'s wardroom, amid the laughter of young men who knew one another like the best of friends, it was always "Captain," "XO," "Mr. Bartles," "Mr. Murphy," "Mr. Luckett," and so forth.*

It is said that attrition of the same adds up to big change. The *Benfold*'s officers had stunned me with a scientific intensity that demonstrated how warfare could be conducted by means other than manly aggression. Here that attribute was further intensified. That, together with the miniaturization of everything, allowed me past another barrier—to a qualitatively different brand of military officer: men who bore

---

* Lt. Michael Murphy of Raleigh, North Carolina, was the navigator; Lt. Comdr. Michael Luckett of Banning, California, the engineer.

expressions so concentrated and screwed tight that each appeared to be wearing glasses, even if he wasn't.

This should not have been surprising, given that these officers, in their twenties and early thirties except for the captain, operated a boat bristling with weaponry and listening devices, which was also a fast-moving, underwater nuclear power plant. Submariners, like Air Force pilots, worked in an unforgiving, zero-defect environment. At several hundred feet beneath the surface, you might as well be in the space shuttle. Anal retentiveness was a matter of survival. Yet to know such a fact was not the same as appreciating it through a sustained close encounter. "It's like being back in seventh grade," said one enlisted man. "If you do something stupid, your crew mates never let you forget it."

If a surface warship was a clean world of sea and steel, especially compared to the dust and muck of Middle Eastern deserts and tropical jungles, a sub-surface warship was cleaner still—antiseptic almost—for no smells could be allowed in such a claustrophobic environment. Sailors showered constantly. Trash was regularly compacted by a machine and attached to weights for its journey to the bottom of the ocean. Sinks were scrubbed after every use. Just as the officers were the most fastidious I had encountered in the U.S. military, the chief petty officers were, too, more punctilious than swarthy: men with tattoos who had high enough math and science scores to be accepted into the submarine service. The sub was the ultimately maintained tool. But unlike a commando or soldier-diplomat operating alone in the wilds, it was under extreme central control from headquarters.

The chiefs' lounge on a fast-attack nuclear submarine was a mere table with a computer screen for movies; no food was served because the space was too small. The chiefs ate on the nearby mess deck (the "Longhorn Café") with the other petty officers and apprentice sailors. The mess deck, in turn, was close to the officers' wardroom. Because everybody on an SSN lived, worked, and ate within arm's reach of one another, distinctions between the officers, senior enlisted men, and sailors were more subtle than on a surface ship even. Despite the blue carpets and tiles in the staterooms and adjacent p-ways, "officers' country" had little meaning here.

Another bond was the fact that all officers, save for the supply officer, as well as seventy of the 130 enlisted men on the *Houston,* had graduated from "nuke school," the Navy's nuclear propulsion school in Charleston, South Carolina—a crucible of six hours' daily instruction in engineering, chemistry, math, reactor physics, and fluid and thermo-dynamics, where one excruciating exam followed another. I was in a steel-hulled cloister occupied by the most intense and driven people I had ever known.

Take Lt. Junior Grade Anthony Williams of Fayetteville, Georgia, a graduate of Georgia Tech and a chemical-radiological assistant in the reactor complex. His sensitive, precise enunciation gave more indica-tion of an academic background than a service one, even as every gen-eration of his family going back to 1685 boasted a member in the American or British militaries. His father was an Air Force pilot and his brother was in the Army. Lt. Williams was very passionate about ideas, as I learned during a discussion we had about the future of American democracy, about which he was deeply worried. His concern for Amer-ica was not affected. It was as though the country were his child that he was willing to physically defend and give his life to. As delicate as he seemed, he betrayed the sort of character that gave rise to bravery. See-ing how disoriented I was at lunch, during a discussion about "wet transmission checks," "magnetic silencing," and "thermoluminescent dosimetry," not to mention a host of acronyms I had never heard of, he took out an exercise board from the closet and explained a few basics to me:*

- *Layer Depth.* A region of the ocean, usually beginning around two or three hundred feet below the surface, where the effect of surface sunlight is dramatically reduced, so stable, colder temperatures ensue. This is conducive to sonar transmissions because the greater the degree of water pressure, the stronger the molecular connectivity that facilitates the movement of sound waves. The

---

* Wet transmission checks refers to checks on the circuitry of torpedoes while they are in tubes pressurized with seawater. Magnetic silencing, or degaussing, is the process of removing the boat's magnetic signature by running electric currents through it, so that it cannot be threat-ened by magnetic mines. Thermoluminescent dosimetry refers to the measurement of radia-tion levels on the body.

ocean has many layer depths, but the term often refers to the first cold region beneath the surface layer. This region, several hundred feet down, was where the *Houston* would be traveling during most of its journey to Guam.

- *Thermocline*. The rate that temperature decreases as one descends beneath the surface, represented by a sloping line on a graph. The straightening out of the thermocline is indicative of the start of the layer depth.
- *Baffles*. A cone of 120 degrees in the water, aft of the boat, where the sonar technicians cannot hear anything specific because of the white-water noise caused by the turning of the propeller—what submariners call the "screw." Because sonar is seeing through hearing, it represents a dangerous blind spot.

Lt. Junior Grade Williams ended his tutorial with a description of the difference between the Cold War and the Global War on Terrorism, from the operational viewpoint of submariners. Because the Cold War was fought mainly in the Arctic, it signified a shallow and uniform layer depth, since polar sunlight does not penetrate very deep in the water. The difficulty was not in identifying the layer depth, but in the unpredictable sonar refractions caused by indented icebergs and "marginal" or partly melted ice. The War on Terror, on the other hand, because it was occurring mainly in the tropics, with more variable sun and wind patterns, meant no problems with ice, but lots of problems with "deeper and more complex" layer depths.

It was time for the *Houston*'s departure. Following lunch and the tutorial I put on a harness. I climbed a succession of ladders to the top of the twenty-foot sail, which, when the sub was above water, functioned as the bridge. Outside, I shackled my harness to a latch and stood atop the highest point of the boat, a narrow space crowded with six crew members in blue coveralls, including the captain, the officer of the deck, and the conning officer. Further reducing the available room were two periscopes, a tangle of antennae and computer screens, a mounted MK-43 light-medium machine gun for force protection, and a "snorkel" device that ventilated fresh air into the boat. All of this constituted the "rigging," which would be either manually removed or hydraulically lowered into the sail prior to descent.

Right below me, extending on both sides at the midpoint in the sail, were two giant wings: the fairwater planes, which, by adjusting their angle, allowed the sub to quickly ascend or descend while underwater. Far aft, by the rudder and hidden under a few feet of water, were the stern planes, smaller wings that allowed for angling and finer adjustments in depth. A submarine operated much like an airplane. The fore and aft ballast tanks filled with water to achieve neutral buoyancy; then adjustment of the wings and tail—the fairwater and stern planes—allowed for most of the course movements.

"Get the ship under way," announced Capt. Zavadil, standing beside me.* "Aye, aye sir," came the reply from the officer of the deck. A tugboat helped nudge us away from the Yokohamas, as crew members in coveralls under green vests stood topside along the length of the hull, "manning the rails" and casting off the mooring lines. The American flag was lowered from a pole aft, and raised on the sail a few inches away from my head, functioning now as "the ensign."

The rudder amidships, we slipped past the *Arleigh Burke* destroyers and the USS *Pasadena,* the sub atop which the ceremony the previous day had been held. In front of us, before we turned, was the battleship *Missouri* with the *Arizona* Memorial off the starboard bow. The boat's whistle sounded like a foghorn as the *Houston* turned to the outer harbor around Hospital Point, and concentric ribbons of water curved green over the bow.

Not even on the bridge wing of a destroyer was there such a feeling as riding atop the sail of a submarine, your feet dangling over the sides, only the harness to keep you from sliding into the water. The sensation intensified as we picked up a few knots of speed, so the water—now green, pastel blue, and navy blue in succession—spilled over topside, with only the sail and fairwater planes still dry.

The boat accelerated to full speed, or "full bell" in submarine language, meaning eighteen knots (flank bell and best bell were faster).

---

* A submarine, like an aircraft carrier, was usually referred to as a "boat." But it was also a warship, so calling it a boat was not a hard and fast rule.

Water cascaded all over the hull in explosions of suds, reaching closer to us. The officer of the deck lit a cigar, and I leaned back against the periscope tower, enjoying the sun and the roar of waterfalls less than twenty feet below now. Two children with their mother, standing at the edge of the shore on the residential grounds of Hickam Air Force Base, waved small American flags as we passed.

Once clear of Pearl Harbor and vicinity, the "maneuvering watch" was over, and the "at-sea watch" commenced. The captain unshackled his harness and went below to the control room, which would henceforth function as the bridge. Down there, others would take over the roles of officer of the deck and conning officer. As I went below, I hit my head against the revolving radar and began bleeding all over my clothes. Seeing me pass into the washroom to clean away the blood, one sailor remarked, "You just came on board and already you have a sea story to tell."

The moment I went below I passed from a world of exhilarating traveler's sensations to one of digital abstractions, from a world of vivid blue tropical seas to a purgatory of dead fluorescent lighting, prison-gray electronic monitoring panels and switching devices, endless entrails of seafoam green ducts and cables, and blinking red LED (light-emitting diode) numbers. The weather on a sub was always the same, "69 degrees and fluorescent," in the words of one chief petty officer. The Formica paneling of the wardroom and some of the p-ways was the closest thing to aesthetic luxury.

Eyeing the industrial-age gray and seafoam green, one sailor remarked, "Yeah, Martha Stewart sure as hell didn't do the interior decorating on this boat." "What's a sub like?" another sailor asked rhetorically, looking up at the continuous spaghetti of pipes and cables in the most dismal, mealy shades. "It's like being stuck in the boiler room of your high school for several weeks."

On the mess deck, sailors were already studying for boards and other qualification tests: settling in for two weeks at sea. I noticed red and yellow signs here and there, warning of the danger of radiation if one passed through a door, or a certain point along a p-way. The Navy was careful to the extreme regarding the protection of sailors from radiation. Between its submarines and aircraft carriers, the Navy had operated many dozens of nuclear reactors for decades—twice as many as the number of nuclear power plants active in the United States—without incident.

The control room, henceforth functioning as the bridge, was a B-52 cockpit writ large—clunky gray, World War II–like consoles that often masked the latest and greatest technology. The helmsman controlled the rudder and fairwater planes. Seated beside him to his left was the "outboard," the equivalent of a co-pilot, who managed the stern planes. Beside him was the chief of the watch, who handled communications throughout the boat, as well as the amount of water pumped into the ballast tanks. Behind all three sat "the dive" (diving officer of the watch), who had overall responsibility for the boat's movement in the water. The goal was RAMOD (reach and maintain ordered depth). That depth was determined by the conning officer, in consultation with the quartermaster, or navigator. Given that the weaponeers and sonar techs also sat nearby, the control room was the pulsing heart of the sub.

Final preparations were in progress for descent, which included retrieving the rigging on the sail, testing the hydraulics and ventilation systems, and bringing down one of the periscopes. The *Houston*'s speed had slowed considerably in the moments prior to leaving the surface, and the boat was rolling about to a much greater extent than a destroyer did in similar seas. I thought I might become seasick: subs were designed for underwater stability, but they could be notoriously unstable platforms on the surface.

"Dive! Dive!" came the command. We descended thirty-five feet at a five-degree angle, at which point the second periscope was lowered. I heard the hissing of water through one of the sound sensors. Then, increasing the angle to fifteen degrees, so my body leaned forward, we descended another four hundred feet. The rolling ceased and my oncoming seasickness subsided immediately as we crossed beneath the wave action. There had been only the faintest feeling of falling, as in a slow elevator. All was now quiet and calm. "It's good to go deep," someone said, just above a whisper.

Speed was increased to twenty-four knots. That necessitated restraining the fairwater planes and steering by the smaller stern planes only. This was a safety measure: if the larger wings shifted precipitously to a steep angle while the boat was moving at full bell or faster, they could quickly bring the sub down to crush depth, a point where the water pressure would bend the hull inward.

Almost four thousand miles underwater to Guam, I thought. It was an amazing prospect, yet utterly routine given the history of this mode of travel. "The sea is everything. It covers seven-tenths of the terrestrial globe. . . . It is a spacious wilderness," says Captain Nemo, the commander of the submarine *Nautilus* in Jules Verne's 1870 visionary epic *Twenty Thousand Leagues Under the Sea.*[6] The first U.S. nuclear submarine, the *Nautilus,* was named after Verne's imaginary ship, which in the novel reaches the South Pole; its American namesake drove under the North Pole in 1958. Verne's story, which only a fool would confuse with one for adolescents, establishes the fundamental tenet of life aboard a submarine: that the boat is a "holy ark" whose cramped space encompasses all of human progress. Inside are victuals, security, calm, and—at least on Verne's *Nautilus*—a library of humanity's twelve thousand greatest books, while outside are only the black and crushing depths, the equivalent of interstellar space.[7]

In fact, every U.S. submarine boasted a prodigious library—of technical manuals. They were everywhere on the boat and referred to constantly. A destroyer in a mechanical emergency could call in expert technicians by helicopter from a nearby carrier, but a submarine crew was on its own deep beneath the surface, so these thick manuals were veritable bibles.

We were now sailing north of the *Nautilus*'s course in *Twenty Thousand Leagues Under the Sea.* Whereas Captain Nemo had taken his boat south from Hawaii to French Polynesia, and then west through Oceania to the Torres Strait, between Australia and New Guinea, we were to end up due north of that longitudinal point, in the Mariana Islands chain.

Again I was struck by how every inch of space counted. The hospital corpsman shared his cubbyhole office with launchers for sonar buoys and torpedo countermeasures, in addition to the usual dense jungle of pipes and cables reaching down to his nose. The lone exercise bike was squeezed between fuse boxes, temperature gauges, and sonar transmitters. Technical manuals were fitted into shallow wall recesses for quick retrieval. Hundreds of cans of food lay in storage spaces that also served as benches in the crew's mess, where the cooks, whenever they were not preparing a meal, were on their hands and knees scrubbing every nook and cranny. With 147 men stomping in and out of the mess, and no outside air for weeks sometimes, cleaning was an interminable necessity.*

Such eighteen-hour-a-day drudgery, absent the sensation of day or night, allowed me the privilege of being with people whose pride depended on not needing to rest. Their escape consisted of porn in the racks, smoking or dipping tobacco aft, watching a movie, playing cribbage, or mainly just engaging in bull sessions.

The U.S. Navy, as I had learned on the *Benfold,* comprised a veritable childhood map of the interior continent, as so many enlisted sailors hailed from the great land sea of the Middle West and Great Plains, with its corn, soybean, and wheat fields, which engendered boyhood dreams of the blue ocean. Machinist's Mate Jeff Meinheit of Auburn, Nebraska, was a typical bald and bulky Navy senior chief, with a mustache and a splendid disposition. He and the nine sailors under him were responsible for fixing everything on the boat that was not part of the nuclear power plant: from the esoteric equipment that converted hydrogen to water vapor and scrubbed carbon dioxide out of the atmosphere, to mundane devices like the laundry machine and clothes dryer. Chief Meinheit ruled over a multi-level maze of screaming boilers, generators, pumps, and valves, negotiated by narrow deck plates that were more like catwalks. "Pretty much anything with a pipe on this boat belongs to me," he said.

Because something was always broken, the labor was unrelenting. Chief Meinheit's dad had been in the Army, his sister in the Air Force, and his uncles in the Marine Corps. The only way to deny that the volunteer American military was not a caste was to avoid the life stories of the enlisted men and women in it. Meinheit was full of details: how a week's worth of emergency oxygen was stored in pressurized banks fore and aft; how the amine used to scrub the air of carbon dioxide was

---

* The cooks—the true heroes of submarine existence—also did the officers' laundry.

odorless inside the boat, but as soon as you left the submarine and were back in your home, you discovered that all of your clothes reeked of the chemical. One more chore for the wives of submariners.

Electronics Technician Gordon Boese of Richey, Montana—another senior chief and farm boy from the Great Plains, with a mug of coffee perpetually in his hand—had spent fourteen years on submarines, including many months above the Arctic Circle as a radioman, and under the North Pole. "I was twenty-three, married, no great job, and always interested in military service. I met the Navy recruiter and then sold the wife on it. The population of this submarine is more than half of that of my hometown. The sub force has really broadened my horizons."

One chief hailed from Cape Girardeau, Missouri—Rush Limbaugh's hometown, he told me with pride. He hoped to return there after reaching the twenty-year mark in the sub fleet. Another senior enlisted man had a stepdad who had served in the Army Air Forces on Tinian in the Marianas, when they brought in "Fat Man and Little Boy," he said, referring, respectively, to the atomic bombs dropped on Hiroshima and Nagasaki.

Electronics Technician 2nd Class Kyle Marshall Limb of Vernal, Utah, was an enlistee with whom I became acquainted at the start of the voyage. At twenty-three, he was the same age as the *Houston.* Enthusiastic to the point of giddiness sometimes, with an innocent voice, he, too, had relatives in other branches of the military and had joined the Navy both to better his social station, and, he told me, as a response to 9/11. "All of us are a little kooky living in this 3-D math world," Limb went on. "Not only are we packed together underwater, but because it's hard to send e-mail we lose touch with the outside world to a greater degree than other sailors."

Petty Officer Limb, raised as a Mormon, was the lay leader of the "eclectic services" on the *Houston,* offered every Sunday morning along with Protestant and Catholic worship. Eclecticism was essentially a "neo-pagan" movement, he explained, which combined elements of old Norse religions, and Druidic, Wiccan, and other covens. Sometimes Buddhists and what Limb called "solitary practitioners" took part. I had heard stories about neo-paganism among marines in Iraq and enlisted sailors on the *Benfold,* but this submarine was the first place where I en-

countered it directly. Limb told me that he had to persist with his superiors to get it officially sanctioned: a wise decision on the part of the
Navy, since only seven sailors attended in any case, and this way it did
not become some subversive, underground youth faction. It was a matter of being tolerant without being indulgent. "We don't sacrifice ani-
mals or pray to the devil," Limb said. "I've never touched drugs. We
stand in a circle and sprinkle salt water, and ask for blessings from the
physical elements. Our moral basis is, do as you will, as long as ye harm
none."

The very compression of this far more intense, squeezed-together
version of the bobbing and swaying universe of the destroyer *Benfold*
made it frightening in its tyrannical possibilities, had iron-fisted discipline not been so total that it barely needed to be asserted—or implied
even. It was just there: the discipline of a true elite, in which the lowli-
est of enlisted men could take great pride.

The personal security I felt among these 147 young males thrown together in the primordial deep allotted me the luxury of ruminating on its
opposite: the mini-universe of men behaving like beasts, with the strong
and less intimidated preying upon the weaker and more intimidated, in
a finely stratified hierarchy of bullies on a small ship in the mid-Pacific.
That is the world of Jack London's *The Sea Wolf*—the story of an inde-
pendently wealthy and bookish scholar captured by a seal-hunting
schooner, on which he is both terrorized and, finally, at the age of thirty-
five, brought to manhood by a captain "so purely primitive that he was
of the type that came into the world before the development of the
moral nature."[8] There is a swift, deeply etched quality to London's characters in the story that might make them seem stark and exaggerated,
and thus unsophisticated by some literary standards. But if you spent
enough time in close quarters with vigorous young men—unrefined by
the wider cosmopolitan world, like many on this submarine—you
would realize that London was merely being realistic: that he had seen
far more of the world than those who relegated him to the realm of the
merely "self-taught."

The discipline that did not even need to be asserted had much to do
with the COB (pronounced "cobb"), the chief of the boat, Command
Master Chief Scott Weaver of Fernandina Beach, Florida, near the

Georgia state line. At fifty, Master Chief Weaver had been in the Navy since 1979, almost the whole time on submarines, much of it spent in the North Atlantic tracking the boomers and other Soviet subs. In the entire world of the Navy, chiefs of the boat had an especial allure, more so even than master chiefs on surface ships. Truly, COB Weaver's authority was more subtle than that of Master Chief Craddock on the *Benfold*. Whereas the latter loomed over you, the former was more like that of a parent or high school teacher whom you did not want to disappoint, or test. The COB had gray hair and round wire-rimmed glasses. The impression he made was trim and neat, not burly. He was an avid backpacker in the Olympic and Cascade ranges (for decades Washington State had been a major submarine hub). The mountain air was the antidote he had chosen to a quarter century underwater.

"My grandfather was a sailor on a Navy cruiser and my dad an Army Ranger. But my grandfather was a better storyteller. I was enthralled by his tales about riding out typhoons, even if they were exaggerated.* And I was named after him, so I joined the Navy and became a sonar tech." The COB gave out the family death messages, knew whose crew members' wives were in the hospital, set the smoking and liberty policy, set the watch bills, was responsible for cleanliness on board ("heads and beds"), and was on the noise reduction and other technical committees— all in addition to the two hours of daily paperwork he had. He napped rather than slept. Like all master chiefs and sergeant majors, COB Weaver had pet peeves: he would not tolerate sailors who went about unshaven or with their hands in their pockets.

———

"We've finished the basic phase," Capt. Zavadil told the group of officers and senior chiefs crammed into the wardroom toward the end of our first day at sea. "I'd say we're now mediocre. We need to focus on navigation, sonar analysis, torpedo strikes, mining, noise reduction, and the like." Raising the boat to periscope depth and holding it steady in a rough sea—to ventilate the air inside with the snorkel—had been a big deal some weeks back. Now it was routine. The *Houston,* having re-

* Because sailors had a habit of telling sea stories whenever they congregated to unravel strands of old line, telling a sea story came to be known as "spinning a yarn."

cently emerged from a three-year overhaul in dry dock that featured a $200 million refueling of the nuclear reactor, was finally back in the water, with the crew reacquainting itself with war-fighting skills.* It was a matter of getting a lot better at them, before the boat could go out on sustained operational deployments. That meant drills, and more drills, which would commence the following morning. As the captain told me, "We're in spring training, preparing for the regular season." The pressure on him was severe: as a forward-deployed sub, the *Houston*'s training and operational treadmill was faster than that of subs based off the mainland and Hawaii, because more time at sea was expected of it.

Whereas Marine generals often looked like Marine generals because of the physical toughness required for close-quarters combat, submarine commanders had no particular look to them, and whatever that look might be, it definitely wasn't gritty. Still, the requirements for being the commanding officer of a nuclear submarine were of the kind that would intimidate the most ambitious of people in the civilian world. Fair-complexioned John Zavadil was forty, but looked much younger. He was cheerful and uncomplicated in the extreme. Sometimes the chemistry of strong leadership is simple. It certainly was in Zavadil's case. Because of a pleasant disposition, he was able to be blunt all the time, without offending anybody.

Zavadil saw the future of submarine war fighting in the following terms: more warm water as opposed to cold water operations, and more SOF (Special Operations Forces) deployments off submarines. While the recent past had been carrier strike group–centric, the future would emphasize force multiplication: get close, real fast, to a coastline to collect data or sink a ship when no one thinks you're there, perhaps even frightening away the enemy before he has time to muster his forces. In sum, it was about preparing the battlespace. It could apply to the defense of Taiwan, the subjugation of North Korea, or much less obvious scenarios like killing a concentration of terrorists in a remote part of the Indonesian archipelago.

---

* A submarine nuclear reactor has a life span of thirty-three years, but requires a refueling after twenty years. The $200 million was reasonable considering that a new SSN could cost as much as $1.4 billion, with even a diesel-powered sub running up to $800 million.

Indeed, the submarine, which could deposit SEALs on a beach at night, and the V-22 Osprey, which could land and take off vertically from a dirt strip and be refueled in the air, were two examples of how the American military might employ technology to circumvent the need for diplomatic permission slips and foreign basing rights prior to the insertion of forces: by gathering intelligence and killing "bad guys" without the media or a host nation even knowing about it. Together with Marine and Army Special Forces training missions of third-world militaries, such hardware was helping to ease a paramount security problem of the early twenty-first century: how to meld the political reality in distant regions of the world without the need for cumbersome, large-scale interventions as in Afghanistan and Iraq—interventions that, because of the big footprint they created, required the approval of a global media to be successful. And of all the big footprint hardware in the U.S. military arsenal (tanks, B-52s, carriers, destroyers), only the sub was completely invisible.

The more powerful the media, the greater the benefit from being able to operate unseen. The height of the anti-war protest movement in the late 1960s was also a time of particularly aggressive American submarine infiltration of Soviet waters, which at the time elicited nary a headline. Because submarines were absent from the media radar to a more significant extent than the Central Intelligence Agency or the National Security Agency, they might, for example, allow a liberal president, publicly committed to multilateralism, to conduct a compensatory, unilateral foreign policy behind the scenes. The sub was where the true intentions of a nation were revealed.

—

"Embrace the suck" was an American military cliché that I had been hearing for years. It meant: accept the extreme bodily discomfort demanded of operational deployments, whether in a theater of actual war or in a rigorous training environment that simulated war. "The suck" wasn't only the dust, the filth, the insects, the heat, and the cold, but also the smaller things like the absence of decent beds or chairs, or tables on which to unfold maps and eat meals. On a submarine—"a sealed people tube," as sailors called it—the suck was the extreme absence of space, of forever rubbing up against other male bodies in narrow p-ways. It meant maneuvering your way into your rack without banging your head against the one above you; sharing a tiny toilet and shower with a large number of other officers or sailors; stepping gingerly between things piled on the floor, because there was no other place for them. The first night on board was rough, but as the nights accumulated my sense of scale adjusted, and the once-tiny stateroom and p-ways became, as on the *Benfold,* gradually of normal dimensions.

I had only a mild taste of the suck of submarine existence. Take the four-month-long undersea voyages, without once coming near the surface to ventilate the air, experienced by Culinary Specialist Otis Hines of Calion, Arkansas. The fabled *Sturgeon*-class spy sub USS *Parche* had won six Navy Unit Citations and one Presidential Unit Citation while Chief Hines was aboard, between 1995 and 2002. He had to plan the meals and, more importantly, store food for 120 days under way. Stacks of canned goods had covered the p-ways, including the floors between the racks in berthing, he told me. With the floors raised, crewmen's heads were closer to the already low ceilings, and soon the ceiling bolts were filthy with tiny pieces of hair and bloody skin from all the minor scalp injuries. "It got worse when we started working our way down through the cans, and sailors started stumbling all over the place." The eggs and potatoes were packed in the bilges, while coffee hung in canvas bags from the ceiling. Standing up straight anywhere was next to impossible. "I've spent eighteen years in the sub force doing stuff that no one would even think or have any idea about," Chief Hines told me.

"We have a bandwidth tracking problem, with enemy totals in the area," Capt. Zavadil announced in the control room. Translation: sonar was scanning transmissions for a hostile fast-attack nuclear submarine. The *Houston* was cruising at a depth of four hundred feet. You didn't want to be at periscope depth when on the hunt; even the tip of a periscope above the water with light reflecting from it could alert the enemy. The enemy SSN did not exist. It was being simulated in a torpedo-firing drill run for the *Houston*'s benefit by the Navy's nearby Barking Sands missile base on the western Hawaiian island of Kauai, which I had visited the previous autumn.

"Resolve ambiguity," Zavadil announced further. The sonar towed array, attached to a thousand feet of cable dragging behind the boat, was the *Houston*'s best eyes and ears. But since the towed array could hear sound in all directions, it was unclear from what angle exactly the enemy's sonar signature was coming. Resolving ambiguity meant doing a zigzag that, by putting the dragged towed array in successively different angles to the boat, allowed the sonar shack to triangulate the enemy's position. This was a game of measuring frequencies that established a pattern of enemy movement. That led, in turn, to a "fire control solution"—killing the other sub with a torpedo, that is. (The choice of adversary, specific to a given country, was mere logic, given the shifting power dynamics in the world. But it is one that I am not allowed to identify.)*

Zavadil closed his eyes and said, "Come left hard rudder 175 degrees." His action was based on finding the enemy SSN at 217 degrees southwest, and he wanted to be about 40 degrees off the latter's stern as he converged from 9,000 to 7,000 yards. Two hours later, after patient tracking, a pattern of movement was established for the SSN, and a fire control solution found: an angle of 295 degrees at 7,000 yards from the target. The torpedo was "smart," meaning that under its own guidance system it could fine-tune its course as it neared impact. But the goal was to minimize the area of uncertainty. Because the loaded torpedo tube was on the *Houston*'s port bow, the captain wanted the boat's starboard side facing the enemy. That way the boat's own sonar signature would shield that of the torpedo until it was too late for the enemy to evade it.

I heard a thud from the torpedo tube. A few moments later the good news came from Barking Sands. Capt. Zavadil announced, "We just sent an enemy . . . to the bottom of the ocean. Not bad." The crew started talking and joking again, signaling its relief.

The XO, Lt. Comdr. Brian Davies, had the most difficult assignment during the exercise. Through headphones, he had to run a three-way conversation between the sonar shack, the watchstanders at computer combat control, and the weapons officer (or "weaps," as he was known), who supervised some but not all of the watchstanders. Each watch-

* In order to embed for an extended period on a fast-attack nuclear submarine, I had to sign a confidentiality agreement with the Pacific Fleet. Certain details about the exercises I agreed in advance not to disclose.

stander had a different function—for example, one evaluated the trajectory of the torpedo, while another tracked secondary contacts in the area so that the torpedo's guidance system would not be confused. Conflicting advice emerged frequently, and the XO had to make quick calls based on often-complex geometry.

Davies was a typically quiet and conscientious Navy officer, of the kind I had met on the *Benfold*. He had loved math and science courses in high school, and didn't think that merely going to classes all day at college would be enough of a challenge, so he applied to Annapolis. At the Naval Academy, he gravitated toward submarines. He was interested in nuclear physics and, as he told me, "When subs go to sea they go to war to a greater degree than surface ships." Davies had to be incessantly curious about every technical aspect of the sub, from the torpedoes in the bow to the reactor aft, so that when junior officers or chiefs were not on top of problems, he knew it before they did.

Upon completion of the torpedo drill, we set sail for Guam, down a preestablished underwater highway, or submarine interstate. Guam was four time zones to the west, but because it was on the other side of the International Date Line, it was twenty hours ahead of Hawaii. Rather than shift the boat's clocks one hour at a time every few days, Zavadil decided to do it all at once. Thus, while the *Houston* was still in the vicinity of Honolulu, 10 a.m. on Saturday, April 23, became 6 a.m. on Sunday, April 24. It didn't matter. Deep under the water there was no indication of night and day; thus you could inhabit any time zone you wanted.* Because Saturday and Sunday became one day, the XO made sure not to delete religious services from the schedule: Protestant, Catholic, and Eclectic.

On this trans-oceanic journey, like the previous one on the destroyer, the drills commenced immediately. "Light smoke in the torpedo room," came the announcement, as a general alarm sounded in the fashion of a police siren. In the control room, the watchstanders all put on EABs (emergency air breathers), a sock-like mask that draped onto your

---

* The crews of SSBNs (ballistic missile subs), wherever they happened to be in the world, used ZULU time—Greenwich mean time not adjusted to daylight savings.

shoulders, with a filter and tube that you snapped into one of the many oxygen manifolds located throughout the boat. The control room filled with the hissing noise of deep breathing. At the same time, the helmsman drove the boat on a fast ascent from 485 feet to 150 feet below the surface. During most emergencies, the submarine had to be in a position to quickly resurface.

I ran down two sets of ladders and forward into the torpedo room, leaping onto one of the stows to observe the action, careful not to hit my head on the ceiling. For the moment, the only ones in the room were the drill monitors, with red ball caps and stopwatches. Then a line of sailors wearing EABs hustled in carrying a pressurized fire hose. They were followed by other sailors in firefighting ensemble—oxygen tanks and helmeted masks, thermal imagers in their hands to identify the source of the fire through the smoke. The stopwatches indicated that the response had been below average. Both the captain and the XO were annoyed because one sailor came storming in with an axe instead of a wooden pole. An axe was a conduit of electricity and thus particularly dangerous. Its only likely purpose on a submarine would be to destroy equipment in case of an imminent enemy takeover of the boat. "Anyone wants to use an axe or crowbar," the captain said, smiling but dead serious, "they can come into my stateroom afterwards to do push-ups."

The crew would have to practice the procedure again, and again. There might be no sight on a submarine more memorable than sitting on the mess deck with every seat occupied as sailors ate, yelled, argued, and exchanged stories, just as the fire alarm sounded and the crew became a single life-form: exploding off cheap vinyl benches and adjacent berthing racks, tearing down p-ways and hatchways to their watch stations, their heads ducking to avoid protruding bolts and pipes, simultaneously pulling on EABs.

There was a simulated oil spill in which the sailor contaminated was given the most expensive medical treatment available, two aspirins and a cup of coffee.* Another drill involved filling the escape trunk with seven hundred gallons of water, so that the pressure inside would equal

---

* The combination acted as a diuretic, which helped the sailor pass the contaminant out of his system.

that outside the sub, thereby blowing the hatch and allowing four crew members at a time to accelerate upward to the surface because of the air bubbles inside their pressurized suits.

There was, too, torpedo and mine mustering. The *Houston* had four torpedo tubes and space for twenty-six MK-48 ADCAPS (advanced capability torpedoes) and MK-67 mobile mines, situated on massive iron tables (stows) moved vertically and horizontally by hydraulics. Shifting the weapons around, sliding them into the tubes with ramming devices, closing the interior hatches, pressurizing the tubes with water, and then opening the exterior hatches was another complex procedure accomplished by one sailor reading out loud from a manual, while others carried out the orders. From the movies, one thought of torpedoes being rammed into ejection tubes. But the ramming devices silently slid the massive weapons into position over greased skids. The very oozing slowness of the procedure made its intent seem even more ominous. The air pressure from a torpedo firing was such that wherever you were in the forward half of the boat, your ears popped.

One of the operators before the mealy gray control panels was TM-2 (Torpedo Man 2nd Class) Kevin Mallory of Coos Bay, Oregon, an "old dog" at thirty-five, who had been in the submarine fleet a decade before leaving the Navy, only to reenlist after 9/11. "Was it worth it to reenlist?" I asked. "Yes and no," he told me. His pay was one-third that of his civilian job, and he hadn't seen his wife in months.

I had met Mallory at breakfast at 6 a.m. in the crew's mess while rap music was blasting as the kitchen staff was busy scrubbing the deck on their knees. He was joshing with another sailor about the feasibility of storing golf clubs on board. With the sub at a steady "trim" at a depth of five hundred feet, you could putt in the p-ways. Crew members were noisily coming on and going off duty. It might as well have been noon.

Early in the morning and again at night we'd come up to periscope depth, raising the antennae four feet above the water to capture messages on the secret net. Then we'd dive deep and fast. Through the periscope in late April, I saw the moon illuminate the rocking sea a "baffling protean gray," in Jack London's words, a gray "which is never twice the same; which runs through many shades and colorings like intershot silk in sunshine."[9] Lying on my stomach in the rack at night reading London's *Sea Wolf*—there was no room to sit up—I reflected that at fifty-two, I stayed young certainly not so much by journeys with the military, but by occasionally carrying around the same paperbacks I had read a third of a century earlier, when I was riding trains through Turkey and Iran, and taking car ferries around the Greek islands. Rediscovering *The Sea Wolf* for the first time in decades was like going back in time.

Through the periscope in the morning, I'd look out at the blue, post-dawn water and sometimes espied a merchant ship ten thousand yards out on the horizon. The invigorating clarity of the scene appeared not quite real, even as it was only fifty feet above the grim, industrial grays of the congested control room. In a submarine, peering through the periscope was the equivalent of strolling amid sunlight and fresh breezes on the outer deck of a surface ship. Or you could go inside the sonar shack and listen to the "biologics," the screeching cries and whistles of whales and dolphins, registered by a spray of dots on the computer screen, as opposed to the solid, bold shapes of commercial fishing trawlers.

Sensations inside a submarine were indirect, making them even more precious and fantastic to consider. "The reactor is critical," would come the announcement sometimes when we were at flank speed. You would feel the powerful shudder of the propeller (screw), along with the pressure against your back (if you were sitting against something), and realize that the boat was traveling at over twenty-five knots against a veritable wall of resistance, five hundred feet below the surface, where the pressure per square inch was the equivalent of a 220-pound man sitting on your thumb.* Flank speed on a surface warship, with a rooster tail of white water rising several stories up, felt like going eighty miles per hour on a highway. But I traveled faster on the *Houston,* in depths where the water pressure would have reduced the destroyer's gas turbine engines to a crawl.

The sub could travel at the same speed for years without ever slowing down, with all the lights, computers, and machinery operating at the

---

* The actual "best" speed of a fast-attack nuclear submarine is something that I experienced, but that I am not allowed to print because it is classified. The same with the deepest depth it can attain.

same time, and with much of the crew taking hot showers. The reactor needed to be refueled only about once every two decades. There was evidently a lot to be said for nuclear power.

———

In a tiny recess amid screaming air vents, signal storage equipment, and a bank of transmitters that created wattage for sonar transducers, I found STS-3 (Sonar Technician Submarines 3rd Class) Steve Spence of Woodlands, Texas, crouched on the floor, notebook in hand, studying for an examination in equipment damage control. Sonar Tech Spence always knew that he would join the military. The only question was which branch. "I had the call in my soul—just like my father, an oil drilling engineer, who got the call from his spirit to be a Baptist preacher." Spence had been in the Air Force's junior ROTC program in high school, but upon graduation decided to join the Navy because, as he told me, the Navy recruiter was more specific about educational opportunities.

Spence had been a crew member of the USS *San Francisco,* another fast-attack nuclear sub that was part of the same Guam-based squadron as the *Houston.* A few months earlier, on January 8, when the *San Francisco* was 350 miles southeast of Guam, traveling at a speed of twenty-five knots, five hundred feet beneath the surface, Spence was in a middle-level p-way, on line for chow, when the sub smashed into an uncharted seamount at a ten-degree upward angle on the port side. He had heard a boom and a shake and the next thing he knew he was on the floor, having hit his head, his glasses missing. A general alarm sounded. Aching and bleeding, he found himself helping more severely wounded sailors.

Another crew member of the *San Francisco* with whom I spoke had had a similar experience. He was in a compartment of the engine room that got kicked out from under him. Regaining composure, he ran to the crew's mess, which soon took on the appearance of a battlefield hospital, with blood everywhere and intravenous bags hanging from the ceiling.

The *San Francisco* had been traveling south toward Australia through the Caroline Islands, near Satawal. Though it was in a designated submarine lane, the charts were contradictory. It would turn out that the chart the *San Francisco* used showed no discolored water—green and light blue water indicating shallow depths, usually accompanied by a shoal or reef. As Lt. Michael Murphy, the *Houston*'s "nav" (navigator), explained to me, when it comes to underwater mapping, lines on a chart "are mere cartography" that do not necessarily correspond to depth soundings. The fact is that much of the ocean floor remains a mystery that has yet to be mapped out nearly to the degree of accuracy of the much smaller, terrestrial portion of the earth's surface. After all, beneath a few hundred feet there is no practical need for surface vessels of any kind to be aware of depth changes. And because the Pacific is deeper than the Atlantic, and also played less of a role in the Cold War, until recently the Navy had paid less attention to its underwater topography.

While the uncharted seamount that the *San Francisco* hit had reared up suddenly like a sheer cliff, the very shoal-laden geography of the Carolines, coupled with the contradictory cartographic information available, might have led the *San Francisco*'s commanders to be extra careful. The *San Francisco* was, at the time, in dry dock in Guam with a crumpled bow.

With the *San Francisco* in mind, Lt. Murphy, a graduate of Duke University's ROTC program, was taking no chances. He noticed a particularly questionable area in the pre-designated submarine lane that we were transiting, around 162 degrees east latitude north of Wake Island. It was an area of some rather dramatic seamounts, with a shoal and reef here and there perhaps, appearing on some charts and not on others. Murphy did not assume that just because the route had been selected by headquarters in Honolulu meant it was safe. Thus, for a few hours, when the *Houston* was in this area, Murphy, with the captain's permission, limited the MOD (maximum operating depth) to 150 feet and the speed to ten knots. He also stood up a modified piloting party—more people in the navigation section, with a sailor required to constantly look at the depth soundings on the fathometer, and note them down every five minutes.

While nothing unusual showed up on the fathometer during the piloting party's watch, a few hours later, two hundred miles east of the Marianas chain, where the charts indicated a seamount rising to 2,641 fathoms (15,846 feet below the surface), the fathometer displayed a steep, cliff-like mountain rising to a depth of 1,173 fathoms (7,038 feet), a whopping difference of 8,808 feet from the charts. In a region of many active, undersea volcanoes, the ocean floor was not only little known but also unstable.

With the Navy's increasing emphasis on unconventional shallow-water operations in crowded sea-lanes, navigation had become an especially critical art, even as the American submarine fleet was rusty at certain aspects of it, at least compared to Cold War days, when cat-and-mouse games with Soviet boomers made American submariners expert at following close behind other boats, by hiding in the latter's baffles.

Shallow-water operations also demanded better-honed periscope techniques. Because the objective was to stay undetected, theoretically you wanted to keep the periscope up for as short a time as possible. That meant getting the most out of the time the periscope was up, which, in turn, entailed micro-managing every second of its use. It was the per-isher navies—the Dutch, Swedes, Australians, and others—with diesel subs designed for patrolling littorals, that mentored their American allies on periscope techniques.

Before rising to periscope depth, the boat would swivel to "clear baffles"—that is, to inspect the 120-degree blind spot created by the propeller-made white water. Then the periscope ("one-eyed lady") would ascend and the officer of the deck would do three eight-second, 360-degree sweeps, followed by a second series of sweeps to check for airborne contacts. Meanwhile, both secret and unclassified message traffic would be uploaded and downloaded on a priority basis, before the boat quickly dove again.

There was also the "dip scope" technique: surface just long enough to snap a photograph through the periscope of a ship that had been detected by sonar, then calculate when you had to surface again to keep visual tabs on the ship, based on its speed and direction.

On the other hand, the longer you had the periscope up, the more intelligence you could pull down through ESM (electronic surveillance measures)—the monitoring of radars on enemy ships, for example. In fact, the American submarine fleet considered itself an "up-scope navy"—that is, an aggressive navy, willing to brazenly ascend to periscope depth to gather as much intelligence as possible while avoiding detection. This was part of a Cold War tradition, when American subs would hover at periscope depth in Soviet waters above the Arctic Circle. For submariners, the Cold War was surrounded by nearly the same halo of risk and glory as World War II. And given the significant role played by subs in operations in the Balkans and the Persian Gulf in the 1990s, it was a service that saw itself permanently at war.

———

"A sub's not a job; it's a way of life," Senior Chief Anthony Maestas of Salt Lake City remarked. His was among the intense, screwed-tight faces I had noticed during my first hours on the *Houston;* his expression told you a lot was going on in his head. Senior Chief Maestas had grown up Hispanic in a white-bread, Mormon environment. "I understood early what racism is, and how to see it coming," he told me. "You can't tolerate even a hint of racism or ethnic innuendo in a sub because of the small community we inhabit, and our dependence on one another." Much of Chief Maestas's family had served in the Army in Vietnam, and he enlisted out of high school, becoming a 13 Bravo artillery gunner. But he wasn't fulfilled in the Army—he just wasn't, though he had a hard time explaining why. After two years he switched to the Navy. Because he didn't know that it was illegal to enlist in one service while serving in another, he spent several days in jail for the infraction. He now had twenty-one years on submarines, and had traveled all over the Orient, the Persian Gulf, and north of the Arctic Circle, in places where the U.S. military denied it had been. In 1999 he spent 310 days at sea. "The wife has to be strong," he remarked.

"In school, I didn't like the kids who got A's in calculus without having to study much," he continued. "School came hard to me." Chief Maestas worked at it though, and was now the department chief in the engine room, a key component of the nuclear reactor complex, with sixty sailors working under him. "It's easy to mold a sailor into anything you want him to be, because on a sub he can't go anywhere. He's yours.

"This crew's going to get a lot tighter and more disciplined when we go out on actual missions, a few months from now," he went on. (The *Houston* was forward-deployed in Guam, two days' sailing from Taiwan.) "During the Gulf War, I saw shitbags turn into warriors after we had fired our first Tomahawks. We're still in the midst of changing the *Houston* from a yard boat to a warship, from a caterpillar into a butterfly: when it will be loaded down with weaponry that we won't be able to confirm or deny we have, when dropping a wrench on a deck plate will have consequences because it raises our sonar signature. Yeah, you think the atmosphere is serious now—just wait."

I got to know Maestas better after I moved into the chiefs' quarters, into a top rack with two inches between my nose and a nest of valves, which I entered by grabbing on to a couple of pipes, pulling my knees up to my chest and then into the mattress. It was worth it, though. I got to listen to the chiefs talk about the individual problems of junior petty officers. What carrots could they offer this one exemplary sailor who was on the fence about reenlistment? How could they rein in this other sailor who was smart but cynical, and was ridiculing younger, more ambitious seamen for "kissing the chiefs' asses"? What about the sailor who was overeating? Could they get him counseling? Nothing—no bullying, no slacking off—was missed on the boat.

"Even if we know they won't reenlist, we still have a responsibility to prepare them for society," COB Weaver explained. He spoke of a sailor on another boat who had been raised by a grandparent, and had gotten a "less than honorable" discharge. Months later, the grandparent—a retired sailor proud of his own military service—called and said that his grandson never came home after leaving the Navy. Did the COB know where he was? No, he didn't. The following year, someone spotted him homeless in the streets of Tacoma, Washington. Weaver used the story to scare sailors about whom he was worried.

The chiefs' discussion happened to occur while the *Houston* was at "test depth" over the Mariana Trench. That is, we had descended at an angle of thirty degrees to a depth of greater than 800 feet in over 28,000 feet of water. Between the ocean floor and the surface you could fit K2, the second tallest mountain in the world. We were somewhere in between.

Two weeks into the underwater voyage, land was sighted through the periscope: the island of Rota, north of Guam in the Marianas chain. The *Houston* passed west between the two islands and then turned south into the Philippine Sea, where we surfaced. The hatch was opened. I scrambled up the sail and into what seemed like the most glaring sunlight I had ever experienced. There was a delicious racket of white water as the bow cut through the ballpoint blue. With the sea right below me, I felt on top of the world. The high cliffs of Guam's northwestern tip, guarding Andersen Air Force Base, lay ten miles abeam. The heat—stifling, humid heat as opposed to the fresh, cool Hawaiian breezes—told me that the central Pacific had been spanned.

Alongside me atop the sail, now serving as the officer of the deck, was Lt. Comdr. Michael Luckett, the boat's "eng" (chief engineer in the nuclear power plant). He was so smart and conscientious—his eyes seemed to register the light more than other people's—that the XO had decided to let him alone and concentrate on the work of other junior officers. Luckett's next sea tour would probably be as an XO himself. Members of his family had served in both World War II and Vietnam. The same story: he wanted something harder than college, and living quarters that were more crowded than college dorms didn't matter to him. He applied to the three service academies and ended up at Annapolis. Later, he got an advanced degree in engineering at Berkeley, where, as he remarked, "The science and engineering students on the north side of the campus lived in a different political universe than the liberal arts students on the south side."

"Why'd you choose submarines?" I asked.

"Because I knew I'd work with the smartest NCOs in the military." He ticked off the names of Chiefs Maestas, Meinheit, and a handful of others, handing out superlatives. He and his wife had recently bought a house in Guam and were looking forward to purchasing a fifty-foot sailboat. Their plan was to retire in this U.S. territory, where there was a sizable American military community.

The *Houston* soon passed Asan Beach, where the Marines had landed sixty-one years before in a bloody campaign to retake Guam from the Japanese. Then the boat turned east toward the shore, into a wall of wind that almost tore my notebook from my hand as the American flag crackled beside me. Rounding Spanish Point into the entrance of Apra Harbor Naval Station, I noticed the smashed-up USS *San Francisco* in dry dock.

A tug pulled alongside us, and the commodore of forward-deployed Submarine Squadron 15, Capt. Brad Gehrke of Odebolt, Iowa, stepped onto the *Houston* along with a small team from his headquarters. We immediately turned around and headed back out to sea. The commodore had come aboard to observe two combat drills scheduled for the next morning.

The mine drill was the big one. The scenario called for the *Houston* to lay eighteen defensive mines around Apra Harbor. In the process of laying the mines, the crew had to be careful not to be counter-detected by two enemy warships, a guided missile destroyer and a diesel-electric submarine, whose mission was to penetrate the military facilities in the harbor. The identity of the enemy was the same as that in the exercise earlier in the journey. A succession of junior officers and chiefs drove the briefing in the wardroom that night. The tension was palpable.

Capt. Zavadil peppered the briefers with questions as Commodore Gehrke looked on: Did they really need to leave the fathometer on? Zavadil asked. After all, why provide the enemy diesel sub with an additional sonar signature? A junior officer responded that the fathometer could work on a high frequency that the diesel wouldn't pick up. Why should the boat turn to port rather than to starboard when outside the harbor? the captain asked, this time just to test the knowledge of one chief. Because the towed sonar array, dragging behind the boat, could get caught by the propeller in the event of a sharp rightward turn, the chief answered. On it went.

The chances of an American sub having to fire torpedoes—complicated by systems' failures that the drill monitors had preprogrammed—and then lay mines the same morning, which (again as the monitors had arranged) would suffer their own mishaps, were unlikely in the extreme. The whole idea, as Commodore Gehrke explained to me, was to make the drills so frustrating and complex that actual combat operations would be easy for the crew. After all, this crew was going to war, in a way that was similar to the way American subs went to war from the 1950s through the 1980s, though few were aware of it.

The morning dragged on. A torpedo misfired. A mine didn't work. Drill monitors in red ball caps smiled furtively at one another as the crew quietly, persistently struggled with getting their weapons off. Lunch was missed. Crawling under the stows in the torpedo room to get a better look at the mine-loading operation, I got green grease all over my shirt. In the crew's mess, a galley worker gave me detergent to try to remove it. We were joking about my ruined shirt when a general alarm sounded, followed by the announcement: "Hot mine in a torpedo tube, there has been a toxic gas release, everyone to their watch stations." EABs were ripped out of closets as sailors leapt over tables, out of racks, and out of toilets. Another pre-programmed drill.

Later, in the control room, I noticed an authentic set of Texas long-horns lying atop a bank of computers. Capt. Zavadil told me that after the crew had reached a higher level of proficiency in these drills, and gone and returned from a successful operation, he planned to mount them on the bridge atop the *Houston*'s sail.

FIVE

NATO'S RAGGED SOUTHERN EDGE

WITH ARMY SPECIAL FORCES

Algeria, Summer 2005

From Guam in the western Pacific, I made my way to Central Europe. Stuttgart, Germany, was the headquarters of European Command (EUCOM). The Pacific might have been the great, emerging military theater of the early twenty-first century, but as I had seen the previous summer in Niger, the U.S. military, with EUCOM then as its executive arm, was expanding in Africa in a manner that, because it went largely unseen, embodied power projection at its most efficient— the antithesis of Iraq.

EUCOM's home was the U.S. Army base of Patch Barracks, an assemblage of sloping, red-roofed buildings graced by birch and oak thickets at the edge of the Black Forest. Constructed in 1936 and 1937, these baronial structures had once housed the men of the Wehrmacht's 7th Panzer Regiment, who took part in the Nazi invasions of Poland and France. In the middle of the Cold War, when I first visited West Germany, American military bases seemed natural to the German landscape. Now, amid the soporific prosperity and attendant pacifism of a united Germany, the sight of U.S. soldiers was an anomaly, a flickering vestige of a bygone era—an heirloom almost. In the early 1970s, when

you met U.S. soldiers here, they spoke highly of the host country whose
dark soil it was their mission to defend. A third of a century later, Germany was just a place where American troops happened to be located,
a place whose population was viewed as politically hostile, while the
military mission had become the near abroad: at first the Balkans, then
the Caucasus, and now the bone-dry Islamic regions of sub-Saharan
Africa. When American officers did look at Europe, it was usually to
probe the Islamic terror cells breeding within it.

Sixteen years following the collapse of the Berlin Wall, it was almost as if Germany—whose defense had once been NATO's principal
mission—had become a *neutral;* whereas a country such as Algeria,
formerly the hub of the officially neutral but hostile "nonaligned"
movement, had become, almost, a friend. As it happened, the Algerian
government was on the brink of destroying an Islamic insurgency over
a vast territory, three and a half times the size of Texas, in an endeavor
that constituted a mini–Global War on Terrorism. While Germany's
center-left government in the summer of 2005 was proving feckless in
the hunt for terrorists at home and abroad, an Algerian government recovering from decades of radicalism was providing the U.S. military
with a stream of intelligence tips.

Because both Algeria and the United States wanted to stamp out the
growth of al-Qaeda offshoots in the African Sahel—on the southern
fringe of the Sahara Desert—a U.S. Army Special Forces A-team was
about to deploy from EUCOM to the extreme south of Algeria. Unlike
the previous summer, when the Marines had taught basic soldiering
skills to a company-sized element of the Nigerien Army, this was not a
Security Assistance mission officially run by the State Department.
Rather, it was a JCET (Joint Combined Exercise for Training) mission
run by the Department of Defense. The bureaucratic distinction was
vital. It implied an equality between the American and Algerian militaries. Not only did Algeria boast a far more sophisticated army than
Niger's, but in regard to the hunt for Islamic insurgents, its troops might
have as much to teach the Americans as the Americans had to teach
them.

The Algerians had killed, divided, and co-opted an extremist movement that specialized in abducting large numbers of civilians and slit-

ting their throats. Like the Muslim Filipino fanatics of Abu Sayyaf, the Algerian ones had imported high-end violence from a cadre trained in the terrorist hothouse of pre-9/11 Afghanistan. The Algerian authorities had demonstrated a high level of aptitude and historical patience. Slowly, meticulously, they had infiltrated terrorist cell structures with operatives who were under little pressure to achieve immediate results. Absolute ruthlessness had been followed by general amnesties, so the number of insurgents in the country had dropped from 27,000 to 1,500. Helping the regime had been a population tolerant of a veritable police state: a police state that was more open-minded, accessible, and favorable to economic growth than any alternative on the horizon. The U.S. military was impressed.

As was often the case, the insurgents still out there were the most hard core. The GIA (the French acronym for the Armed Islamic Group) had morphed into the Salafist Group for Preaching and Combat, the same Salafists that the Marine mission to Niger the previous summer had been designed to suppress. The Salafists were heading "offshore," in American military lingo, to the "under-governed" countries of the African Sahel and to the "over-governed" countries of Europe.

In the Sahel, the Salafists were leveraging a north-south divide that pitted Arabs (who lived closer to the Mediterranean) against less prosperous, darker-skinned desert tribesmen such as the Tuaregs— smugglers of cigarettes, drugs, arms, and people. It was to the Tuaregs that the Salafists had affixed themselves. Northern Mali was now a Salafist sanctuary of the first order, Niger still a major access portal. While people in Washington, in the words of a EUCOM official, were obsessed with "wandering Pakistani preachers" and "Saudi Arabia as the root of all evil," EUCOM was "not turning up much of that order." Rather, it was turning up an inextricable relationship between Islamic fervency and community self-help: a universalist ideology grafting itself onto the local problems of the world's poorest countries.

"The pacifist governments of Europe," in the words of another EUCOM briefer, "believe only in rebuilding societies in Africa. That's a slow, linear function," he went on. "You're going to have to pour a lot of water into the Sahara before any boat comes off the bottom." In the meantime, all you needed was a few insurgents to instantly puncture such a dreadfully gradual trend.* Meanwhile, inside Europe itself, the Salafists had joined terrorist cells dominated by ethnic North Africans with European passports and quasi-European identities. Said yet another briefer: "Forget blond, blue-eyed Swedes. The new face of Europe is darker skinned, with hybrid names and passports ensuring easy entry to the U.S. People are going to come at us out of places you never dreamed of."

So here I was, in a forested German fortress of a long-defunct Nazi Panzer unit, with American military officers talking feverishly about shadowy and turbaned tribesmen in the Sahel at the southern fringe of the Sahara Desert, and their offshoots within working-class sections of European cities. However serious the Salafist threat turned out to be, one thing was clear: without major terrorist attacks in the heart of Europe—of a type and scale that would make the average German once again embrace the American military—these corridors would in the foreseeable future become twice haunted, as they emptied themselves of another army.

As one general told me, "I'd relocate U.S. forces south or east of the Alps: to Tunisia or Morocco, perhaps. But I'd get out of here." The setting up of Africa Command in 2008, which might eventually replace EUCOM, could only quicken this process.

—————

Near Patch Barracks was Panzer Kaserne, once home to Erwin Rommel's 8th Panzer Regiment. Its cobblestone roads had supported the weight of World War II–era tanks. Eagle crests adorned lintels. I noticed a partially chipped-away swastika. Here was located the barracks of the forward-deployed 1st Battalion of the U.S. Army's 10th Special Forces Group.

Tenth Group was the original SF group, established in 1952 at Fort Bragg, North Carolina, as one of the successors to the Office of Strategic Services, (OSS). Manned at first by East European immigrants, 10th Group's domain had always been Europe. In the early days of the Cold

—————

* EUCOM was working with other branches of the U.S. government to construct transmitters for an FM radio network throughout the Sahel, in order to counter messages broadcast by the Salafists. But this was a targeted information operation, designed to achieve fast, measurable results, rather than traditional, broad-based nation-building.

War, it worked actively to destabilize the Soviet Union. Now based at Fort Carson, Colorado, in recent years it had been kept busy in the Balkans and the Caucasus.

Special Forces groups, as I had learned in Latin America, the Philippines, and Afghanistan, took on personalities peculiar to the region in which they operated. In 10th Group's case, the European theater had given it a slightly more formal, cerebral tinge than, for example, the more physical, salsified Spanish speakers of 7th Group in Latin America, at least as far as the officers and the most senior noncoms were concerned. Whereas submariners were math geeks with tattoos, SF officers from 10th Group had a tendency to be wine connoisseurs with tattoos.

Yet Algeria was new, exotic terrain for the A-team from Bravo Company of the 1st of the 10th. The team leader, Army Capt. Michael Adorjan of Canton, Ohio, was typical. A strapping, dark-haired twenty-nine-year-old, fluent in German and Hungarian, he had an intense and affectingly awkward intellectual curiosity that, because it was not calculated, left an overall impression of gangly innocence. He had grown up on a family farm and came from a central European immigrant family of soldiers: his great-grandfather had served in uniform for the Austro-Hungarian monarchy; his father was a Vietnam veteran. He had been educated at Catholic schools, and in 1998 he was in the last all-male graduating class at the Citadel in Charleston, South Carolina.

"I'm a nostalgic sort of guy with a romantic love of history," he told me when we met at Panzer Kaserne. "The southern military tradition just appeals to me. The Citadel is weaker academically than West Point, but it makes up for it with a particularly hard physical regimen. It prepared me well for Army Ranger school." Later, as a member of the 10th Mountain Division, Adorjan worked in a civil affairs unit in Bosnia, where he learned that if you did not drink slivovitz with the locals, did not know an East European language, and did not know the local history, "you just didn't get it. The Big Army certainly didn't get it," he said, "so I joined SF."

Capt. Adorjan's apartment in the Swabian town of Leonberg told you about him. There was no television. Instead, there was a library about the Habsburg empire, next to other books on army tactics. Paper currency from the days of the Dual Monarchy in Austria-Hungary and

the Kerensky government in Russia lay beside World War II bayonets
and Citadel memorabilia. A wall map of the Holy Roman Empire hung
near a portrait of John Wayne. Adorjan was an avid gun collector. He
owned forty guns, he told me, even as he had a volume on ancient Greek
history on his bedside table. In short, he was a typical 10th Group team
captain, a mixture of history buff and good old boy.

His eleven-man A-team would constitute the first U.S. military mission to Algeria since its independence in 1962, and the most important
there since the Allied invasion of North Africa twenty years before that.
"The aim is to grip-and-grin, drink a lot of *chai,* forge bonds with their
officer elite, and Adorjan and his team are the best used-car salesmen
we have. It's impossible not to like him," remarked Chief Warrant Officer III Bill Gunter, the 1st of the 10th's gruff, ball-of-fire noncom from
Roanoke, Virginia, himself fluent in several central European and
Slavic languages.

For U.S. Army Special Forces (also known as "Green Berets") to be invited to Algeria represented, in its own modest way, the ultimate triumph of America's liberal vision over the totalitarianism of the former
Soviet Union and its allies in the developing world. In the 1970s and
early 1980s, when I had last visited Algeria, the capital of Algiers, with
its sprinkle of white stuccoed art nouveau buildings majestically front-
ing the Mediterranean, had been the throbbing heart of third-world radicalism, just as the Syrian capital of Damascus was at the same time the
throbbing heart of Arab nationalism.

Until the late nineteenth century, both Algeria and Syria had been
little more than vague geographical expressions, their very place-names
carrying more significance to European travelers than to local tribesmen. Because the borders of the Algerian and Syrian states that emerged
in the mid-twentieth century contradicted ethnic ones, the new polities
gave rise to extremist, universalist ideologies that carried the benefit of
traversing such regrettable artificial frontiers. The anti-Western rhetoric
that emanated from Algiers and Damascus, it now turned out, had been
necessary to compensate for seething tensions just below the surface of
these unhappy societies. Both states claimed to be nonaligned, even as
each was a veritable tool of the Soviet Union.

Algeria's secret-police regime—with its steel grip over the local economy that undermined every Arab entrepreneurial tradition—had its origins in the bloodiest colonial war ever fought: a grisly struggle against France from 1954 to 1962 that left a million Muslims dead and a million French settlers homeless. It was the last great war of European imperialism. From its ashes arose an Arab political cadre that was as paranoid as it was perverse, even as it enjoyed a unique moral standing throughout the newly independent countries of Africa and Asia. Nevertheless, despite all the talk about the Algerian regime's moral and ideological purity, there was the little inconvenient fact that the army ran the country—period.

The "Zionism is racism" resolution that the United Nations General Assembly passed in 1975 was a partly made-in-Algiers affair. It would turn out to represent the high-water mark of Algeria's worldwide diplomatic influence under its austere and remote leader, Houari Boumedienne, over whom the world media gushed for a time in the 1970s; and who, it should be said, provided his people with free education and medical care, which prodded the creation of a middle class. By 1978, Boumedienne was dead: According to some rumors, he had been poisoned. According to others, he had been poorly attended to by his Soviet patrons in a Moscow hospital, where he had gone to be treated for what turned out to be a rare form of cancer. In 1980 and 1981, Algeria briefly regained the media spotlight when it served as a conduit for the Carter administration to the radical regime in Iran, thus aiding the release of the American hostages on the eve of Ronald Reagan's presidential inauguration. "But the only reason the Algerians were able to be helpful," a State Department official explained to me, "was because they were friends with the worst sort of people." From then on, Algeria followed a path of deterioration that bore striking resemblance to what was transpiring in the Soviet Union.

Like the Soviet Union, Algeria was a sprawling, geographical mess of a country. It stretched from the Mediterranean Sea to the deepest reaches of the Sahara Desert, with not only Arabs but also unruly Berbers and Tuaregs living secure in their mountain fastnesses. The stability and consequent political moderation that Morocco, Tunisia, and Egypt enjoyed along the southern littoral of the Mediterranean had been the gift of civilization clusters that reached back to antiquity, whereas Algeria and Libya—the two radical states of North Africa—represented only weakly governed transition zones. Algeria essentially had no national identity until the war to oust the French.

My last sojourn in Algiers in 1982 had coincided with the final glimmer of the regime's trendy, revolutionary zeal. Back then, the lovely cityscape of wrought-iron balconies and fiery white facades was already bursting at the seams with hundreds of thousands of migrants from the desert, merely a day's bus ride away. Exactly a decade later, concurrent with the collapse of the Soviet Union, an Islamic uprising erupted in Algeria that was a partial reaction to the regime's socialism and fierce secularism, even though the immediate cause had been the abrogation of a second round of voting by the army, after the first had threatened to bring to power an Iranian-style theocracy. Chaos reigned in this country of 32.5 million as the regime was revealed for what it always truly was: a secular, ideological abstraction that the military indulged. Well over a hundred thousand people were massacred. By the end of the 1990s, the regime, tempered and having lost much of its radicalism, was able to regain control over most of the country, something partly legitimized by an ongoing democratic process. It was a stunning feat to which Western militaries had paid close attention.

⸺

The day I departed for Algeria with the A-team's advance element (composed of Capt. Adorjan and his warrant officer) six other A-teams were also departing Stuttgart to fan out across the African Sahel: to Mauritania, Mali, Niger, and Chad.* They were following up on the Special Forces and Marine training missions of the previous summer. One Romanian and one German special forces team were also included in the exercise. Despite frustrations with a leftist German government, EUCOM had not given up on the German military, whereas Romania's was always grasping at opportunities like this one. Running it all was a Combined Joint Special Operations Task Force (C-JSOTF), whose purpose was to get the military elites of the individual African countries to coordinate operations and information-sharing with one another under

---

* The official name of the effort was Operation Flintlock.

a EUCOM umbrella. The location for the C-JSOTF was Dakar, Senegal, the westernmost point on the African continent, where European imperialists, arriving by sea, had begun their conquest of the interior.*

In the middle of the nineteenth century, the French had successfully exploited Senegal as a base for the takeover of the Sahara Desert, creating the structure of weak West African states that the U.S. military was now trying to shore up. France's strategy, the Victorian-era explorer Richard Francis Burton writes, was "to shake hands with Algeria, to link the North African possessions with their future conquests south of the Sahara, and eventually with the rich mineral lands lying east of Senegal."[1] Without seeking to govern or conquer anything, the American military's strategy of security linkages was identical to that of the French 150 years back.

The strategy also bore comparison to the hub-and-spoke Bismarckian arrangement in the Pacific. Company-sized EUCOM elements located in Dakar and the Malian capital of Bamako were to reach out to smaller units scattered throughout the region, which would, in turn, work with specially trained indigenous forces in each country. Because most of these countries had little or no military tradition to speak of, they were easily moldable by American noncoms. To further ease penetration, there would be humanitarian activities such as MEDCAPS (medical civil action programs) and VETCAPS (veterinary civil action programs). Thus had imperialism progressed from something all-encompassing to something spare and lean—from an intricate and lavish oil painting to minimalistic modern art.

Ultimately, this is how NATO planned to move south. No permanent bases would be needed, just contractor-supported cooperative security locations owned by the host country, and used quietly and austerely by the Americans.

—

Capt. Adorjan, his warrant officer, and I stopped first in Algiers: vaster than I remembered it a quarter century before, and grayer thus, on account of more undressed concrete. Yet, it was still an architecturally stunning city, especially by the harbor. The American ambassador's

---

* For an explanation of JSOTFs and C-JSOTFs, see Chapters 4 and 5 in *Imperial Grunts*.

residence was a jewel of Andalusian magnificence, graced by delicious unruly gardens, though sadly surrounded by high walls and concertina wire. From the outside, the embassy compound, where we spent the night after a series of meetings, might well have been a prison. But the ambassador was determined to get his people out and about town and to bring back dependents after years of a security lockdown, now that the civil war was over.

The next day we left the Mediterranean behind and flew to the far south of the country, to Tamanrasset: to Africa. We arrived there late at night, greeted on the tarmac by a team of Algerian Army majors and colonels. I knew one of them, a former exchange student at the U.S. Army's Command and General Staff College at Fort Leavenworth, Kansas, where I lectured periodically. He was Brahim Gouasmia of Souk Ahras, in northeastern Algeria, near the Tunisian border (the boyhood home of Saint Augustine). Maj. Brahim commanded the 41st Algerian Special Forces Company, with which Capt. Adorjan's A-team would train. Like other Algerian officers I would meet in coming days, he had learned English at the Defense Language Institute on Lackland Air Force Base outside San Antonio, Texas. Afterward, he had attended the Special Forces Qualification (Q) Course at Fort Bragg, North Carolina, before studying at Fort Leavenworth. The experience of driving with their families from one American military base to another, and taking automobile holidays at Disney World, had given these Arab officers a familiarity with the South and southern plains that many Americans from other parts of the country lacked.

Soon we pulled up in a procession of Land Cruisers to a military guest house with Mediterranean motifs, a small indication of just how much the Algerian Army was a stranger here in the Sahara Desert, which was dominated by ethnic Tuaregs. As I would discover, there was little civil authority. We had to travel everywhere in a heavily armed convoy. Algeria, in a real organic sense, had ended much farther north.

Over a four-course midnight meal, the Algerian officers, Capt. Adorjan, and Chief Warrant Officer II Orlando D'Amelio of Queens, New York, slipped easily into a bull session about topics of mutual agreement: the desire for male children; how air force pilots everywhere were prima donnas; the need to control the northward flow of economic migrants from Mali and Niger into Algeria, and from Mexico into the United States; the necessity of fighting and killing terrorists; and the beauty of Russian women. Algeria's army was still dependent upon Russian equipment from the Cold War era, and some of the officers had visited Moscow; and Chief D'Amelio had married a Russian girl he had met in Germany.

There was already talk of future, more extensive exercises between U.S. and Algerian special forces detachments. The conversation drifted. We took up the tactical relevance of America's nineteenth-century Indian Wars to the War on Terrorism, as two of the Algerians had studied not only at Fort Leavenworth, but at Fort Huachuca in Arizona, the advance headquarters of the U.S. Cavalry during the Geronimo campaign of the 1880s.

The Algerian officers' open enthusiasm for the two American soldiers—the opposite of the suspicion with which I had thought they would be greeted—harked back to the enthusiasm evinced by Romanians and Bulgarians upon their first contacts with the American military after 1989. I thought, too, of Libya, where the first American tourists in decades reported being mobbed by friendly people. The anti-American radicalism proclaimed by the Algerian and Libyan regimes during the Cold War was a flimsy facade that had never reached beyond the governing class.

Algeria's historical experience made it particularly amenable to a relationship with the American military. Algerian officers associated imperialism with France, not America. Moreover, the local military had just successfully concluded a decade-long struggle against an Islamic insurgency that for years seemed unwinnable, with little or no help from the outside world, including from their fellow Arabs. "Even before 9/11, we knew terrorists were importing tactics and weapons from Europe, but in the 1990s nobody wanted to listen to us," an Algerian colonel told me.

The next morning there was a larger welcoming ceremony for Capt. Adorjan and Chief D'Amelio at the regional military headquarters, with heaps of almonds, tea, and fruit juices. Adorjan apologized for his lack of French and Arabic. He candidly told the officers assembled on boxy sofas that the mission had been originally assigned to the 3rd Battalion of the 3rd Special Forces Group, which had many French and Arabic language speakers.* But that battalion had been diverted to Afghanistan. The truth was that the wars in Iraq and Afghanistan were cutting into more effective democracy-stabilization exercises elsewhere, even such a historically ground-breaking one as this. But with the Balkans at peace, however tenuously, Adorjan was assuming an Africa orientation for 10th Group and he consequently planned to recruit an Arabic speaker or two into his detachment.

He went through the program for the coming weeks, including visits to Tamanrasset by EUCOM officials, with help in the details from Chief D'Amelio. The perfect SF warrant officer, who had worked training missions everywhere from Spain to Azerbaijan, low-key Orlando D'Amelio, who looked more like a schoolteacher than a commando, liked to operate quietly behind the scenes, whispering in people's ears.

Next we hit the airfield to await the arrival of the vehicles, equipment, ammunition, and the other nine members of the A-team. On the way I got a look at Tamanrasset, perched a mile above sea level, at the foot of the Hoggar—those crazy black and twisted Alps of the Sahara, soaring up several thousand feet. From here the trans-Saharan highway linked Algiers 1,200 miles away to the north, while a network of unmarked trading routes stretched in other directions deep into Mali, Niger, and Libya. I was as close to the Gulf of Guinea as to the Mediterranean, yet the Algerian border with Niger was still two hundred miles to the south.

Tamanrasset was not an oasis; water came from a nearby aquifer. There were no date groves to soften the landscape, only pine and some eucalyptus trees planted in the style of a colonial outpost.[2] The bleak streets, lined with one-story cement structures in crude Arab and African patterns, were mainly populated by Tuaregs, with an interspersing of black Africans. The Algerians called the Tuaregs the "blue men," on account of the color of their dazzling robes and the blue vegetable dye (*nila*) they smeared on their bodies. With their camels and immense helmet-like turbans that covered half their faces, they once again—as

---

* I had been embedded with the 3rd of the 3rd in southern Afghanistan in late 2003. See the last part of Chapter 5 in *Imperial Grunts*.

they had in Niger—reminded me of figures out of a medieval tapestry. Tamanrasset was their capital. They controlled everything here that the over-governed West considered illegal, and which the under-governed third world considered, well, just commerce. The Tuaregs knew the desert, where it was better to have a Tuareg with you than a GPS (global positioning system) device.

The massive U.S. Air Force C-17 Globemaster snuck down onto the runway. The rear hatch opened and out slid the pallets and Humvees, followed by Adorjan's team wearing tan desert uniforms, looking like a bunch of big, overgrown farm boys. There was no ammunition, though. The French had not allowed it across their airspace until more paper-work was filed. It was petty, but not unusual. "The other European countries do it to us all the time," Chief D'Amelio told me. "That's why we want to get out of those places and move elsewhere."

The convoy began its one-hour movement northwest into the desert, which began past a new military base that Kellogg, Brown & Root was building for the Algerians. "Immense, beautiful, sudden, savage and harsh; one gropes inadequately for the right adjectives to describe the country," writes the British historian Alistair Horne about Algeria.[3] We were smack in the middle of the Sahara, the crucible for Algeria's insta-bility as a nation, and for Europe's social instability in the foreseeable future. Tamanrasset marked the first major way station for the clandes-tine movement of immigrants north from sub-Saharan Africa to coun-tries like Germany and France. Because many of the migrants got delayed here, and needed money for the onward journey, they drifted into smuggling and prostitution. Tamanrasset accounted for half the AIDS cases in Algeria.

Through the pasty dust I saw the broken vertebrae of buttes, mesas, and slag heaps, like indecipherable symbols, or faces emerging from the past. The vast bleached distances between each vertical eruption cre-ated a shimmering curvature of landscape, empty except for swirling patterns of blackish, apricot-colored sand. One mesa, an Algerian offi-cer told me, reminded him of a Tuareg lying on his back with his elbows extended. Upon seeing a Tuareg with his camels by a water well, marked only by a stone, Maj. Brahim remarked that the Tuaregs subscribed to KISS. A U.S. military acronym that I had first heard from marines in Djibouti, KISS meant "Keep it simple, stupid."

The Land Cruisers and Humvees now left the asphalt and rumbled deeper into the desert, where the sand was like cigarette ash blotched with black, volcanic outcroppings. After fifteen minutes of more driving came ranks of pointed green canvas tents, our home for the next three weeks. The temperature in the late afternoon when we arrived was 105 degrees, but that was only because of the cloud cover. Tomorrow it would be hotter. For a year now, it had been two kinds of extremes for me, those of the world's largest ocean and its largest desert. Among other things, great power projection was about the regulation of vast amounts of space—space that was not necessarily livable.

Assembled upon our arrival at the camp were the 103 troops, or four platoons' worth, of the 41st Algerian Special Forces Company, with whom the eleven-man A-team would train. They were dressed in dark green and maroon uniforms, clashing with the tan of the Americans. Early the next morning the Stars and Stripes was raised alongside the green-and-white Algerian flag with its crescent and star. It was the first time that the American flag had flown over a military base in this country since Operation Torch, the 1942 American-led sweep across the Maghreb.

The A-team and I began to settle in, getting accustomed to the clammy puddles of body sweat that would soak our cots for the next twenty days. Staff Sgt. James Lewis of Middletown, Rhode Island, the team's 18 Echo (communications specialist), was frustrated. The communications had gone "tits up"—that is, they weren't working the way they were supposed to. "The Army can't make a radio without a cascading matrix of things that can go wrong," he said. That got us into a discussion about how the U.S. military was becoming too dependent on "toys," even as the real base of soldierly knowledge, like using a map and compass, was dissipating. The communications weren't the only problem. "My computer took a shit so I had to download my CDs on my iPod," said another team member. Nevertheless, the strawberry milkshake powder in the MREs was fantastic. As someone exclaimed, "That bitch is banging." The conversation shifted next to relationships: "I married a liberal, but I'm going to take her back to North Carolina, teach her how to shoot, and make a good Republican out of her." There were nods of approval throughout the tent.

Such interludes notwithstanding, there was also wholesome talk about family and being good parents. "My wife's the boss in our house, I admit it. I don't take a big decision without talking it through with her," said Sgt. 1st Class Mike Salzwedel of Marshfield, Wisconsin, the 18 Charlie (demolition engineer), the most massive member of the team. "Despite all my talk," he went on, "I'm just a cuddly bear." Everyone agreed that the kind of father they all hated was the guy who showed up at his kid's sports game in a business suit and then loudly humiliated his son or daughter for not playing well. Because most of Operational Detachment Alpha 023—the bureaucratic designation for this particular A-team—were parents themselves, and had experienced real violence as part of their work, behind the profanities lay an innate maturity.

It was now 108 degrees in the tent, so hot that on the nearby volcanic slag heap the lava rocks were cracking, and we were sweating out through our pores the onions that we had just eaten in the Algerian army mess. "It's hot as balls," Chief D'Amelio wrote on the dry erase board. The Saharan wind came through the flaps like bad breath. Even though the Algerians had provided four tents for the SF hootch, the team wound up cramming all the cots and much of the equipment into one, so conversation—"jaw-jacking," as team members called it—never flagged. Nobody decided it, but moving the cots and equipment to spend three weeks in crowded proximity to one another, rather than enjoy a little more privacy and space in separate tents, was instantaneous, unconscious, and collective, every bit as much so as listening to CDs of Creedence Clearwater Revival, the favorite sixties band of the American military. For the team to split up, if only for sleeping, would have led to a decline in morale.

Because of their small size, SF A-teams were highly intimate affairs. Unlike the Navy, Marine Corps, and regular Army, SF guys called themselves by their first names, or just "dude." Like, "Hey, dude, where's my Copenhagen [chewing tobacco]?" Even Capt. Adorjan was addressed as "Mike" and Chief D'Amelio as "Orlando." (Unlike in the Marines or the surface and sub-surface navies, nobody here called me "sir.") This was mainly why nobody in SF wanted to admit women to their ranks. Objective reasons be damned, it would have meant separate sleeping quarters for team members, and consequently a threat to morale.* An SF team was one inextricable organism or it was nothing. If you had to be polite, if you had to watch your language, or in any way edit what you said while jaw-jacking, the warrior spirit would have suffered, it was believed.

"Once we get our ammo tomorrow we'll be happy," said the team sergeant, Master Sgt. Ken Butcher of Springfield, New Hampshire. Staff Sgt. Michael Hair of St. Paul, Minnesota, the 18 Bravo (weapons specialist), cut in derisively, "Any soldier who doesn't like to shoot all the time should leave the Army, and unfortunately there are a lot of those around." "Everyone in America should own at least five guns," someone else said. More nods.

Master Sgt. Butcher owned thirty-eight guns. Everyone agreed that whenever you read in the newspapers about a kid shooting someone with his father's gun, it was because the father kept the gun in a closet and told the kid never to touch it—which of course he would! Rather than a working gun, it served as a macho item that the father owned to show off to his friends. With one or two exceptions, these sergeants all owned working guns and had taught their sons and daughters gun safety. "My son is too young to shoot," Ken Butcher explained, "but whenever he hands me his plastic cap gun, he knows to disarm it first."

Ken Butcher had handled humanitarian and military emergencies in seventy-three countries in the course of seventeen years in the Army. Accepted to Dartmouth, he enlisted instead, and never regretted it. He never even wanted to go to Officer Candidate School at Fort Benning, Georgia. He had worked with anti-Saddam Kurds in northern Iraq. Then, for nearly a decade, he was all over the former Yugoslavia, interrogating local politicians and suspected war criminals, helping Romanian and Hungarian elements of the international security force, providing

---

* For an argument in favor of admitting women to Special Forces, see Chapter 6 of *Imperial Grunts*.

protection for visiting heads of state, and so forth. He was in Zaire in 1997 when it fell apart; in Liberia in 2004 when it, too, disintegrated. He was in Sierra Leone twice during mayhem there, and had tutored the cabinet of Azerbaijan in disaster management. He had called in a JDAM strike in Spinboldak in eastern Afghanistan in 2001, helped Armenia recover from an earthquake, and traveled on horseback and snowmobile through Canada's Northwest Territories, among a plethora of other assignments and experiences that would make Harrison Ford drool.* (Months later in Mali, I would mention Butcher's name to an SF buddy of his, who told me how Butcher had "MacGyvered" a solution to a frozen fuel line on a snowmobile using only a Leatherman.) This all was after guarding Pershing-II nuclear missiles in Germany in the last days of the Cold War. Butcher's musculature seemed slightly crushed in, on account of years of rucking and parachute jumps. Under short, dirty blond hair, he had a blunt, ground-down, rural New Hampshire way of speaking that recalled the poetry of Robert Frost. This was enhanced by a no-bullshit expression that at proper moments turned wistful, reminding me of tough and reserved kibbutzniks of yore. Butcher was happiest embracing the suck.

As our first evening in the desert drew near, a light breeze cut the heat down into the nineties. A game of beach volleyball commenced. Rather than the Americans playing the Algerians, again there came another collective, unconscious decision on both sides—in favor of mixed teams. Following the game, I took a hike to the top of an outcropping, and saw a sandy sea as stormy and endless as the Pacific. With me were Sgt. 1st Class Buck Wilford of Cleveland—the 18 Delta (team medic)—and Capt. Habib Akermi, the supply officer, who, like Maj. Brahim, came from Souk Ahras. The three of us were still strangers to one another, but that was to change. You became intimate by doing things with people, especially in an isolated setting like this one.

Buck Wilford, especially, turned out to be a real character. He was big, with a large-sized head that was always nodding and stamped with a smile, as though he were in a permanent state of laughter. Buckley

---

* JDAM: Joint Direct Attack Munition, a massive GPS-guided air-to-ground bomb.

Erie Arthur Roy Wilford, to give him his full name, had joined the Army to pay his way through Bible college. He had a tattoo of Jesus wearing the crown of thorns on his right shoulder, one of the Lion of Judah on his right thigh, and a Pentecostal cross on his left shin. He had been a street-corner preacher in Columbus, Georgia, when he was stationed at Fort Benning. He owned twenty-seven guns, and was an active Mason. Buck's church was the evangelical Assembly of God. But he warned me, "I'm not the man I was. I've fallen since." Yet having married, and given up drinking and dipping and cussing, he now had more money in the bank with a child at home than he had had when single. "Oh Lordy" was the worst language I ever heard him use. An Army Ranger before joining SF, Buck had been in the thick of the fighting in Mogadishu, Somalia, on October 3–4, 1993, when nineteen American soldiers were slain, a battle made famous by the book and movie *Black Hawk Down.* Yet he harbored no resentment toward the Somalis. Buck was just a good soul.

Capt. Habib Akermi, on the other hand, was as small and sinewy as Buck was big and fleshy. While Buck was quietly competent and easygoing, Akermi seemed as if he had something to prove. His hospitality could sometimes appear overbearing, in a particular Middle Eastern way. But he was also fast, nimble, indefatigable through the worst, hottest parts of the day, and frighteningly driven. I could imagine him in the army of the indigenous warlord Jugurtha, 2,100 years ago, fighting the Romans in the naked hilltops and savannahs of the Tunisian-Algerian borderland. His pride caused him to conceal his vulnerabilities, so he was almost impossible to imagine as a civilian. Buck didn't mind, though. He liked Akermi, just as he would like all the Algerians he came across—without knowing barely a word of Arabic. You could conquer the world peaceably with an army of Bucks, I thought.

A pattern of daily existence emerged, as we got used to hitting the shitters a hundred yards away from our tent in the sand that was infested with scorpions and camel spiders, washing our faces and clothes in sinks filled with moths and grasshoppers, sweating through the afternoons when the tent affected the aura of a tropical disease ward, and washing our own trays and eating utensils after every meal in the Algerian mess. Living exactly like the Algerians helped break down barriers.

————

Following a two-mile run and breakfast, the eleven A-team members laid out their toys for the host-country soldiers to inspect. The summer before in Niger the Marines had only M-16s and basic communications and medical equipment. That had formed one kind of bond with the troops of a backbreakingly poor country, who saw that you did not need fancy stuff to be good. But the Algerian military was more advanced than the one in Niger, and was looking for a stronger, deeper relationship with their American counterparts: an appetite that the morning display whetted.

There was the small and light M-4 assault rifle with a rail system that included the latest EOtech hologram sight and PEQ-2 infrared laser for calling in close air support at night. There was the ballistic eyewear, body armor, pistol rigs, CamelBaks (hydration backpacks), MBITRs (multi-band intra-team radios), various types of shotguns and machine guns, and enough medical equipment to do minor surgery, including partial amputations, intubations, tracheotomies, and gun debridements—all of which Buck Wilford and the team's other medic, Sgt. 1st Class Kevin Carlson, were experts at.*

Trouble was, it meant that each SF soldier had to carry fifty pounds of weapons and web gear, plus a rucksack that might weigh as much as ninety pounds. Whenever I'd ask an American soldier how much he carried, he'd always reply, "Too much." SOF equipment was getting to be like information technology: every year a new gadget was introduced that soldiers felt they couldn't do without. Yet to carry as much as they did made it impossible to fight efficiently.

The A-team was aware of the problem, which resulted in another jaw-jacking session. The Americans were struck by two things during the early days of the deployment: how little equipment the Algerians had compared to them, yet how good at soldiering they seemed to be. An Algerian soldier out on a counter-terrorist mission in these desert

---

* Sgt. 1st Class Carlson was born in Iowa and moved from place to place growing up in Illinois, as his father, an engineer, kept getting better and better jobs.

borderlands might carry only a Russian-designed AK-47, water, and some food—usually dates. He would be neither protected by body armor nor slowed down by it. In any case, in this heat body armor made a soldier on the move virtually worthless. The first few days here, the hulking SF troops, who could drop a bad guy at several hundred yards, were somewhat intimidated by the 120-pound Algerians in dark camouflage and bush hats, who could run up and down hills in the middle of the day, turn somersaults with their guns in the sand, jump through burning tires, throw knives expertly, and, most importantly, did not need to drink nearly as much water in the desert as the Americans did, dependent as the Americans had become on their CamelBaks. Maj. Brahim and Capt. Akermi noticed this weakness on the part of their guests immediately.

The Algerians, who had fought a full-fledged counterinsurgency war throughout the 1990s, clearly were a different class of third-world army than any I had experienced while traveling with SF and the Marines. The first full training day the Algerians were unflagging. It became a test of wills as to which side would cry uncle first in the shadeless heat and dust. Finally, after eight straight hours in hundred-degree-plus heat, the two armies began the police call: picking up the brass cartridges that signaled the end of range work. Everyone was smoked.

"Holy sheep shit, Batman. Jesus Christ, it's hot," said one American to another, when the thermometer hit 110. But this came more in the way of joking than complaining. Said Mike Hair, the weapons specialist: "It could be worse, we could be training with some other African armies. The Algerians are motivated. They're full of ambition. They keep getting at the back of the line to shoot again and again."

Part of what had lured me here was the advanced nature of the training, compared to the simple skills taught by the Marines in Niger. Yet the first day was basic rifle and pistol work. Trying out the American M-4s with the rail systems, the Algerians were impressed by their lightness and precision, and their night-fighting capabilities. But the M-4 was difficult to maintain compared to their own AK-47, which was a simpler, more forgiving instrument, and worked even if you dropped it in the mud. Again, the American way was to seek a technical solution to every challenge, even as the Algerians demonstrated that victory in the desert in the early twenty-first century could also mean fighting with less on your back and unique cultural skills in your head.

Cameras were everywhere that first day and all the ones following, as individual Algerian soldiers took Polaroid photos to show off to friends and family how each had trained with the Americans. There were also military cameramen documenting the mission for the Algerian Army.

The next day the training lasted even longer, as one ammo case after another—each containing eight hundred pounds of "whoop-ass" (7.62mm rounds)—was used up in firing the Americans' 240-Bravo Belgian-manufactured medium machine guns. The Algerians, who were short on ammunition, appreciated the unlimited quantities provided by SF. It was already 3 p.m. when the Americans demonstrated transitioning: shooting with an M-4 rifle and then a 9mm Beretta in one fluid movement. The Algerians preferred the Italian-made Beretta (which held fifteen rounds) to their own Russian Makarov, which held only ten.

"The way you're firing, you'll hit only two things, jack and shit," one Green Beret remonstrated an Algerian. But later on, impressed with the Algerian's improvement, he said, "You turned that steel target into lingerie." And after using one of the Algerians' Russian-made Draganov sniper rifles, this Green Beret provided the ultimate compliment: "When I get back home to the South, I'm going to buy me one of them."

When we returned to the camp before sunset, the sky was the color of salt from the heat. By then each of us had consumed four large bottles of mineral water since breakfast, almost without having to urinate. At night, after washing my clothes and eating dinner in the Algerian mess—and observing the Green Berets stomp around in the powdery dust and close air of the tent, preparing to clean their weapons—I was gripped once again by the grim, poverty-stricken world of the American soldier. Buck Wilford, whose cot was the second over from my own, had just found a large scorpion at his feet. This was after a brief but ferocious sandstorm, succeeded by gucky rain. Oily guns and smelly socks and underwear lay all around, mixed with electric cables and communications gear. The only luxury we had was the locally made soda sold at the Algerian PX, which we all shared out of the same large bottles since we lacked cups.

The saving grace in all of this continued to be the company: simple, uproariously funny noncommissioned officers, who could not be calculating and selfish if they tried. Buck Wilford never stopped smiling even after discovering that scorpion. If you didn't like Buck, it was you who had the problem. It was nearly the same with other members of the team. Yet why would anyone with the possibility of a reasonably high income and good chances in life want to have anything to do with such an existence? Here and there, reporting on the Army and on the Marines, I had met people from prosperous, upper-middle-class families, and from prestigious schools. But their numbers were too small to constitute a trend.

Noncommissioned officers—the sergeants of the Army and the Marine Corps, the chief petty officers of the Navy—were sort of like writers. Because they loved what they did so intensely, career advancement was not their most important priority. This made them at times naïve about the competitive world outside their own domain. Here was one member of the team, a former marine who had worked as an embassy guard: "State Department people pretend to like each other, even while they're stabbing each other in the back. They take quiet pleasure in watching one of their own fall. I want no part of that."

The most well-educated, well-traveled, and linguistically adroit noncoms were precisely the ones most critical of the diplomatic and relief aid establishments. After all, they knew much of what the diplomats and NGOs knew, occasionally more. But because of their hardscrabble backgrounds and military experience, they just interpreted reality differently. Rather than a disadvantage, the hands-on circumstances of their own upbringings helped break down barriers with host-country nationals. Mike Adorjan, Ken Butcher, Mike Salzwedel, and Kevin Carlson had all grown up in a vanishing rural America. Butcher had raised oxen in New Hampshire as a boy, and worked as a logger. Salzwedel had worked on a succession of pig farms in Wisconsin. Carlson's family had only sixty-three acres to raise corn and soybeans in Iowa. This was an economically tenuous existence not that far removed from the men of the Algerian Special Forces company. Over lamb couscous one day with Master Sgt. Butcher, Maj. Brahim noted a truth familiar to classicists: "The best soldiers have been farmers."

Army Special Forces still depended upon a backbone of rugged individualists who constituted the last remnants of the continental frontier in North America, the type historically associated with agriculture, exploration, and soldiering. But as America's urbanization, subsequent suburbanization, and finally ex-urbanization proceeded apace, I questioned whether the warrior spirit of these elite units could survive. While Special Forces needed to evolve, with more racial variety and women—for the sake of operating unconventionally in a more coffee brown–mestizo world—that was not necessarily an argument for a weakening of its aggressive mindset.*

One long day rolled into another. On day three, the two countries' special forces units spent eight hours firing RPGs (rocket-propelled grenades), LAWs (66mm light anti-tank weapons), AT-4s (84mm anti-tank weapons), and M-2HB .50-caliber heavy machine guns. The Algerians insisted on teaching the Americans how to use their own Russian-made RPGs, and the Americans, who already knew how to use them, pretended to learn. Just as diplomats regularly practiced diplomacy by means other than negotiations, so did SF.

The barrels of the .50-caliber heavy machine guns became so hot from firing that they had to be separated from the rest of the firing apparatus and put in the shade to cool off, a process that took hours in the 110-degree heat. My open palms registered the intense heat of the barrels three inches away. Touching them was like touching a flame, so they could be handled only with heavy gloves. It made several members of the team bring up the consequences that would have befallen the American military had Operation Iraqi Freedom been delayed a few more weeks, from spring to early summer 2003, when the temperatures in the Mesopotamian desert would have been comparable to the Sahara.

"The diplomats at the U.N. don't know or care about small things like gun barrels," said Staff Sgt. James Lewis, who in addition to handling the communications was one of the team's two snipers.† "Yet they complain whenever American troops don't perform perfectly."

---

* See Chapter 6 of *Imperial Grunts* for a more detailed discussion of how Special Forces needed to evolve.
† The other sniper was Mike Salzwedel.

On day four, the Algerians did have a lot to teach the Americans: about booby traps used by their own domestic terrorists; jerry-rigged anti-personnel mines set off by syringes in the road; and bombs concealed in coffee thermoses, gas containers, and Korans even. "The very people blaming us for mistreating the Koran think nothing of making booby traps out of them," Buck Wilford remarked. For their part, the Americans demonstrated how to make a bomb out of white, taffy-like C-4 plastic explosive. It turned out to be as easy as hanging a picture or making scrambled eggs.

The subject of Guantánamo Bay ("Gitmo") and the alleged abuses of prisoners there by the U.S. military, including the desecration of prisoners' Korans, would not go away. "Shouldn't it be taken into account," implored James Lewis, during another bout of jaw-jacking, "that we're allowing these prisoners to pray five times a day, and providing them food that is not contrary to their religion? Shouldn't it be regularly reported how much worse they would be treated in their own countries?"

Lewis had enlisted in 1993, at the age of nineteen, burdened by mounting bills despite holding down four part-time jobs. His father and uncle had each spent a lifetime in the Navy. His way of being an individual was to join the Army. He appreciated the discipline it enforced on him, as well as the fact that he could now pay his bills. Because he did not want to mark time, he volunteered for Special Forces. The truth was that in his late twenties he had suddenly become ambitious after becoming aware of his own ignorance. "I realized that I could be influenced by a lot of things other than just the people around me." Thus he began to read, and read more—about history and politics. What he had learned, he told me one night when the heat in the tent made it impossible to sleep, even as some of the other team members were "cutting logs" (snoring), was that while he himself had lived a narrow-minded existence growing up working-class in Rhode Island, so did a lot of higher income people who, at least in his mind, saw the world as a playground for their comfortable views. He said that when he left Special Forces, it wasn't a commendation or a plaque he wanted, just an official Green Beret Yarborough knife.*

---

* The 12.5-inch combat utility knife was named after Lt. Gen. William P. Yarborough.

At 5 a.m. one day during the second week of training we awoke to a sandstorm. Even after sunup, the sky was like a death shroud, grimmer than the blackest part of the night. A convoy of American and Algerian special forces drove out to a rocky field in the desert that sloped down into a coarse, sandy bottomland studded with pine copses—indication of a nearby underground water source.

"Bad weather like this is great for fighting," Maj. Brahim told Capt. Adorjan and Master Sgt. Butcher. Brahim related how in 1994, south of Algiers, his platoon had killed fifteen terrorists whose hideout was lightly guarded because they never expected an assault in fog and rain.

We surveyed the sandy area before the Algerians and the Americans took turns assaulting an imaginary terrorist hideout in one of the pine copses. The imaginary hideout was typical of real ones in Algeria: the places for cooking, ammunition storage, and headquarters command were all separated, so that the smell of food would not necessarily give away the exact location of the terrorists; nor would the fall of one area in the compound necessarily mean that of the others. Brahim said that the smaller the number of the assault team the better; the more personnel you used in an attack, the less control you had as a commander, for this was not a war between two armies.

From then on opinions diverged. The Algerians were going to assault the compound in single "Indian file," the lead man armed with a portable minesweeper. The Americans favored a lateral sweep with each man responsible for watching out for mines. "After contact [the first shot], you spread out anyway, so you might as well start wide apart," Ken Butcher told the Algerians. Still, he wasn't dogmatic about it. "Tactics are like assholes," he remarked. "Everybody has one."

Using blank bullets, the Algerians commenced their attack. It looked like something out of a Hollywood movie, with men firing all around. It was confusing to follow. The Americans were not impressed. "I would not feel safe fighting with those guys," Buck confided. "Guys in the rear were firing in the same direction as their teammates in front of them. There was no way they could have avoided friendly fire with real bullets." He explained that the Americans, upon contact, employed the buddy system: two-man teams advanced and dove on the ground in sequence, with only the guy in front firing.* But Capt. Adorjan, the diplomat, congratulated the Algerians on a "great performance" as they lined up in formation after the mock raid. Then one of the Algerian soldiers let out an AD, or "accidental discharge," on full automatic, with several bullets blasting into the ground. He had not put his AK-47 back on safe. Even with blanks, in the U.S. military that would have led to a judicial proceeding. Not here.

Fundamentally, it was the same problem that I had noticed with other third-world militaries: weak noncoms who never offered advice up the chain of command to their officers, so the officers had to manage everything and every man, and thus did so badly. Meanwhile, the same officers were loath to admit mistakes. You needed squad and platoon leaders—sergeants and staff sergeants—to discipline corporals and privates, not captains and majors to do it. The more decentralized the nature of command, the better a unit performed.

"How should you guys look during your assault?" I asked Buck's buddy, Staff Sgt. Tim Haines of Placerville, California, an 18 Charlie (engineer). He was a huge, dark-complexioned twenty-five-year-old who had played junior college football in Nebraska. "We should look simple, boring," Haines replied. "That Hollywood crap doesn't work."

Chief D'Amelio gave the brief before the Americans' attack. "We'll be using live bullets, not blanks," he said. "The emphasis will be on accuracy of fire: one shot, one kill."

The American A-team separated into two "splits" of several men each. One hid in a pine cluster while the other moved out along a dried riverbed to flank the imaginary hideout where targets had been set up. This second split stopped at the LCC (last place of cover and concealment). Suddenly a barrage of fire erupted, including that of a 240-Bravo medium machine gun. Unlike the Algerian attack, where there was a lot of confusing movement and sporadic fire, now there was an intense explosion of firing and nothing to see, since the second split had completely concealed itself.

Now the first split, which hadn't moved since the beginning of the

---

* It was the same principle when fighting from Humvees. The fire would come from a stationary Humvee while another advanced.

exercise, suddenly swept around behind the imaginary hideout, executing IMTs (individual movement tactics)—that is, buddy teams advancing in tandem so that despite the live fire, no one accidentally got hit. It
was easy to follow, with not much to see, dull and efficient as Tim
Haines had predicted. When the targets were pulled out of the hideout,
they were completely shredded with bullets like "lingerie." The fire had
been that accurate.

The Algerians were stunned into silence. For the first time since the
JCET had commenced over a week ago, they realized just how good
this SF team was, and how much they themselves had to learn, despite
the fact that they were better acclimated to the harsh landscape. It
wasn't a bad performance for a bunch of clowns who, while adjusting
their web and communications gear prior to the assault, were carrying
on about the cartoon series *South Park,* and such inane comedies as
Team America and *Office Space.*

A few days later, the Algerians performed more impressively, as
they demonstrated with live fire how to react to an ambush. Indeed, it
was something that occurred several times a day in Algeria during the
1990s. One moment a convoy of several vehicles would be moving un-
exceptionally along a road; the next moment there would be a series of
explosions, with smoke everywhere. A barrage of fire would ensue seconds after that. After another forty-five seconds, it would be as though
the gun battle had been raging for an hour.

The A-team followed up with a "down driver drill," in which the
driver of a lead vehicle was "killed" after the detonation of an improvised explosive device. Another soldier took his place and led the convoy out of the kill zone, while engaging the enemy ambush from a
steadily lengthening distance. Again, because the Americans boasted
better equipment and more accurate fire, their response to the ambush
was less kinetic and visually less spectacular than that of the Algerians,
yet more effective. Rather than leave their vehicles and dive into a defilade position like the host-country troops, they remained inside their
up-armored Humvees and nailed the ambushers with medium machine
gun fire, even as they used smoke grenades to conceal their movements
while withdrawing. If they had to leave the vehicles, as they did in a
follow-up drill, they took the medium machine guns with them. Be-

cause the .50-caliber heavy machine gun could not be transported by one man, it was one team member's job to remove the trigger mechanism from it so that it couldn't be used by the ambushers if they captured the Humvee. All this was standard operating procedures. The Algerians had their breath taken away.

As the Algerians and the Americans complimented each other in exercise after exercise, and played more volleyball as well as dominoes together, the relationship strengthened. The Americans rode camels. Some had their hair cut by an Algerian barber. They ate Algerian MREs, better than U.S. ones, as they were essentially French with tins of tuna and fondue instead of oversalted meats. One day we all walked around Tamanrasset, bargaining for Tuareg trinkets, then eating couscous at a local restaurant that was decorated with native rugs, swords, beaten brass, and a large reproduction of the *Mona Lisa*. "And I thought the real *Mona Lisa* was in Paris. Who would have known it was here all along?" Buck joked, with his trademark broad smile.

I saw that the ratty cafés in town were never more than a quarter filled. Tuaregs and shady characters in cheap Western dress sat around with sullen expressions and thousand-yard stares, listening to scratchy music. It was like one big bus station. An ashen veil of dust robbed the streets of color. If you were a traveler who had just arrived from the desert, you might luxuriate in the small air-conditioned supermarkets filled with fresh cheeses, fruit juices, and ice cream. Otherwise, Tamanrasset was a mournful place at the edge of nowhere.

In the afternoon we drove with the Algerians in a convoy of Land Cruisers deep into the Hoggar, through towering curtains of basalt, shale, and limestone, and along prehistoric riverbeds where we encountered Tuaregs with their camels, busy baking bread in holes beneath the sand. The majestic back-of-beyond peaks brought to mind Father Charles de Foucauld, the ultimate imperialist: French soldier, missionary, linguist, and eccentric.

A modern Saint Augustine, "Père Foucauld" was half mad with visions of evangelizing the whole of Saharan Africa, so as to reverse the Islamic conquest that had come in the wake of Augustine's death. Chronologically he was a man of the late nineteenth and early twentieth centuries; spiritually he was closer to the fourth-century Byzantine monks of the Egyptian Thebaid, like Saint Anthony. Born in Strasbourg in 1858, Foucauld studied under the Jesuits at Nancy and Paris before attending the Saint-Cyr Military Academy. His first experience of the Maghreb was at Sétif, in Algeria, where he was sent as a young officer in 1880. Discharged for indiscipline, he was reinstated in the French Army to help against a native revolt south of Oran near the Moroccan border. There, he became infatuated with the Arabs. He resigned his commission and moved to Algiers to study Arabic and Hebrew, before traveling throughout Morocco as well as through southern Algeria and Tunisia. Back in Paris, writing up an account of his travels, he slept on a native carpet wrapped in a North African burnoose. Later he would live the ascetic life of a solitary monk: first on the Moroccan-Algerian border, where he dreamed of Christianizing Morocco; and finally in Tamanrasset, where he arrived in 1905 and lived at first in a *zeriba* (reed hut). After moving into a mud house, he devoted all of his time to prayer and writing a lexicon and grammar for Tamachek, the language of the Tuaregs. In 1916 he was killed by Tuaregs who had come under the influence of invading Senussi tribesmen from Libya. His was the imperial experience taken to its logical extreme, in which a solitary individual cast away all personal ties to his homeland and withdrew into a remote and hostile landscape—an act of nihilism almost—while attempting to remake this same hostile landscape into a moral likeness of what he had left behind. Imperialism could be a form of escape.

That evening in the tent, Buck and Orlando decked themselves out in Tuareg headdresses and Saharan tunics that they had purchased in Tamanrasset, waxing enthusiastic about how well they were being treated. The following night, the Algerians translated two French- and Arabic-language movies for the Americans, *The Stick and the Opium* and *The Battle of Algiers,* about the rural and urban aspects of the independence struggle against the French. Among the last black-and-white films of the 1960s, they were much less graphic than the films of today; for that reason their effect was more powerful. They captured in extraordinary vividness the existential hatred between the French settlers and the Arab inhabitants of Algeria. Painting the French as the bad guys went over well with the SF team.

In the context of *The Battle of Algiers,* a pretty young Arab woman calmly placing a bomb in a crowded discothèque filled with French teenagers seemed perfectly normal; the same when a crowd of French adults beat unconscious a little Arab boy who they assumed had planted another bomb. What struck me about both movies was how much Algeria had changed since both films were made. The carnage and hatred of the 1950s and 1960s had given rise to a quarter century of dysfunctional, radical regimes that ruined the country's economy—to say nothing of its social peace—so all the population now cared about was security and material improvements. "The young people don't want to hear old men talk about the great struggle anymore," one Algerian soldier told me, "they just want a better life." In part, it was such mundane desires that were forcing the government into a closer relationship with the Americans.

Capt. Akermi saw little irony in pointing out to me the similarities between the tactical situation that the French had faced against Algerian freedom fighters in the 1950s and the one faced by the Algerian Army against Islamic terrorists in the 1990s. In each instance, he confided during the screening, the challenge was to pin down guerrillas who had indigenous inhabitants on their side. Another Algerian officer told me that it had taken a month to clear a village of booby traps, with local women eerily warbling in the streets against the government army, just as they had done against the French over three decades earlier.

———

At the beginning of the third and last week of training, a south wind arrived that blew sand for several days straight. The sky was a gaseous, daguerreotype yellow, like the atmosphere of a distant planet in a science fiction movie. Dust was everywhere, yet despite the constant wind the heat did not abate. But with limited time left, the training continued.

A tape drill for military operations in urban terrain (MOUT) provided another example of the differing mentalities of the two armies.* The American way of entering a hostile room was counterintuitive and methodical: several soldiers assumed interlocking sectors of fire while seeking points of domination, even as they ignored someone standing directly in front of them, since the person you saw was not the problem,

---

* Lines of tape were spread over a flat surface to simulate partitions in a building.

it's the person you didn't see who would kill you. The Algerians were more impulsive, going for the first person they saw. They were obsessed with booby traps and suicide bombers in terrorist-occupied buildings, because that had been their experience in the 1990s. As they told us, their terrorists rarely stood and fought, but fled on contact and set traps instead.

Yet the Americans demonstrated their way, and the Algerians were impressed. Burly and red-haired Mike Salzwedel, the farm boy from Wisconsin, told them, "Once you're in the building you have to be methodical, you can't be terrified of bombs. That's why you and we are special forces."

The debate about tactics continued after the morning training. Adorjan, Butcher, Brahim, Akermi, and a few other Americans and Algerians stood around, underneath their two countries' flags, exchanging stories and ideas. Butcher told about how in Sarajevo he had learned never to stop his vehicle wherever it looked as if the road had recently been repaired—a telltale sign of a bomb. Adorjan explained how to plant minefields and lay obstacles to turn the enemy in the direction you wanted him to go. Brahim mentioned that the first thing you did when you found out that terrorists were in a building was to cut off the electricity, which terrorists used to set off bombs. An Algerian captain with much combat experience in the 1990s remarked that tunnels were a popular escape method for local terrorists. Everyone agreed that perfection was the enemy of good enough. Said Adorjan: "A plan that is 70 percent complete today is better than one that is 98 percent complete tomorrow, because the sergeants can use the extra day to rehearse. It is only through rehearsal that nitty-gritty problems are exposed." Nods all around. Capt. Akermi added: "If you win, it is always because of firepower. If you lose, it is always because of comms [failure to communicate]."

The discussion continued for an hour in the midst of the sandstorm. There was never enough of a break in the conversation for someone to suggest moving inside. Officers and senior noncoms on both sides were that comfortable with one another.

A field training exercise was the culmination of the JCET. It entailed a more complex assault on a make-believe terrorist hideout than the one ten days before. Both the reconnaissance and assault teams would be composed of Algerians with a sprinkle of Americans. The Algerians would plan the operation. A few days earlier, Maj. Brahim had taken the A-team to the exercise site thirty-five miles north of the hootch, pointing out the hills from where his forces would stage the assault. The Americans would have done it differently, they told me.

As I knew from my own experience in southern Afghanistan, you would never have had the luxury of taking an entire assault team ahead of time to the site of an attack. Instead, you would have rehearsed and rehearsed at your own base, even as you sent out a two- or three-man sniper team to hide for forty-eight hours close to the actual site. The snipers would be armed with telephoto lenses, and would have the ability to electronically send photos of the site and surrounding terrain back to the A-team. They would also be able to call in air strikes, if necessary, before the main assault. But the Algerians did not have such technological assets, nor such faith in two or three individuals. Their way, rather than wrong, was simply a reflection of their own strengths and weaknesses. For example, in order to guard against an ambush with hills on both sides of a road, the Americans employed a "bounding overwatch," pulling a vehicle off to a side to provide cover for the others. But the Algerians couldn't do that, because it slowed down a convoy, and they had thousands of miles of desert to patrol, with such hills everywhere.

I stuck with Ken Butcher, who was part of the exercise's reconnaissance element. We arrived at the assault site as dawn was breaking. With the Algerians there was noise, confusion, and a lot of milling around. "They should have been inserted silently in the middle of the night," Butcher confided. "When these things go right, they happen fast. You un-ass the vehicles, hit the high ground, and set in." Worse, the helicopter bearing the actual assault squad landed too far up the valley, and the overwhelmingly Algerian squad made too much noise in the process of advancing toward the objective. There were also three accidental discharges.

"What the hell is going on down there? It looks like a cluster fuck," Butcher said over the intra-team radio. As I climbed down the hill at the conclusion of the disappointing exercise, I spotted the battalion commander of the 1st of the 10th, Lt. Col. Scott Eaddy of Knoxville, Tennessee. He had flown in the night before from Mali, by way of Algiers. The A-team gathered around the tall lieutenant colonel with the clean tan uniform (unlike everyone else's) as he listened to their complaints. But then he had to listen even longer about the things that had gone right over the past three weeks:

The Algerian troops are motivated as hell. They've ended their one-handed Hollywood-style shooting with their Makarovs and are correcting themselves on the two-handed style. They now know how to take cover without being told to. Yeah, for some of their officers everything's a dick-measuring contest, but others are like sponges. They just want to learn, and absorb the information we give them. They take their commitments seriously, unlike other places we've been. Whether it's food, clean water, shitters, personal security, we've never had to ask for anything. The host-nation troops are in incredible physical condition. They've taught us about booby traps and desert survival. We'd come back here in a minute.

Of course, the biggest problem (that led to all the others) was the noncoms who did not make decisions. And Algeria had it in spades, a consequence of authoritarian Arab culture made worse by Soviet influence. Because officers did not delegate, nothing happened until the last minute, thus constant delays and confusion, like this morning.

But as this was a familiar headache to 10th Group Green Berets—from past experience training Albanians, Romanians, and other ex-communist armies—they weren't particularly bothered by it. They knew, for example, that producing a proud noncommissioned officers' corps took many years and lots of money—years to train competent staff and first sergeants to run platoons and companies; money for the benefits that good noncoms required for their families. Thus, the bitching (like Ken Butcher's remark about the "cluster fuck") was just something the guys did all the time. I would be suspicious of any SF A-team (or Marine platoon for that matter) if I had walked into its hootch at night and did not hear a flamboyantly vulgar litany of complaints.

That evening over *chai* and Pepsi, Lt. Col. Eaddy and Capt. Adorjan met with several of the Algerian officers and visiting higher-ups about more and bigger JCETs in the near future. There was a suggestion from one Algerian general about joint American-Algerian operations against Salafists in the Sahara. The Americans did not need to remain focused on training exclusively in Algeria's border areas like Tamanrasset, where every bad guy in the vicinity soon knew about their presence. Rather, they could be housed in permanent army bases like the one farther north in Biskra, the home of Maj. Brahim's 41st Special Forces Company, from where helicopters could transport both them and the Algerians on joint missions close to Mali and Mauritania. "The great benefit of this country," one American soldier observed, was the state-controlled media, which would allow such operations to remain low-key, if not altogether secret.

Later, over in the A-team's tent, the noncoms condemned "the dicks" in the U.S. Air Force who still hadn't made arrangements for their flight home. "I wouldn't say they're totally worthless . . . ," said one team member, "but their planes always seem to develop mechanical difficulty when the crews are over a nice spot like the Canary Islands." The conversation turned to "the generals and other fuckheads in Mother Army," who cared more about whether SF troops were wearing nonregulation ball caps than about what SF was accomplishing in the field.

"They told us to always wear name and rank on our DCUs [desert camouflage uniforms] down here," said one team member, his anger and sarcasm building. "So what happens when they open the hatch of the C-17 on the tarmac at Tamanrasset? The Algerian military has its cameras rolling. Who's to say Al-Jazeera doesn't have our names and faces matched up by now?" To SF, Al-Jazeera journalists were synonymous with international terrorists. "But Mother Army doesn't care about that," he continued, "as long as in the photos we're not wearing ball caps."*

It was a good JCET, in other words. The grumbling of the noncoms was directed at their own higher-ups, not at the host-country troops.

---

* There was another side to this argument, provided to me by an Army sergeant major some months later in another theater. The Army was about structure and discipline, he explained, not self-expression. If Green Berets had to grow beards and wear *pakols* to ease their relationships with Afghans, or if civil affairs officers at a Kenyan beach resort had to grow their hair long to look more like tourists and NGOs, that was accepted and encouraged even. But wearing ball caps served no practical purpose in terms of a mission.

SIX

THE GURKHA STANDARD

Nepal, Summer 2005

The defining truism of realism from Thucydides onward has been that liberty is impossible without authority—something often conferred by uniformed men with guns. Take Algeria, where political and economic freedom was beginning to sprout, but only on the heels of a military defeat of Islamic insurgents. Likewise in Nepal, where a military defeat of a Marxist-styled Maoist guerrilla movement was, by itself, certainly not the solution to the anarchy in the Nepalese countryside; yet, at the same time, no solution was ultimately possible without at least some sort of setback for the Maoists on the battlefield. Nepal was not far removed from other places where I had seen the American military grapple with a country that was not a country.

Here was a place on the brink of collapse, even as its 27.7 million people were squeezed between the two rising economic and demographic behemoths of the age, China and India. Nepal had been a buffer territory of the British Empire much like Afghanistan, left backward and isolated, while India, which Afghanistan and Nepal had been fated to protect, reaped the rewards of colonial development. The monarchy had been the glue holding together Nepal's dozen ethnic groups, with their forty-eight languages and dialects. But this Hindu monarchy, which had ruled the country for over two hundred years, had been undermined when, in 2001, a mentally unstable crown prince, distraught at not being allowed to marry his beloved, killed nine members of the royal dynasty before he himself committed suicide. Then there was the country's political parties, bases for feudal politicians unable to rise above tribal and caste loyalties. Like the Scottish Highlands as described by Samuel Johnson in 1775, "To this general distemper . . . was added the peculiar form of the country, broken by mountains into many subdivisions scarcely accessible but to the natives, and guarded by passes, or perplexed with intricacies, through which national justice could not find its way."[1]

This depressing state of affairs was abetted by the Maoist rebellion, ignited in the mid-1990s in the heavily forested mountains of western Nepal. The upshot of fifty years of communist influence in the region, it was triggered by an earlier ban on hashish, the main cash crop for farmers.* The Maoist revolt had led to the deaths of many thousands. It reached a peak in the period between 2001 and 2003, before surging upward once again just prior to my arrival.

Some of the killings had been especially gruesome. Called "mutilation atrocities," they featured breaking most of the victim's bones, followed by gouging out his eyes, cutting off his tongue, ears, and nose, sawing him in half, and finally burning the remains. Nothing in Nepalese history or culture accounted for such barbarism, which was always inflicted by a small number of young Maoist men and women on a single victim.[2] The remoteness of the terrain, the Maoists' lack of a real governing apparatus, and the fact that their ranks were filled with unsocialized youth from the lowest castes brainwashed by elderly ideologues brought to mind elements of the Cambodian Khmer Rouge, the Filipino Abu Sayyaf, the Peruvian Shining Path, and the Colombian narco-terrorists.

The Nepalese government no longer controlled the countryside, where 85 percent of the population lived. The police barely functioned

---

* See, among other articles, Pankaj Mishra, "A Nation Out of Time," *The New York Times,* June 10, 2001; and Stanley A. Weiss, "China and India Face Off in Nepal," *International Herald Tribune,* July 21, 2001. Among the best studies of the Maoist revolt is Robert Gersony, "Sowing the Wind: History and Dynamics of the Maoist Revolt in Nepal's Rapti Hills," submitted to Mercy Corps International in 2003.

beyond the capital of Kathmandu. Nepal had never constituted a coherent bureaucratic state. Colonialism, however derided, often bequeathed a strong bureaucratic tradition. Thus, it was no accident that Nepal, Afghanistan, and Yemen—all beset by various levels of anarchy—had never truly been colonized.

No political resolution to the crisis was possible without Indian acceptance. On the one hand, the authorities in New Delhi were nervous about an insurgency that threatened to evolve into another Kashmir on their weakly policed northern border, especially as the bulk of Nepal's population lived in the lowlands beside India. Could, for example, Bihar, India's poorest and most chaotic state, absorb large numbers of refugees from a collapsed Nepal next door? On the other hand, the Indians were not averse to a weak and henceforth dependent Nepal. Moreover, there were congeries of leftist groups within the byzantine Indian party system that sympathized with the Maoists, whom, because of the porous border, they were in a position to assist.*

The Chinese strategy was quiet patience, in the hope that, as in the case of Uzbekistan, human rights violations would make it increasingly harder for Western democracies to help Nepal militarily. That would allow Beijing to move in, sell arms, and gain influence without regard to their new client state's moral improvement.

The Chinese bet was a good one. Days before my arrival, the Bush administration had canceled an Army Special Forces training mission to Nepal—of the kind that I had observed in Algeria—because of the king Gyanendra Bir Bikram Shah's failure to move quickly in reinstituting democracy, something that in nuts-and-bolts terms meant returning power to the same political parties representing feudal castes and Indian moneymen that had brought the country to its knees in the 1990s. Of course, it would be hard to exaggerate just how inept and autocratic the king's rule was. But it was also possible that had he not grabbed power away from the party system in 2002, the state might have already collapsed.

The situation bore resemblance to El Salvador twenty years before,

---

* Experts also assumed that the Maoists were receiving aid from the Tamil Tigers of Sri Lanka.

where murderous right-wing forces that, nevertheless, represented a legitimate state were pitted against murderous left-wing ones that represented the geopolitical ambitions of the Soviet Union and Cuba. While the media of the day tended to record the atrocities of one side, the U.S. government's only choice was to try to work with the other.

Alas, Nepal was another poor country fighting a dirty struggle against an enemy that did not play by the rules. The Royal Nepalese Army (RNA) had no previous experience in fighting a war, let alone a counterinsurgency. Its human rights violations were considerable, including many unaccounted-for disappearances. Still, it had a human rights lawyer in many divisions and a colonel under house arrest, as well as several majors under investigation, for alleged human rights abuses. But because it had at least some transparent bureaucratic structure that could be held accountable, the Royal Nepalese Army was an easy target for the United Nations and various human rights groups.

It was the same old story. Because the U.S. military had to operate in a world of power, to be effective it occasionally had to appear as the bad guy.

—

Army Maj. Larry Smith of Savannah, Illinois, whom I had met at the Command and General Staff College at Fort Leavenworth, Kansas, had lured me to Nepal—something that was easy to do given the country's fascinating situation. When I had encountered Larry at Fort Leavenworth he wore a uniform; when I saw him again in Kathmandu he had on jeans, cowboy boots, and a flowing white *kurta*—an outfit he called "Texan-Hindustani"—and was surrounded by an extensive home library that included many Hindi, Tamil, and Urdu grammars.

Larry smoked a lot of cigarettes. He had grown up on a family farm in Illinois along the Mississippi River, near Ulysses S. Grant's hometown of Galena. At sixteen, he spent a year as an exchange student in western Germany and learned German fluently. Now forty, he had been married for twenty-two years to a beautiful New Delhi–born Indian woman whom he had met at Highland Community College in Freeport, Illinois. They had a twelve-year-old daughter and a twenty-one-year-old son. The son was also in the Army, about to enter the Special Forces Qualification (Q) Course at Fort Bragg, North Carolina.

After community college, Larry enrolled at Rockford College, near where he grew up. In October 1983, after hearing about the suicide bombing of the Marine barracks in Beirut, as he told me, "I got up and walked out of a class on French literature, went straight to the local recruiter's office, and joined the Army as a buck private. I have nothing against French literature. But at the time, it didn't mean much to me."

Over the next five years, while working as a military policeman in Alabama and Germany, he rose to sergeant. Then he enrolled in the ROTC program at Illinois State University in Normal, graduating as a second lieutenant. Tours at Fort Bliss, Texas; Fort Lewis, Washington; Fort Polk, Louisiana; and Fort Carson, Colorado, followed in succession, as he rose to the command of a military intelligence company. Next, he decided he wanted to be a foreign area officer for the Indian subcontinent. That led to a year of studying Hindi at the Foreign Service Institute in Arlington, Virginia, and a year of graduate school in subcontinental Asian studies at the University of Texas at Austin.

From Texas, Larry and his wife moved to southern India, where he spent a year at an Indian Army staff college. His impressions of it were mixed. Despite the extensive battlefield experience of his fellow students in Kashmir and along the Indian-Pakistani border, the Indian military, in his opinion, put "tremendous emphasis on form over substance, with an unwillingness to self-critique." After-action reviews of the 1962 Indian-Chinese border war were still classified, and Indian generals expressed criticisms of military tactics and policy only in the most oblique terms, making for an academic straitjacket. There was, too, the usual problem of a third-world army—weak noncommissioned officers "who were essentially privates with seniority." At Indian Army messes, enlisted men served tea to the officers. Larry, an officer who had once been a noncom, remarked that if he were still enlisted and an officer ordered him to bring tea, he'd spit in the cup. He said, "You want real democracy in a country like Nepal? Then empower the NCOs in the Royal Nepalese Army. That's where democracy starts."

Larry's was a typical Army résumé: years and years of training before the job even commenced. He was just starting to feel his way around Kathmandu when I arrived.

I found Kathmandu a ragged, jungly, hilly confection of moldering walls set amidst stage-prop bluish mountains, which in August were half swallowed by monsoon clouds that had the look and texture of dirty sponges. As crowded and polluted with motorbikes, automobiles, and rickshaws as it was, Kathmandu never quite gave up the atmosphere of a small town that had simply grown too big. Durbar Square, notwithstanding its rambling clutter of Hindu and Buddhist temples, appeared small and intimate, unmanageable in its number of gods but quite manageable in its absence of yawning space.

Durbar Square had been an off-duty hangout for Peace Corps volunteers. The Peace Corps, from its start under President John F. Kennedy in the early 1960s, evoked a rugged tradition of service requiring both discipline and idealism. Unlike the hippie movement, it had lost little of its legitimacy over the chasm of the decades. It was still much respected, and accounted for many of the new crop of American ambassadors. As one embassy staffer told me, "Nepal is important to the United States because, among other things, it represents one of our oldest Peace Corps legacies."

That legacy seemed to demand rescue. For the most part, the Peace Corps volunteers were gone from Nepal, as the countryside beyond Kathmandu, courtesy of the Maoists, had become too dangerous to operate in. There was a hard lesson here, especially for the U.S. Agency for International Development, a lesson that I had also caught indications of in Niger—a place where civilian aid workers, including Peace Corps volunteers, were mainly restricted to the area of the capital city. If civilian aid was to have any kind of future in countries like these, it would have to be at least partially militarized.

My first night in Kathmandu, Larry took me to a gathering of a U.S. Air Force medical aid team dispatched by PACOM in Honolulu. The aim of the nine-man mission, explained Capt. Jason Deese of Linden, Michigan, who had relief experience in twenty other Asian countries, was to train Nepalese first responders and paramedics in the event of anything from a bomb blast to an earthquake (Nepal was on a major seismic fault line). Tech. Sgt. David Eubanks of Saint Cloud, Minnesota, a member of the National Guard, worried that while at his level, "the Nepalese suck up knowledge," the problem was that the higher-ups were feckless. "Government agencies," he said, "are not talking to each other here. And without synergy you can't have an adequate disaster response." Sgt. Eubanks mentioned that the caste system had created an unbridgeable wall between officers and noncoms in the local military.

Larry and his colleagues in the military wing of the embassy did not kid themselves that they could reform the Royal Nepalese Army. Rather, they were investing their hopes in one Ranger battalion of 897 men. This battalion, consisting of four rifle companies, was modeled after the U.S. Army Rangers based out of Fort Benning, Georgia. One evening in Larry's house, over a dinner of wine and Indian curry dishes, I met two of the battalion's officers, including thirty-year-old Capt. Anup Phayal, who had played a role in establishing the unit two years earlier.

Capt. Phayal and his superior, thirty-two-year-old Maj. Subash Thapa, were smartly dressed in pressed slacks and polo shirts. Their engaging manner and knowledge of literature and policy studies reminded me of the foreign students one encountered nowadays at Ivy League universities. Like the late King Hussein of Jordan, both had gone to the Royal Military Academy at Sandhurst. Capt. Phayal was also a graduate of Ranger School at Fort Benning; Maj. Thapa of the Q Course at Fort Bragg.

Both Capt. Phayal and Maj. Thapa were from military families. Capt. Phayal had grown up listening to his grandfather's stories of being a British Gurkha in Singapore and the Malay Peninsula. Maj. Thapa, on both his mother's and father's side, boasted eight generations of army officers. These two young men, who discussed with me Camus's *The Rebel,* and who had arrived at the house on late-model motorcycles and wearing light body armor, were, by taste and education, a subcaste of global cosmopolitans to which the attendees at Davos and other international conferences had doubtlessly been little exposed.

Capt. Phayal said, "The Nepalese army must set an example for society by breaking down class divisions. What I'm particularly proud of," he added, echoing Larry, "is the strong role of NCOs in our particular battalion."

As for the state of affairs with the Maoists, Capt. Phayal stated, "Terrain-wise, Nepal is twenty times Afghanistan. We fight in a vertical jungle landscape. We see the enemy [the Maoists] on an adjacent hilltop and it takes us three days of rucking to reach him, by which time he is long gone. We need a few helicopters, that's all. Nothing fancy, Russian Mi-24s will do.

"There are large tracts where the Maoists have ruled for five years," he continued, "yet they've done even less in terms of improving the lives of the people than our own government." Then there was their cruelty, which, rather than being a result of bad discipline, was intrinsic to their operating procedures. "I'm convinced that morally it's a black-and-white situation," he said.

Though Capt. Phayal looked younger than his thirty years, as a company commander he was a veteran of several combat sorties in the western hills, and had been wounded in the thigh.

Because of the incompetence of the Royal Nepalese Army in its dealing with the media, it had taken much pleading on my part to gain access to the Nepalese Rangers' training camp. The Ranger battalion was doing its training at Surya Binayak, in the oily dark, heavily wooded foothills east of Kathmandu. I left the teeming sprawl of the capital behind and drove up a maze of careening mountain roads into a realm of pristine air graced by pines and oaks and studded with small Hindu temples, amidst fields as perfect as any golf course.

The camp was spotless, right down to the new trees and plants that the members of the battalion had been tending, punctuated by dazzling red hibiscus in brass pots. Maj. Thapa and Capt. Phayal, along with some other officers, greeted me in a shed. They wore woodland camouflage fatigues, emblazoned with crossed Gurkha swords, suns, and half-moons—traditional Nepalese symbols denoting rank. The briefing they delivered was standard Pentagon PowerPoint: a swift overview of little substance, but with one significant exception.

The most frustrating weakness of third-world armies confronting counterinsurgencies was here being admitted and dealt with. From Colombia onward, I had encountered host-country militaries that, because they lacked confidence and because their morale was questionable, were only comfortable engaging the enemy in large numbers, at the company level (150 men roughly) or above. But here in Nepal, the nine-man squad or "section" was the preferred point of contact. Moreover, this concept was being farmed out within the RNA, as these Rangers, the recipients of previous U.S. Army Special Forces JCETs, were, in turn, providing squad-level training in similar twenty-one-day cycles to other infantry units. As Maj. Thapa noted, "We train to fight at the squad level, with squad leaders. The company level is the highest at which we'll ever fight. We don't want panicky, trigger-happy soldiers."

I walked up and down hills, watching live-fire, movement-to-contact drills with Colt Commandos (short-barreled M-16s). The squads were subdivided into teams of five and four, led, respectively, by a sergeant and corporal. The teams burst out of 360-degree cigar-shaped formations, charging up steep hills in the intense heat and humidity, using the buddy system of alternating fire to prevent what the Rangers (employing an American term) called "blue-on-blue" (friendly fire) incidents. The fire was controlled, one shot being used to draw enemy fire before further bursts were ordered. The grading of each squad was often done by noncoms. In the midst of thick vines, I came across two privates lying prone in opposite directions, their rifles cocked in guard positions. Their Mongol-like faces were lathered in grime, sweat, and green camouflage stick. They resembled Buddha statues, barely breathing.

As exemplary as the performance of these enlistees was, they were, nevertheless, simple boys intimidated by authority. Rarely were they the advice-giving, middle-level managers of Western militaries—and these were the best enlistees the RNA could produce. You could give these boys lectures on human rights, as well as on civil affairs and disaster relief, as the officers of this battalion were dutifully doing, and that would result in a heightened concern for human rights. But a situation with few or no violations, as Western governments and international authorities were demanding, was simply unachievable until the society itself evolved to a level that would take it years to reach.

Capt. Phayal told me that "only our officers have linguistic access to Western literature and military field manuals. Thus, they inhabit different mental universes than the enlistees. And yet," he went on, "it takes so little to make my men happy and motivated."

So far, the battalion had suffered twelve killed and fifty-three wounded in action. Twenty-one-year-old 1st Lt. Ashok Khadka told me of one engagement the previous April in which he had been wounded by shrapnel in the neck.

The firefight "happened as it always does," he told me, "when you are most uncomfortable: before we ate, before we had drunk sufficient water, with full battle order of twenty kilograms [forty-four pounds] on our backs. Bursts of fire came from spot height [the top of the hill]. We charged uphill. IEDs went off. I was on the point [lead] squad. A rifleman and the SAW [the man bearing the squad automatic weapon, a Belgian M-249 light-medium machine gun, in this case] were both wounded. Two platoons eventually relieved us, and we took the hill, but only with air support."

"The worst aspect is that even with night-vision goggles we don't know the terrain like the enemy," another officer told me. Continuing with the same admirable honesty, a third officer said, "We distributed chocolate to the kids in a village and they refused to take it. The Maoists had convinced them that it was poison." A fourth officer: "A wounded, dying Maoist told his comrade, 'Don't waste a bullet on me, use it to kill the enemy. Kill me with a knife, or choke me before you retreat.' "

Capt. Phayal summed up: "While men join the RNA with the goal of serving overseas in a U.N. peacekeeping mission, with all the extra income that brings in to their families, the Maoists have a mystical willingness to die. We're an all-volunteer battalion. But ultimately, all we can do is train and bond with each other, train and bond."

─────

I did not kid myself that the Maoists didn't have real allure. Like the Eritrean guerrillas about whom I had reported in the 1980s—and who eventually triumphed—the Maoists had taken a cluster of ideals and launched them into a full-fledged cult. With culthood came discipline and dynamism, two attributes the RNA, except for specialized units like the Rangers, lacked. The Maoists were known to have good communications, and to attack from three sides in human waves. A journalist wanting to visit with them had an easier time gaining access than a journalist wishing to visit with the RNA. Like all post-modern movements, the Maoists were media savvy. In modern warfare, information was another form of battle maneuver. The free economy, coupled with destructive party politics in the 1990s, had exacerbated social inequalities in Nepal from which the Maoists drew sustenance. Their uprising was another rebuke to globalization.

American officials knew that the RNA could not by itself restore stability to Nepal simply because the government had no presence in the villages. So the villagers, faced with threats from the Maoists, were easily intimidated. The RNA, with more training and equipment, might liberate the countryside, but only the presence of civilian authorities building such things as schools, roads, and medical clinics could hold it. Nepal was the Philippines and so many other places all over again. The popular uprising that would occur the following year, which successfully forced the king to restore democracy, could not by itself be a solution to the anarchy in the countryside. It was a good start, though, one that ultimately could be consolidated only with a Western-oriented military, a military that would keep up the pressure on the Maoists, so they would participate in good faith in the democratic process, rather than manipulate it in order to grab power.

————

I could not think about Nepalese fighters—whether the RNA or the Maoists—without thinking about the fierce and fabled legacy of the Gurkhas.* Throughout my travels, I had been experiencing and ruminating upon the challenge of training indigenous troops, and using them to project American power in a more efficient way than I had seen in Iraq in 2004.[3] The story of the Gurkhas shows how the British were past masters at this.

The term "Gurkha" stems from a British mispronunciation of the town of Gorkha in western Nepal, from where the first units of these warriors were initially raised among Gurungs and Magars—Nepalese tribes of Mongolian origin.† Rather than an ethnic group of their own, the Gurkhas represent what, since the early eighteenth century, British

---

* The Gurkhas of the British Army have had nothing whatsoever to do with either the current Royal Nepalese Army or the Maoists.

† Gorkha was also the place from where the current monarchy set out to conquer the country and establish the Nepalese state. Because it was the kings of Gorkha whom the British initially fought, they referred to Nepalese soldiers as Gurkhas.

officers have considered the fighting classes of Nepal that emerged out of the feudal anarchy endemic to a poor mountainous country.

The British first encountered them during the 1814–16 war between Nepal and the Bengal Presidency of the East India Company. Impressed by the cheerful disposition of these Nepalese even when they were wounded, the British bonded with their erstwhile adversaries. The relationship was solidified during the Indian Mutiny of 1857, when Gurkha recruits to the Indian Army did not revolt, and in fact came to the aid of British civilians.

Afterward, the Gurkhas fought for the British in the Sudan during the Mahdist uprising, in China during the Boxer Rebellion, in Mesopotamia during World War I, and in Burma during World War II, to name but some places. There were tens of thousands of Gurkha casualties in the two world wars. In addition, the British Army had used Gurkhas in the Falklands, the Balkans, and Iraq. The Gurkha tradition of discipline and professionalism, because it had seeped culturally into the RNA in a few instances, was key to why Nepal currently had both battalions and companies of peacekeepers in Burundi, Congo, Haiti, and Liberia.

Gurkha enlistees in the British military tended to come not only from the same tribes, but also from the same clans and families. In the 1970s, in a single battalion, the 6th Queen Elizabeth's Own Gurkha Rifles, forty-six sets of brothers were serving at the same time. In the history of Great Britain, both imperial and post-imperial, the Gurkhas have been its most valued mercenaries—a profession at times unfairly sullied.[4] As the poet A. E. Housman writes,

> *Their shoulders held the sky suspended;*
> *They stood, and earth's foundations stay;*
> *What God abandoned, these defended,*
> *And saved the sum of thing for pay.*[5]

"The toughness of Gurkha skulls is legendary," writes historian Byron Farwell. In 1931 on the North-West Frontier, when a mess mule kicked a Gurkha *havildar* [sergeant] in the head with his iron-shod hooves, "the *havildar* complained of a headache and that evening wore a piece of sticking plaster on his forehead. The mule went lame."[6] The wild and woolly "Pathan" warriors of Afghanistan feared only two things: the Prophet Mohammed and a Gurkha with a *kukri* (short curved knife). Farwell writes that "no living thing is faster than a Gurkha leaping downhill." But such toughness should not be confused with harshness. Among Gurkhas, the bullying and intimidation common to many Western armies was absent.[7]

Retired Cpl. Balbasdar Basnet was the most memorable of the old Gurkha pensioners I interviewed in Kathmandu—men who were veterans of the World War II Burma campaign, of Japanese prisoner-of-war camps, and of the British counterinsurgency in Malaysia in the 1960s. He was in his seventies, with a raspy voice that fought against time. He had joined the Gurkha Rifles of the British Army when he was sixteen. He had teeth only on the right side of his mouth, and a shriveled, nut-brown face capped by a *topi*. There was something indisputably antique about this gentleman warrior, who told me his life story in a room under a black-and-white photograph of Queen Elizabeth II.

Cpl. Balbasdar, despite age and a back brace, had a sinewy musculature, with large, capable hands. He was from a village so impoverished that he had never had tea before joining the army.

"How was basic training as a youth?" I asked.

"Oh, I enjoyed it so much, it was good living," he told me, smiling.

After basic training, he had served for eight months on the North-West Frontier of British India, guarding the border against "Pathans." (He used the old British term for what today we call Pushtuns.) From there he went to Bombay, and by ship to northwest Malaya for three months of jungle training, just as World War II was gathering force. Finally he was fighting the Japanese in close combat.

"Were you scared?" I asked.

"No, I was thinking only to do and die," he answered, still smiling.

For fifteen days, he and other Gurkhas marched in the jungle, retreating from a larger force of Japanese. He was taken prisoner early in the war, and for four years subsisted on beatings and two hundred grams of rice per day, moved around from labor camps in Malaya, Java, Sumatra, and New Guinea, wearing nothing more than a loincloth. Hiroshima liberated him from his sufferings, he told me. Suddenly he was being fed and clothed, and a few weeks later New Zealand troops arrived to formally release him. He was proud to have served Her Majesty, he said.

The more prosperous the society, the harder it was to produce men like this, I thought. We were a softer, less fatalistic culture than the one he represented and, overall at least, morally the better for it. But good deeds, whether in Sierra Leone or the Balkans, still required such men.

Comparing these old Gurkhas with contemporary American infantry soldiers and marines, I found the difference great, yet at the same time bridgeable, for I had met many in the combat arms community whose fighting spirit, coupled with their humble backgrounds and their ability to suffer, narrowed the psychological space with these antique warriors. The real difference had to do with the civilian constraints under which they operated. No matter how much the combat arms community of the American military with its warrior ethos believed in its worldwide mission, the American governing class, unlike that of nineteenth- and early-twentieth-century Europe, had less stomach for it. Nepal was a telling example of what this meant for the American military.

The notion persisted among the left and some isolationists that our military training missions were somehow still propping up dictators, but Colombia, Mongolia, the Philippines, Afghanistan, Kenya, Niger, Thailand, Algeria, and every other place I had visited (and would visit) with the military had one thing in common: they were internationally recognized democracies, however imperfect. And we weren't pushing military aid on them; they were requesting it of us. If they were not democracies, Congress would not have permitted these missions in the first place.

But Nepal was no longer in this category, ever since 2002 when the king had suspended the political party process. Nevertheless, Maj. Larry Smith, along with others, believed that the suspension of aid to the Royal Nepalese Army (because of its own human rights violations and the suspension of democracy in Nepal) would only further empower the Maoists, and that would make a stable democracy in Nepal only more elusive. The U.S. State Department and Congress did not agree, and elements of the Bush administration were on their side. It was an honest policy dispute, the bottom line of which was that my journey to Nepal coincided with a halt to U.S. military aid, even as the Chinese were offering the Royal Nepalese Army an extra million dollars in assistance, an amount that went a long way here. The Nepalese defense minister had just been invited to Beijing, to be followed by the king. This American empire, to say the least, was a weak and hesitant one compared to that of the British and almost all others before it.

Larry Smith, who had come to Nepal hoping to replicate the work of Tom Wilhelm in Mongolia, was worried that he might soon be out of a job.[8] A year later, after riots curtailed the king's power and put the country back on the road to democracy, military aid would be resumed, and Larry would be back in business: getting the promised thousands of sets of body armor out of mothballs, filling slots at the National Defense University in Washington, D.C., for Nepalese officers, and helping the Nepalese Rangers get funding for an NCO academy. But for now all that lay in the future.

Meanwhile, in the midst of this bad turn of events for him, when military aid had been stopped, Larry and I made a visit to Pokhara, to the west of Kathmandu, to meet a British Gurkha legend. The flight took only half an hour. We couldn't go by car or bus because the ground in between was either controlled or threatened by the Maoists.

Pokhara lay in a dank and humid valley, in the shadow of the glittering snows and granite of the Annapurna Range of the Himalayas. This time of year, though, it was snuggled in monsoon clouds and choked by greenery so dark that it was as if the whole landscape had been filtered through tar. Water buffalo meandered amid black mildewed walls that were almost completely covered with moss, further obscured by dripping banana leaves. Government paramilitaries sleepily guarded their installations, which were topped by concertina wire. While the town was considered secure, atmospherically it conjured up signs of state collapse.

Eighty-year-old retired British army Col. John Philip Cross greeted us outside his compound in Pokhara, wearing a *topi,* dark glasses, a smart cravat, pressed shorts, and high woolen socks pulled up nearly to his knees. His knees, I noticed, were tanned and powerful. He had covered ten thousand miles on foot through the Nepalese hills over the years, and still hiked twelve miles a day, though he could barely see because of cataracts. He had enlisted in the army on April 2, 1943. On "D-day plus two," June 8, 1944, he boarded a troopship for Bombay. Except for short visits to England, he hadn't been back from Asia since.

His first memorable experience in the army had been a briefing on sex from a medical officer prior to sailing, which frankly shocked him. The officer, without a trace of a smile, said: "Don't forget, a woman for children, a boy for pleasure, but for real ecstasy, a goat."[9] At the tail end of World War II, Col. Cross was assigned to the 1st Battalion of the 1st Gurkha Rifles based at Dharamsala.* Thus, his lifework commenced.

From there it was on to Burma to fight and disarm Japanese soldiers; to Cochin China (Vietnam) to fight the Viet Minh; and to Laos, where, as the last British defense attaché before the king fell, he became the de facto eyes and ears of the U.S. Embassy tracking the communist Pathet Lao (for the British ambassador, he sneered, "was a fellow traveler"). Next he went to western Nepal to become a recruiting officer for the Gurkhas. Future years would find him parachuting into Borneo to fight a communist insurgency, and in the Malay Peninsula to train Americans in jungle warfare. "A certain BBC reporter—God rot his soul—accused me of teaching torture." All in all, he had spent a total of ten years in the jungle, often carrying the equivalent of his own weight on his back, which he called "a delightful way of life." He spoke French and nine Asian languages.

Col. Cross was a confirmed bachelor, because of "hot blood and cold feet," he explained. His library of battered books, medals, and *kukri* knives, each object charged by a memory, was decayed by heat and humidity, for he had no air-conditioning. He slept on a spartan bed in the next room. Here was another antique man of empire—a man who, in his youth, had befriended old British officers who had joined the Gurkha service before Kipling wrote *Kim.*

Writing books on irregular warfare and Himalayan history that de-

---

* Dharamsala, an Indian town near Nepal, was now the home-in-exile of the Dalai Lama of Tibet.

served to be read even if they weren't, he was a minor and far more eccentric offshoot of a British imperial species that had reached perfect culmination in the person of the former soldier and literary travel writer Patrick Leigh Fermor.* Both were inveterate walkers: Fermor across Europe, Col. Cross across Nepal.

"Late-nineteenth-century warfare never stopped," intoned Col. Cross, "though it was masked for a time by the Cold War emphasis on atomic bombs. And in this type of warfare that you Americans must now master, only two things count: the mystic dimension of service and the sanctity of an oath. It's about the giving 'of one's best when the audience is of the smallest.'[10] It's not about sugar-coated bullets and dispensing condoms in PXes. You can't fight properly," he went on, "until you know that you are going to die anyway. That's extreme, but that's the gold standard.

"Now take your Gurkha," he continued, motioning to Buddhiman Gurung, his muscular Gurkha retainer and beloved, adopted son, who had been with him for the past twenty-eight years. "He's a hungry peasant with a knife who is out for the main chance. There are none finer. I placed these western hillsmen in the Singapore police and they never failed me. The Mongoloid doesn't die easily. Plainsmen will never defeat such people in hill battles without field artillery—Clausewitz had said as much."

This was bad news for the Royal Nepalese Army, though Col. Cross was careful not to make explicit political statements, given his circumstances: the Maoists were in the nearby mountains, and government forces down the street. The fact was that the Maoists came from the same sturdy hill tribes that for decades he had recruited, while many of the Royal Nepalese Army's forces were plainsmen who couldn't employ artillery, since even a handful of civilian casualties would ignite protests from international organizations. Moreover, the Maoists were fortified by "the mystic dimension of service and the sanctity of an oath," whereas RNA recruits joined for a salary and a career. The Ranger battalion that I had visited, while a stellar exception, was com-

---

* I had interviewed Fermor three years earlier. See the last chapter of *Mediterranean Winter: The Pleasures of History and Landscape in Tunisia, Sicily, Dalmatia, and Greece* (New York: Random House, 2004).

promised by domestic and international politics. Laos in Col. Cross's day had been similar: another landlocked country with a king and a communist insurgency.

When I asked him about Iraq, all he said was: "You don't join the army to wipe your enemy's ass. You join to kill, or for you yourself to be killed, and above all to have a good sense of humor about it."

Col. Cross could be brutal, perverse almost—in this he was totally unlike Fermor. He was near blindness, living in the threatened back-water of the only country he could call his own. Yet there was an unde-niable logic, however cruel, to some of his truths. War was still about killing people. While this might be a truism to civilian observers, it cer-tainly was not to those who actually practiced for it, and particularly not to their trainers. For example, to say publicly that marines liked killing people did not go over well, but it was something marines said among themselves all the time.

About special forces the colonel said, "They're introverts at heart, happy to be by themselves, shit-hot on the outside during operations, but pathetic cuckoos on the inside." That was SF all right.

The United States was never going to produce troops like the Gurkhas or officers like Col. Cross, nor should it. It would have to get the most out of what, by the traditional standards of warfare, were indi-rect half measures, under the guidance of enlightened, liberal-minded officers who, when it was necessary, could nevertheless kill with the best of them. Those on the political extremes imagined an imperial bully and global busybody, but the reality of the American military in so many places was how restricted it was. Only at sea, from what I had seen so far, were we still relatively unfettered by global and domestic politics.

SEVEN

TRIBAL MAFIAS

WITH AN ARMY STRYKER BRIGADE

Iraq, Autumn 2005

hether I was with the American military in the African desert, the Pacific Ocean, or the Himalayan foothills, Iraq cast a shadow over it all. In the spring of 2004, I had traveled to Iraq with the 1st Battalion of the 5th Marine Regiment, moving overland from Kuwait to the Sunni Triangle, observing weeks of security and stability operations, and then the First Battle of Fallujah.* Now, eighteen months later, I decided to embed with the regular Army farther north in the country, in Mosul, the capital of Nineveh Province, near where the mountains of Kurdistan reared up against the Mesopotamian desert. This was the area of responsibility (AOR) of the 172nd Stryker Brigade Combat Team, the same "Arctic Wolves" brigade that I had visited the previous autumn at Fort Richardson and Fort Wainwright in Alaska.

Getting to Mosul was the usual hurry-up-and-wait hassle. I gave up a hotel room in Kuwait City at midnight to shiver all night outside a Kellogg, Brown & Root (KBR) shipping container at a Kuwaiti air

---

* See Chapter 8 of *Imperial Grunts*. The Second Battle of Fallujah occurred in the autumn of 2004.

base, waiting for a C-130 flight to Baghdad that did not leave until daylight. My passport was handed back to me at the last moment by a
taking-his-sweet-time KBR employee who told me with delight, "Don't
it suck when you can't get a meal [at the all-night dining facility] because you only just got your ID back?" Exiting the C-130 into the suffocating, mud-filled air of central Mesopotamia, fiddling with my body
armor and backpack, I learned that there was no room on the helicopter
to take me from BIAP (Baghdad International Airport) to the IZ (International Zone, or Green Zone, the nerve center of the American military
occupation), where I had to go to get press credentials. This was something I had not had to do in Iraq in 2004, because then I had come in
overland with the Marines.

That meant waiting for sixteen hours at the "stables" for the "rhino"
(a prison wagon retrofitted with heavy armor) that sped people in the
dead of night from the airport to the Green Zone. Security was perceived to be that bad, the U.S. military and State Department that para-
noiac. My fellow passengers were sleepy, grizzled contractors of several
nationalities, including Filipinos and Kosovars. Some of their jobs might
have gone to Iraqis, but because of the security situation American contractors felt more comfortable with non-Arabs. I thought of decades before when American oilmen began hiring Filipinos and other non-Arabs
in Saudi Arabia, and when Israelis did the same to replace Palestinian
workers. In both instances, it had led to worsening relations with the
locals.

To stop the rash of attacks in the territory between the airport and the
Green Zone, a virtual tunnel-like corridor of massive concrete, bomb-
blast Alaska barriers had been erected. Once inside the Green Zone, the
landscape was so dominated by mazes of these tall concrete barriers
that they now overshadowed the Stalinist-cum-Babylonian architecture
of Saddam Hussein. As with any gated community besieged by some
form of crime, the Green Zone had been secured by turning the area surrounding the U.S. Embassy into a fortress, rather than by making inroads into the insurgency. Just bring in enough poured concrete and
private security guards and you might buy the appearance of progress.

Returning to the airport for the flight to Mosul, I was able to catch a
ride on a U.S. Army Black Hawk helicopter, which along with the rhino

operated as a shuttle of sorts between the two safe havens. Careening a few hundred feet above the ground at high speed in the Black Hawk, two machine gunners at the ready, I had a glance at America's latest version of Mogadishu-like hell: a ratty cinder-block jigsaw of streets interspersed with dust-bleached palms and crummy old cars and market stalls.

I had a third shivering all-nighter in order to make an early morning C-130 flight north to Mosul. Mosul was a different country than Baghdad. The air was cold and clear following the first rainstorm of the season, revealing a hardened plateau of aching, sculptural distances. Though the altitude was only a few hundred feet above sea level, it was a relief from the choking mud vapors of the Mesopotamian desert. Studded with pine, fir, and cypress trees, the landscape communicated the closeness of Anatolia. I noticed kebab stands and all kinds of Turkish products, from generators to fruit juices. Near the airfield was a roadblock manned by Massoud Barzani's Kurdish Pesh Merga.

Mosul, like Aleppo in Syria, was an age-old caravan city whose history defied the concept of the twentieth-century nation-state—the very nation-state that the U.S. military occupation of Iraq was trying to hold together and keep from descending into full-scale civil war. Historic trade routes linked Mosul to cities in Syria, Turkey, and Iran. The Arabic language in Mosul was influenced by Kurdish and Syriac. There was a large community of Chaldaeans—Christians who had been converted from Nestorianism to Catholicism.* For a long time this city of 2.1 million had been a seat of Catholic missionary activity. Seljuk Turks held Mosul in the Middle Ages and Ottoman Turks in the modern era, with a Persian occupation in between. Mosul's degenerating old quarter, with its beetling Ottoman walls and elegantly stuccoed twelfth-century Seljuk minaret, was testimony to this cosmopolitan lineage. The incorporation of the oil-rich Turkish vilayet of Mosul into the new Iraq in 1926 meant that the Arab polity of Sunnis and Shiites would henceforth be a place where a quarter of the population was non-Arab Kurds, Turcomans, and Assyrians. Mosul symbolized the ethnic and sectarian

---

* Nestorians are a sect that originated in the fifth century, based on the teachings of Nestorius, who emphasized the difference between the divine and human qualities of Christ.

divisions that had made Iraq so untenable, helping it to fall victim to the most suffocating of dictatorships.

Straddling the banks of the Tigris, Mosul occupied the site of ancient Nineveh, now a barren, sandpaper emptiness of crumbly hills and vegetable plots across the river from the city center. The Assyrian capital had been the mortal enemy of the biblical nation of Israel. It was the Assyrian tyrant Sennacherib who had destroyed Babylon and laid siege to Jerusalem in the early seventh century B.C., prompting the prophet Isaiah to counsel the Hebrew king Hezekiah to pray for deliverance. Eventually Sennacherib's forces withdrew from Jerusalem. Nineveh also conjured up the Hebrew prophet Jonah (Nebi Yunus in Arabic), who, as the story goes, after being vomited up by the whale on dry land, made his way here and beseeched the population to dress in sackcloth and ashes, in repentance for its sins.

Assyria met its end at the hands of the Medes in 612 B.C. The collapse of Assyria as a great military power was "one of the completest yet known to history," according to historian Arnold Toynbee. The Assyrian war machine, one of history's most terrifying, had dominated the Near East for centuries. Yet, when the Greek general Xenophon passed through here only two hundred years following Assyria's demise, even the name of Assyria was unknown to him. Assyria, top-heavy with military might, was, in Toynbee's words, "a corpse in armour," a phrase that conjured up such overly militarized, centrally controlled states as Syria and Pakistan, and, until 2003, Saddam Hussein's Iraq.* If the past in this part of the Near East had a theme, it was the impermanence of states and the malleability of their borders.

I came to Mosul after one set of national elections, and would leave just before another: the former had elected an assembly to draft a constitution, the latter would select political parties for parliament. The former had seen a voter turnout of more than 80 percent in the Mosul region, representing the largest increase in voter participation in Iraq since another election ten months before in January 2005. Mosul was a success story, albeit relative, partial, and extremely tenuous, the credit

---

* Arnold Toynbee, *A Study of History* (Oxford, Eng: Oxford University Press, 1939, 1946). Toynbee's source is Xenophon's *Anabasis*. I write more on Assyria's collapse in *Eastward to Tartary* (New York: Random House, 2000).

for which belonged to the Stryker Brigade Combat Team that had recently departed: the 1st Brigade of the 25th Infantry Division based out of Fort Lewis, Washington.

When the 1-25 "Lancers" had arrived in Mosul in September 2004, the city and surrounding area was a violent no-go zone, having seen several thousand insurgent attacks, not to mention over a thousand explosions from improvised explosive devices. The local police had largely deserted, dropping from a force of 10,000 to 300. But by the time 1-25 left a year later, mortar attacks alone had fallen from 300 a month to less than 10. It was a figure that carried significance since among my most vivid memories of Iraq in the spring of 2004 were the constant mortar explosions.[1] Other forms of insurgent activity had dropped to the point where international journalists no longer considered Mosul part of the Iraq story, evinced by their absence here in recent months.

The local police force was now back up to 9,000, with the number of police stations having expanded from 5 to 24. More importantly, the number of intelligence tips called in by the local population had risen from near zero to 400 per month.

The sort of chaos that 1-25 had alleviated was an abiding interest of mine. It had been nearly twelve years since I had published an article in *The Atlantic Monthly,* "The Coming Anarchy," about the institutional failure of third-world countries stemming from ethnic and sectarian rivalries, demographic and environmental stresses, and the growing interrelationship between war and crime.* The Mosul region, of all places, might offer some way of coping with parts of that thesis, I thought.

The 1-25 Lancers' shaky success bore credit to the brigade-level transformation of the United States Army: Big Army or Mother Army, as the Green Berets of Special Forces derided it. And they were right. Big Army was still too much of a vertical, dinosauric industrial-age organization. Yet it was changing, partly because of the new emphasis on brigades. A brigade was only a third or a half the size of a division, to say nothing of a corps. Thus, its headquarters element was less bureau-

---

* "The Coming Anarchy," *The Atlantic Monthly,* February 1994. The article was completed in autumn 1993.

cratic and top-heavy with colonels. The very size of a brigade could be custom-fit to the situation. Putting brigades first represented an organizational means for dealing with a more chaotic, unconventional world. It was the kind of reform that the military was embracing faster than the State Department. The credit for the emphasis on brigades belonged to succeeding Army chiefs of staff, particularly Eric Shinseki and, to a lesser extent, Pete Schoomaker.

There was, too, the phenomenon of how new hardware, in this case the Stryker combat vehicle, was facilitating a change in relationships between captains in the field and majors and lieutenant colonels back at battalion headquarters. The Stryker, with its added safety features that drastically cut down on casualties from IEDs and suicide bombs, its ability to travel great distances without refueling, and its FBCB2 computer system that gave captains and noncoms situational awareness and the latest intelligence for many miles around, had helped liberate field units from dependence on their headquarters, making them more autonomous.* Rather than compete or bicker with Special Forces, the ground-level reality was the co-option of the Special Forces model by the regular Army. This would put pressure on SF to innovate further.

Such autonomy was further encouraged by the Stryker brigades' flat intelligence architecture, another reform that was happening to a lesser extent throughout the Army. Information now came to captains less and less down the vertical chain of command from their own battalion headquarters, and more and more horizontally, from other junior officers in other battalions via informal e-mail networks, as well as directly from Iraqi units. The lieutenant colonel who commanded an infantry battalion and the major who was his executive officer did not always have to be consulted.

One evening the previous March, a tip from an Iraqi source had led a captain—without seeking permission from any vertical command chain—to carry out six raids in Mosul over the next few hours that netted the capture of fourteen out of twenty members of an insurgent cell, plus the confiscation of large numbers of weapons and several vehicles. A second night, a tip that insurgent leader Abu Zubayr (Mohammed

---

* FBCB2: Force Battle Command for Brigade and Battalion.

Sultan Saleh) was planning to assassinate a local police chief led a company captain to develop a plan to trap the insurgent by using the tipster as bait. The captain had Abu Zubayr's movements tracked with an unmanned surveillance plane. Abu Zubayr was killed along with two other key area insurgents.

Such successes did not indicate that overall things were going well in Iraq. What they did indicate was that in the midst of bad situations, individual innovations were possible that steepened the military's learning curve.

And they showed that in the early stages at least, ending anarchy was, well, about ending anarchy. States both democratic and not had to monopolize the use of force. Here that meant killing particular people and apprehending others. "You're dealing with a gang mentality," explained Capt. Phillip Mann of Antioch, California, a thirty-two-year-old intelligence officer and graduate of Fresno State University. "There is a pool of young men in Mosul without jobs who sell drugs and do kidnappings. With a high inflation rate and little economy, being an insurgent *pays*. You've got to make the insurgency a very unattractive profession to people who are not motivated by religious ideology." Indeed, pornography was a common item found by the battalion whenever it overran insurgent hideouts. "So we adopted a gang-tackle approach," Capt. Mann went on. "If we get shot at like in Palestine [a retirement community of former regime generals in southeast Mosul that had supported the insurgents], we surround the area and go house to house, every time. We keep doing this till people get tired and start helping us. Our message: 'We don't give in—we're not going away, so work with us.'

"It's a matter of suppression. You do kinetic ops until you find that magical balance—an acceptable level of violence that allows you to shift resources to nation-rebuilding. Don't overdo the killing of bad guys. Ending the violence completely is a foolish goal without development."

And in a large unconventional battlefield with relatively few combatants on it—a battlefield where killing the enemy was easy but finding him difficult—that meant pushing power out to junior officers and noncoms, by giving them immediate access to vital intelligence and the authority to act on it. Capt. Mann was getting instant reports from the highest levels of the military bureaucracy, but also generating intelligence himself upward through the command chain.

For years at the Army intelligence "schoolhouse" in Fort Huachuca, Arizona, young intelligence officers were taught how to receive and collate reports from various parts of the battlefield and build a narrative from them. That system worked when the battlefield featured masses of men and machines in an organized fight. Now, as Capt. Mann explained, "I've got my own urban battlespace in a part of Mosul populated by 450,000 people, and I'm trying to find a hundred insurgents who can slip in and out of that battlespace. Rather than satellites and other strategic assets feeding information down to division, to brigade, to battalion, and finally to me, I'm under pressure to get the stuff first by being a detective who pieces together crimes."

The very military that had caused the anarchy in Iraq was now worth studying as a way to end it, both here and elsewhere in the third world. Keep in mind that the conventional infantry invasion of Iraq was a policy decision made by civilians, even as the restoration of some semblance of order was being driven by young officers who were learning lessons as they went along.

The real change I experienced upon arrival in Mosul was with the soldiers themselves. It never failed: the closer you got to a frontline infantry unit, the greater the pride and intelligence, and the more erect the bearing of the individual troop. Rather than the nasty, young female enlistee at Baghdad International Airport who had grumpily lifted her eyes from a paperback to tell me that she didn't know the flight times to Mosul, though knowing such information was the sole purpose of her being in Iraq, I now found myself in a TOC (tactical operations center) staffed with noncoms, and junior and middle-level officers, whose whole identity seemed to be their jobs, as revealed through the game-on clarity of their expressions.

Some of these soldiers had high-and-tight buzz cuts like marines. The shaved Mohawk-style heads were less a Marine thing than a combat infantry thing. The Marine Corps was a small elite organization; the Army diverse. Soldiers could make the worst impression on you or the best, depending upon the unit. Even in frontline Army units, privates and noncoms in support positions, more so than their marine equivalents, often appeared to be marking time, sleepwalking through their jobs. This was testimony to the Army's stratified society in which clerical staff were given different training, used different acronyms, and could be made to feel like dirt by infantrymen. But as for Army officers and noncoms who went outside the base perimeter on daily missions, the differences between them and the Marines and Green Berets were subtle rather than basic.

A further similarity with the Marine Corps was the pixilated camouflage uniforms these soldiers had recently been issued to replace the Army's old desert fatigues. Again, like the Marines, the uniforms were emptier, as soldiers had stopped wearing their skill badges near their collars.* These were more small steps toward the convergence of the armed services and the replacement of a specific soldier or marine identity with—at least among frontline infantrymen—a generic warrior one. Because all marines, cooks and clerical workers included, had always thought of themselves as warriors, this slow-but-sure identity change was having a greater effect on the Army. Soldiers now wore an extra dog tag around their necks with the "warrior ethos" inscribed: "I will always place the mission first, I will never accept defeat, I will never quit . . ."

And as I kept hearing, "Every soldier's now a rifleman." Well, that had long been the Marine motto. It was the old story: you win not by being praised, but by being copied.

The tactical operations center, decorated with pin-ups of San Diego Charger cheerleaders, belonged to the 4th Battalion of the 23rd Infantry Regiment, based out of Fort Richardson outside Anchorage, Alaska. The 4-23 "Tomahawks" were among the 172nd Stryker Brigade's four fighting battalions. The Tomahawks, in turn, were built around three rifle companies, referred to as "Apache," "Black Hawk," and "Comanche." Because of the Cavalry's storied nineteenth-century history, Army units more so than Marine ones consciously maintained the legacy of the In-

---

* A telling complaint about the new uniforms was that they were too dark for the desert and too light for the jungle. The Marines still had it right: tan camouflage uniforms for the desert and greenish ones for the jungle.

dian Wars. The 4-23 battalion coin mentioned the "Indian Wars" along with the Philippine Insurrection, World War II, Vietnam, and other conflicts in which 4-23 was proud to have fought. The motto of the Stryker brigade's support battalion was *"Opahey,"* Cherokee for "It's a good day to die."

The commander of 4-23 was Lt. Col. John G. Norris of Louisville, Kentucky, a short and stocky former Marine noncom who had sold lemonade at the Kentucky Derby as a kid. He transferred to the Army early in his career, doing ROTC at the University of Louisville. Arriving on the heels of 1-25's success in late summer, his battalion had so far sustained only twelve wounded in action and no deaths. The fighting that had occurred was mainly in the run-up to the election the previous October.

Since then, Lt. Col. Norris told me, "We've done twenty-three patrols or so, mounted and dismounted, every day, and have never been attacked. They're not passive presence patrols either. We scout for trouble. We're always acting on intel tips and consequently bringing people in. There's just not much fighting here. It's become a political and development challenge."

My first days in Mosul I spent alongside Lt. Col. Norris, watching him facilitate relationships between local rulers who had once been hostile to one another. Historically, this had been an unconventional Special Forces job. But as combat gave way to politics in Mosul, regular Army officers found themselves dealing increasingly with situations familiar to the attendees of the Special Forces Q Course at Fort Bragg. These were also situations that would have been familiar to officials of the British and French nineteenth-century colonial services.

The days began with a meeting of the notables of Hamman-al-Alil, south of Mosul. First we drove east across the Tigris to pick up journalists from a reopened Iraqi television station who would cover the event. Sitting in the roomy interior of the Stryker, I saw the Tigris through the thermal imagery, while smelling the freshness of the river through the air hatch. Then came the smell of raw sewage as we entered a wilderness of automobile chop shops that had months back been a haven for insurgents. Kids waved and ran after the Strykers with "gimme-a-soccerball" pleas. The television station had a brand-new five-hundred-foot tower. A second one was going up, paid for with coalition funds. Re-crossing the river in the other direction, I saw the mosque holding Jonah's tomb on a hill above Mosul's vast clutter of stone and cement.

We drove down a road that had been paved originally by the 101st Airborne Division, only to be "IEDed to shit by insurgents," then repaved by Iraqi contractors hired by the American military. That was another tool against chaos: be relentless, particularly in the face of bad trends. If foreign aid to Africa could be justified, as well as inspire idealism, despite decades of failure and corruption, how could it be otherwise for civil affairs projects in Iraq in the face of a few years of difficulties?

The Stryker convoy passed through ashen brown, dome-shaped hills along the Tigris, bordered by fields of melons and sunflowers. The water was divided and redivided by islands and sandbars of massive reeds. The sharp contours gave every feature of the landscape an iconic quality. I saw brick hovels with new satellite dishes on the roofs—a sig-nature detail of post-Saddam Iraq.

Insurgents had made Hamman-al-Alil, a town of twenty thousand, another no-go zone, destroying the council officers and killing the mayor's nephew, then cutting off his head and delivering it to the mayor at his office. The mayor and the town council went to ground. Continu-ous raids by the Americans and the newly stood-up Iraqi Army and po-lice, trained and equipped by the Americans, gradually put an end to that. A clinic, a new police station, and new city offices were now near-ing completion, and the same mayor was back: Khalif Khader Mo-hammed Hussein al-Jabouri. Lt. Col. Norris planned to build a badly needed bridge across the Tigris here.

Not that the town looked good; it was a dismal pageant of muddy, garbage-strewn streets awaiting the first meager fruits of a very prob-lematic new stability. The council members adorned in their traditional keffiyehs and gold-braided regalia pleaded with Norris for more proj-ects. The town didn't just look awful through my eyes, but through theirs, too. Their offer was blunt: "We'll provide twenty-four-hour se-curity and workers if you'll pay for the projects." The claim of safety was backed up with the muscle of the dominant Jabouri tribe, which had decided to go with the Americans against the insurgents—after the

American military had demonstrated its resolve for month after month after month. The fact that the new police chief, Khaled Hussein al Hamdani, was a Hamdani tribesman—related to the same Hamdani tribesmen who had been bodyguards for Uday and Qusay Hussein—made for a coalition in the town.

This was easier done in a town than in a city. In the rural areas everyone knew one another, and therefore the tribes—a tangible form of authority you could get your hands around, unlike the new democratic governing bodies—were a potential counter to the insurgents.

Mayor Khalif walked in. His expression was at once tired and indefatigable. He looked the epitome of the rumpled, preoccupied politician, with roughed-up hair, who went through a checklist of points. "There had been a bridge here in antiquity, but not under Saddam. The bridge would confirm the American commitment" and so forth, he droned.

Norris said that help was coming in the form of PRTs (civilian-military provincial reconstruction teams). "The American military will continue, we will facilitate. We will not leave prematurely." "*Inshallah* [God willing]," they all replied.

Throughout the meeting I sat between two council members: Mohamed Najim Shakara had had three brothers killed by the insurgents; Khamis Mohamed Jassim had been attacked twice and pulled up his robe to show me, in LBJ style, the bullet wounds on his hip and lower abdomen.

"Some love us. Some hate us because we've accidentally killed their relatives," explained the lieutenant colonel from Kentucky in a quiet and reflective manner after the meeting. "Others would rather we just leave. But whenever we kill a terror hideout and return an area to some semblance of normalcy, people come out and say thank-you. A big problem is the daily low-level kidnappings of professionals, like doctors and lawyers, that don't make news but help provide a cash flow for the insurgents."

He and other American officers felt that a car bomb a day that killed a few dozen people in a country of twenty-six million was, while awful for the individuals and their families, easily sustainable. It was the flight of the middle class and the random crime that worried them more. "But if we can pull off the third nationwide election here without a major offensive by the insurgents, then we've won, though it will take the outside world quite a while to realize it," Norris believed.

Of course, the third nationwide election did go well, from an organizational point of view. But because the voters chose candidates completely along sectarian lines, it would be months before a unity government was formed, and thus Iraq would slide backward toward chaos. Norris could not have known that, however. His belief in the election reflected an optimism without which he would have been ineffective in his job. Indeed, the very chaos that democracy would later engender in Iraq would lead to the battalion's redeployment from Mosul to Baghdad the following summer, in order to deal with the upsurge of violence in the capital.

Inside the Stryker en route back to the TOC, I had a conversation with Maj. Doug Merritt of Venango, Pennsylvania, the battalion's assistant operations officer. He had grown up in a rural part of the state near the Ohio and New York borders, doing horse farming and construction work. He eventually joined the Army Reserves to afford college. Merritt now lived in Alaska and absolutely adored the hunting and hiking. "Every corner there's another awe-inspiring view," he told me. "The blues and the grays . . . I never take pictures because I'd lose it if I did. I'd lose the meditation, I mean. I have all these private memories of beautiful landscapes. Pictures would only make me forget."

One day Merritt had been hiking in Alaska with his company and collapsed. It turned out that he had an unstable angina with 90 percent blockage in his heart arteries, though he was only in his mid-thirties. He had four stents inserted and recovered completely, competing in the Anchorage marathon. "I was terrified that I would not get the opportunity to serve in Iraq. Now that I'm here, I carry with me my buddy's KA-BAR knife from Vietnam," he told me.

I never thought of these stories as corny. Nearly everyone I met in frontline infantry units, soldiers or marines, had the same commitment. If the stories sometimes appear to be repetitious, I mean them that way. You often can know or experience a fact only through repetition.

The next morning Lt. Col. Norris traveled east of the river to the region of Nimrud, to put in place another piece of a political reality in the micro-region under his command.

While Hamman-al-Alil had relative peace and development projects, Nimrud had only relative peace. That was because its relative peace was brand-new—a result not just of the relentless aggression of the U.S. military and new Iraqi Army, but of a political deal that Hamman-al-Alil Mayor Khalif had brokered for Nimrud with the support of Lt. Col. Norris. The deal involved an informal power-sharing agreement between the Nimrud mayor, Ahmed Obeed Isa, an ethnic Kurd, and the district police chief, Salim Salih Mishal Needa. Not that relations were good between the two men—they hated each other. Mayor Isa seemed to be a transparent, modern fledgling democrat. Chief Salim had the reputation of a thug. But reestablishing order in Nimrud following the high-water mark of the insurgency in 2004 meant allowing Chief Salim to be the real power in the area. Only recently had Lt. Col. Norris begun nudging him aside to allow Mayor Isa to truly govern.

This was classic political science theory. Sudden transitions are generally bad. Russia went cold turkey from communist authoritarianism to Western parliamentary democracy and got chaos as a result. Iberia, on the other hand, had gone from iron-fisted authoritarianism to succeedingly milder versions of it in the later Franco, Salazar, and Caetano periods, so when democracy did arrive in Spain and Portugal it did so competently. Harvard professor Samuel Huntington's *Political Order in Changing Societies* has been judged one of the great political science books of the twentieth century because, among other things, it lays out the principle that the real difference in political systems is not between those that are democratic and those that aren't, but between those that have strong institutions and those that have weak ones.[2]

Lt. Col. Norris had not read Huntington's four-decade-old book, nor had he been following discussions in Washington about the imposition of democracy. He was simply being commonsensical. He had figured out on his own that Chief Salim might have been a bad guy, but one who for the moment served a useful purpose. Salim was a less lethal thug than the ones in control prior to the American-led invasion of 2003.

Thus, he constituted a transition figure, one who could set the stage for the emergence of the lawyerly Mayor Isa. The invasion of Iraq, while arguably necessary, was at the same time cataclysmic for the country's politics down to the village level. Stabilizing the country meant reversing directions before you could move forward. It was what the Marines had learned in 2004 in the Sunni Triangle, when I saw them going behind the backs of new democratic governing councils to make deals with the tribal sheikhs.

Too, it was a matter of personalities and local situations, in which no guidance from books or from generalized policy discussions could help. Lt. Col. Norris and others in the 172nd Stryker Brigade had made the call to temporarily favor Chief Salim based primarily on a reading of his character—thuggish but capable and trustworthy. It was a reading backed up by Hamman-al-Alil Mayor Khalif. This had nothing to do with giving too much power to middle-level officers. Rather, it was about trusting the experts on the ground: something Foreign Service officers had been recommending for decades. The same principle applied to the military.

Here was Lt. Col. Norris: "Nimrud eventually requires a politician like Mayor Isa because of the mix of Arabs, Turcomans, Kurds, and Christians there. Mayor Khalif can afford to be more of a tough guy in Hamman-al-Alil because that town is ethnically more monolithic."

Mayors Khalif and Isa, Chief Salim, and others convened at a regional security meeting in Nimrud, held at a fifth-century Syrian Catholic monastery that, with its pagan Greek stucco work, Aramaic calligraphy, and bas-reliefs of early church fathers reminiscent of Assyrian and Hittite statuary, was testimony to the birth of Christianity and to the eclectic cultural stew of northern Iraq, which, after all, was central to the governing challenge.

Lt. Col. Norris, wearing pixilated camouflage with his Mohawk-style buzz cut, sat on a boxy red sofa between the two mayors and opened the meeting. He spoke for a minute or two about how honored he was to do this, how he believed in a free and democratic Iraq, and how the United States wanted nothing more than to help the Iraqi people achieve this. Power and authority flowed from him not merely because of his uniform, but because he appeared to simply believe the things he said, without nuance or embarrassment, or a sense of irony. Don't agonize, don't be complex in your spoken arguments. Believe and act starkly on your beliefs. Simple belief can be a dangerous thing, but you cannot wield dynamic power without it. Reducing anarchy was later on about root causes. Initially, it was about the reassertion of authority.

It was the first time I met Chief Salim. He had a fixed stare that never changed, no matter who was speaking, and thus gave little away, except for a sort of mournful intelligence about human affairs that could not be measured by standardized tests. In the first round of speeches everyone praised everyone else. The meeting was covered by the reopened local television network. American military officers had told me that the presence of the media might mean less candor, but it would serve the larger purpose of committing these officials to what they said.

In the second round, everyone attacked a recent release of insurgents from the Abu Ghraib prison that had been meant as a goodwill gesture. They argued that it could only worsen the security situation here. Then came demands on the Americans for more development projects. One notable said that if the Americans promised more aid, then people would be happy to vote on December 15. When the 101st Airborne Division had left this part of Iraq in 2004 and was replaced by a Stryker brigade, a significant amount of the development money went away with it. This, in turn, was part of a bigger story: the lack of continuity in assistance when one Army unit replaced another, and when a Marine unit replaced an Army one. For the Department of Defense, the occupation of Iraq was a grand conception never properly worked out in nitty-gritty detail—unlike the original invasion.

In the third round, one official attacked another for pocketing development money, which he said was the real problem. Local television put it on the record. So much for the lack of candor. There was another dispute about a missing $10,000. Here Lt. Col. Norris interjected, "I observe three people with three different understandings of what happened to the money. We will put them in a room to achieve one understanding. We will work this out, and then we will move on." Steel smile.

Back at the TOC, there was a BUB (battle update brief). An Iraqi Army unit had fired all its AK-47s in the air to celebrate alongside a wedding party. "At least they didn't fire at the wedding party, that's progress," one officer remarked. Washington categories mattered less here. It was less of an issue if the new army or police had uniforms, or even if they had fired their guns in celebration. As long as they acted professionally when doing searches, as long as they were not acting like thugs who jumped the line at gas stations, and were increasingly trusted by the population, Norris and his staff didn't complain. But the problem was, as I began to learn, that even by these ground-level standards the performance of the new Iraqi security forces was mixed.

It was Thanksgiving Day, but the main meal at the dining facility was over by the time we had returned from Nimrud and completed the BUB. Nobody complained. Norris's sergeant major for the battalion, Dennis Zavodsky of Mapleton, Oregon, got over to the gym in time to speak at an evening evangelical service. I went to observe. Lt. Col. Norris, Capt. Mann, and others were in attendance.

The audience at the service was strikingly multiracial. It began with evangelical country music songs like George Bennard's "The Old Rugged Cross," reminiscent of the music of Roy Acuff's Great Smoky Mountain Boys from the 1930s, and sung by prisoners of war at the so-called Hanoi Hilton POW camp during the Vietnam War. People sang and shouted. A Hebrew psalm was read. Soldiers began to testify about what they were grateful for. One gave thanks for the lowest casualty rate in any American ground war (excepting Desert Storm). Another thanked "the Lord for giving us a moral purpose in Iraq." A third was grateful for e-mail connections with families back home, "which our fathers did not have in Vietnam."

Sgt. Maj. Zavodsky got up to speak. He gave several factoids about Thanksgiving, including the information that ninety-one Indians had been at the first Thanksgiving, which "was a good thing," and that the Indians were later massacred, which "was a bad thing." Then he told the audience that the Pilgrims during the first winter in the New World suffered a 54 percent casualty rate from disease and cold. "That's a casualty rate that would render any of our units combat ineffective. But did the Pilgrims sail back to England? Did they give up?" he went on. "No. This country isn't a quitter. It doesn't withdraw. It doesn't give in."

Building on the conference in Nimrud was the first-ever regional "targeting meeting," held the following day at the TOC. Under 4-23's supervision, Iraqi Army and police detectives from throughout the area were brought together to exchange the latest information on particular suspects. Decisions were made about whom to ignore and whom to apprehend or kill. Facilitating were storyboards: spot visual reports aided by satellite imagery that created a narrative of each suspect's activities that went right up the chain of command on secret websites to Gen. John Abizaid, the combatant commander of Central Command in Tampa, Florida. Two of the translators working for the Americans wore masks because they didn't trust some of the Iraqi officials present.

There was talk of "Elvis sightings"—that is, local sightings of the terrorist Abu Musab al-Zarqawi (AMZ in military lingo). The term caught on because people had gotten tired of hearing false or dated reports concerning Zarqawi's whereabouts. An intriguing thing about some of the reports, though, was that Zarqawi, the master of disguise, was not always in disguise. He still had the same clipped beard, and was at times viewed easily inside a vehicle. He was brazen, confident, suicidal perhaps, or simply disdainful of the Americans' ability to catch him. Sighting him was less the challenge than enabling informants to communicate the information in real time and react fast enough to the intelligence. Of course, U.S. forces would find and kill him the following June.

In a number of the cases discussed, the insurgency was a family business: a father, son, and uncle formed the core of a cell that also had a record of small-time criminal activity. The most interesting new suspect was a female suicide bomber about to act if she wasn't apprehended first. She was the young, stylish second wife of Abu Zubayr, the insurgent leader killed by the previous Stryker brigade. She was known to have many Syrian connections and financed her own cell. Because the police chief of Hamman-al-Alil had provided some of the intelligence that had led to Abu Zubayr's death, it was thought that Hamman-al-Alil would be the target. "I'll have a photo of her in a few days," one of the Iraqi detectives promised.

This particular detective was very aggressive and always coming up with tips that panned out. Later, he would meet privately with members of the battalion to provide more detailed information about what had been discussed more generally during the meeting. Lt. Col. Norris wanted to encourage cooperation among the Iraqis, but he wasn't a fool. He simply didn't trust a bad apple or two in the room. Moving forward in a straight line was not progress but foolishness.

Another obvious lesson of the meeting was that when you squashed a network you rarely killed it; elements of it dispersed and were able to regroup from a lower level of activity. Progress rarely meant victory but moderate suppression. To wit, in Colombia, as the American military succeeded in weakening concentrations of narco-terrorists there, the terrorists were escaping in smaller numbers to adjacent Venezuela, Ecuador, and Panama. But very few American troops I met around the world got discouraged about such developments. Again, it was a matter of the simple virtues—dogged persistence, what soldiers shared with relief workers.

The next morning I went out on a seven-hour patrol with a three-vehicle platoon from A (Apache) Company. Except for getting shot at by someone with an automatic weapon and catching someone else selling bootleg gasoline that might or might not have been used to help finance the insurgency, nothing happened. The rifle shots did constitute a short-lived morale boost, though. Said one sergeant: "This deployment's bullshit. It's not like the last time in Iraq when we were always fighting." A long line of cars waiting to be searched at the eastern entrance to the city was an indication that the Iraqi Army was doing its job. "Outstanding," said the lieutenant. Inside the Stryker a specialist read a Louis D'Amour novel. The dullness of the day pointed toward the appearance of progress.

To wit, the platoon did a dismounted, or foot, patrol with an Iraqi Army counterpart. You could not help being impressed with these Iraqi troops. Their TOC was as neat and well organized as 4-23's, with flow-charts on the walls and satellite maps under table glass. They seemed to have strong noncoms with game faces who flooded out of their white pickups, and covered corners and fields of fire almost as well as the Americans. When one Iraqi soldier was about to mount the stairs to search the second floor of a suspicious house, his fellow noncom told him, "Don't go alone, take a battle buddy." That was the correct procedure.

There was only one problem—these troops were all ethnic Kurds, who in their TOC had pictures of the Kurdish leader Massoud Barzani. Would this unit stay loyal to Iraq in the event of a weakening of the state following an American drawdown of forces? Or were the Americans merely helping along the possibility of what some called "creeping Kurdistan," in which the Kurds would extend their de facto line of control to the Tigris River, lopping off the eastern side of Mosul? Was the possibility of a creeping Kurdistan actually a means of pressuring Sunni Arabs to participate constructively in the political process?

I was surprised to learn that this Iraqi Army platoon was rated next to the bottom by American military training teams (MTTs) in terms of its fighting capability. When I asked for an explanation, I was told that the unit was bureaucratically underdeveloped at the battalion level. Though fighting well at the platoon level was more important than "battalion ops," because counterinsurgency was about small-unit warfare and developing snitches, any nationwide unity of military effort was impossible without organized battalions and divisions. If this was a bad unit, then the Iraqi Army—at least in terms of professional development—was doing better than many supposed, or so I thought. Later, I heard of another platoon that stole from the places they searched and, as one American captain told me, "shit in the side rooms."

One Sunni Arab shopkeeper told me: "When American troops patrol the streets with the Iraqi Army it is so awful and humiliating for us, because we know those Iraqi soldiers are really Kurds, not Arabs. Your occupation has strengthened our enemies." This young shopkeeper, the son of a former general in Saddam's army, engaged me in conversation for more than half an hour. He was uncannily objective in his own way. He had just come back from Syria, which he heaped praise on. "Syria now is so much better than Iraq," he told me. "It is under tight control, so people there feel safe and can go about their lives with dignity. You Americans think you have brought freedom; you have just allowed the thugs from the villages to kill and rob from the educated people whom Saddam had protected."

"Your father liked Saddam?" I probed.

"My father hated Saddam," he replied. "He spit on him, in the home, that is. As long as you obeyed the rules by not criticizing the regime outside of your home, you were fine. With Saddam there were clear rules; now there are none. Now we are caught between the Americans and the insurgents. Everybody hates terrorism, but we're more vulnerable than you."

"Should the Americans leave?" I asked.

"No, that would only make things worse," he responded. He told me that he was impressed with the American military, as long as it was alone and not with the Iraqi Army. But he admitted that the Iraqi police had improved, and that Mosul was no longer a battle zone like the year before. "Your soldiers are disciplined. They don't scare people by shooting their guns in the air like ours," he said.

"But that discipline," I argued, "is an indirect effect of a free society that allows the military to constantly criticize itself."

"No, no," he said. "What good is voting if the Shiites and Kurds will vote, too? Elections are useless without water, sewage, electricity, and safety."

"So you won't vote on December 15?"

"Maybe I will vote. What else is there to do?"

He was a mass of understandable contradictions. More confusing was that another shopkeeper recommended the opposite: that U.S. soldiers should always patrol with the Iraqi Army. If you applied every recommendation you got talking to Iraqis on just one street, you'd wind up doing exactly what you were doing before. When an infantryman encountered Iraqis on patrol, the best that he could do was take off his sunglasses and his helmet too, if possible, look people directly in the eye, give them a lot of deference (especially if they were older), ask them for advice, here and there interject an opinion so as to actively engage them, and plead his case without trying to lecture. That was the only way to build trust among a population that had been taught for decades and centuries how to be subjects rather than citizens.

The method did build sympathy. Another Iraqi told me: "I like your soldiers. They are poor, simple people. The Army was the only opportunity they had. I can tell that by looking at them. In a way, they are in the same boat as us. They mean well, but what can they do?"

On a different patrol, a Sunni Arab, this one a school principal, would tell me regarding Syria: "Sure, the people there don't like the regime. But the last thing they want is the kind of freedom you Americans have brought to Iraq." In truth, these supposedly poor, simple soldiers always made it a point to introduce me to the Iraqis who they knew were the most critical of the occupation. "We want you to get the full flavor of how people feel," one captain said. No matter how hurtful the message of these conversations, the soldiers always thanked the locals for their opinions before delivering their own upbeat message.

It was simply impossible for the soldiers to be wholly liked. There was no nice way to barge into people's houses bristling with weaponry, stomping your dusty boots on their Oriental carpets, and expect it to be a pleasant experience for them, even if you handed out candy to their kids and replaced a lock you had to break with a new one. On most of the occasions there was only a woman and her children present. The soldiers would find an assault weapon that had recently been fired and half a magazine of 7.62mm bullets empty: very suspicious. Did the woman know anything about it? No, she would tell the Americans, staring past them at the wall, her eyes peering out below her kerchief. She might have been completely unknowing. She might have known a lot and was lying. She might have been hiding cellphones and identification cards of wanted criminals on her person. Only a female soldier was allowed to search her, and one usually wasn't present.

Such numerous, seemingly ineffectual searches did work to the extent that they kept terrorists on the run and at the very least inconvenienced them, as the insurgents now had to hide their guns and bomb-making paraphernalia outside the home. While this was reflected in the temporarily improved security climate, it was an inefficient way to make progress, and it bred hostility. If this kept up, I thought, the Americans would end up being as hated in Iraq as the Israelis were in the West Bank. But it would be worse for the Americans, because they would be hated even as they were not feared.

By that time, morale among the American military in Iraq would have deteriorated. Yet as long as there was sustained combat, morale was high and anyone who spoke of withdrawal was considered a defeatist. But if the current situation existed indefinitely, one of little combat and little rebuilding, then the warriors might start bitching.

In the midst of one search, I asked the Sunni Arab woman of the house about the Americans. She told me: "They do this from time to time. Some have clean tongues, some dirty tongues. But they can't stop the criminal gangs from occasionally putting a bullet in my kitchen window." She showed me the shattered window.

Under Saddam such things had not happened. The violence occurred behind closed doors, had a specific purpose, and was absolutely hideous, with people dragged away in the middle of the night, so everyone not mistreated was utterly terrified of breaking the law. Saddam's system, albeit efficient, begot obedience, not a social contract.

For its part, the U.S. military was plugging a dike of potential unrest following a hard-won remission in combat, but with still no large-scale public works projects on the horizon to soak up the crime. Only such public works projects could make Sunni Arabs—politically weaker than ever in Iraq—see the tangible benefits of democracy. Indeed, for three weeks I went out on at least one patrol a day, and the typical scenery riding air guard, my upper body sticking out of the top of the Stryker, was of a shot-to-hell cityscape of bullet-marked and half-finished buildings, gray- and rust-colored, in which every object—sign, streetlight, telephone pole—was bent or broken, and garbage filled every open lot. The only bustling commerce I saw was in the markets near the old city, which was of the subsistence kind that did not create employment.

Here and there we were attacked by small-arms fire, though rarely seriously. One local police chief told me that there were now Iraqi police and soldiers on streets where six months before there had been none, and murders and kidnappings had been reduced substantially. Security was as good as it was going to get without a major jobs program, I thought.

"That's why I like Iraq, it's always a challenge," said 1st Lt. John Turner of Indianapolis. Lt. Turner was a massive, fair-complexioned soldier with blond hair that his buzz cut made barely discernible. He looked like a simple farm boy until you heard him talk to Iraqis: about the promise of America, and about how he and his sister had grandparents who hadn't finished high school, and yet she had graduated from the Air Force Academy and he from Purdue.

"Sir, I am willing to die for a country that is not my own [Iraq]," he told a former *mukhtar* (local leader) of a section of Mosul. "So will you resume your position as *mukhtar*? Brave men must stand forward. Iraq's wealth is not oil but its civilization. Trust me by the projects I bring, not by my words. Will you stand with me against the insurgents?" softly pleaded the thirty-one-year-old lieutenant. "The men who threatened you are just sixteen-year-old boys with guns but no jobs. These projects will bring jobs to your streets."

The former *mukhtar* seemed to like the American lieutenant, as we continued to sit on his machine-made carpets, lean against undressed cinder blocks, and drink tea in his home. But he said no. "I cannot resume my role as *mukhtar*. They will kill me. The contractor down the street was threatened if he continued to repair the neighborhood. If you are so serious about security, why," he went on, "did you Americans release prisoners from Abu Ghraib?"

Lt. Turner said that the decision to release prisoners from Abu Ghraib was one made by Iraq's own new government. The former *mukhtar* wasn't convinced. Because many of the detainees at Abu Ghraib were known to be hardened criminals from the Mosul area, the release had undermined the credibility of American troops here. Abu Ghraib had a different connotation for Iraqis meeting with Americans in Mosul than it had back in the United States. Here the words meant American weakness and lack of resolve, not human rights violations.

I thought of a conversation I had had the previous summer in Algeria with one of the Algerian special forces officers. I had asked him how his government had put down its Islamic insurgency: a military success that was rewarded by the country fading out of the news without explanation. The Algerian insurgents were arguably more brutal than those in Iraq, beheading bus passengers at roadblocks on a regular desultory basis, making Algeria in the 1990s among the unsafest places in the world. What's more, the sprawling, mountainous country constituted a geography that during the best of times was a challenge to govern. The

Algerian officer told me it had been simple. Government forces, with the full support of a population devastated from constant terrorism—the psychological equivalent of a 9/11 every week—had killed many people (a portion of them innocent, I suspected) without journalists present. This was followed by internationally sanctioned elections and a steady, ongoing trickle of European investors back to Algiers. The country was impressively back on its feet. The United States, though it desired the same end-state in Iraq, could not and would not apply the same means. In Iraq the same sort of success would have to be accomplished with the most restrictive of half measures.

The former *mukhtar* said the visit had endangered his life and told Lt. Turner not to return. In the countryside the tribe could protect him, not in the city. Lt. Turner pleaded further, probing what specific security and political actions could get the former *mukhtar* to change his mind. Finally, the old sheikh said, "If the elections go well, everything will be better afterwards. We will see then."

Lt. Turner departed, saying, "I will be back. I will not quit." It hadn't been an altogether wasted afternoon. It had taken three months of pleading before anyone in the surrounding area would even tell the platoon where the former *mukhtar* lived, and after several false leads that day the soldiers had found him.

"I was a D student in high school," Turner told me. "I didn't show up to class much. I straightened out as an enlisted man in the Coast Guard, and then switched to the Army and did ROTC at Purdue. My dad was military." The corporal with Lt. Turner, Cody Thomas Faust of Morro Bay, California, also had a dad in the military and an uncle who had fought in Vietnam. Cpl. Faust could have played strong safety at Fresno State or the University of Oregon, but had enlisted instead. Before this deployment he had fought on the Afghanistan-Pakistan border. "All I ever heard growing up was 'airborne,' " he told me. It was the same with almost everybody else in this Stryker: sons of veterans.

The patrol wasn't over. After darkness we went house to house in another neighborhood from where mortars had been fired at a new Iraqi police station. Finally, someone in the fifth house cooperated and supplied information about the make of the car, the men inside it, and from where they had set up the mortar. The next step would be if the unit

could deploy snipers there for several days running, in order to elimi-
nate the culprits when they returned to a nearby field, which had a clear
line of sight to the police station. If they could do that, the people in the
other four houses might start cooperating. "I hate to say it," said Turner,
"but sometimes the best confidence-building measure is to kill certain
people."

Another thing you could do, I was told, was to pay people significantly for tips that turned out to be accurate. None of this was new, or
inspiring. But these young soldiers were learning by trial and error that
such tactics worked, assuming you had a lot of patience. It was like the
old clichés of watching the grass grow or paint dry.

The large amount of patience required for such a small measure of
success was among the many hard-to-communicate frustrations that
separated these soldiers from the civilian home front, which, in turn,
had the effect of bringing them closer and closer to one another. Such
togetherness, if accompanied by death and loss in combat over a sustained period, created the deepest of bonds.

I remembered a Marine sergeant I had met at Quantico the year before, who told me that after each nighttime combat sortie, his men
would not go to bed until the debrief was completed, and the equipment
cleaned and refit for the next day. Near dawn they would wash away the
blood and grime, and sleep a few hours. "Even when the lieutenant
praised them after a mission, I knew they had fucked up and I chewed
the hell out of them," the sergeant told me. In a loud, deliberate voice,
he then declared, "I love my men. For seven months they put up with
my shit and still loved me for it."

The late historian William Manchester writes that he and his fellow
marines at the Battle of Okinawa in 1945 fought because of the "love"
they felt for one another. That love was connected to pride, something
sacred, that only in recent decades has been "derided as machismo."[3]
Indeed, when men who had been together for months at a time in the
front lines in Iraq or Afghanistan began to go their separate ways, they
told me of a loss akin to losing their wives, or their children almost.

F. Scott Fitzgerald believed that such love among American soldiers
and marines had been extinguished in World War I. But Fitzgerald
died a year before Pearl Harbor. Manchester, writing in *Goodbye, Dark-*

ness: A Memoir of the Pacific War, also believed that his generation—toughened by the Depression and "the absolute conviction" of the moral superiority of the United States—would be the last to see combat as an act of love. But that turned out not to be the case. Army Brig. Gen. James E. Shelton (Ret.) writes: "I never expect to see again in my life young men of eighteen, nineteen, or twenty years of age who understand the true meaning of the word 'love' as I saw it in Vietnam, in the men who cared about each other and would sacrifice for their buddies."[4] So it was, too, in Iraq.

The troops with whom I spent time spoke constantly about heroes, which the world media had shown limited interest in covering. Take Army Sgt. 1st Class Paul Ray Smith of Tampa, Florida, thirty-three, married with two children. He had advanced alone under withering enemy fire near Baghdad airport on April 4, 2003, so that he could man a .50-caliber machine gun atop an armored vehicle and protect his wounded comrades from being overrun. Killed in the process, he was awarded posthumously the nation's highest, rarely bestowed decoration, the Medal of Honor, with his wife receiving the award. This first Medal of Honor in the Global War on Terrorism had drawn only 90 media mentions, though. By comparison, there had been 4,677 media mentions of the supposed Koran abuse at Guantánamo Bay, and 5,159 of the court-martialed Abu Ghraib guard Lynndie England.[5] While the exposure of wrongdoing by American troops is obviously of paramount importance, less obviously it can become a tyranny of its own when taken to an extreme.

On another occasion I accompanied Lt. Col. Norris to the office of the acting Mosul police chief, Wathiq Mohammed Abdul Khader. We walked in on a heated discussion the chief was having with two Americans in polo shirts and cargo pants, and packing 9mm Berettas. The chief sat behind a massive wooden desk that faced a television showing an old black-and-white Arab movie with the sound turned off. Ashtrays overflowed. In the back of the cavernous room an aide seemed to be dozing. The Americans were private contractors who had been detectives back in the United States, probably with military backgrounds. Seventeen Iraqi policemen were suspected of involvement in a terror ring that was accused of kidnapping, beatings, and a dismemberment.

"Don't worry, if they are immoral I will finish them," the chief said.

"I need evidence," explained one of the Americans, a bit exasperated. "All I've heard is hearsay, which I believe. But to mount a case, I need witnesses. I realize American standards don't apply here, and we are working by your rules, but I have to live with my conscience."

"Don't worry, we will take care of it."

"I need the ringleader separated from the others," the American went on, "and I need to interrogate them all separately. I need access."

"We will get the weakest one to confess," the chief said.

"Without beating him," the American advised. "When will you arrest them?" he added.

"Soon," the chief said.

Finally the chief, who was a dramatic improvement over his predecessor, agreed to put all seventeen under house arrest immediately and to provide the Americans the access they needed. The American had pleaded for fast action but within proper standards. The chief, worried about political and tribal fallout, had been a bit less eager to take action, but was also less anxious about how the accused would be handled once they had been apprehended.

In this corrupt and rudimentary democratic system, the police would be a particular challenge. Third-world police work usually meant watching television, sipping *chai,* taking a nap, sipping more *chai,* and collecting a paycheck. In such countries, police were little more than traffic cops. For a citizen to get a policeman to do anything for him, whether in today's Mexico or in Saddam's Iraq, he had to bribe him. Countries with venerable political patronage systems, however corrupt and undemocratic, could survive like that, but a created-from-scratch affair like post-Saddam Iraq could not. Nonetheless, with the police, too, there were some bright spots to be exploited. Take the Hamman-al-Alil police chief, Khaled Hussein, who had been stabbed and IEDed by insurgents, and whose brother had been killed by them. He was known by 4-23 to be "committed to the fight," and maintained a meticulous filing system of area "bad guys." Even in a dismal environment, you could find and empower force multipliers.

The flight in a Black Hawk south to the Qayyarah-West forward operating base (FOB) took fifteen minutes and was marked by small-arms fire directed at the helicopter, which one of the side gunners responded to with a short burst. It had been little more than a nuisance. Upon landing I found myself with the 4th Battalion of the 11th Field Artillery Regiment, another part of the 172nd Stryker Brigade. The 4-11 "Arctic Thunder" was a busy battalion. Though almost all the work it did in Iraq was infantry related—shepherding the development of an Iraqi army brigade, while cat-herding twenty-one new Iraqi police stations along the Tigris River valley—it still had to work nights to renew its artillery certification on the 155mm howitzer.

The first place I traveled with the soldiers of 4-11 was to the town of Om al-Mahir, an area under the command of thirty-one-year-old Capt. Jeff Ferguson of Columbus, Mississippi, a graduate of Mississippi State University. The desert was like an unending sheet of cardboard, a dirt lot that never ended. New construction was everywhere, along with brand-new plastic café chairs and satellite dishes. Throughout the journey, crowds of kids gave the Americans the thumbs-up symbol. Streets were also cleaner than in Mosul because of a trash removal program that employed some of the area's teenagers, started by Capt. Ferguson. Safety was helped by periodic Iraqi Army and police roadblocks. Just as in 2004, when I had last visited Iraq, the rural areas were safer than the urban ones. Of course, the rural areas mattered less in the scheme of things.

At Om al-Mahir, amid a patch of grass and faded oleanders, a large crowd of American soldiers, tribal elders, and young Iraqi men and boys sprawled over Oriental carpets for what the troops called a "goat grab," a meal of grilled meat on a bed of unleavened bread that you ate with your hands. Iraqi Gen. Ali Attalah Malloh al-Jabouri, commander of one of the battalions under 4-11's tutelage, spoke to the assembled. The Americans had left their helmets and body armor in their Humvees a few hundred yards away and their weapons against a wall, entrusting their safety to Iraqi soldiers.

"The hands of men who are without work will end up cooperating with the devil," said Gen. Ali, addressing the Americans and Capt. Ferguson in particular. He followed with details of this young man and that one who were unemployed, and who had drifted north to Mosul to take part in the insurgency.

"Where is the investment money, now that our area has been safe for months?" The American soldiers essentially had no answer for Gen. Ali. They were as frustrated as the Iraqis. Even the safe areas were absent of any sign of civilian relief work or private development. The soldiers admitted that while they had the money to gravel over a particular road, they lacked the funds to pave it, even as all agreed that graveled roads were easier to conceal IEDs on.

It was surreal. The stability of Iraq would likely determine history's judgment on President George W. Bush. Yet even in a newly secured area like this one, there appeared to be little available money for the one factor at the center of generating that stability: jobs.

Out of a landscape flattened by anarchy in 2004, the American military had constructed a flimsy house of cards by late 2005 that, in order to be fortified by wood and cement, now required a massive injection of aid—of a type and scale that even America's increasingly unconventional, civil affairs–oriented military could not provide. But because the official statements from Washington did not match the reality that I saw firsthand, this flimsy house of cards was threatened with collapse.

Gen. Ali, seconded by one of the *mukhtars,* next spoke about the need for vigilance against a return to the terrorism that had recently plagued the area. It was a terrorism he had largely stamped out by a combination of theological arguments to the *mukhtars,* the hunting down and killing of insurgents so that the inhabitants would fear his men more than the terrorists, and calculated displays of bravery like not wearing body armor.

He gave a stack of money to a little boy who had noticed two men stop by a road with a motorbike and dig a hole, to plant what turned out to be an IED. "See this money," the general said as he held out the stack to a group of young men. "It could be yours if you catch a terrorist in the act or shoot him in the face. Why not?" Like Lt. Turner, nobody here quarreled with the need to kill certain people.

That night I accompanied 4-11's battalion commander, Lt. Col. Scott Wuestner of Philadelphia—a former tight end on the West Point football team—to the home of another sheikh. The town that this sheikh controlled had recently become unfriendly, with fewer cheers from the kids and an increasing number of "stink stares" from the grown-ups whenever American soldiers passed. The sheikh had prepared an extravagant dinner for us. He denied with smiles that anyone he knew had become unfriendly. Then he excused himself for a moment, and one of his subordinates casually mentioned to Lt. Col. Wuestner that people were becoming impatient. They wanted loans for a cotton gin, chicken farms, and so forth, yet nothing was happening. Wuestner wrote it all down in one of those field books covered with green cloth that American soldiers and marines carried, but it was unclear if he could find the funds. The newly released "National Strategy for Victory in Iraq" was merely a document; the difficulty in finding money at ground level when a battalion commander needed it was real.

"We can race around the battlefield and fix little problems, but where is the State Department and USAID [United States Agency for International Development] to solve the big problems?" one Army major complained to me. President Bush's list of projects under way and accomplished in the Mosul area—communicated in his December 7, 2005, speech to the nation—was accurate. Yet such individual projects simply disappeared into the immensity of Mosul's cityscape and its environs.

Meanwhile, these battalion commanders had no choice but to encourage Iraqis to seek help from their own, barely functioning ministries. The Americans sought genuinely to transfer power and responsibility to the Iraqis. But for the Iraqis themselves, history had taught them to think of power not in any formal or legalistic sense but crudely, in terms of who actually wielded the authority to help, and to punish severely.

Yet the military might still do more, I thought. For example, I hadn't noticed the Army holding MEDCAPS (medical civil action programs) for the local population as I had seen it do in Mongolia, the Philippines, Kenya, Djibouti, and other places. No activity developed relationships (and hence intelligence assets) like treating people for disease and illness.

As long as the U.S. military was still, to all intents and purposes, trying to save Iraq by itself, staving off anarchy meant essentially drinking a lot of *chai*—that is, think of any excuse you could to get out of the base in order to meet and jawbone with the locals. To wit, Wuestner, a conventional artillery officer, told me of a meal he had eaten with thirteen *mukhtars*. "When everyone lined up to wash their hands, I gave them the towel [a mark of extreme politeness in Iraqi culture]. I've learned that gestures like that count for more than a lot of the raids we do." As necessary as killing insurgents was, establishing relationships was more important still. "Ninety-nine percent of my time is on the go, outside the FOB," one major would tell me. "I don't bother to write down convoy numbers, to get written approval, I just leave the base whenever I can to meet locals."

Truly, the regular Army in Iraq had been forced into a classic unconventional mode, even as the Green Berets themselves were still stuck, to too large an extent, in the macho culture of direct action. The rank structure of the Stryker battalions was also becoming more like that of the noncom-oriented Green Berets, for as the Stryker battalions remained intact, promotions within the battalions made them top-heavy with sergeants, much like the SF A-teams with which I had been embedded.

It was near midnight when I returned to 4-11's TOC with Lt. Col. Wuestner. He was not discouraged, though he had to write officer evaluation reports that would keep him up into the wee hours before another grueling day of visits with Iraqi commanders and sheikhs. Wuestner, who was so gregarious that I simply couldn't imagine him discouraged or unhappy, told me, "We can win this thing even if it takes ten years." It might have been Bush's war, it might have been a gargantuan mistake, but none of that mattered to him. "The media wants to feel sorry for us. But I don't want to be safe. Has anyone noticed that we now have a volunteer army? I'm a warrior. It's my job to fight. How can quitting in Iraq be in my interest or that of any other American soldier's?"

I thought of a conversation I had eighteen months earlier with Lt. Col. Brennan Byrne, the commander of the 1st Battalion of the 5th Marines, who had told me the same things. That earlier conversation had occurred before the First Battle of Fallujah, before the Abu Ghraib scandal, and before a lot of other deeply discouraging news about Iraq.

Yet the dogged determination of these officers persisted. They could win if only the home front would let them. After all, look at the progress they had made since 2004. The fact that such progress was modest and ephemeral did not mean that it wasn't real to them.

My next visit was to Forward Operating Base Crazy Horse, named thus by the 101st Airborne Division, which had previously occupied the site. FOB Crazy Horse, east across the desert from Qayyarah-West, was within sight of the front range of the Kurdish mountains and not far from Gaugamela, where in 331 B.C. Alexander the Great had defeated the Persians under Darius III. The ancient battlefield was just another tract of desert, without anything to mark it. The FOB was occupied by the first Iraqi Army battalion in northern Iraq that would assume command of its own battlespace. It had only a handful of American officers and trainers embedded with it, though, once again, the complicating factor was that the battalion was ethnically Kurdish, with Kurdish flags and pictures of the Kurdish leader Barzani in evidence.

Nevertheless, the battalion's area of responsibility had a population evenly split between Kurds and Sunni Arabs, and under the leadership of its Kurdish commander, Lt. Col. Hogar Salahidin Abdul, it had drastically reduced the level of violence in the region. Whenever Lt. Col. Hogar went to a village, large numbers of Sunni Arab sheikhs came out to greet him, praise him, and bluntly complain to him—the mark of an honest and healthy relationship.

I went with Lt. Cols. Hogar and Wuestner to the village of Tal Ashir, in the Tigris River valley, to meet with the area sheikhs. This visit, more than the previous ones, summed up for me the immensity of the challenge facing the American military in Iraq.

Upon arrival, the Americans left their helmets and body armor in their vehicles. Lt. Col. Wuestner held hands with the leading sheikh, another sign of respect and friendship. Two long lines of aging men wearing white-and-red-checkered keffiyahs lined up to greet us. Nearby were tables with greasy lamb and chicken on flat bread.

Then the hand-holding was followed by hugs, followed in turn by the words of the leading sheikh: "We say thanks up to God for your visit. We are pleased that you care about us. But with all due respect, we have no electricity. And though we live along the river, we have no water. All we ask is that you restore services in this village to the levels they were under the former regime."

In fact, there had been electricity in Tel Ashir until a few days before. The power line, according to the villagers, had been cut by soldiers from another Iraqi Army battalion, the one of Gen Ali. Lt. Col. Wuestner said that this was ridiculous. The villagers continued with more theories and accusations: one was that the power line could not bear the load of new villages that had been added to it, and that those other villages should have their electricity cut for the sake of Tal Ashir. "The sub-district manager is useless because he can't impose his will on the Jabouri tribe," warned one old man. Tal Ashir, it happened, was populated by the rival Sabawi tribe. "Please don't escalate this into a tribal dispute," the Kurd, Lt. Col. Hogar of the Iraqi Army, pleaded. According to another suspicion, a local radical leader, Sheikh Hussein Abdel-Azziz Hamed Naif, whose party was contesting the upcoming elections with an anti-American platform, and who had gotten control of a local television station, was also involved.

The simple matter of an electricity cut, which might have had the most mundane of technical causes, aggravated by the very extension of electric power to nearby villages, had ignited a groundswell of divisive suspicions, for which the villagers of Tal Ashir, it was clear, expected the American officer more than the Iraqi ethnic-Kurdish one to fix. The situation in Tal Ashir, more than any particular election process, was the daily reality of post-Saddam Iraq in a part of the country that was a relative success story at the time.

In every place we went and took off our body armor, we did so under the assurance that this sub-tribe or that sheikh had guaranteed our security. It was a classic mafia system, the kind that for centuries, in many parts of the world, had constituted an efficient contrivance against anarchy. Iraq under the old regime had been built on succeeding, compacted tiers of these tribal mafias that culminated at the top with Saddam and Sons. The cost was high: the violent death, direct or indirect, of several times more people than the number killed by the former Yugoslav dictator Slobodan Milošević. But now the place was functionally ours, whoever happened to win the elections.

The Bush administration had confused elections with authority. Elections were a day-long procedural event, while authority was a legitimate system of control that could take an exceptionally long time to build. For years, fearful of anarchy, I had warned in print about our over-zealousness in promoting Western democracy abroad. Yet I had also supported the invasion of Iraq, as the old regime here was so awful (as bad as Stalin during the worst of the 1930s) that it went far beyond the bounds of normal dictatorship, and thus itself constituted a form of anarchy masquerading as tyranny. The arguments of those who felt that the toppling of Saddam was a blunder destined to go wrong had to be taken seriously, given what had transpired. On the other hand, to say that the outcome would have been just as bad no matter how the occupation was handled—that it would have failed abjectly even if there had been many more American troops on the ground, and even if we had done a lot of other things differently, too—was an extreme form of determinism with which I could never agree. Nothing was destined. But the bigger the risk being taken, the more meticulous and self-critical the planning had to be at every stage. And while small, light-footprint deployments worked in most places as a means to avoid full-scale invasions, once such an invasion was thought to be necessary, the larger the footprint the better.

—

While soldiers could hope only to stabilize such a country by getting outside the base perimeter, it was doubtful that more than one out of ten did so. Of the 150,000 or so American troops in Iraq, only a very small fraction dealt with Iraqis in any substantial way. Back in Mosul with the 4-23 Tomahawks at FOB Marez, I had lunch in the massive chow hall with Capt. Brad Velotta of Alexandria, Louisiana, a graduate of the New Mexico Military Academy in Roswell. He and I figured out that with all the support troops and private contractors who kept the base running, the total population of the FOB was roughly three thousand, whereas no more than two hundred or so troops and civilian operatives ventured into Mosul on any given day. The result of this support was amenities like heating and the Internet, as well as crab, lobster, steak, and ice cream in the chow hall. Capt. Velotta commanded one of the battalion's three rifle companies. His whole purpose in Iraq was to be constantly outside the wire, where he could get shot or IEDed. He spoke about the Marine detachments sent to fight near the Syrian border. They slept in the dirt and their force protection, rather than guard posts as at the FOB (which sucked yet more manpower from the fighting units), was just themselves, fanning out into a 360-degree formation at night. Zero support tail, in other words. No ice cream, no Internet, no nothing except sleeping bags and MREs.

Now that wasn't a wholly fair assessment, he quickly admitted, since the Marines relied on fuel, ammunition, equipment, and MREs that, in turn, required the support of large bases like this one. But it did capture a truth—that there might be some leeway to reduce the American presence in Iraq without proportionally undermining the war effort. The need for lobster, steaks, and ice cream was part of an occupation mentality, as in West Germany during the Cold War, even as Iraq still required a fighting mentality. Sparer bases meant more people outside the perimeter, because the very comforts inside the base subtly lessened the incentive of commanders to take troops outside for too long. There was an undeniable contradiction between the high living standard the Army felt it had to provide for the sake of soldiers' morale and the new warrior ethos it was trying to promote. Staying with the Marines in the Sunni Triangle and in sub-Saharan Africa in the spring and summer of 2004, living substantially on MREs, I had learned that often the worse the conditions, the better the mood of the troops, at least in the short term. In the field, troops lived for the moment; at the base, eating good chow, they counted the days.

The Army thought differently, though. It planned to reduce troop strength by consolidating FOBs into super-FOBs, so that there would be less duplication of support services, even as the same high living standards could be maintained. In an atmospheric sense, then, these enlarged FOBs were about to become like the vast, little-America Burger King bases in Europe and Turkey. At the same time, by turning over the commands of various regions to Iraqi forces, the Army planned to reduce the American footprint and wean the Iraqis off dependence on the Americans.

In one sense the Army was right. There weren't any great logistical efficiencies out there. You couldn't substantially reduce the total number of American troops in Iraq without also reducing the number who went outside the base perimeters. While you could save on support troops here and there with enlarged FOBs, in fact most of the logistical element of the occupation was already being handled by civilian contractors. The American face in Iraq in the early twenty-first century was as much the rough-and-tumble KBR employee as the American soldier. It was KBR that provided items like lobster and ice cream, not some long and imagined support tail of men and women in camouflage. Because so much had already been outsourced, it was hard to reduce the support tail without also undermining fighting elements like the Stryker brigade.

Thus, as my days in Iraq multiplied in late 2005, I had become increasingly leery of any but the most cautious and calibrated of drawdowns.

Whereas the colonels I met were confident that the Iraqi Army and police were capable of bearing the burden of a reduction of American forces, the staff sergeants and other noncoms who worked on a daily basis with the new Iraqi security elements were less so. "Trust me, sir," one staff sergeant confided about an Iraqi Army unit with which his platoon had just completed a three-hour patrol, "if we leave, they won't show up again in this neighborhood. They'll never leave their base." On another occasion, while surveying a school slated to be a polling station, the local Iraqi Army commander kept insisting that his men be able to camp out at the school overnight. The American captain kept telling him no. One of the noncoms remarked quietly, "It's the same old story, all they want to do is hunker down and play defense, but they will not be able to hold off this insurgency unless they play offense." As for the Iraqi police, once again, there was even less confidence. The most generous quote I got was from a junior officer, who said: "Some IP [Iraqi police] units are good, others are as crooked as New York City cops around 1850."

The best scenario I could then anticipate was a colonial-like situation years down the road that would never be referred to by name, in which there might be ten thousand American troops left in Iraq, embedded in various ministries and throughout the military and police, propping up the security structure behind the scenes. It would be much like in the Philippines in the early twentieth century, following the American invasion and our protracted counterinsurgency campaign there. If you were now to visit any number of places in the Balkans or the Caucasus, you would find quite a few American military officers or private contractors working in this and that defense ministry, and in this and that army unit, all very low-key, so it never became a political issue.

But the United States wasn't even remotely close to that point in Iraq.

Iraq's other legacy might be on the future of American leadership itself. One afternoon I observed a group of junior officers and a few noncoms plan the upcoming elections in the part of Mosul under the battalion's command: the ballot convoys, the sniffer dogs for the polling stations, the security for the ballots up until the moment Iraqi officials counted them. Essentially, they were managing a process behind the scenes for which the Iraqi Army and police were to take public credit. If you wanted to locate America's future elected leaders, I thought, it might be here in this room and all over Iraq.

When Col. Michael Shields of Kennebunk, Maine, the commander of the 172nd Stryker Brigade, went over a map of Mosul with me, he referred to each area not according to the lieutenant colonel in his forties whose battalion it was, but according to each captain in his late twenties or early thirties whose company it was—each of whom he knew personally, and each of whom he referred to as a "soldier-statesman," for that's what they were.

What other group of young people, I asked myself, could possibly compete with these officers as future leaders? These young men not only had military experience like the veterans of World War II and Vietnam, but they also had acquired hands-on knowledge of governance and civil affairs of a sort somewhat rare in American military history. Being a veteran had always carried a terrific advantage for political candidacy in America. But it would be more so in coming decades, given that future veterans from the Global War on Terrorism would boast a résumé of lessons learned applicable to the practice and development of democracy itself.

There were quite a few of them, to the extent that the young captain

who was a de facto mayor of an Iraqi town or village had become almost a commonplace for a time in newspaper feature articles. Voters
loved stories and anecdotes, and these young soldiers, as well as the veterans of Bosnia and Kosovo and Afghanistan, would have the best
stump pitches about combining the frontier ethos of practicality and
idealism in the service of the national interest. Nation-building, well,
they had done it—or at least tried it—through a tightly organized operational planning process in which failure was not (according to their
value system) ever an option.

Given their own experience on the ground, as future leaders they
would be extremely skeptical of forcibly implanting democracy in a
place with no experience of it. Yet they might be just as hostile toward
those who advocated a surrender strategy in the face of adversity, before
all the facts were in. They had learned in the field to be internationalists
rather than isolationists, but internationalists of a very pragmatic sort.
Not for them the beauty of ideas, unless those ideas survived testing.
Their specific tendency would be to pull both political parties toward
the center, and thus they bore the hope of a renewal of American politics.

A final impression of Iraq: one day I had gone with a group of American soldiers to the sprawling ruins of Hatra, a city founded upon the fall
of Nineveh at the end of the seventh century B.C., and which reached its
peak in the second and third centuries A.D. Hatra lay in the midst of the
desert southwest of Mosul, empty of other visitors, without even a
guardrail or derelict ticket stand, as though awaiting rediscovery by
some Victorian-era explorers. Indeed, the only sign of the twentieth
century was the initials of Saddam carved into bricks throughout the
complex, which now appeared like the marks of just another tyrant from
antiquity.

Hatra had flourished as a Silk Road nexus of trade and ideas, reflected in its mix of Assyrian, Hellenistic, Parthian, and Roman styles,
which set the stage for early Islamic architecture. The ruins encouraged
the notion that Iraq's best available future was as a similar East-West
crossroads, in a Middle East of weaker, decentralized states, states that
would succeed the tyrannical perversions of the modern nation-state

system still in the process of crumbling. In decades ahead, cities like Mosul and Aleppo would be oriented (as they had been in the past) as much toward each other and toward cities in Turkey and Iran as toward their respective capitals of Baghdad and Damascus. Obviously, borders would matter less, as old caravan routes flourished in different form. Something comparable had already begun in the Balkans, a more developed part of the Ottoman Empire than Mesopotamia. In Mesopotamia, this transition would be longer, costlier, and messier. We were in for a very long haul. Excepting the collapse of Turkey's empire, the creation of the State of Israel, and the Iranian Revolution, neither anything nor anybody in a century had so jolted the Middle East as had George W. Bush.

EIGHT

A DEPENDABLE BLUE-COLLAR PLANE

WITH AN AIR FORCE A-10 SQUADRON

Thailand, Winter 2006

After Iraq, it was back to the Pacific to embed with the Air Force. It would be my fifth trip to the Pacific Rim and my seventh to the PACOM area of responsibility in three years. On none of these trips did I bring a jacket and tie. I felt a bit incongruous on commercial airliners crossing the Pacific, wearing cargo pants, surrounded by men and women in the latest business attire, at a time in history when the words "Pacific Rim" signaled unprecedented economic growth. Yet it was precisely because of its surging economies that the Far East was also seeing extraordinary military buildups.

The world of men and guns might have been an afterthought to my fellow passengers. Trade, finance, and the burgeoning consumer power of India and China dominated media coverage of Asia. At the conferences I had attended around the world in the 1990s, military matters were relegated to a briefing or two by a retired general, even as dozens upon dozens of seminars were devoted to political and economic issues. It was an age when the elites of America, Europe, and Asia had, in the main, little or no experience—let alone meaningful social contacts—with the uniformed ranks of their respective countries. Intellectually, they might have grasped the importance of military transformation in Asia, especially as it concerned the problems of Taiwan and North Korea. Still, it was human nature to see reality in terms of one's own daily experiences and the people one encountered.

To see how trade and technology were transforming Asia you didn't necessarily have to travel in well-heeled circles—it was all around you, and on every newsstand. Contrarily, the military situation lay hidden behind a screen of bases, and aboard ships, boats, and airplanes.

My plan was to link up with the 25th Tactical Fighter Squadron stationed at Osan Air Base in South Korea, and fly with it to Korat Royal Thai Air Force Base in Thailand to participate in Cope Tiger, an annual exercise that the air forces of the United States, Thailand, and Singapore had been conducting for thirteen years. The point of Cope Tiger (Combined Operation Exercise Tiger) was as much diplomatic as military. Again, it was about China. From a geostrategic standpoint, relatively strong countries enveloped China to the north, east, and southwest: Russia, Japan, Korea, and India. The easiest outlet for China's ambitions was the relatively weak countries of Southeast Asia.[1]

China was dominating trade in Southeast Asia through a new summit architecture. It was forging bilateral military relationships with longtime U.S. allies Thailand and the Philippines, protecting the military dictatorship in Burma, initiating a strategic partnership with Indonesia, putting all sorts of pressure on Singapore, and using trade as a wedge between the United States and Australia.[2] The growing Chinese business community in Bangkok had plans to build a canal across the Isthmus of Kra in Thailand, connecting the Andaman Sea with the Gulf of Siam and the South China Sea. The Chinese military saw not only Taiwan but also the Philippines as a potential forward base from which to project power farther out into the Pacific. "The Chinese are making the Filipinos increasingly dependent on their economy, and that will come back to haunt us," a three-star Air Force general told me.

For the sake of a stable, regional balance of power, Cope Tiger was not the answer to managing China's political and economic expansion in Asia. But given China's rise, the exercise was, at the very least, a necessity.

Yet, American participation this year had been cut by half. A squadron of F-15s was to have participated from Elmendorf Air Force Base in Anchorage, Alaska. So were Marine F-18s that had been forward-deployed in the Pacific. Both cancellations hit the local economy in northeastern Thailand hard. The reasons given were lack of money related to the increased price of jet fuel—a pathetic excuse. It was ultimately because of Iraq, though no one would admit it officially.

Thus, the 25th would be the only American jet squadron participating. The Thais and Singaporeans could not have been pleased, especially as the A-10s flown by the 25th did not integrate well with their own F-16s and F-5s. If the reduced American presence at Cope Tiger became more than a one-year aberration, it would signify another small victory for Beijing, and would be a sign that America's fragile virtual empire could handle many small wars and deployments, but not a messy large-scale one.

I had first been exposed to the Air Force in late 2004 during a windshield tour of American bases and austere outposts around the Pacific. Now I would embed with airmen for several weeks. The 25th Tactical Fighter Squadron, known as the "Assam Draggins," was actually just what I had been looking for. Its first aerial combat mission was flying over the "hump" in 1942, from Assam in British India to northern Burma, to bomb the Japanese. The 25th saw intensive aerial combat in the Korean War with F-80s (the first fighter jets), and in the Vietnam War with F-4s. Since 1982 the squadron had been flying A-10 Thunderbolt IIs, nicknamed "Warthogs," because they hunted low to the ground "in the dirt." This was the same A-10 that had provided close air support (CAS) for Army Special Forces in Afghanistan and Iraq, which I had seen on the tarmac three years earlier at Bagram Air Base.[3]

Since 1975 the A-10 had been performing a role similar to that of the fabled Flying Tigers of the Asian theater in World War II. It was originally designed to operate in the crappy weather of the Fulda Gap in Germany, whose low cloud cover made it necessary to fly close to the ground in order to kill tanks. The plane's bent-up, Hershey bar wings provided stability in heavy air. It was antiquated, and yet more up to date than the latest fighter jets in an age of counterinsurgency and unconventional war.* Rugged and relevant, at $10 million apiece it was a third the price of most fighter jets, and a twentieth of that of the F-22. Army Special Forces liked the plane much more than did the Air Force bigwigs, who were often former F-series pilots with a prejudice against the A-10. Nevertheless, such attitudes were changing in light of the A-10's impressive performance in Afghanistan and Iraq.

The A-10 wasn't fast and high-tech, and that was the point. A-10 pilots loitered over the battlefield, risking ground fire, and thus had real situational awareness. "We pride ourselves in being able to see the battlefield from the point of view of the commander on the ground," one of the pilots told me. Army Special Forces considered Air Force A-10 pilots true warriors. A-10 pilots reciprocated with a mentality that was more *joint* and pro-Army than other branches of the Air Force.

A-10 pilots represented a Special Forces culture fitted to the air. After a high-ranking officer had upbraided two A-10 pilots for flying too low over an airfield, a third pilot came up to me and said, referring to the high-ranking officer, "He's from the B-1 bomber community, he doesn't know what 'low' is." Then he went on, "We're a culture that asks forgiveness after the fact, rather than permission before the fact. That's the only way to accomplish our mission."

The A-10 pilots of the 25th would be at the forefront of close air support in the event of any ground war on the Korean Peninsula. They were oak trees—cemented to the DMZ. Cope Tiger was a monumental change for them, the first time that they would train outside Korea.

Getting the A-10 squadron off the Korean Peninsula, even for a few weeks, was not a decision made lightly. It had gone all the way up the chain of command at the Pentagon. For years, the South Korean government had been increasingly restricting A-10 training sorties in order to satisfy domestic anti-Americanism. It had become a game. Aware that deployment times of such squadrons was a year, the South Koreans would keep delaying flight requests until a new squadron arrived and the process started again. At the same time, the South Koreans claimed to be providing the U.S. Air Force with all it needed to defend the

---

* The A-10 was more properly called an "attack" jet, but the word "fighter" was applied liberally to it.

country. By deploying the 25th to train in the less restricted airspace of northeastern Thailand, the U.S. Air Force had called a bluff, stating publicly in effect that Seoul could not provide it with what it needed to defend South Korea.

———

Embedding with the Air Force for the first time, I had to familiarize myself with a whole new bureaucratic hierarchy. For example, the rank above senior airman was staff sergeant; a plain sergeant did not exist in the Air Force. Nor were there warrant officers. Instead of a sergeant major, there was a chief master sergeant. Rather than battalions, regiments, and divisions, or fleets and carrier strike groups, there were squadrons, wings, and "numbered air forces." An average squadron (if there were such a thing) comprised 50 planes and anywhere from 500 to 1,000 airmen, including logistics, maintenance, medical, and administrative elements. Three squadrons usually but not always formed a wing, which might comprise anywhere from 1,200 to 5,000 airmen. A wing was part of a numbered air force, essentially a war-fighting headquarters for a large geographical area. In this case, the 7th Air Force handled the Korean Peninsula with its two wings, the 8th Fighter Wing ("Wolf Pack") stationed at Kunsan, and the 51st Fighter Wing ("Mustangs") stationed at Osan. Nicknames of Air Force units did not hark back to the Indian Wars the way that those in the Army did.

Located at Osan, only forty-eight miles from the demilitarized zone with North Korea, the 51st Mustangs constituted the most forward-deployed, permanently based Air Force wing in the world. It comprised only two squadrons: the 36th Fighter Squadron, which flew F-16s, and the 25th, with its A-10s, with which I would embed.

All this bureaucratic terminology mattered because it was central to the Air Force's identity, and as such was referred to by airmen constantly. Though begotten by the Army following World War II, the Air Force was more easily compared to the Navy than to the other services. Both the Air Force and the Navy served as transportation systems for the Army and the Marine Corps. Indeed, among the four armed services under the Pentagon's domain, there was a further division: between the Navy and Air Force on the one hand, and the Army and Marines on the other. The world of the first two was dominated by technology to a greater degree than that of the second two. With obvious exceptions, like the Navy's *über*-macho SEALs, sailors and airmen were simply less physical than soldiers and marines. More than their Army and Marine brethren, the self-images of sailors and airmen were determined by the technology they had mastered more than by the number of push-ups they could do, or by the number of guns they owned. Sailors and airmen, again as a generality, seemed at first glance to be less *ancient* and warrior-like than Army and Marine grunts.

Because they did not occupy territory, navies and air forces were thought to be inherently more democratic than the other services. As I mentioned earlier, navies had been a tool of diplomacy in ways that armies had not. Navies and air forces needed to occupy only a limited amount of territory to project power, whereas for armies, taking territory was the whole point. Yet air forces could travel faster and dominate even more territory than navies, and also required more highly centralized, global coordination. Thus, it remained to be seen whether air forces (and the space forces that would follow later in the twenty-first century) would prove to be quite as politically benign as navies. Because it took so long for navies to get somewhere, navies urged on the diplomatic process, rather than short-circuited it.[4]

A recent visit I had made to the Air Force Academy in the foothills of the Rocky Mountains, outside the conservative, evangelical bastion of Colorado Springs, evinced a radically different atmosphere than the East Coast–based service academies. Compared to that of West Point and Annapolis, the architectural ambience of the Air Force Academy was alienating, austere, and technological. The combination of extreme isolation, a nearby evangelicism, and a heavy, science-based curriculum carried the danger of an authoritarian mindset. Yet when I actually got to know academy cadets and graduates on an individual basis, I realized that such a danger was still theoretical. Yes, faith was something emphasized by the chaplains, but that was to be expected, since a cadet could not get through such a tough four-year curriculum without something deep inside him or her.

The Air Force was created by Congress in 1947. Had there been no Air Force, the old Army Air Forces would have executed tactically oriented land campaigns and naval air wings strategic ones, like covering oceanic spaces and protecting sea-lanes, as well as conducting littoral operations.* But even before Vietnam and Iraq, the Korean War had shown the value of this new armed service, which, together with naval air, provided the principal military means of forcing the North Korean communists to the negotiating table. By the turn of the twenty-first century, the Air Force had evolved into a global bus system for the U.S. military, deploying to 182 out of 210 countries annually, holding exercises with 65 countries, and assisting 98 in humanitarian crises. The Air Force was now central to peacekeeping operations in 20 countries. It had identified mass graves in Bosnia and Kosovo, and proved indispensable in both the Balkan and Iraq wars. It also operated 700 space-based satellite systems, which provided surveillance for the entire earth. Even as it was still young and without the tribal tradition of the Marines, the United States Air Force was, in military and planetary terms, ubiquitous.

Concerning the Pacific, just as the Navy wrestled with China's submarine expansion, the Air Force wrestled with China's exponential increase in the acquisition of fourth-generation jet fighters like the MiG-29 and Su-30, and of double-digit SAM missiles. This complicated the Air Force's basing schemes. Even from Guam, places like Taiwan, Korea, and Okinawa were still three to four hours' flying time away, with all the gas guzzling that entailed. Aerial tanker requirements were going through the roof. Consequently, there was a need to park planes in places such as Thailand, the Philippines, and Japan. That meant building relationships, as well as gathering intimate knowledge of local conditions in obscure airfields—where private contractors who had gone native came in. "Whatever you pay one of these guys isn't enough," remarked one officer.

The Air Force needed a more expeditionary mindset. Col. Jeff LeVault of Thomasville, Pennsylvania, told me, "It's about figuring out billeting and force protection in each site, about who you can call and be on a first-name basis with in such and such a country. We need to land, say, in Colombo [Sri Lanka]. Well, who do we know on the ground

---

* The military analyst Ralph Peters goes so far as to suggest that the Air Force be eliminated and broken up into these two new-old components. See *New Glory: Expanding America's Global Supremacy* (New York: Sentinel, 2005), p. 269.

there? What are the airfield conditions? Flying is easy, it's the logistics tail that's hard. The tsunami was like a big exercise," he went on. "We got access we never dreamed of in remote parts of Indonesia. We got the State Department to fund repairs of Indonesian C-130s. The next step should be doing exercises with the Indonesians. It's drills like Cope Tiger, Cope Taufan in Malaysia, and Cope India where, tactically speaking, the rubber meets the road for PACAF [the Pacific Air Forces]."

As technological as the Air Force was, as with the other armed services, it was human skills on the ground that had never been in such high demand.

———

Osan Air Base lay twenty-five miles south of Seoul. It was in Osan in early July 1950 where American Army units had first seen combat and began to form up for the retaking of South Korea, after North Korea's late June invasion of that year. And it was from Osan in January 1951 that the U.S. Army began to repel the second invasion of the South, this time by Chinese communists. The Delta and blast barriers I noticed driving into the base were the first I had seen in the world that were not there for protection against terrorists, but for protection against the special operations forces of a national army—of North Korea in the event of another invasion of the South.

I had only a day in Korea, since the 25th Fighter Squadron would fly the next day to Thailand for Cope Tiger. It would do so by way of Kadena Air Base in Okinawa. Showtime was 2:45 a.m. for the 8 a.m. liftoff to Kadena. There was a brief about filling out departure cards for South Korean customs. "Remember, your nationality is American, not Black or Caucasian." Otherwise it was quick and straightforward, not the elaborate video brief for idiots that the Army was famous for.

I passed the wee hours at an all-night pancake house with four enlistees, part of the maintenance crew accompanying the pilots. They were white: from northeastern Pennsylvania, northwestern Idaho, central Nebraska, and southern Georgia. The two from Nebraska and Georgia had grown up on family farms, and had joined the Air Force to escape home and learn a profession. One waxed nostalgic about his favorite place in the world, the woods outside Alaska's Elmendorf Air Force Base: stripping down, tying your clothes in a garbage bag, jumping naked into a glacier-fed stream and floating the bag across to the other side to shoot a bear; taking care not to drink from the stream or risk getting beaver fever—the worst form of shits. "Why did I join the Air Force? What other job pays you to live in Alaska?"

Whether I was in boats, ships, or Stryker combat vehicles, it made no difference: in all these situations I encountered the manifest representation from the interior of rural America, and the absolute love of Alaska as a last frontier. The very repetition of these things made them significant for an observer. What was commonplace provided a fairer description of an institution much more than what was rare.

Six A-10s and a KC-10 Extender would take part in Cope Tiger. I flew to Kadena with the maintenance team in the KC-10, which was basically a DC-10 modified for air-to-air refueling. In service since 1981, the KC-10 was another Air Force mainstay, like the B-52 and C-130. It had flown 409 refueling missions during Operation Allied Force, the effort to push the Serbian military out of Kosovo in 1999. The two-hour flight southwest to Kadena Air Base in Okinawa entailed a refueling of the A-10s. I sat in the observation seat of the KC-10, facing backward in the bottom rear part of the plane, and watched.

The procedure was strangely ordinary and quite undramatic, masking the skills required to execute the operation, as one A-10 after the other appeared through the large window in front of me, as if on puppet strings, to get gas over the East China Sea. The boom was lowered with its attached wings that stabilized the boom in the winds of 14,000 feet. The boom's inner telescope then slid out, as the A-10 pilot traveling at 210 knots crept forward to meet it. I felt as if I could reach out and touch the pilot. Because the telescope could eject as much as 12,000 pounds of fuel per minute, depending upon the type of aircraft it was servicing, it took only a few seconds for each plane to be topped up.

Latching the telescoping probe to the A-10's receptacle was akin to latching a sailboat to a mooring in rough seas. Staff Sgt. Michael Hinton of Grafton, Iowa, instructed Airman 1st Class Michael Meitz of St. Louis on how to do it. On one occasion, it took about twenty attempts to attach the probe to an A-10. Over the communications system nobody sounded frustrated, though. The voices were quiet to the point of being disembodied. "Just hold steady," Staff Sgt. Hinton said, as Airman Meitz worked the two sticks controlling the massive boom inches from the plane. In the Air Force, speaking dully and calmly in a "radio voice," especially in the worst situations, was a sign of machismo.

Finally all the planes were topped up. *"Pilsung,"* one of the pilots announced, Korean for "certain victory," the motto of the 25th. We descended through silken cloud strands to the sight of encrusted atolls, the Ryukus and Okinawa. The nine-hour flight the next day to Thailand would see six separate refueling operations. Each A-10 required enough fuel all the time to get to the nearest friendly base in case of an emergency, and by all means without having to land in China.

—

Because Korat Air Force Base did not have K-loaders for the pallets, we landed at the Royal Thai Naval Air Station at Utapao to unload them, and truck the pallets up to Korat. The plane door opened at Utapao and there was my old friend Dan Generette, the private contractor who made it all happen between the U.S. and Thai militaries at Utapao. Dan wore a ball cap, a gas station shirt with "Dan" inscribed over the pocket, and a big smile.

"You're good," he told the pilot in his soothing voice. "No hassles here." He dealt with one issue after another in the space of two minutes: pallets, customs, buses, ATM machines, restaurants, and "entertainment"—everything required for a memorable night in Thailand for an American airman—even as he fielded cellphone calls from his Thai contacts.

A few weeks after I had left Dan in November 2004, he got a text message on his cellphone saying, "Massive tidal wave." Within days the tarmac at Utapao was packed with American military aircraft, and Dan's staff was working 24/7 as marines poured in to execute tsunami relief.

"Did the marines behave themselves?" I asked.

"There were a few scrimmages at the bars in Pattaya, fighting over something there's plenty of in Thailand—beautiful women. See that Navy C-4?" Dan continued, changing the subject. "There is a sailor in my office who's there to guard it. The Navy of all the services insists there be U.S. eyes on its aircraft all the time. Do you know what kind of condescending message that sends to the Thais? That their security is not good enough. In many little ways we're ugly Americans, and it's these details that are just killing us around the world," Dan said with the same smile.

Dan pointed out an Air Force master sergeant in civilian clothes driving a K-loader. "He's new. JUSMAG [the Joint United States Military Assistance Group for Thailand] is making Utapao an official OL [operating location]. The people at JUSMAG are cool, but I worry that we'll become too conspicuous here. Less is more, keep it low-key. Washington never understands that."

The bus ride north to Korat took over four hours, through a raggedy carpet of coconut palms, banana and tapioca groves, and secondary-growth forest mixed together with gas stations, iron-roofed markets, and Buddhist shrines, before ascending into smoky hills. As soon as we arrived in Korat there was another brief:

"If you bring a girl back to the hotel, you'll have to register her in the logbook at the reception desk, and pay a 500-baht joiner's fee. That means there will be a paper trail that could find you later in life. When you get her up to your room, and you've exhausted yourselves discussing world politics, and nature takes over, as nature tends to do, and you reach into her pants and find something that you did not expect to find, and *she* turns out not to be a *she* . . . , just kick her or *it* out, and pay the five hundred baht. It's not the time for an argument. All that's going to be hurt is your ego. By the way," the briefer continued, "every kind of STD [sexually transmitted disease] exists here including HIV-AIDS, and the chances of getting something is high. So practice abstinence. DOD [the Department of Defense] says that human trafficking is illegal. Do I make myself clear?"

Meanwhile, several boxes of condoms had been brought down on the pallets.

I went out to a local bar with the pilots: cans of Red Bull mixed with bottles of Tennessee Jack Daniel's. The caffeine kept you awake, allowing you to drink more. "We're not the trim, in great shape, penny loafer– or topsider-wearing F-15 pilots," I was told. "We're the sloppy, relaxed, sometimes a little overweight, whatever guys who fly A-10s, the bastard children of the Air Force." And yet, as Maj. Chris Price of Schererville, Indiana, added, while we were still on our second drink, "You don't get to be a pilot if you don't have your shit together. Part of that shit is faith and spirituality." Being a warrior meant being a believer; the two were inseparable to him.

Price was thin, gawky, ate all the time, and rifled through his briefs with a voice huskier than his physiology suggested. Having just pinned on major, he was consciously intense. Like a lot of these guys, he didn't look Hollywood, which showed how inaccurate Hollywood was.

Maj. Price's grandfather was a master chief petty officer in the Navy at Pearl Harbor on December 7, 1941. His dad, too, was in the Navy, and his brother also in the Air Force. "I was brought up to love the military," he told me. "And I wanted to help the guys fighting on the ground. There was never any doubt that I'd fly an A-10." Price, thirty-three, did ROTC at Purdue, and would later fly A-10 missions over Iraq and Afghanistan. In Iraq, during Operation Iraqi Freedom 1, the Marines marched up the right side of the Euphrates and the Army the left, meeting in Baghdad. "The Marines were flexible," Price said. "Even if there was no immediate tasking, they'd find stuff for you to bomb. They were always thinking ahead, of what they needed taken out on the ground a week in advance even. Because they had their own air component, they were more efficient at using air than the Army. The first time I dropped ordnance over a live target I was too busy trying not to screw up to think about it.

"Afghanistan was like the baseball season," he went on. "Fighting would start in April and wind down in early November. In Afghanistan, unlike Iraq, the A-10s were nearly the only show in town. It wasn't large infantry that we were supporting, but small teams, SF. We were basically a QRF [quick reaction force]. The terrain along the border with Pakistan was, well . . ." He couldn't find words, but his eyes spoke of majesty. He told me stories about hiding on one side of a mountain and flying down the other side for a bombing run: loiter and hide, loiter and hide.

"It was constant TIC [troops in contact]," he said. "Some days we worked so hard it was 'Winchester,' " meaning the A-10s had run out of ordnance. "But everyone else in that squadron [the 75th out of Pope Air

Force Base, North Carolina] has better stories than mine, and did a hundred times more than I did."

Keith Bonser was a fair, red-headed, thickly set, almost flabby first lieutenant from the Ridgewood section of Queens, New York, the pilot who had had trouble attaching his plane to the boom the day before—the first time he had been refueled by a KC-10. I vaguely knew the area where he had grown up. Bonser, twenty-nine, had played baseball in the Catholic youth leagues in Rees Park. His brother was a cop, working the beat in "Bed-Stuy" (the Bedford-Stuyvesant section of Brooklyn). His father worked a forklift at a steel factory in Brooklyn. His mother cleaned the house of late Mafia boss John Gotti in the Queens neighborhood of Howard Beach. "My parents were broke as a joke," he told me. "They were married twenty-six years before they owned their first home." Bonser went to Arizona State after turning down a bowling scholarship from Oklahoma State. (He had several 300 games to his credit, and had actually bowled 272 once with a ten-pound house ball.) He claimed that it took him eight years to graduate. "The guys who went to the Air Force Academy, they're no fun, they don't know life. They're programmed too early. You have to screw around for a few years first to have your shit together." He was joking—well, somewhat. Almost half of his A-10 buddies in Thailand had gone to the academy.

Bonser's half brother was killed in the World Trade Center on 9/11. "That's why I joined up. I had an uncle who was an Air Force colonel. He was the distant relative I never talked to, then he suddenly became important to me." Bonser went to Maxwell Air Force Base in Alabama for officer training, and then listed the A-10 at the top of his dream sheet. "It was a plane without airs," he said over blasting country music in the bar, as if describing himself. He would be flying A-10s in Afghanistan the following autumn while his wife was giving birth.

Each of these pilots had a call sign that was his real identity: "Thrill," "Bull," "Rage," "Turk," "Tex," "Sniper," "Binford." Choosing a call sign for a pilot was a ceremonial event. The other pilots would kick you out of the room and propose a name for you based on some buffoonery in the jet. Precisely because it was new, the Air Force emphasized ritual. To wit, pilots wore their flight caps slightly crunched at the top to commemorate the days when the hats were squashed by headsets.

Pilots in other air forces also had call signs. Some of the names of the Thai and Singaporean pilots I met: "Stuntman," "Exciter," "Chucky." But whereas the Thais and Singaporeans named themselves, the American pilots had their call signs chosen by their fellow pilots, and they were meant more in the way of ridicule than as a macho thing. "Our call signs are ego-deflating. They commemorate an instance where we screwed up," one pilot named "Ape" explained.

"Sniper" was so named because the first time he fired the A-10 Gatling gun he was so scared he got off only one round. "Turk" was an ethnic Greek. "Thrill" was quiet except when drinking. "Smash" tripped in a bar in Denmark and pulled down a TV that exploded. "OLE" was an acronym for a pilot who had demonstrated Obsessive Love for Elvis. "Gyro" had argued that it was his flight lead who was upside down in the air, when in fact it was he. "Tex" really had nothing to do with Texas, but with an incident very embarrassing for a male. According to Tex, "a call sign should be cool enough to get you laid at a bar, yet bring laughter to your fellow pilots who know the story of how it came about."

The call sign for Capt. Brandon Kelly of Cairo, Georgia, was "Custer," because his wife was half Indian "and she beats my ass every day." Capt. Kelly's extended family, he told me, hot-rodded and made moonshine. Quite a few of his relatives were cops. "It's a military family with service from the Civil War to Vietnam. We have a lot of pride in country," he said purposely.

"It's about pride in country," Custer repeated. "I always knew I'd be in the military. I cried when President Reagan died. I know how lucky I am to be flying an A-10, and yet I know how much the wife sacrifices when I'm away." Service before self was not some hokey concept. It was what these A-10 pilots lived by, declared the squadron commander, Lt. Col. Scott Caine of Vero Beach, Florida. Lt. Col. Caine's father was a farm boy in New Hampshire's Connecticut River valley who had enlisted in the Air Force during the Korean War. He went on to become an officer and flew 258 combat missions over Vietnam. Lt. Col. Caine graduated from Georgia Tech as an electrical engineer but found civilian life uninspiring. "My father never pushed me toward the Air Force," he told me. "I came to it on my own."

Unlike the other services, in which enlisted men did most of the fighting, in the Air Force it was the pilots—the officers, that is—who put iron on targets. In an Army or Marine infantry battalion of under a thousand men, there were only about ten captains, and only about four or five of them were company commanders.* Captains were rare in the infantry, surrounded as they were by hordes of enlisted men whom they led into battle. You didn't normally encounter a group of captains together. But the Air Force was radically different, since the pilots were usually captains or first lieutenants, with an occasional major or second lieutenant thrown in, all commanded by a lieutenant colonel.†

Officers simply mattered more in the Air Force. Whereas in the Army and Marines, captain was the highest real field, in the Air Force it was lieutenant colonel, for the squadron commander flew just another jet. And because in the air a lieutenant colonel might take orders from a lieutenant, rank mattered less here. You heard call signs like "Tex" and "Custer," or simply "dude," much more than you ever heard "sir."

Of all the officers, Custer Kelly had been pointed out to me as truly brave, not because of what he had done in the air, but on the ground. To understand how better to support ground troops, A-10 pilots frequently worked as forward air controllers, embedded with Army ground troops to provide close air support. After flying A-10 missions in Afghanistan, Custer became a forward air controller in Iraq south of Baghdad. He lived with an Army sniper team a few feet from the Euphrates, in a power plant where there never was any power, on MREs and cold showers in the autumn of 2003, mortared every night.

"An RPG came across my head, the dude behind me was hit by an IED, another dude said to the officer, 'Sir, they're shooting at us.' 'Yes they are,' the officer said, 'feel free to shoot back.' It was as normal as that. A specialist was killed in his soft-skinned Humvee and we did a

---

* For example, there were three line companies, a weapons company, and a headquarters and support company.

† Navy lieutenants (the equivalent of captains) clustered only in the wardroom, otherwise at sea you usually found them among their petty officers and chief petty officers. Major was the go-to rank in the Pentagon and in staff headquarters at battalion level and above. But in the Army and Marines, outside the base perimeter, majors were much less in evidence.

ceremony with his boots, rifle, and helmet. It was fucked up," Custer continued. "The up-armor we needed for the Humvees was still in Bosnia. But nobody I knew complained. We had it made. We were in combat, fighting for our country."

They say not to trust the stories you hear in a bar, no matter who tells them. I disagree. Emotions, perceptions, attitudes honestly rendered are more important than facts. And who said the facts I heard were wrong?

Custer Kelly spoke in a mild, melodic drawl next to my ear, as though ducking under the loud American country music, with Thai hostesses squirming around him. "I was embedded with the 1st Battalion of the 32nd Regiment of the 10th Mountain Division, based out of Fort Drum, New York, and fragged out to the 82nd Airborne Division," he related, knowing how important these facts were to those with whom he had been an Air Force embed. "That's what I do, that's my identity. I am an Air Force pilot who serves the Army. Providing CAS for the 10th Mountain Division was the defining moment of my life. I befriended and loved people, and saw them killed. I was a new captain and there was this very experienced first lieutenant who would never call me anything other than 'sir.' That does something to you. He had been married for a few weeks and then was killed by an IED."

———

Cope Tiger began the next morning. Like military bases I had seen in Colombia and the Philippines, only more so, Korat Air Force Base was neat to the point of perfection, with modern facilities in all respects. Joint air exercises required partners who were economically and technologically developed enough to fly jets. That meant a high level of education, which, among other things, translated into cleanliness. This wasn't the Marines or Army Special Forces living in the Sahara amid frogs and scorpions. The mess hall at Korat served excellent Thai food.

Counting the two briefings before we left Korea, we now got the fifth on sex, this one from a grizzled contractor. More about logbooks, joiner's fees, two-hundred-Baht girls who failed their STD test at the massage parlor and were working the streets, and about reaching down and finding something you never expected to find. For the times when you did find what you expected to find, the sixth briefer, who had followed the contractor, in a moment of honesty, said, "Cover up. Your member, I mean."

In the morning the pilots were different people. They had drunk hard only because they weren't flying today; instead, they were getting oriented to an airfield from which they had never flown. There was a rule for flying—no alcohol within twelve hours of entering the cockpit.

"At an altitude of 790 feet, I've added an additional 890 feet to your BDU mils," began Capt. John "Tex" Lesho of Newnan, Georgia, in a brief to the other pilots. "It will be a 180-degree run-in for DMPIs the first day of the exercise. I'll get you some good pop references. In the high TDAs, the air mass is thinner, so you'll pick up a lot of smash. We don't know yet what the DMPIs will be, so the possibility exists to shack chassis."

Translation: BDUs were bomb demonstration units, practice bombs that would be used in Cope Tiger. Mils were a sight setting in the pilot's HUD (heads-up display). There were 17.45 mils per degree in a circle.* DMPIs were the desired mean points of impact. Pop meant popping up steeply from low altitude and rolling out to the other side of a hill to hit the enemy by surprise. TDAs were target designated areas. Smash was speed. Chassis meant old tanks or cars that might be the targets themselves. To shack meant to bomb.

This was one of the easiest parts of the brief for a layman to follow. The language of fighter jet pilots, a combination of slang and technical jargon, was as abstruse as that of submariners. But whereas in the subsurface Navy, war was reduced to math since you couldn't see anything, and thus became totally cerebral, fighter pilots remained gunslingers, who flew by seat-of-the-pants hand-eye coordination equal to that of major league hitters. They had to translate an extraordinary amount of data into arm and finger movements with a stick and trigger buttons. It was no accident that Ted Williams was an ace pilot in both World War II and the Korean War. This was especially true of A-10 pilots, whose only radar was, in Custer's words, "our Mark One eyeballs." Popping up from one side of a mountain to the other was not what they concen-

---

* The measurement began with Army field artillery. In the air the circle is vertical rather than horizontal.

trated on; they did that by instinct. What they concentrated on was shacking the target.

Flying was nothing they thought much about. To use another sports analogy, whereas spectators marveled at the skating skills of professional hockey players, the players themselves thought only about passing and hitting the puck.

Fighter pilots represented the last stage of the physical warrior before war was relegated to moving a mouse on a screen. And of all combat pilots, A-10 pilots remained the most physical and low tech. They were truly an extension of the infantry, operating an airframe and technology that were essentially three decades old.

———

"All I ever wanted to do was fly a Hog [A-10 Warthog]. It was the plane I played with as a little boy," Capt. Tex Lesho told me. He had just finished a brief to three Thai pilots, apologizing to them that he didn't speak their language and hoping that they would understand. Tex had grown up Southern Baptist in Georgia. His mother was a math teacher and his father an electrical repairman. His educator-mother forbade him to "speak southern" in the home. She was the factor that ultimately got him to the Air Force Academy, where he was exposed to the other fighter jets. He wanted none of it.

Here's what he said: "The F-16 is cool in air shows, but it's limited on gas. Take away its air-to-air capabilities and all it can do on the ground is kill a couple of targets. The Hog can do a lot more damage. As for F-15C pilots, you've heard of type A personalities. They're AAA. The F-15E is a two-seater, and I'm a rebellious loner. Only the Navy and Marines fly F-18s, and I joined the Air Force because I didn't want to be on a boat [aircraft carrier]. The F-22 I love, but not as a job. The debriefs for all these planes are too theoretical. With the A-10, you hit the target or you don't, nothing to argue about. Basically, what I really wanted to do was fly a gun, not a plane, to help soldiers on the ground. And the Hog is a flying gun, the Gatling."

Tex's point could not be emphasized enough. The Air Force was not—or at least should not be—primarily about flying. It should be about killing from the air. The A-10 really was a plane fitted to a gun: the GAU-8/A Gatling gun, whose seven barrels fired 3,900 30mm rounds per minute, designed by a bunch of guys in a bar writing on a napkin. Opening the airframe from the bottom, you saw how the massive barrel extended from the nose all the way past the plane's midpoint.

"The other planes are high-priced Lamborghinis," Tex went on. "I'm a redneck from Georgia. I want an American muscle car," Tex continued in a self-mocking manner. "Think of the Hog as a '69 Ford Mustang, or a Dodge Charger. It's like the original 1952 Russian SKS [machine gun], a real dependable, blue-collar plane. There's no better feeling in the world than smelling the gun gas in the cockpit after you've fired the Gatling. You remember the Highway of Death where we bombed those Iraqi troops fleeing Kuwait in Desert Storm? That was all Hog. On Assignment Night at Columbus [Mississippi] Air Force Base, after you've finished most of your T-38 training and you stand up in front of your family and declare what you want to fly, I said, 'I want a Hog.' "

A noncom working maintenance put it more succinctly: "If you're in the Air Force, why would you want to be associated with a plane that doesn't blow shit up?"

The A-10 Thunderbolt II, alias the Warthog, was the plane that the Air Force brass had wanted to kill after the first Gulf War. So the Army said, Okay, you don't want it, we'll take it. The Air Force quickly changed its mind. The plane constituted an argument against beauty. It could loiter amid enemy gunfire because it was tough. It was tough because it had so much built-in redundancy: separate engines, separate hydraulic systems, double tails, and double everything almost. If one part faltered, another took its place so that the pilots could make it to "good-guy land." The two engines were mounted high so that the wings shielded them somewhat from ground fire. Because the engines were mounted high, they were less susceptible to foreign objects like gravel. That was one reason the A-10 could work out of dirt airstrips.

All this made the A-10 ugly but trustworthy. Right/left interchangeable parts allowed it to be serviced easily from austere bases with limited facilities. Its retractable crew boarding ladder made it unnecessary to have a ladder on hand to get the pilot into the cockpit. As planes went, it was quiet, giving the A-10 the element of surprise. If the fuel tanks were hit by bullets, the foam inside expanded, plugging holes and minimizing damage. Cheap, old, and reliable, it was suited to an era of low-tech, irregular maneuver warfare. Of all the fighter jets, it was what Rudyard Kipling called "the cheaper man," whom the odds often favored. Yet because it had only one seat, influential generals and civilian defense officials couldn't experience a ride in one, making it hard to impress people who controlled budgets.

The A-10s of the 25th were more properly designated A/OA-10s, because the squadron's mission was not just combat, but forward air control. That's what Tex and Rage did.

Rage was Capt. Colin "Rage" Donnelly of Utica, New York. I caught Rage during a brief he gave to two Singaporean pilots, whose call signs were "Diablo" and "Furby."

"You understand the term 'shit-filter'?" Rage asked the Singaporeans.

"Yes," they responded, smiling.

"A FAC [forward air controller] is a shit-filter. I expect him to filter all the shit coming from the AWACS [E-3 Airborne Warning and Control System]. Shit are all the targets, threats, and other information not specifically related to our mission. The FAC gives the other pilots the 9-line [location, elevation, description, egress point, etc.] for the target. But I'm not going to demand all nine points of the line from Marine and SOF dudes who need us to immediately deliver fire. The FAC is not loaded down to the gills with weapons, or raging around at max speed. He's conserving gas so he can deconflict and rack-and-stack the next group of fighters, and the next, arriving on scene."

The forward air controller orchestrated the entire battle from the air. In addition to all the other information coming at him in compressed bursts, and the instincts he required simply to fly and pop, he had three radios going: one to the ground FAC embedded with the soldiers or marines, another to the airmen on the AWACS, and the third to the pilots themselves whom he was directing. He managed everything through cadence. For example, there was TTFACORB (targets, threats, friendlies, artillery, clearance, ordnance, restrictions, battle damage), the order in which you mentally processed the battlespace situation. There was a cadence for everything. Cadence allowed you to prioritize. Since as Tex had explained, "as a FAC you're always entering a busy traffic circle at high speed in fog and writing numbers with a grease pencil on the windshield at the same time." Never for a split second could you get flustered and say to yourself, "What do I do next?" It got as simple as, the first thing you did was fly the plane. That was, in the basic brief, called "Motherhood."

The air, like the sea, was a blank space that both pilots and submariners drew road maps on, with superhighways, intersections, and holding points. To them there was nothing empty or abstract about it. "Hold in a block and keep your head down in the drool cup," one pilot explained, in reference to being "stopped" in the sky. Indeed, there were similarities between flying and being on a sub: the time spent in the air was short compared to that spent in small windowless rooms on long briefs and debriefs, with columns of data and instructions to go over.

Tex and Rage were four-ship flight leads, meaning they were mini-FACs for four planes. Capt. James "Sniper" Krischke of Chatham, Illinois, explained it to me: "Think of a bar fight. The FAC is the guy who goes outside to call for help on the pay phone. When his buddies arrive, the flight lead tells them where the pool cue is to use as a weapon." Being a four-ship flight lead was exponentially more complicated than being a two-ship flight lead because you had to vertically split the sky in order to manage egress and deconfliction issues for two groups of two.

———

At Korat, during the two weeks of flying sorties, I moved back and forth from the pilots' hangout to the flight line. As the A-10 was a one-seater, I couldn't fly.

I noticed that it wasn't only the pilot who had his name painted on the side of each A-10, but the dedicated crew chief and his assistant, too. These were the maintainers, the airmen who serviced the engines, hydraulics, and weapons systems, and signed their names to everything they did so that there was a paper trail in case of a malfunction. Consequently, there was a lot of stress. "I'm a character and a half," Staff Sgt. Stephen McDonough of Lehighton, Pennsylvania, told me. "I'm the class clown because everything has to always be done perfect, and if you didn't have fun on the job you'd simply worry yourself to death."

"Why did you join the Air Force?"

"My real dad was in the Navy. I raced stock cars in high school and my friend, who was retired Air Force, died of cancer the day I won a race. He had been a C-5 engine mechanic and willed himself to live long enough to see me win. I joined in his memory."

Working on the flight line was not easy. In the winter, it was the windiest place imaginable, and in the summer the hottest. A common uniform for the crew chiefs was woodland camouflage trousers and black T-shirts "for a farmer's tan" on your arms and neck. Often you couldn't wear "cover"—caps, that is—because they might get swept off your head and sucked into the jet engines. (Throughout the military, unless you had on a helmet with straps, it was considered bad form to wear any kind of cover on an airfield.) Of the eighty-five airmen from the 25th participating in Cope Tiger, only fourteen were pilots. The rest were maintainers.

There was Tech. Sgt. Larry Driver of Carrollton, Georgia, a big, towering kid with a baby face and a tattoo of a flying black Vulcan on his left arm. Tech. Sgt. Driver had twelve years in the Air Force. In a rapid-fire southern accent, moving his fingers to show me each part, like a gas station mechanic diagnosing a problem to a customer, he explained how the weapons store on the A-10 wing was released: "This is an impulse card. It generates gas pressure which works the entire rack. Two of these cards go into a cartridge block. When the pilot pickles [presses the trigger button], he electronically signals two firing pins in the back of the cartridge block to send gas pressure that actuates the slave piston, causing the bell crank to rotate. This rotation causes linkages to retract the hooks. These retracted hooks release the remaining gas pressure, which splits into two tubes. The tubes go through orifices that regulate the pressure downwards. That, in turn, pushes down the ejector feet, and the weapon is released

"It's a down-and-dirty plane, the A-10 is," he continued, slapping the wing, ending his oration and eyeing the black gun gas smeared all over the airframe's belly. Every time a pilot began to taxi out to the runway, the crew chief would touch the end of the wing as it moved forward under him for good luck.

Tech. Sgt. Driver was the fifth rural Georgian I had met thus far here.

They included a master sergeant from Fitzgerald, Georgia, and a staff sergeant from Cairo, Georgia, the same hometown as Custer. There was only one high school for Custer's entire county with a few hundred students, and two from Cairo had ended up in this squadron. The staff sergeant, William "Cleetus" Davis, was from a family of peanut and cotton farmers, saw no future in it, and like so many others just wanted to get away. There were other rural Georgians in the squadron I still hadn't met.

Noncoms like Larry Driver helped rekindle the spirit of adventure in me. Only on the surface were their lives monotonous. Adventure is relative; the most jaded and depressed people I ever met were in the business-class cabins of intercontinental flights. But take Tech. Sgt. Walt Mardis of Coeur d'Alene, Idaho, who fixed jet engines for the A-10. I discovered him in the middle of diagnosing an engine problem.

The pilot had noticed fluctuating RPMs (revolutions per minute) on his gauge. Avionics changed the gauge. The problem persisted. The pilot's only choice was to abort the mission. Tech. Sgt. Mardis, a tall, hovering presence with a serene and sympathetic manner, ambled onto the flight line and plugged his Panasonic Toughbook into a terminal underneath the plane. Downloading data from the EPU (electronic processing unit), he saw that there were no RPM readings at all, which had to be wrong since the engine was spinning. So he took his Toughbook into the cockpit, where he could read what the engine was doing in "real time" by circumventing the gauge system. This allowed him to compare the Toughbook's numbers to those on the cockpit display.

Seeing Mardis in the pilot's seat with headphones on was funny because even on commercial flights, as he told me, he got airsick. The Toughbook indicated that the RPMs were all over the place, from 63 percent of optimum normal to 4,000 percent. That was impossible. Mardis decided that the tachometer generator was spitting out bogus signals and needed to be replaced. At least he hoped that was the problem. The "tach" generator could be replaced quickly, whereas if it was a wiring problem it would take hours to fix and he might have to miss the weekend elephant ride to a waterfall he had signed up for.

Mardis had been marking time at North Idaho College when his dad developed cancer. The only family member at home who could drive,

Mardis would regularly take his dad for therapy to the hospital in Spokane, Washington. "That's when I grew up. Life becomes serious when one of your parents gets sick." His dad eventually healed and Mardis decided to join the Air Force, to get away and do something with his life. His decision was not out of context. He had a brother in the Marines, and three other brothers and a sister in the Army.

After basic training at Lackland Air Force Base in San Antonio, Texas, and technical training at Chanute Air Force Base in Champaign, Illinois, he was sent to Barksdale Air Force Base near Shreveport, Louisiana, to fix engines on B-52Hs. For the next nine years through 2001, Mardis fixed engines at Barksdale and at Pope Air Force Base in Fayetteville, North Carolina. He was happy. He assumed that's all there was to do in the military. It was about what he expected when he had enlisted in Idaho.

"Then came 9/11, OEF, and OIF," in his words. Mardis was eating with a friend in a restaurant in Fayetteville when they got the "recall": be ready to deploy in twenty-four hours to Iraq. His friend's squadron deployed first, his followed a few months later in the summer of 2003.

"It was a time I'll never forget," he began wistfully. "The C-130 popped flares after takeoff from Kuwait and did a combat landing in Iraq. They took our pictures for the various IDs we'd need on the flight line. They gave us mosquito nets and assigned us a tent, and we dragged our B-bags to it. Nine of us in that tent for five months. We scrounged for livables. I used a poncho as a curtain. I was so nervous and scared the first days in Iraq. But I'm really glad I did it. Once there was an explosion. It sounded so close, but the car bomb was miles away. That was all the violence I ever experienced there."

Not much of a story. For a journalist, let alone a fighter pilot or infantryman, Mardis's experience didn't count. It was so in the rear as not to be worth a line in a reporter's notebook. But it did count. To him. To judge by the way he spoke, the dust in the tent, the very strangeness of it all, made it extraordinary, and thus he had remembered every detail of his arrival in Iraq.

Next he went to Afghanistan, where every night he was mortared. "But then I got home and went to a NASCAR race, and realized that while I and my buddies in the military were at war, the country wasn't," he reflected. Later he was deployed to South Korea, and was now in Thailand—in his case, an epic adventure. "I never thought I'd get around so," he said.

Life in the Air Force, as in the other services, meant drifting from base to base. Sailors and marines were always on the coasts. The Air Force, by contrast—even more so than the Army, with its forts on the Great Plains that were legacies of the Indian Wars—inhabited the large and empty spaces that not by accident happened to be in deeply conservative parts of the country. There was the complex of Eglin and Tyndall Air Force bases, and Hurlburt Field, all in the Florida Panhandle of the central time zone, George Bush territory in the 2000 Florida recount: then Maxwell Air Force Base in Montgomery, Alabama; Vance Air Force Base in Enid, Oklahoma; Barksdale Air Force Base near Shreveport, Louisiana; and Nellis Air Force Base outside Las Vegas, Nevada— all places where airmen spent years of their lives.* Yes, there were big global transport hubs near Dover, Delaware, and San Francisco; and National Guard and Reserve outposts in places like Springfield, Massachusetts, and Hartford, Connecticut, but those places did not constitute the world of active-duty combat pilots. The effects of location had something to do with why troops thought the way they did politically, even if they didn't get off the base much. Sailors and marines might have been on the coasts, but usually not in the fashionable parts; in the hotel gift shops of Norfolk, Virginia—the Navy's biggest hub—there was always chewing tobacco on sale.†

Nevertheless, pilots weren't as redneck as they talked, or rather as they aspired to be or joked about. Only two of the fourteen in the squadron chewed tobacco. And despite their claims, they didn't curse nearly as

---

* Air Force tradition demanded naming bases after deceased fliers. To wit, Army Air Corps Lt. Col. Frederick I. Eglin was killed in 1937 when his plane crashed. Lt. Frank B. Tyndall, a Florida native and World War I ace, was killed on active duty in 1930. First Lt. Donald Wilson Hurlburt was killed in an air crash in 1943 in northwestern Florida. Second Lt. William C. Maxwell of Atmore, Alabama, died on August 12, 1920, in the Philippines when his DH-4 aircraft hit a flagpole after he had turned to avoid striking a group of children. Lt. Col. Leon Robert Vance, Jr., a native Oklahoman, was a World War II hero and Medal of Honor recipient. First Lt. William Harrell Nellis of Las Vegas, a P-47 pilot, died in action during the Battle of the Bulge.

† The big exceptions to this rule were the naval bases in San Diego and near Seattle.

much as marines or Army infantrymen. All had high SAT scores. Almost half had graduated from the Air Force Academy, and had that clean-cut, intense manner common to graduates of the service academies.

They fondly referred to the Air Force Academy as the "Zoo," because visitors there were always looking in and gawking at the cadets as they ate in the dining facility. Capt. Zach "Thrill" Laird of Billings, Montana, who went on to get a master's degree in Russian from Indiana University, had this story:

"Walking between classes one day I saw a visitor. 'Oh, look at the cute cadet,' the girl called to me. 'Can I take your picture?' I said sure. After all, she was pretty. Then she threw me a candy bar, like I was an animal in a real zoo. I thanked her. Hey, I was hungry."

What defined the pilots was their closeness to one another. Call signs and a conscious attempt to preserve Air Force history enhanced the bonding. For example, Capt. Jeremiah "Bull" Parvin of Rocky Mount, North Carolina, a big guy with a bald head, had a "Misty" patch on his arm. "Misty" was the call sign for A-10 FACs in the Korean Peninsula today. It commemorated the Misty call sign used by FACs flying over North Vietnam and Laos between 1967 and 1970. Bull Parvin explained it to me:

Nothing was more dangerous for a pilot during the Vietnam War than to be a FAC. Other pilots dropped their bombs over enemy airspace and got out. FACs loitered for hours over enemy airspace directing the raids. The Air Force had been losing too many O-1s and O-2s (slow single- and twin-engine Cessnas), so it created a program, Operation Commando Sabre, a FAC program using reliable F-100Fs. The F-100F pilots would spend eight hours daily over North Vietnam and Laos, searching for convoys, SA-2 missiles, and "triple-A pieces [anti-aircraft artillery]."

The leader of Commando Sabre, who would later be shot down and spend years in the so-called Hanoi Hilton, the infamous North Vietnamese prison, was Maj. George E. "Bud" Day of Sioux City, Iowa.

When Bull mentioned the name Bud Day, I had a shock of recognition. A few months earlier I had been at the Jacksonville Naval Air Station in Florida and happened to walk in on the middle of a speech that

Bud Day was delivering to Navy pilots. It was an inspirational speech about never giving in, laced with colorful profanities. Day was old and repetitive. It wasn't the greatest speech I ever heard, but the Navy fliers were deeply moved by it. After all, they knew exactly who he was, a Medal of Honor winner who had been tortured for years by the North Vietnamese. Bud Day had undergone a mock execution, escaped, and hiked over twelve days alone in the jungle back toward South Vietnam, only to be recaptured. Once when guards burst in on him and other POWs during a clandestine religious service, he stared into their muzzles and sang "The Star-Spangled Banner."

After his speech at the naval air station, Day sold copies of his book, *Duty, Honor, Country,* brought out by a small publisher.* He took payment in cash for each copy. The book wasn't listed on Amazon even. I thought it demeaning for him, especially as it was infinitely more significant than so many memoirs brought out by major publishers.

Bull showed me a coin commemorating the Misty FACs of the Vietnam War, with Bud Day's name on it. It was a tradition in the squadron that the youngest and oldest members always carried the coin on their person. Whenever there was a reunion of Misty FACs from Vietnam, held usually in the Florida Panhandle, where Bud Day now lived, the pilots of the 25th sent a representative.

The Korean and Vietnam wars held special meaning to the Air Force because they were the first wars in which it fought as its own service. This feeling was particularly strong in the case of Vietnam, because so many of the prisoners of war at the Hanoi Hilton had been Air Force pilots.

Though one should not overestimate the living memory of Vietnam as a means for bonding among pilots. Unlike the Army and Marines, as I've written, the Air Force was more technology- than tradition-oriented, because technology drove tactics to a far greater extent in the air than on the ground. The Army might still glean lessons from the Spartan victory at Plataea in the Peloponnesian War or from Napoleon's ill-fated inva-

---

* George E. Day, *Duty, Honor, Country* (Fort Walton Beach, Fla.: American Hero Press, 2002). It is an updated and expanded version of *Return with Honor* (Mesa, Ariz.: Champlin Museum Press, 1989).

sion of Russia. But for today's Air Force, there were almost no lessons to be gleaned even from the air battles of World War I.

The Air Force was so future-oriented that even some of the pilots admitted that the Air Force's life span would be the shortest of any service because sometime in the twenty-first century it probably would be converted to a space force.

And so the real way, aside from flying, that these pilots bonded was by carousing together. They visited strip joints that left you speechless, even though they were tourist traps compared to what was available in the Philippine Islands. The squadron, the Air Force, and U.S. troops in general adored Thailand, whose principal attraction was that it was not Korea. Thailand was tropical, whereas Korea this time of year had a foot of snow. The bases in Korea were on a permanent war footing for a war that never happened, meaning an operations tempo almost as grueling as in Iraq, but with many of the stupid, petty regulations that did not exist in Iraq, because the crucible of real conflict led to a Darwinian process of survival of the fittest in regard to bureaucratic rules. On bases in Korea such as Osan, you had to wear a reflector belt even when jogging during the daytime; nor could you get a haircut off base because you might get an infection from the barber. Some A-10 pilots told me that flying combat missions in Iraq and Afghanistan was liberating compared to the daily grind in Korea, where during the frequent war exercises the squadron flew five sorties a day.

Capt. Rage Donnelly was constantly in demand by the Thais and Singaporeans to give briefings on close air support and CSAR (combat search and rescue), particularly close air support, because of the U.S. Air Force's use of it in Afghanistan and Iraq. When there were boots on the ground in a theater of combat, A-10 pilots were busy, and that had been the situation since the autumn of 2001. Rage went through the steps necessary to avoid hitting friendlies. "Without confirmation from the ground, you don't shoot. You'll fire a round in a safe area and the ground controller will say something like, 'Okay, fire twenty-five meters [about twenty-five yards] northeast of that hit.' You bracket. You need to know the weapon's footprint. If the footprint overlaps with the position of friendlies, the guy on the ground has to sign his initials to the order."

Afterward there were no questions. Perhaps the Singaporean and Thai pilots were shy, just too polite and deferential. Maybe some of them did not sufficiently understand English and consequently had gone on auto-nod. Maybe they were in awe of the Americans for being veterans of combat for over four years now, the way the Americans had been secretly in awe of the Israelis decades back. Rage didn't know. He knew only that after briefs in the U.S. Air Force, it was rank off, meaning a lieutenant could vigorously cross-examine and disagree with a lieutenant colonel.

The Thais and, to a lesser extent, the Singaporeans shared a common trait with airmen from South Korea and the former Warsaw Pact countries. They were scripted. They were used to getting exact instructions for everything. If it was a low deck (low cloud cover), and they hadn't been briefed for it, rather than do a low show they would just cancel the mission. "I can read their eyeballs in advance," one A-10 pilot told me.

There were other problems with the Thais, all related to the linguistic divide: ground controllers you couldn't understand, vague and incomplete briefings on combat search and rescue, and the general confusion of an LFE (large force exercise), in which runways were stacked with dozens of F-16s having to take off every fifteen seconds and A-10s every twenty. If only one plane was late there was a cluster fuck. Meanwhile, a pilot would call, "Oscar, Oscar, Oscar [Thai ground control]," and sometimes no one would answer.

"The only way the communications gap is going to narrow is through more exercises and interactions like Cope Tiger," said Jim Traywick of Anniston, Alabama, the private contractor who had, essentially, arranged Cope Tiger for the U.S. Air Force. Traywick, like Dan Generette in Utapao, was retired Air Force. Gray and overweight, with jeans and a fishing vest, he had settled in Thailand with a Thai wife, having first visited the country during the Vietnam War. He spoke basic Thai. "The first time I heard of Thailand was in high school," he told me. "The teacher mispronounced it, calling it 'Thigh-land.' Well, that's kind of really what it was. I mean, guys go crazy here. They arrive in this place and it's like in *The Wizard of Oz,* when the black-and-white changes to Technicolor. I've seen guys divorce wives and marry the first local girl they meet on the street. But there is more to Thailand than Patpong and Soi Cowboy [the red light districts of Bangkok]."

I saw that Traywick, like Generette, was extremely calm. He spoke slowly in a monotone, to the point where his whole demeanor seemed to be on a lower RPM speed than other people's. "What's the trick to getting things done here?" I asked him.

"Patience," he replied, smiling, pronouncing the word slowly in a Zen-like near whisper. "The Thais don't understand why we do things the way we do, and we don't understand them. They are never in a rush. It's an attitude that's worked well for them. The most you can do here is repeat your request with a slightly firmer voice. If you get angry, they just shut down and ignore you.

"Remember," he continued, "they have to live here. They have to get along with the Chinese and their other neighbors. They want the American military here, but they don't want to broadcast it."

Traywick talked about getting more Thais to PACOM conferences in Honolulu and to more exercises like Cope Thunder in Alaska, "so they could observe us and how we operate among ourselves." He wanted the Air Force to send more ethnic Thais on missions to Southeast Asia and to emphasize Thai language programs. Though this view was self-serving, he was right. He was simply calling for more area expertise. "The guy who's gone native," I heard one airman deride Traywick behind his back. But whenever there was a problem with the locals, he was usually the only one to whom you could turn.

———

"Misty" wasn't the only call sign immortalized by the Vietnam War; so was "Sandy." As Capt. Custer Kelly told me, "If you meet an old air guy from Vietnam and you tell him you're a Sandy-4, he'll buy you a beer. If you tell him you're a Sandy-1, he'll offer to put your kids through college." Custer got real emotional about Sandys in Vietnam. He began to speak faster and his accent got more southern. He ticked off a list of books about the air war in Vietnam, which, like the names of books that soldiers and marines had given me about the ground war there, were just as heroic in a black-and-white sense as the books about World War II. Bud Day's book was part of this different Vietnam library, read

by a different geographical and cultural subdivision of American society than the one usually represented by major opinion-makers.

In Vietnam (and in A-10 squadrons today), Sandys essentially performed the same role in combat search and rescue as Mistys did in
regular bombing missions. For example, in Vietnam, when a Misty like
Bud Day had his plane shot down, it was a Sandy-1 who led the rescue
operation, and who was the only pilot allowed to talk to "the objective"—
the downed, ejected pilot, that is. (Sandy-2 was the flow manager, who
coordinated the communications between the rescue planes. Sandy-3 and
Sandy-4 arranged the rendezvous with the rescue helicopter.)

The second week of Cope Tiger saw a pre-planned combat search
and rescue. It was eerie. The day was February 13, 2006, three years to
the day that three American private contractors had been captured by
narco-terrorists in southern Colombia while I was there. Had the Green
Berets not been stalled twenty-four hours for diplomatic reasons from
carrying out their own CSAR, those three contractors might well have
been rescued hours afterward, rather than still being held hostage as
they were.[5]

The CSAR brief was dull, not emotionally moving as a layman
might expect. Nothing was said about a downed American pilot in
enemy territory or anything like that. The brief was delivered by 1st Lt.
Miya Rivera, an ethnic Chamorro from Guam.

"BUICK or one times F-16 was shot down at 6 a.m. by a Rapier
SAM at the border of CT-6. The wingman had eyes on the landing location but bingoed out for fuel." Translation: an F-16 pilot with the code
name "Buick" was shot down by a surface-to-air missile in a geographical area previously gridded as CT-6. A fellow pilot saw where he
landed but had to depart the scene to be refueled. The Thai and Singaporean pilots understood perfectly this code language, and in the Thais'
case, better than they often understood normal English. It was a civilian
like me who had to have it explained to him.

Lt. Rivera continued: "The word for the day is DINGO. The letter is
M. The number is 1. The color is blue. The duress word is BUD-
WEISER. The SARNEG is Blacknight, numbers one through nine."
Every time a pilot hopped into a cockpit, he was given a word, letter,
number, and color that changed daily. Asking a pilot downed in enemy

territory to recite these things was a way to verify that it was in fact he, not a bad guy who had overtaken him and was using his radio. It was like asking someone his mother's maiden name and the last four digits of his Social Security number before executing a stock transaction. By working the duress word into a sentence, the downed pilot could communicate that somebody was holding a gun to his head. The SARNEG (search and rescue number encryption grid) allowed the pilot to transmit his GPS coordinates in code without giving away his location to anyone but the Sandys.

Thrill Laird got to be the downed pilot. Because it was an exercise, Senior Airman Tanya Suloff of Lincoln, Delaware, and I went along with him. The pilots tried to motivate enlistees by including them in exercises whenever they could, and Airman Suloff was the lucky one today. A Singaporean CH-47 Chinook helicopter deposited the three of us at a site in the forest, in the CT-6 area, where Thrill was to have landed by parachute. We jumped off the helicopter and followed Thrill away from the clearing, through thick brambles snapping across our faces, over boulders, and through a muddy stream, running for a full ten minutes, until Thrill located a bamboo thicket that we quickly crawled inside of. Smearing dirt over our faces, we lay silent as Thrill retrieved his AN/RRC-112 survival radio. We prayed that the sound of the Chinook had made the cobras and vipers scatter from the wider area. We really were trying to hide. Hunting us down were four JTACs (joint terminal attack controllers), airmen who specialized in survival on the ground, and who were usually embedded with ground units to provide close air support.

The forest around our ears was dark and screaming with animal and insect life. Spiders landed on our faces and the dirt was moving everywhere. We dared not budge, though, as we spotted two JTACs combing the ground nearby. It was more claustrophobic than being in a closet. The half-hour wait in that thicket seemed like hours. Living thus for weeks, which downed pilots had done in World War II and again in Vietnam, you could easily go insane. It was a humbling experience.

Using the survival radio, Thrill had Airman Suloff communicate our GPS location to Rage Donnelly, the Sandy-1. She got a bit confused working the radio, and Rage calmly walked her through the steps the way an expert who knew it all by heart walked you through a software problem over the phone. At the same time, he was the flight lead over-head, with all that that entailed. Rage, whose personality could be tense and severe at times, truly became himself when multi-tasking in the cockpit. He was a graduate of the Weapons Instructor Course at Nellis Air Force Base in Nevada, the equivalent of the Navy's "Top Gun" school, though it went on for more weeks. As was typical with him, he never spoke about it. It was the other pilots who told me.

The JTACs never did find us. We found them in the clearing prior to being retrieved by a Thai UH-1H helicopter. They were dressed like Abu Sayyaf guerrillas, carrying big knives and wearing kerchiefs over their heads and necklaces with teeth. One of them had worked with Spe-cial Forces on the Afghanistan-Pakistan border. Thrill had used a mir-ror, catching the sunlight reflecting off Rage's low-flying A-10, to bring the planes to our exact location. The Thai para-jumpers from the UH-1H put guns in our faces until we correctly recited the letter of the day and the other information. The CSAR was then over.

On the final day of Cope Tiger, Capt. Matt "Turk" Kouchoukos of Bloomingdale, Illinois, made his last A-10 flight as an active-duty pilot. He would be leaving the Air Force and joining the Air National Guard. After he climbed down from the cockpit, in keeping with tradition, the other pilots tackled him, bound him with duct tape, sprayed him with a fire hose, and poured Thai beer all over him—since they couldn't find champagne. The fire hose wasn't necessary, as a thunderstorm had un-leashed gobs of rain and soon everyone was sliding on their backs on the tarmac. That night the American pilots entertained their Thai and Singaporean counterparts with old-fashioned beer hymnals. "I used to work in Chicago, in an old department store . . ."

If the loud and rude camaraderie was reminiscent of anything, it was the movie *Memphis Belle,* about the B-17 pilots of the Army Air Forces in World War II. As Tex, who was raised on Zane Grey novels in the Deep South, told me, "I'm old school. I believe in the kind of guys who don't care whom they piss off. The older guys were the better aviators. They didn't have GPS. The arts of old-fashioned flying and bombing are being lost."

Just as there were different navies (surface, sub-surface, naval aviation, and the SEAL community), there were different air forces. And what I had been witnessing the past few weeks was a unique pilot community that, in terms of personalities, was a throwback to World War II.* These guys were spiritually as much a part of the old Army Air Forces as they were of the new Air Force. Indeed, at a quick glance, the ungainly A-10s lumbering out to the runways even resembled the B-17s that bombed Germany from bases in England.

Like the pilots of the Second World War, the A-10 pilots didn't agonize about what they believed. Theirs was ultimately a world of black-and-white faith. It didn't mean they were necessarily conservative (though most were), or that they didn't get mad at their own government (they often did). In fact, their worst fear was that they might kill innocent civilians by mistake. It meant only that as a group they weren't cynical, and retained a heroic, almost naïve outlook on life.

Their commander, Lt. Col. Caine, summed up their attitude for me by reciting almost by heart a passage from President Theodore Roosevelt's "Man in the Arena" speech, in which Roosevelt paid tribute to his forefathers who had settled the North American continent:

It is not the critic who counts; not the man who points out how the strong man stumbles. . . . The credit belongs to the man who is actually in the arena, whose face is marred by dust and sweat and blood; who strives valiantly . . . who knows great enthusiasms, the great devotions; who spends himself in a worthy cause; who at the best knows in the end the triumph of high achievement, and who at the worst . . . fails while daring greatly, so that his place shall never be with those cold and timid souls who know neither victory nor defeat.[†]

And of those in the arena, these pilots whom I befriended were, alas, not the best. "You want to see the best, the real Air Force?" one of the

---

* The A-10 pilots who participated in Cope Tiger 2006 not otherwise mentioned in the text were Maj. Brian "Milli" Gross of Phoenix; Capt. Michael "FAAC" Bullard of Crofton, Maryland; Capt. Ryan "APE" Hayde of Massapequa, New York; and 1st Lt. Michael "Beaker" Kump of Flint, Michigan. The flight surgeon was Capt. Martin "Tails" Harssema of Houston.

† Delivered at the Sorbonne in Paris on April 23, 1910.

A-10 pilots admitted to me in a nightclub in Korat, in the wee hours after many drinks. "Hang with the F-15E pilots for a while. You want to know how to recognize the A-10 pilots at Nellis during Red Flag?* We're the fat fucks." Of course, none of them were fat and a few were quite lean. Again, it was a form of self-deprecation, as with the call signs.

The nostalgic world of the A-10 was definitely not about where the Air Force was going. The A-10 was a tactical instrument, which might have a future for a few more decades. But the Air Force, I knew, was ultimately about controlling the space above the planet, where technology would increasingly provide the means to hit targets on the ground, no matter how small and specific, with planes manned or unmanned, or with satellites. While you would certainly still need armies, air and space forces would over time be able to do more and more, more subtly, with less collateral damage.

⸺

I caught a glimpse of a whole other side of the Air Force a few feet from where the A-10 pilots were headquartered at Korat Air Force Base. There was a large, portable satellite dish with lines connecting it to two mobile trailer units. Inside the trailers was a computer array that ran Eagle Vision, a mobile satellite ground station that mapped a given area in real time and in tremendous detail from space, and could immediately transmit the images anywhere in the world that also had such facilities.† The development of Eagle Vision had been spurred by the Global War on Terrorism—the need to map and remap parts of the Afghanistan-Pakistan border in order to identify the addition of even one new hovel. Yet, it had widespread humanitarian applications during natural catastrophes, when topographical features changed radically, and for the observation of refugee migrations and the growth of squatter camps.

Because this technology was available commercially, there were no classification issues. Thus, everything Eagle Vision offered could be shared with nongovernmental organizations. At the same time, there

---

* The Air Force's principal large force exercise held at Nellis Air Force Base in Nevada.
† The Internet lacked the bandwidth for reasonably fast transmission of such high-quality mapping.

was little chance that another nation or group would soon be able to do with Eagle Vision what the Air Force could. That's because this commercially available technology was useless in a fast-developing emergency without force protection, fuel bladders to run the portable generator, lift assets, and everything else that a military could do but civilians couldn't to deploy such a unit into a zone of anarchy and keep it up and running.

The Air Force was offering Eagle Vision for indirect diplomatic advantage. Ostensibly, Eagle Vision had been deployed to Cope Tiger to help the pilots with their bombing targets. In truth, the Air Force saw the exercise in Thailand as an opportunity to exhibit its humanitarian products, as a stream of visitors from not just Thailand and Singapore, but also from India, Australia, and other countries in Asia filtered through the trailer units, interested in coping with future tsunamis and with monitoring piracy in the Strait of Malacca. Countering Chinese military expansion, I was told over and over again during Cope Tiger, was about intangibles, like building relationships on the ground.

En route home I stopped in Honolulu and met with Maj. Gen. Lloyd Utterback of Llano, Texas, vice commander of PACAF (the Pacific Air Forces). He told me: "Tsunami relief succeeded because the Air Force and Navy already had a close working relationship with the Thais, who provided basing facilities. Our relationship with the Indian Air Force is growing dramatically, so that in future humanitarian emergencies we may be able to stage out of India. The tyranny of distance in the Pacific will, at the end of the day, be shortened not by technology but by personal ties."

The emerging situation in the twenty-first-century Pacific was the following. The United States Air Force, like the United States Navy, would need to upgrade its war-fighting capabilities to match any theater threat. At the same time, it would rely on disaster relief and humanitarian assistance packages that were second to none to give it a diplomatic edge over any emergent power.

Even so, great powers weren't measured by their foreign aid budgets, but by their ability and willingness to use their comprehensive military, economic, and political power, helped by proximity, to force their will on their neighbors.[6] In other words, it might turn out that the United

States would provide the wet blanket of aid, even as Beijing would subtly force dependent political-economic relationships upon adjacent states.

China was the unstated organizing principle for everything I saw the Air Force do in the Pacific. When I had asked a member of the squadron if there was a future for manned air-to-air combat, as an A-10 pilot who concentrated on air-to-ground I expected him to say no. But his reply was, "Ask the Chinese; they're quick learners, and increasingly will have the budgets to challenge us."

In fact, just as we had sought détente and transparency with the Soviet Union for the sake of stability during the Cold War, Pacific commanders were now seeking the sort of exchange programs with the Chinese military that they had with the Thais and Singaporeans. They would have liked nothing better than to include China in Cope Tiger. One reason businesspeople could proclaim the Asian century was that military men and women were practicing a constructive brand of pessimism in regard to the region.

NINE

TIMBUKTU, SOVIET STONEHENGE, AND GNARLY-ASS JUNGLE

MALI, GEORGIA, THE PHILIPPINES, AND COLOMBIA

Winter and Spring, 2006

Five days after I had arrived home from the Pacific, I left New England for Africa. In the midst of the crisis in Iraq, which threatened all-out sectarian war, the U.S. military was following up on earlier deployments in the Sahara and Sahel, culminating a long deployment in the Caucasus, expanding another in the Philippines, and continuing yet another in South America. Rather than take a deep, vertical look at a single operation as I was accustomed to doing, this time, accompanied by a three-man British film crew, I would do a quick, horizontal sweep of four separate deployments on different continents.

I started in Timbuktu, Mali, a place that even in an age of globalization and tourist clichés lived up to its reputation, suggestive of the ragged edge of the earth. An Army Special Forces A-team had requisitioned an old hotel there that had the air of a foreign legion outpost, with archways fortified by sandbags, overlooking desert and the scarred remnants of a Niger River tributary. I slapped the mattress in my room and the air went black with dust. Blinding sandstorms stole away the landscape, except for the mournful sounds of donkeys and banging doors. "The donkeys carry rocks and are beaten all day by kids with sticks," one Special Forces sergeant told me. "They must have been child molesters in an earlier existence, and this is their punishment." My teeth crunched grit when I closed my jaw. You could set fire to the air.

A smattering of vegetation, neem and acacia trees mostly, consti- tuted the last flickering reports of the great Niger itself, which lay about seven miles to Timbuktu's south. The river was wide enough to gener- ate its own micro-climate, so pale in its blueness that it exaggerated a sky whitened by dust. Pirogues lined its shoreline, disappearing into the distance like scattered toothpicks. Beyond Timbuktu, in the oppo- site direction toward the Sahara Desert in the north, this thin coat of vegetation—of civilization, really—all but vanished. From this point all the way to Tamanrasset in Algeria, where I had been the previous sum- mer with another 10th Group A-team, there was nothing for a thousand miles but a tyranny of distance, much like the Pacific. Simply put, there were too few landscape features to funnel the movement of human traf- fic, so the borders of these Saharan countries became uncontrollable, next-to-meaningless lines on a map, discernible only by GPS.

Taking off a few days from training with a Malian infantry company, five members of the A-team left Timbuktu to survey the desert a third of the way to the Algerian border. They wore civilian clothes and packed 9mm Berettas under their shirts, as well as a few M-4s in the trunks of Toyota Land Cruisers. Capt. Bill Torrey, a West Point graduate from Winter Springs, Florida, who had logged many months on the ground in Iraq and in the Balkans, wanted to meet local tribal leaders and identify potential landing strips, as well as sites for humanitarian relief work. As he put it, "We want to set the conditions that will prevent the emergence of terrorist activities."

Mali's government didn't so much rule the north of the country as maintain a ceasefire with the Tuaregs there. Once again, the point was for the U.S. military to get into a place early, fast, and with a small foot- print to try to do some good, so that it wouldn't need a bigger one later on. Even if the Salafist terrorist threat was exaggerated, much like the Cold War, it served as a useful pretext for military engagement with obscure parts of Africa: something that helped stabilize newly civilian regimes and got relief aid to places otherwise forgotten. It also fostered relationships with local intelligence assets of the kind the American military wished it had had in Afghanistan and elsewhere following 9/11.

From the standpoint of where we were headed, Timbuktu—a cosmopolitan caravan nexus before it was overrun by the Moroccans toward the end of the sixteenth century—with its gray, mud-brick houses, a couple of paved roads, a little museum of medieval Islamic manuscripts, and an occasional satellite dish—represented the modern world that we would be leaving behind. Rather than being the ragged edge of the earth, Timbuktu was actually next door to it.

The convoy consisted of five Land Cruisers and pickups, three of which were Special Forces and the others Malian Army escorts. Mine was driven by an 18 Delta (medic), a staff sergeant who was, in his own weird way, typical SF. A foster child shuttled from one home to another as a kid, he had found love and stability with an evangelical Christian family in rural Oklahoma. As he told me, his foster father, a policeman, was "a real man." That is, he loved and protected his family, was at ease with risk, and didn't need an audience to be heroic. This staff sergeant believed that such manhood also required religious virtue. Like others in SF, he had an abiding respect for the Marines. He didn't think much of the regular Army, though, except for its Alaska-based infantry battalions. As he put it to me, the brutal climate of Alaska made for unit cohesion and personal excellence. "Alaska's a real frontier," he kept repeating.

He didn't want his name used because, as he told me, he thought of accomplishment in terms of personal anonymity. Getting credit for something spoiled it for him.

He and the driver of the other Land Cruiser, a sergeant first class from rural Minnesota, who was an 18 Bravo (weapons specialist), had recently served together in Iraq. The pair had assisted marines during Second Fallujah in November 2004, and afterward trained Iraqi soldiers outside Baghdad. They had also worked as a two-man human intelligence team (HIT), going out alone dressed in beards and civilian clothes to meet with Iraqis who were too scared to meet publicly with Americans. It was a risky assignment, in which it was easy to be set up. The pair that followed them in the job were killed.

These two Green Berets had left for Mali almost immediately after returning from Iraq. They had families whom they missed, but they called those who complained publicly of overly long deployments "parasites." As I said, they were typical SF sergeants—the kind I had been meeting again and again for the past four years.

We were headed for Araouane, not so much a town as a few wells with some inhabitants that was a name on a map, as though it were the size of Cleveland. The information age created the illusion of knowledge where none existed. Nobody in Timbuktu really knew if anyone still lived in Araouane, and if so, what the security and health situations were there. Did the inhabitants have worms? Did they need eyeglasses? Was there a functioning school? Nor did anyone in Timbuktu seem to know who had been passing through Araouane—a former French colonial outpost for the regulation of nomads on the caravan route to Algeria in one direction, and to Mauritania in the other. Information as to what route to take from Timbuktu to Araouane was also confusing. Roads did not exist so much as "tracks."

We thought it would take four hours to reach Araouane. It took eleven. We averaged under fourteen miles per hour. We passed camel trains bearing salt to Timbuktu. We got stuck in the sand, had flat tires, suffered overheated batteries, and so on. The bumps and skid-outs were relentless. The sand spread like water under the tires, as we passed one micro-terrain after another: going from shining, hard-packed flats to normally fine sand, to flour, to moon dust. The African-American team sergeant from Far Rockaway, New York, called it a "shaking-out process. You find out all your weak points," he told me. Our Malian escorts got stuck just as often. They leveraged the fact that they were native to the area, but in fact, coming from Timbuktu, they were also city boys who were less comfortable in the desert than the Tuaregs.

Araouane, which we reached just after sunset, turned out to be a huddle of ruins on a bleached, khaki emptiness. As far as the horizon there was only an unending sandpit. An ancient man in dust-stained Tuareg headgear greeted us. He explained that the men of the village were either mining or trading salt in the desert, so only the women, children, and old people like himself remained, with just enough to survive. The Malian state did not exist here. With the coming of democracy, there was even more pressure on politicians to spend all the aid money in the populous south, near the capital of Bamako, where the votes were. The default situation for a Tuareg was movement: conducting raids, banditry, and commerce on the caravan routes. So the absence of working-age men was normal. It took seven days by camel to reach Timbuktu, the old man told us.

"What kinds of people live here?" Capt. Torrey asked.

"Tuaregs and Songhai," the man said. "And outside," he continued, pointing to the surrounding vastness, "Arabs." By that he meant lighter-skinned strangers who spoke varying degrees of Arabic.

We laid out sleeping bags after a dinner of cold-weather MREs: tastier, more filling, and with even more calories than the MREs I had become accustomed to, but awkward to prepare since they did not self-heat with water like the normal kind.

Following sunup, Capt. Torrey and the evangelical staff sergeant from Oklahoma set up an eye clinic inside one of the ruins. They unpacked little boxes of adaptable eyewear, an ingenious low-tech device manufactured by the U.S. Agency for International Development. These were round, Harry Potterish, horn-rimmed glasses of zero prescription which increasingly strengthened as you pumped a clear gel solution attached to the frame inside the glass. The SF guys called them "never-get-laid-again" glasses, because of how they made you look.

At first, only the old men came to have their eyes checked and get glasses. They would not let the SF guys touch their women. Luckily, also among us was Army Maj. Holly Silkman of Colorado Springs, Colorado, visiting from European Command (EUCOM). As soon as she entered the hut women began appearing with their children, as though by magic.* Wearing loose civilian clothes and a purple headscarf, Maj. Silkman looked as if she might be a Peace Corps volunteer. The sergeant first class from Minnesota, recently back from Iraq, snapped pictures for a photo album that he planned to give the villagers on a succeeding visit—a visit for which Capt. Torrey was already making a to-do list. The next time the team came here, it would have to

---

* In *Imperial Grunts,* I argue for the introduction of women into Special Forces precisely for missions like this one. See Chapter 6.

bring smaller-sized eye frames for the children, school supplies, and medicine for worms and so forth, in order to conduct a full-scale medical civil action program (MEDCAP).

"We could conduct a JCET here," Torrey told me—that is, camp out nearby and train with the Malian Army for a month to hone desert survival skills. For a small amount of money you could do a lot with this outpost and others like it spread across the Sahara. As in the Pacific, it was through relationships more than through technology that you conquered the tyranny of distance. But setting up a network took time. Progress would be slow and organic, and measured subjectively in successive layers of trust. Such things you could not quantify or objectify; thus they were the very things that congressmen and generals in Washington had the least interest in, because of the pressure to show "concrete results fast." And yet you could cover most of Africa with A-teams in places like Araouane for the price of only one F-22 fighter jet, for which it was easier to get funding.

Hours passed. More women and children kept streaming into the hut. By late morning, the evangelical staff sergeant, who had driven eleven hard hours the day before, and had slept only a few hours in the sand—a sleep interrupted by guard duty—was still smiling and joking by way of sign language with the patients.

Meanwhile, Capt. Torrey had disappeared for an hour to meet with the elders. He drank a lot of *chai,* and made a monetary gift of $100 to the village that he would justify to the U.S. Army bureaucracy by claiming it was for the overnight sleeping accommodations. "What can I tell the higher-ups that I accomplished here?" he asked rhetorically. "Only that I drank tea and turned a bunch of kids into Harry Potters. It's the intangibles that you can't measure. If we don't spend a little money in this region, sooner or later the bad guys will."

Two days later I was on a bleak, rippling plain, my boots stuck in gluey mud, shivering in a cold drizzle outside Tbilisi, Georgia. Before me was a Soviet Stonehenge of half-finished, pebbly-cement structures from the 1980s that U.S. Marines were using to train a Georgian Army battalion in military operations in urban terrain (MOUT). Smoke bombs, flash bangs, and artillery simulators all went off at once as marines mounted an ambush against the Georgian soldiers with whom they were working. The marines had role players mimic screaming, abusive civilians, since the Georgians had to learn not only how to fight in urban areas, but also how to handle noncombatants in a civilized, professional manner, regardless of how much they were provoked.

On this same bleak plain of Krtsanisi in 1795, a Persian army had defeated a much smaller Georgian one. The Persians had invaded only because the Russians under Catherine the Great did not live up to their treaty obligations, so when Russia withdrew its troops from Georgia a vacuum was created that Persia filled. The Persians went on to destroy Tbilisi and massacre its inhabitants. Laid bare to the Persians from the south and to Dagestani marauders to the northeast, the various Georgian kingdoms and principalities had no choice but to allow the complete annexation of their country by the Russians, who stayed for the next 190 years, until the collapse of the Soviet Union.

This only led to another series of attacks on Georgia's historic borders, as Abkhazians in the northwest and Ossetians in the north ethnically cleansed their Georgian communities and established breakaway republics. At the same time, predominantly Muslim Ajaria in the southwest emerged as a semi-independent warlordship, even as Chechen raiders from the northeast infiltrated through the Pankisi Gorge. The Georgians had not helped their own cause by tearing themselves apart in a civil war.

It was thanks to the Machiavellian deal-making of the former Soviet foreign minister and ethnic Georgian Eduard Shevardnadze that a semblance of normality was restored here, and the separatist rebellions quieted—that is, until Shevardnadze himself was toppled in a peaceful, democratic uprising in late 2003, known as the Rose Revolution. The advent of full-fledged democracy in Georgia was what allowed for the ramping up of the Marine-led training mission, under the control of EUCOM in Stuttgart.

The Marines aimed to professionalize the Georgian military so that it could stabilize its own borders. Deploying Georgian detachments to Iraq and Kosovo would fast-forward their learning curve. As for the Marines, who had recently contributed a detachment of their own to Special Operations Command (SOCOM), the Georgia train-and-equip mission constituted a prototype for the Special Forces–type training missions in which the leathernecks would henceforth be involved.

"There was nothing here a few years ago—no army, no security force—the Russians could have simply walked in and nobody could have done anything about it," said Lt. Col. Billy McGowan of Land O' Lakes, Florida, the Marine commander in Georgia. Now, in addition to Marines, there were Navy corpsmen training Georgians in combat medicine, and private contractors training a Georgian Army reconnaissance company. Indeed, there were actually young Georgian officers who had been to both TBS (The Basic School) at Quantico, Virginia, and Ranger School at Fort Benning, Georgia, respectively the best and toughest schools the Marines and regular Army had to offer. Very few Americans in uniform had been to both.

An age of democratization was also an age of military professionalization, for without a disciplined military developed along Western lines, it was doubtful that a new democracy like Georgia's would remain one for very long. Nevertheless, you had to wonder about what was being created here. Going in with a small footprint as in Georgia and Mali meant there was relatively little at stake in the event the deployment went sour. But the very fact of a small footprint also meant that you had little control over the product being produced. True, U.S. military assistance was provided only to recognized democracies, the exceptions being such places as Pakistan and Egypt, where the alternative seemed worse. But Georgia illustrated the risks of military aid in support of democratic uprisings in places with nonexistent institutions and border disputes, even though these same revolutions, in and of themselves, had to be admired.

In fact, democracy did not necessarily signify stability or economic growth. Tbilisi, since the last time I had visited in 1999, had grown from a charming little city to a better-lit, more substantial one, with a smattering of new hotels, restaurants, and nightclubs.* And if you didn't journey far beyond downtown, you might even call Georgia a success story. Beyond the capital, though, this was a mean, ruined ex-Soviet re-

* For an account of my previous visit, see the chapters on Georgia in *Eastward to Tartary: Travels in the Balkans, the Middle East, and the Caucasus* (New York: Random House, 2000).

public ruled by muscle rather than by the rule of law, with knots of men who looked more comfortable wearing black ski masks than business suits. Nor had the border situation improved much. While the crisis with Ajaria seemed alleviated, the one with South Ossetia was worse.

New democracies had populist tendencies. Georgia's democratic president, Mikhail Saakashvili, had used the tensions with South Ossetia to deflect attention from Georgia's economic woes. There was a rich legacy for him to exploit. In the nationalist rebellions in the Caucasus that followed the breakup of the Soviet Union, the Russian-backed Ossetes had expelled ethnic Georgians in a bout of ethnic cleansing. The South Ossetian capital of Tskhinvali had not improved since I had visited there seven years ago. It remained a shabbier, more untamed version of the worst parts of Georgia. The women in the street were beautiful and the men looked like gangsters and slobs. It was a chaotic region where politics were inseparable from criminality.

The Georgians hated the Ossetes and wanted the autonomous territory back. Meanwhile, under Vladimir Putin's low-calorie dictatorship, the Russian empire was attempting to reconstitute itself in the North Caucasus and had placed "peacekeepers" on Georgia's border with South Ossetia, a mere hour's drive from where the Marines were training Georgian troops. American imperialism was about going abroad in search of security at home and, as a consequence, enmeshing itself in all the world's anxieties.[1]

Of course, volatile borders and rebellions existed in many of the places I had been with the U.S. military. But everywhere else, the problems were terrorist-related. Here they were less so, despite the infiltration of some Muslim Chechens. In fact, training the Georgians was the quid pro quo for their helping us in Iraq, as well as a means of encouraging democracy in the Caucasus and linking Georgia more directly with NATO. Even so, a further NATO expansion eastward to include a country like Georgia was unlikely. Georgia did not have a European tradition beyond Tbilisi's architecture and circle of intellectuals. The rest of the country was heavily Oriental. The strength of Georgia's mafias and the weakness of its governing institutions attested to the predominant influence of Persia's clan and tribal system over that of Russia's bureaucratic tradition, which, however coarse, at least represented the rudiments of an impersonal, law-based system.

Yet, the Marines loved this place. The red wine was rich and good. A bottle of good vodka at a restaurant cost $5; a meal for six with alcohol was $25. The women had sad, intoxicatingly dark expressions and the noble bearing of Eastern princesses. And they were always on the lookout for Western husbands and boyfriends, much like German women had been on the lookout for GIs in the late 1940s and the 1950s. The problem in Georgia—a milder version of what I had seen in the Philippines three years before—was keeping the guys in check.[2]

Intensifying the situation was that young marines were sent to Georgia not for three or six months but for a year, so obviously there was a tendency to go native. As one marine told his commander, "I'll reenlist if I can stay in Georgia." The commander, Lt. Col. McGowan, later complained to me, "That's not at all what being a marine is about!" I wondered if the Marines themselves would change, given that joining SOCOM meant more such exotic deployments like this one. When site survey teams planned such deployments, the most important thing to do was to scout out the bars and nightclubs, I thought. Once again, it was the intangibles that mattered more than the objective facts. To wit, how attractive and friendly were the local women?

———

Next stop, the Philippines. Since the summer of 2003, when I had last visited Zamboanga, on the southwest tip of Mindanao, the unconventional warfare operation against the Islamic insurgents of Jemaah Islamiyah and Abu Sayyaf had been extended southwestward, from the island of Basilan to Jolo, the other large island in the Sulu Archipelago.*

The Philippines was the flip side of Iraq. In Iraq, the failure of the interagency process in Washington had been in plain sight. I had seen not just the U.S. Army but the whole Potomac River bureaucracy as an industrial-age dinosaur in which one massive governmental department had little coordination with another. Because the original invasion of Iraq had been a purely military affair, it succeeded. (Whether it was also

———

* See Chapter 4 of *Imperial Grunts* for a full account of Army Special Forces operations in Mindanao and the Sulu Archipelago, and a historical-cultural overview of the region.

a strategic mistake or not was something that would be debated for years.) But the occupation was a civil-military affair—that is, an interagency affair—and that was one reason, among others, it failed.

But in the Philippines the effort to marginalize the al-Qaeda–linked Islamic insurgents of Jemaah Islamiyah and Abu Sayyaf was succeeding precisely because it was a civil-military affair. The interagency process was working here for two reasons. First, there was the advantage of scale. The operation was initially confined to one island, Basilan, and then to another, Jolo, so the number of bureaucrats and troops involved was limited, and therefore so was the interference from Washington. Second, there was the colonial legacy of the United States in what American troops nostalgically referred to as the "P.I.," the Philippine Islands. Like nineteenth-century European colonialism around the world, this particular colonial legacy highlighted a seamless relationship between diplomats, aid workers, and men in uniform. Thus, there was a long-standing tradition among diplomats inside the American Embassy in Manila to psychologically view the military not as "the other" but as one of them. The same went for the soldiers. As Col. Jim Linder of Fort Lawn, South Carolina, told me, "To do my job right, I am embedded inside USAID [the United States Agency for International Development]."

Col. Linder was the commander of the Joint Special Operations Task Force (JSOTF) in Zamboanga. A graduate of Clemson University, he was from a family of farmers and had gone to school to become a better one. But he joined the Army instead and never looked back. Linder illustrated something crucial about the military:

The military was a world of structure to an extreme extent. For example, it could take a teenage hoodlum and turn him into a command sergeant major by the time he was forty. Structure, in the military's case, was not democratic. In fact, it was vaguely authoritarian. Men who exuded an almost vestigial sense of authority had a distinct advantage. Jim Linder had it. His stony, unblinking expression could be intimidating.

Such a vestigial sense of authority also featured a simplicity of expression: a clear advantage in communicating a commander's intent down through the ranks. Civilians understandably found American military expressions like "good guys" and "bad guys" childish, corny, and off-putting. This was true not only of civilians but also of military men from other countries, such as Great Britain, who, while also exuding manly authority, thrived on understatement. But whereas the British tradition was the product of a millennium of an island nation's sea-based defense, the American military tradition also featured an army one: of settling a frontier in a very short space of time, barely a century and a half ago. Because of its very violence, crudity, and singularity of purpose, the Army's frontier legacy helped breed a black-and-white way of talking.

All this came together in the person of Jim Linder, the South Carolina farmer. Col. Linder's simple talk was doubly effective—inside and outside the ranks—since he also had to play the role of a politician in selling the American military to the Muslim Filipino civilians of Jolo and Basilan. He was a warrior-diplomat to the extent that he did almost no fighting but a lot of public speaking.

"We were told that the Muslim Tausugs [the ethnic group on Jolo] would steal from us, and knife us in the back after we gave them aid. After all, for hundreds of years on Jolo there were clan wars, banditry, piracy, kidnapping for ransom. The Tausugs would kill you because, just because. . . . But," Linder went on, "I have the luxury of being a soldier. That means I have a mission in which I do not intend to fail."

He told me this over dinner the first time we met, at a restaurant in Zamboanga. Everything he told me that night I heard him repeat over and over again before crowds of Filipinos in Jolo and Basilan.

"I will fortify the moral high ground. People will attack me with stories about Abu Ghraib and the killing of Filipino civilians a hundred years ago by American troops, actions which I cannot defend. And I will respond that my troops can build a school, or fix a little girl's cleft palate at a MEDCAP, whereas all the guerrillas of Abu Sayyaf and Jemaah Islamiyah can offer is a suicide vest. I will build my fortress on deeds, because I know that the only force protection I have is the goodwill of civilians. All the guns in the world won't keep an IED from going off."

This was much the same message that Marine Maj. Gen. James N. Mattis had given me at Camp Pendleton, California, prior to the deployment of the 1st Marine Division to Iraq's Sunni Triangle in the late winter of 2004. Jim Mattis had told me that our best eyes and ears would be the locals of whom the Marines had to win the trust. Ultimately, that did not happen, not because of want of trying by Mattis's marines, but because of events outside their control in a theater of war in which his marines were just one element on the American side.* The Philippines was a different story, though.

As one SF A-team captain on Jolo would tell me: "The majority of people on Jolo have never seen a Westerner, let alone an American, and their form of communication is word of mouth, not newspapers and certainly not the Internet. So they have no preconceptions about us. And we're bringing them things like health care which they don't have."

A hundred years ago to the month that I would visit Jolo, Capt. John "Black Jack" Pershing defeated the Muslim Moros (actually Tausugs) in a counterinsurgency campaign that eventually led Pershing to the command of American troops in Europe during World War I. But modern development had left Jolo behind, and this same population had little ill will toward the Americans who were here to help it.

The insertion of American forces into Jolo in late 2005 and early 2006, like the one into Basilan in 2002, was accomplished under the auspices of Balikatan, Tagalog for "Shoulder to Shoulder," an annual American-Philippine joint military exercise. I had heard that the top civilian leadership in the Pentagon hated the fact that they had to hide such troop insertions under the cover of annual exercises, as if the United States had to apologize for hunting down terrorists. But if true, these leaders had it backward. The whole object was to downplay the American military footprint. The more indirect and softer the approach, the more likely that it would be accepted by the local media and population.

I flew with Col. Linder from Zamboanga to Jolo on an Army C-12. Through the gloomy cloud cover the island revealed itself as raw, dense jungle with a lot of primary hardwood forest. From the air, Jolo Town was just a sprawl of corrugated shanties. On the ground, I was immediately oppressed by a rotting, grimy humidity that spoke of mold and snakes and dirty towels. With the exception of coconut palms that signi-

---

* Though Mattis once came to the media's attention when he mentioned that marines like to kill people, ironically, the fact was that he was among the most well-read, intellectual, and civil affairs–oriented generals in the military.

fied secondary growth tracts, the island probably looked much as it did when Pershing had been here—the first time in history when American troops fought Islamic guerrillas.[3] "It's a gnarly-ass terrain," Linder said.

Jolo had a larger, more predominantly Muslim population than Basilan, with a more rugged landscape, all of which made it easier for insurgents.* Jolo truly had a tendency of being beyond the law. To understand why, all one had to do was look at a map. It was halfway between Mindanao and the Malaysian part of Borneo, with which it historically did much trade. Before the coming of the Spaniards, Jolo had been an independent sultanate. Manila and the rest of Luzon, from which the Philippines was governed, had little reality on this island. Just as Fallujah's obstinacy and independence were partly a product of its being on a historic smuggling route from Mesopotamia to Syria, Jolo's was similar: it was located on a historic smuggling route between the Philippines and Borneo.

I traveled around Jolo for several days, visiting base camps that had once been hideouts for Ramzi Yousef, the organizer of the first World Trade Center bombing in 1993, and Radulan Sahiron, an Abu Sayyaf leader, both of whom were now behind bars. The fact of their presence on Jolo was testimony to the organic links between a worldwide group like al-Qaeda and a local one like Abu Sayyaf, as well as to the efficacy of the remotest, most primitive locations as camps for the planning of terrorist operations of global consequence.

I stayed with Special Forces A-teams embedded with Philippine Army and Marine detachments, as well as with active-duty civil affairs teams out of Fort Bragg, North Carolina. On Jolo and on more distant islands closer to Borneo were also Marine engineering units, Navy Seabees, and SEAL teams. The USS *Mercy,* one of the Navy's only two hospital ships, was planning a stop here, a place where USAID projects were interwoven with military ones. Every project was directed at two target groups: military-age males, who could make the wrong choices as to their loyalties; and women of childbearing age, who were the motors of cultural change.

---

* Though smaller in size than Basilan, Jolo had a population of 620,000 as opposed to Basilan's 380,000. Whereas Basilan's population was over 60 percent Muslim, Jolo's was over 90 percent.

The Americans here were all in uniform, with red, white, and blue flags Velcroed onto their sleeves, no less. This included the Marines, who normally eschewed the wearing of flags and other insignias. Col. Linder had given the order for all American troops in Mindanao and Sulu to wear flags, which he called the real symbol of "jointness," and of "our idea of freedom."

Context is everything, and because American troops in Basilan and Jolo had never overtly taken part in combat operations but had overtly participated in MEDCAPS and other humanitarian projects, the uniforms and the flags had not only been accepted by the indigenous Muslim populations, but by the Filipino national media as well, despite the legacy of American colonialism.

Of course, the picture wasn't altogether pretty. As Linder kept repeating to me, "This is a no-shit war zone, and we will spill American blood here." He was openly afraid that one day an IED, courtesy of the remaining insurgents hiding in Jolo's dense jungles, would kill some of his men and the American public would suddenly become nervous about the military presence on these islands. As if on cue, the day after I left Jolo a bomb went off in a grocery store, killing a handful of civilians and wounding many more.

"We're at war here," Linder's command sergeant major, Tim Strong of Concord, New Hampshire, told me, emphasizing the potential dangers of this deployment. While one could be forgiven for thinking this a bit of an exaggeration (given the near absence of American military casualties in the Philippines since 9/11), it was such an attitude in and of itself that had helped keep the Philippines out of the news. Whenever traveling by road in Jolo, Americans were in full kit and body armor. It looked ridiculous, but it also made them such hardened targets that it helped dissuade the insurgents from attacking them.

It was difficult to calibrate the extent of the threat. But as the failure to deploy massive numbers of troops in Iraq following the invasion had attested, it was better to over- than to under-compensate. In any case, as one team sergeant on Jolo told me, "If I have one hand on my pistol grip, I make sure the other hand waves. The meaner we look, the softer we have to act to the local people, to show them we're not just a bunch of bullies." Added Col. Linder: "Our image is fragile. If we so much as spit tobacco in the wrong direction, we will break the rucksack of responsibility and trust that we carry."

The sergeant major's comment about being at war had another connotation, of which he was quite explicit. While the term "Global War on Terrorism" was something the American public was skeptical about, since all it ever saw on television were Iraq and Afghanistan, for the troops themselves, deployed all over the world, it really was a "global" war in terms of their personal experiences.

Maintaining goodwill required the most restrictive rules of engagement (ROEs). One night I found myself on a beach in a thatched hut, where an A-team was billeted alongside a Philippine marine detachment. The A-team commander was yet another clean-cut and earnest West Pointer. He had a face and expression that Americans would trust instantly. Too bad he insisted on going on camera with a boonie hat and sunglasses, to conceal his identity.* He called himself "one of the last of the pure," who joined SF before 9/11, before Special Forces became trendy, as he put it. Anyway, the restrictive ROEs really hit home upon encountering this A-team. Though the team was here to "advise and assist" the Philippine marines, it turned out that it couldn't train them, train with them, or go out on missions with them—officially, that is. In point of fact, it couldn't be seen doing any of those things. But whatever it might or might not have been doing behind the scenes, it was striking how its mere presence constituted a confidence-building measure for those in the immediate vicinity.

Indeed, it is said that half of life is showing up; the same often with deployments. Unlike the Afghanistan-Pakistan frontier, a thousand-mile stretch of lawless badlands with seamless egresses to the great urban areas of Pakistan, where anyone could disappear, Jolo was an island. Escape by sea was possible, but not nearly as easy as slipping beyond the Afghanistan-Pakistan border. Unlike that region, the relationship here between the inhabitants and the American military was very good thanks to an emphasis on aid projects. Therefore, sooner or

---

* Despite guidelines from SOCOM, I had found that there was no hard and fast rule regarding the use of real names and faces in SF. You could reveal more in print than on television. Some Green Berets were comfortable being quoted by name; others not. Whatever they were comfortable with, I respected.

later, the Americans, like this A-team, seemingly doing little, might well get lucky with actionable intelligence regarding the capture of the remaining Abu Sayyaf leaders.

Back in Zamboanga I paid a visit to the JSOTF located on the Philippine Army base of Camp Navarro, where I had stayed in 2003. At that time, the JSOTF was a grim, spartan camp in the doldrums, with an air of impermanence: mud everywhere, trashy food, and portable toilet and shower units. With the main operation on Basilan over, it was unclear what exactly the Special Operations task force was doing. The JSOTF was now smaller, but with proper walkways and creature comforts that spoke of a more hardened, permanent arrangement, evinced by the operation on Jolo that it was now overseeing, and the continued involvement of the U.S. military on Basilan and other islands.

I went next with Col. Linder for a visit to Basilan. In 2003 the island was peaceful and relatively safe following the U.S. military operation there, but without an economy and with an air of uncertainty.[4] There had been legitimate questions as to whether the Americans and the government in Manila would stay engaged. Linder went from one venue to another on Basilan, from a Philippine army base to the local governor's office to a charity organization, harping on the same themes as he had with me: about the importance of the American and Philippine militaries working together and with civilian aid agencies. It was a bit of a dog-and-pony show. This was especially apparent when under armed guard we visited Jollibies, a Filipino fast food chain that had recently opened a branch in the island capital of Isabella. As corny as this seemed—overwhelming force in order to eat fast food—it punctuated a point that the dog-and-pony show could not obscure: the air of uncertainty prevalent in 2003 was now less so, to a point where big business in Manila such as this restaurant chain felt safe enough to invest. Basilan now had cellphone towers, more asphalt roads and bridges, more schools, and higher agricultural production. Power outages occurred because of demand surges, a sign of uneven development, but of development nevertheless.

The Philippines, perhaps more than any other place in the world since 9/11, was a success for the American military. It wasn't a dramatic or large-scale success, but something had happened that had a continuing upward curve. A significant and strategic island chain with a Muslim population, which had been outside the law and whose local bandits and insurgents were demonstrably linked to world terrorist organizations, was being reclaimed by a legitimate central government, a government that was, in turn, a U.S. ally and a democracy.

That democracy was not a healthy one. The Philippines remained coup-prone, though such a coup would not necessarily undermine progress in the remote Muslim south. In any case, reverses were still possible on all these islands, even though Abu Sayyaf seemed to be on its way back to the low-level banditry from which it had first emerged, before going big-time in the early 1990s with kidnappings and beheadings of Westerners. Nevertheless, progress against terrorists in the southern Philippines was surer than in Afghanistan or Iraq.

From the Philippines, after a short break back in the United States, I flew to Colombia, where the Army Special Forces mission that I had observed over three years ago was still in progress.

I had forgotten how beautiful Bogotá was, with its clean streets, smart cafés, stunningly dressed men and women, and bicycle lanes and ramps for the handicapped. Yet it was surreal, because the city also featured bomb sniffer dogs, constant searches by private security guards, and sprawling nearby slums. Colombia was three times the size of Iraq, with nearly double the population, and a geography so mountainous that it was like Afghanistan covered by jungle. But with only a few hundred American troops, including a significant Army Special Forces component, undeniable, measurable progress had also been made here.

The country was safer than in 2003. You could now drive from Bogotá to Medellin and Santa Marta. Three years before you couldn't. Whereas road attacks on these heavily populated routes had been the norm, now they were rare and treated as unacceptable by the government. In 1999, there had been 3,500 kidnappings. That number had steadily dropped to 600.

In 2003 one Special Forces sergeant and warrant officer after another had told me that the most practical way to end the almost four-decade-long struggle against private drug armies was for the Colombian government to align itself with one group of thugs in order to defeat the other groups of thugs. And if such a strategy could alleviate the bloodshed and kidnappings, how was that not virtuous?[5]

In fact, the same week I arrived in Colombia in late April 2006, the Colombian government announced that the right-wing Autodefensas Unidas de Colombia (AUC) was demobilizing, with the paramilitary group's 30,000 members laying down their arms. Thus culminated a process that had begun with a ceasefire between the government and the AUC in 2002. No doubt it had led to many seamy deals, by which some members of the AUC were admitted to the government security services and others got assurances that they would not be prosecuted. "Think of it as a massive plea bargain," one foreign observer told me. Nevertheless, rather than fight three private armies of narco-terrorists, the government now had to fight only two. Meanwhile, the left-wing Ejército de Liberacíon Nacional (ELN) was also on the ropes, leaving only the left-wing Fuerzas Armadas Revolucionarias de Colombia (FARC)—by far the most formidable of the three—for the government to actively deal with. Because the FARC would not go down easily, Colombian President Alvaro Uribe Vélez had little choice than to try to co-opt the other two. It wasn't neat, it wasn't pretty, and it was certainly slow-going, with reverses always possible, but it seemed the only plan that in the real world stood a chance of success. Said the same foreign observer, "You can't set expectations here based on the moral standards of Vermont."

Voters in Latin America's oldest democracy agreed. Three weeks later they reelected President Uribe by a 62 percent plurality.

My first morning in Bogotá, I attended a meeting of U.S. and Colombian military and civilian officials at President Uribe's offices. This was interagency coordination of not just one country but two. The subject was Chocó, the province abutting the border with Panama. The goal: how to prevent the FARC from moving into this barely governable jungle region that had recently been given up by the AUC. Social and educational services would be brought to bear, along with traveling judges—protected by the military—to adjudicate crimes. President Uribe did not want to repeat the mistake of former Peruvian President Alberto Fujimori. Fujimori had rightly cracked down hard on the left-wing guerrillas of the Shining Path, but he never followed up with social programs in the areas he had liberated, so similar insurgencies later reemerged.

The U.S. soldiers and aid officials at this meeting not only all spoke Spanish, but also often communicated with one another in Spanish. It was impressive how immigration patterns in the United States had produced a cadre of area experts who understood a place like Colombia down to their fingertips. Every American officer and noncom I would meet in the coming days spoke Spanish, and many had Hispanic last names. I tried to imagine what Iraq and Afghanistan would be like with the same level of language expertise and input from our exotic immigrant communities.

Of course, progress was more easily made here. Although there were large, ungovernable spaces in Colombia, Colombian institutions existed on a much more sophisticated level than in the Middle East, let alone the countries whose governmental structures we were trying to create from scratch. Yet the U.S. military was making Colombian institutions work better still. For example, the Planning Assistance Training Team, a regular Army element out of Fort Bragg, North Carolina, had arranged for every Colombian at this interagency meeting to have an assistant who would work in the same room with all the other assistants, thus creating a horizontal layer of interagency coordination among fourteen Colombian government ministries and departments that had not existed. If only it were that easy in Iraq—or Washington.

My time was short so rather than drive, I flew to Medellín. As everywhere in Colombia, the landscape was overpowering: an almost vertical, crinkled, and intricate junglescape the color of glistening black-green felt. This was the most active military region of Colombia, with hundreds of combat deaths and operations in the first three months of 2006 alone. When international drug kingpin Pablo Escobar's Medellín cartel collapsed, following his killing at the hands of government security forces in 1993, the FARC, ELN, and AUC all emerged from the lower depths of the cocaine economy to fill the breach in this rich coca-growing region, which was relatively close to the cocaine corridor of Panama's Darien Gap.

Now with the AUC disbanding and the ELN weakened, the Colombian Army was intensifying the pressure on the FARC in Medellín. The effort had begun three years before, when the army moved into a number of massive slum neighborhoods built on the scraggly mountains just outside the city, which in the mid- and late 1990s had become virtually extraterritorial crime kingdoms. Bunkers had stood atop ridgelines, and the entrances to the neighborhoods down below had been blocked by school buses so that government forces could not enter. Gun battles were constant as the various drug armies battled for control. "Express kidnappings" were also common, whereby if a ransom was not arranged within two hours the victim was executed.

Three years after the state had taken control of these neighborhoods, I spent the day in one of them: Comuna 13, formerly the worst slum of the cocaine capital of the world. Twelve-year-old girls were dressed like whores and the men looked like vagabonds in this claustrophobic maze of corrugated iron crawling up a forty-degree hillside. I observed a Colombian Army med-ready, the equivalent of a Green Beret MED-CAP. Doctors and dentists provided free medical care to people who had stood in line for hours. Neighborhood schoolchildren sang Colombia's thumping national anthem. The area commander, Maj. Gen. Oscar Enrique Gonzáles Peña, told the crowd that the job of the military was to bring social services to the neighborhood, because that was the only way the state would keep control of these streets. Nearby were Green Berets from the 7th Special Forces Group with American flags on their uniforms. Of course, the reason crime statistics were way down was that soldiers patrolled the streets here regularly. As Maj. Gen. Gonzáles admitted to me, it would take several years more of continuous military operations to consolidate the government's hold. Nevertheless, what the local army, with help from U.S. Army Special Forces, had achieved was still more than what had, by the spring of 2006, been achieved in Baghdad.

Though progress was slow, it was still progress, and as in the Philippines, the American flag on a camouflage uniform was associated with that.

The following day I went to southern Colombia to see another part of the country reclaimed from narco-terrorists. First I flew to Larandia, a Colombian military base that I had visited in February 2003 the day after one American private contractor was executed by the FARC and three others taken hostage. Their plane had gone down in guerrilla territory a few miles outside the base while it was in the midst of mapping coca fields for future eradication. In 2004 the Colombian military replaced an army division here with a combined joint task force advised by Americans, mainly 7th Group Green Berets. Though the three hostages still hadn't been located, the task force had been successful in breaking up FARC concentrations for hundreds of miles around Larandia.

In particular, in April 2004, the government had taken control of Peñas Coloradas, a major cocaine-trafficking center to the south, close to the border with Ecuador. The journey to Peñas Coloradas in a Russian-built Colombian Army helicopter took forty minutes. As we flew south along the wide and looping, brown and mighty Caguán River, the jungle and grasslands became flatter and vaster, as well as emptier of any sign of human habitation. It might as well have been the Sahara north of Timbuktu. The difficulty of controlling this region by a government located several hundred miles and several mountain ranges away was written into the landscape, absent of asphalt and of all but the occasional dirt trail.

Suddenly the helicopter began a steep and circling combat descent to avoid the guns of FARC outposts. We dropped so fast it was as though the glittering greenery jumped up to grab you. The medieval-like arrangement of green sandbag walls with machine gun emplacements got larger and larger as we dove. The sandbag walls surrounded a shattered cluster of corrugated shacks by the Caguán River, which from the air looked like sludge, but now revealed itself as swift and turbulent.

The Alamo. Fort Apache. Choose a cliché. Peñas Coloradas was the real thing, a Colombian army post with two small battalions—four hundred soldiers—living amidst jungle and FARC guerrillas. Larandia, a less besieged base, was the nearest friendly place. Here had been a deserted gold rush town of sex, booze, and fast bucks. But instead of gold it was cocaine. So much money had poured through this place that the FARC counted it by simply weighing the stacks of $100 bills. Millions upon millions of dollars of coke profits piled up here, yet no infrastructure had ever been built save for the streets of scrap-iron and cinder-block shacks that were now completely deserted. It was the ultimate false economy, which, nevertheless, had proved difficult to defeat. A sign in the makeshift bull ring read: "Coca—the Alternative to Peace."

I saw other ratty signs: "Gym," "Cosmetics," "Restaurant." Family pictures still hung on walls and children's toys littered the floors, as the whole town had cleared out in a hurry when the FARC ordered a retreat of every family into the jungle. I was haunted by a very personal, human sadness, even if generations here had been exploited and brutalized by the FARC, and even if the takeover by the Colombian Army had been, in a larger sense, the right thing to do. You simply couldn't wander through these haunted shacks without being affected by the turned-upside-down lives.

Across the smoky river was a compound of two large sheet-metal houses, formerly the home of Nayibe Rojas Valderama, alias "Sonia," one of the FARC's leading cocaine traffickers, who in 2005 had been extradited to the United States and was now in an American prison. The national army was currently in partial control of these cocaine badlands. It seemed to have inherited a void populated by snakes and insects.

The last place I visited in Colombia was Arauca. In February 2003, when I had last been there, Arauca Province was considered the most dangerous region of the country. Narco-terrorist attacks with IEDs, cylinder bombs, and car bombs occurred not every few days, but every few hours. Before the U.S. military began to cope with IEDs in Iraq, 7th Special Forces Group was coping with them in Arauca. Green Berets had left the base only in full battle-rattle. The town of Arauca, on the muddy Arauca River, which marked the border with Venezuela, had been a ratty sprawl of tacky storefronts and café awnings made of black plastic, the kind used for garbage bags. Attacks on the pipeline carrying Colombian oil from here to the Caribbean coast were constant.

To say that there had been dramatic change since then would be a serious understatement. Proper cafés were now open, storefronts painted, crowds flooded the streets—at night too. Rather than a rathole, Arauca looked like a normally poor and unsophisticated provincial town. Three years ago I journeyed through these streets inside a convoy of Humvees armed with light-medium machine guns. Now I rode in the open back of a pickup truck with a handful of American and Colombian soldiers, armed with nothing more substantial than Beretta pistols, and motorcycle escorts with a few assault rifles. Three years ago I did not leave the Humvee in the middle of town. Now I got out and walked the streets with Army Capt. Troy Terrebonne of Houston, who told me, "Wherever you want to go, we can go, on foot. It's safe here."

The last IED attack in the town had been eighteen months ago. In the whole province, there had not been one attack on the pipeline, and only two car bombs and two fatal IEDs over the previous seven months. Instead of two functioning police stations in the province, there were now eight.

There had been no magic bullet solution here, no new twist, no newsworthy technique that you could write about. It was just bread-and-butter, never-give-up attrition of the same. The Green Berets had provided small-unit training that raised the combat quality of the Colombian Army, making it more aggressive in hunting down the ELN and the FARC, as well as making it more aware of human rights as a pivotal tool in a counterinsurgency. Meanwhile, the funds appropriated by the State Department had come with an implicit proviso: the national army would put much more emphasis on medical, educational, and social programs to secure the goodwill of the inhabitants. The goal was simple: the narco-terrorists should have more to fear from the national army than the local population should have to fear from the narco-terrorists, while the national army would be seen by the locals as friends rather than just as another group of thugs with guns.

Meanwhile, independent prosecutors were brought in from Bogotá, who, because they did not live here, could not be intimidated. Development aid was distributed from the capital, where there was much less chance that it could be stolen than if it had been controlled by local officials. Money from local oil revenues was less and less being diverted into the pockets of corrupt officials, and had become the main revenue source to fund construction.

There was still work to be done. The ELN was in disarray, but the FARC was trying to move into this former ELN stronghold. President Hugo Chavez's Venezuelan government across the river was still providing a rear base for the FARC and ELN. More generally, despite all the specific instances of progress I had seen, cocaine was still flowing into the United States at prices not much different than three years before. "We're moving slowly forward," an American official admitted, "and 'slowly' is not a word that the U.S. Congress and the American public like very much."

Between risk-prone invasions like Iraq on one hand and isolationism on the other hand, there were the low-cost, low-risk, tediously unspectacular options of Colombia and the Philippines, of which Mali, Georgia, and other places were variations in a minor key. Particularly in the cases of Capt. Torrey in Timbuktu, who wanted "to set the conditions that will prevent the emergence" of terrorist activities, and Col. Jim Linder in Jolo, who said, "I will build my fortress on deeds," here was the Global War on Terrorism as preventative rather than as proscriptive, more productive than Operation Anaconda or First Fallujah. If there was another model out there that would keep the American military engaged without being over-extended, and that would help move along the interagency process, I hadn't seen it.

As I had been seeing on several continents for four years, the overwhelming majority of our deployments are generally not bellicose, not utopian, not a distortion of our values and, to the contrary, are the epitome of half measures: full of compromises with the host nation, as well as recognition on a daily basis of our own limitations. The host nations in question have been overwhelmingly democratic, and have evolved as such over the years, rather than have us impose systems upon them. In many (if not most) cases, these nations have specifically requested our assistance. Imperfect and pathetic though they might often be, not to assist such democracies would be irresponsible, given our resources and historic responsibilities as a great power.

Such a hidden, responsible hand was very much in evidence in eastern Europe in the 1990s, in the form of military training missions, conducted primarily by the United States, that were similar to those I observed in the developing world. Such missions helped ease the path of former Warsaw Pact satellites toward democracy. The partial Westernization of the militaries of Poland, Romania, and others was crucial to their political reformation.

The threat of anarchy in parts of the world was broadly acknowledged, but so were the vast expense and uncertainty associated with nation-building. Therefore, was there anything more morally prudent and cost-effective than crisis prevention? Crisis prevention had many facets, and the deployments I had been following represented a military aspect of it.

The subtlety of all these missions has been evinced by the near absence of news coverage about them, even though none of them had been secret. As for some of the more high-cost deployments we conducted, such as sailing carrier strike groups through choke points like the Strait of Malacca, where would international trade and globalization be if the U.S. Navy suddenly ceased such activities? To define these missions by their imperfections, or to lump everything together with Iraq, was to tempt isolationism.

I understood and respected the impulse of those who, because of our troubles in Iraq—and the strain Iraq was putting on the armed services—wanted to reassess our commitments worldwide. But there was a danger in taking that idea too far. As Bill Torrey, the West Pointer, told me in Mali, "I really believe that most of the places where we're deployed, we leave better off."

———

Before leaving Arauca, I paid a visit to the SF hootch where I had stayed in 2003, populated at the time by several dozen Green Berets. Now there were fewer than half a dozen American troops here. The place seemed haunted. The reason was not that Green Berets were no longer needed; rather, it had to do with the manpower strain imposed by Iraq and Afghanistan.

It wasn't only Colombia that was suffering because of the demand for high troop levels in Iraq and Afghanistan. In many places I had been—Algeria, Thailand, the Philippines—troops and equipment were missing because the other area commands were being sucked dry by the ongoing wars in the Middle East. Yet, in all these same places, the individual soldiers themselves had used their ingenuity to overcome many of the difficulties. As for the 7th Special Forces Group, which in the first years of fighting in Iraq and Afghanistan had been confined mainly to Latin America, causing frustration and morale problems, the diversion of personnel and resources to the Middle East was actually welcomed. As one Green Beret after another told me, "Now more of us can finally get in on the fight."

TEN

THE BIG GLIDER AND THE JAGGED BOOMERANG

WITH AIR FORCE PREDATOR AND B-2 PILOTS

Las Vegas and Guam, Spring 2006

To embed on some of the most critical air missions over Iraq and Afghanistan, I had to fly to Las Vegas. I drove out of town past Caesars Palace, the Bellagio, and the MGM Grand, and checked into a low-end hotel-casino complex in North Las Vegas for $59 per night. It was crowded with obese people in sweat suits and seniors driving motorized wheelchairs, desperately yanking one-arm bandits, and smelling of whiskey, cigarettes, and popcorn. Ten minutes away, within Nellis Air Force Base, I found a cluster of camouflaged trailers. "Inside that trailer is Iraq; inside the other, Afghanistan," explained Air Force Lt. Col. Christopher Plamp of Louisville, Kentucky. "Either way, you go in there and you enter the CENTCOM AOR [area of responsibility]."

That is, inside those trailers you left North America, which fell under Northern Command, and entered the Middle East, the domain of Central Command. So much for the tyranny of geography.

The MQ-1B Predator drone, or the "Pred" as its pilots called it, was flown from here. Underground and underwater fiber optic cables linked these trailers (ground control stations really) to Europe, where a satellite dish made the connection directly to every Predator in the air over Baghdad, the Afghan-Pakistan border, and wherever else they were needed. Local airfields in places like Iraq and Afghanistan handled only the ascents and descents, otherwise the controls were handled from Las Vegas.

The Predator was the most famous of several dozen unmanned aerial vehicles (UAVs) that the military operated. It first saw action in the 1990s in the Balkans, but made its bones in November 2002 in Yemen, when a Predator fired an AGM-114P armor-piercing Hellfire missile that incinerated a car in which an al-Qaeda leader, Abu Ali al-Harithi, was traveling along with five others through the desert. The Predator also helped track the terrorist supremo of Iraq, Abu Musab al-Zarqawi, in the final days of his life in early June 2006.

When people hear of an unmanned drone, a model airplane comes to mind. Actually, the Predator looked like a big glider. At twenty-seven feet in length and with an almost fifty-foot wingspan, it was comparable in size to a Cessna Skyhawk. Because the Predator's outer skin was made of composites that contained almost no metal, it weighed only 1,130 pounds without fuel or bombs, and could stay aloft for twenty-four hours on a four-cylinder engine. It was so light that I lifted the end of a training model off the ground with one arm. With no life support for a pilot required, and without redundant safety systems, it cost only $4.2 million: for the price of one F-22 you could build over forty Predators. A third of that $4.2 million was spent on "the ball," a rotating sphere on the bottom of the plane where the optics, lasers, and video cameras were located.

But the most impressive thing about the Predator was that it flew slowly. That's right, in a world of counterinsurgency, where you hunt and kill individuals or small groups of fighters rather than attack mass infantry formations, the slower a plane flew the better. Also, the slower it flew, the less wear and tear on it, which is why the Predator required almost no maintenance. Making them was quick and easy; it was the trained pilots who were in short supply.

Slow-flying planes like the A-10 and the AC-130 were particularly useful in the crowded cities of Iraq. Able to hover over complex urban battlespaces, their pilots had situational awareness, and were therefore trusted by Marine platoon commanders and Special Forces team sergeants on the ground. But while those planes still had to fly at 180 knots, a Predator could travel at only 75 knots and remain airborne. Though other UAVs had to fly low, making their trademark lawn mower or snowmobile sound, a Predator flew at 15,000 feet, so no one from the ground could hear, see, or hit it. Think of a satellite that did not need to remain in a fixed orbit, armed with Hellfire missiles.

I had been traveling to Iraq and Afghanistan for a quarter century, yet some of my most revealing moments in those countries were in Las Vegas. Each day began with a pilots' brief, no different from those I experienced with the A-10 pilots in Thailand, with a similar nervous edge to it. To wit, the brief began with "Motherhood"—that is, the idiot-proof basics. Then came an intelligence backgrounder, followed by a detailed weather report (for Iraq and Afghanistan, not Nevada), and concluded with the "brevity" (code words) for the day. The wall clocks focused on three time zones: Iraq, Afghanistan, and ZULU. ZULU was Greenwich mean time not adjusted to daylight savings, the time the U.S. Air Force used worldwide for deconfliction purposes.

Those who flew Predators were pilots, not operators. They wore flight suits. Each was a veteran of an A-10, F-15, B-1 bomber, B-52, or a host of other aerial platforms. Thus, they came from different tribes within the Air Force that were suspicious of one another. They were still in the process of forming their own bureaucratic—that is, Predator—culture. Lt. Col. Plamp was a former Hog pilot. Indeed, the scrappy, lumbering, low-tech A-10 Warthog constituted a perfect preparation for the high-tech "Pred." Both planes were about closing in on small targets and gunning down individuals in dirt alleys.

"If you want to pull the trigger and take out bad guys, you fly a Predator, not an F-15," one pilot told me. Air Force pilots usually worked in twenty-month cycles, sixteen months of training followed by four months on deployment; here it was twenty months of combat. The savings on training were enormous to the taxpayer, but it made for a grueling, truly expeditionary cycle that built up high levels of visual area expertise. Predator pilots knew the telltale signs of an improvised explosive device, the wadis and other egresses, the entrances to the mud-walled compounds, the look of an Afghan "jingle" truck, and so on. Throughout the day they could offer advice to troops on the ground who were deployed for only four to twelve months overseas.

Yet, these pilots faced absolutely no danger. Inside the trailers, there was not even the sensation of flying that one experienced in flight simulators. As one pilot told me, the Predator raised the moral issue of being able to kill someone without you yourself being at risk. True, bombing from 10,000 feet in Kosovo was similar. But as the military saying goes, attrition of the same adds up to big change.

The real tension for these pilots came from the clash with everything outside the trailers. Nellis Air Force Base was full of the same stuffy regulations on driving, dress codes, inspections, saluting, etc., that were common to other bases far removed from war zones. In war zones, informality reigned because the mission was everything. Moreover, beyond Nellis was the world of wives, kids, homework, soccer games, not to mention the absurd banality of a city where even the gas stations had slot machines. To say that entering or leaving one of these trailers was disorienting was an understatement.

The pilots did not identify the trailers by "Iraq" or "Afghanistan" so much as by "OIF [Operation Iraqi Freedom]" or "OEF [Operation Enduring Freedom]." The words indicated more than just an instinctual use of acronyms by the military. They carried meaning—the belief in the original mission of making these countries free and stable. These pilots were warriors, like the best Marine and Army infantry commanders I had met. They were not jaded, not discouraged.

To embed with Predator pilots I had obtained "secret" clearance, but not "top secret" clearance. Thus, I was barred from the best ("highside") missions, and had to settle for the "low-side" ones. The first trailer I went into was OEF. I felt as if I was back in a submarine: grim, mealy-colored computer bays in freezing, pulsing darkness; a three-dimensional math world of flashing, LED digits. Like sub drivers, Pred pilots flew blind—by math only. The camera in the rotating ball focused on the object under surveillance. Thus, the crew's situational awareness was restricted to the enemy on the ground, though much of the time the Pred flew a pre-programmed hexagon, racetrack, bow-tie, or other circular-type holding pattern.

It was a two-man crew inside the trailer: a pilot (an officer) and a sensor (usually a noncom). The sensor operated the ball. There were half a dozen computer screens, including map displays and close-up shots of the object under observation. As in any plane, there was a flight stick with various buttons that the pilot kept using. It was nighttime in Afghanistan, and two small mud-walled compounds near Kandahar were under observation thanks to infrared rays, which appeared like the darker and lighter tones of a photo negative.

Still, the screens swept me back into a familiar world: of knife-carved hillsides terraced with fields of rice, alfalfa, and cannabis, and sectioned by poplar trees on raised banks; and of compounds with inner courtyards where, in the intense heat and dust of late spring in southern Afghanistan, people slept on roofs under magnificent starscapes. The alley between the two compounds, as I knew from experience, was just wide enough for a pickup truck.

The pilot and sensor were waiting for a vehicle to emerge, which they would follow. At least, that's what the "customer" had told them. The customer in this case was a Canadian ground unit. Because the Predator was in such demand, it was taken for granted that every mission tasked was important. Often the more high value the target, the duller the aerial stake-out, since the top echelons of al-Qaeda, the Taliban, or the Iraqi insurgents were the most likely to practice good operations security (OPSEC), and thus go to extreme lengths not to be observed. Predators could go days in shifts observing one compound where nothing seemed to be happening. It was like going on a reconnaissance mission with a sniper unit, except that the boredom was not made worse by heat or cold, or by the need to hide behind a rock.

Whereas a satellite was a disembodied object in space that could take only a snapshot, a Predator was part of the tactical battle element. If a vehicle had appeared, it would have been followed by the UAV, which might then establish who and what the vehicle was linking up with, and consequently follow it, leading perhaps to another stakeout and an eventual raid that the pilot and sensor in Las Vegas could arrange. The Predator dramatically increased the military's ability to "pattern."

Of the two keyboards in front of the pilot, the one he used most was the chat keyboard. He was writing messages to others involved in the mission, while talking into his mouthpiece to the joint terminal attack controller (JTAC), usually a Marine or Army staff sergeant on the ground, who was with the infantry unit near the site under surveillance.

The Pred that was now watching the two compounds had, in fact, only one of its two Hellfire missiles left. The other had been fired some hours earlier, taking out a vehicle in the vicinity that, it turned out, was filled with explosives, causing an immense blast that filled the screen.

The pilot beside me remarked, "Sometimes you get spun up, you fly to a site, you wait for the A-10s to arrive on scene, ready for a kill. Then the whole thing gets called off, and you wind up watching a house for hours and all you see is a guy walk into the courtyard at night to take a crap, registered by the heat signature picked up on the ground after he gets up from his squat."

The pilots and sensors included nineteen Britons attached to the Predator squadron for three years, as well as reservists and national guardsmen along with the active-duty airmen. In the next trailer I entered Iraq (OIF), where an African-American woman, an Army brat from Texas, was operating the ball over a big oil complex west of Kirkuk. Insurgents were thought to be laying IEDs or larger bombs inside it during the night. She saw three suspicious trucks and zoomed in. But there was no heat signature, indicating that the vehicles had been there for many hours without using their engines, so she rotated the ball elsewhere. As she explained, the heat signature allowed you a view back in time several hours, which a good sensor could use to establish a narrative.

It wasn't only what the Predator could do on its own that was significant, but how it could be integrated with existing technologies to magnify their role. For instance, the Predator's camera couldn't quite see the face of an individual. But merged with satellite communications it could listen to him speak, and then by watching him walk, establish an identity for him that could then be tracked.

Yet the real value of UAVs was something that was still developing, and which few outside the military noticed: how these new assets would merge with (and thus expand) the tactics of bread-and-butter elements like Marine infantry platoons and A-10 attack planes. With more and smaller UAVs, platoons would be able to see behind enemy lines and, consequently, find safer ways to defeat an ambush rather than charge directly into it. Because the Predator could "sparkle" a target at night—mark it in infrared so that A-10 pilots and grunts on the ground could see it with their night-vision goggles—it opened up a range of options that fixed-wing and helicopter pilots, as well as infantry, had never had before.

A video of a Hellfire attack that had occurred several days before I arrived demonstrated this. Some Army helicopters had been brought in to attack a building in eastern Afghanistan—nothing fancy. About a dozen Taliban escaped into a field, but that was the intention. The helicopter attack was a feint: to flush them out into the open where the missile from the Predator killed them without the civilian casualties that would have ensued had the building been fired upon.

Future Predators would be able to deliver bigger and heavier ordnance than the Hellfire, as well as fly at 50,000 feet, above the weather. But because it could provide more and more "stuff," as another pilot told me, the Predator carried the danger of being able to immobilize decision-making. "No general will want to attack something without visual confirmation from a Predator. It's the old story: by the time you have all the evidence it's too late to affect the outcome." Rather than expand the opportunities for operations, ironically the Predator could restrict them, even as we fought enemies who had no compulsion about waging total war.

In fact, the more I sat in on missions, the more I realized what the Predator could not do. The Pred's ability to track individuals could fill only a small part of the gap resulting from our abysmal shortage of human intelligence. One nighttime mission (it was morning in Las Vegas) said it all.

We were flying (virtually, that is) over Sangin, northwest of Kandahar. The pilot was given the grids for the town hall, supposedly besieged by 450 Taliban. A B-1B Lancer, the heaviest and most high-tech bomber in the Air Force arsenal save for the B-2 Spirit, was about to do a flyover as a show of force. But the Pred pilot saw nothing "except a few guys on the roof chilling out" in what we knew from the instruments was almost 100-degree heat, though it was near midnight there.

"We're seeing life, just not seeing anything unusual," the sensor reported. "You sure you got the right grids?" He then moved the camera over to observe the police station nearby: still nothing.

The pilot spoke through his headphone: "This is crazy—450 Taliban! Are you high or something? And they're sending in a B-1. To impress whom? These dudes chilling on the roof?"

Watching the three moving figures in robes on the roof, I could imagine the scene: the heat, the tea they were likely brewing. Including the JTAC, the pilot and sensor in the trailer, the image specialists in Qatar and at Langley Air Force Base in Norfolk, Virginia, there were about half a dozen people talking to one another using the latest and greatest technology, yet no one seemed to know what was going on. It was likely that the very number of people with electronic access to the mission further confused things. Circles were being run around them by men in turbans and AK-47s who could melt into the landscape.

Scanning the area, the Pred still found nothing. Then we were ordered to another detail: provide force protection for a convoy of trucks delivering food and supplies. We did that for a bit, inspecting the wadi egresses where an ambush might be laid, and ruts in the road ahead that might be IEDs. Finally we were told to search for a specific "g-truck." That led the Predator to a line of trees where it seemed a number of trucks were being concealed. This was just to the west of Kandahar. But it was impossible to know what or who was inside them, or what their intentions were.

I had had days like this, embedded with Green Berets in the same area near Kandahar. Such days always ended with sergeants barking that "nobody knows the fuck about what's going on."

"Yeah," said Lt. Col. Plamp. "We're in the thick of these ground missions, and as a result we're just as confused as anyone sometimes. It's the typical fog of war."

The Predator and the A-10 represented the two extremities of the Air Force's tactical arsenal: the super-high-tech, anti-heroic remote-controlled UAV and the romantic, lumbering attack plane. I next went to Guam to experience the top of the line of the Air Force's strategic arsenal: the flying-wing-designed B-2 Spirit, which looked like a jagged boomerang and, at a price tag of $1.157 billion per plane, made the F-22 look cheap.

It would be my third visit to Guam in two years. Given the island's growing significance in deployment scenarios, this was not coincidental. The occasion was Valiant Shield, in which the B-2s would be participating. An annual exercise, this year it had grown to immense proportions, providing the largest array of U.S. military power in the Pacific since the Vietnam War. Valiant Shield 2006 featured nothing less than three aircraft carrier strike groups: those of the USS *Abraham Lincoln*, the USS *Ronald Reagan*, and the USS *Kitty Hawk*, with all of their attendant destroyers, cruisers, frigates, and submarines; plus 295 aircraft including B-2s, Marine F-18Cs, Navy F-18Es, and Air Force F-15Es. Never mind the official rhetoric, the point of such a show of force was to impress such adversaries as North Korea and competitors like China. At the same time, PACOM was going out of its way to engage China diplomatically. On a recent visit to Beijing, the PACOM combatant commander, Adm. William Fallon, had invited the Chinese to send a military delegation to Guam for Valiant Shield. The day before I embedded with the B-2 squadron, Chinese officials themselves had been inspecting the bombers from the outside.

Andersen Air Force Base in Guam always had a squadron of heavy bombers on hand, forward-deployed close to Taiwan and the Korean Peninsula. When I had visited Andersen in the autumn of 2004, I had spent some time with B-52 pilots from Barksdale Air Force Base near Shreveport, Louisiana. They were young, happy-go-lucky, uncomplicated. But I was profoundly curious about the B-2 pilots. For a gamut of reasons, they had to be different.

At over a billion dollars per plane, the B-2 Spirit cost as much as a nuclear submarine and a guided-missile destroyer. But whereas a *Los Angeles*–class submarine required a crew of 150 and an *Arleigh Burke*–class destroyer a crew of 330, the B-2 had a crew of just two: one pilot and one mission commander. And there were only twenty-one B-2s in the entire Air Force, flown by two squadrons both located at Whiteman Air Force Base near Kansas City, Missouri. Nobody in the U.S. military—in terms of sheer dollars—was entrusted with as much responsibility as these bomber pilots. If a single B-2 went down, even in training, it would be a banner headline story. So far, none had.

So who were these guys?

The pilots with whom I embedded were from the 393rd Bomb Squadron, out of Whiteman, currently on a four-month deployment rotation in Guam, less than four hours' flying time to the Taiwan Strait. This was the same 393rd Bomb Squadron whose B-29 Superfortresses had dropped atomic bombs on Hiroshima and Nagasaki. In fact, the current commander of the 393rd was the grandson of Army Air Forces Col. Paul W. Tibbets, Jr., the pilot who had dropped the bomb on Hiroshima. His namesake was Lt. Col. Paul W. Tibbets IV of Montgomery, Alabama. Nearly forty years old and a graduate of the Air Force Academy, "Nuke" Tibbets was one of several B-2 pilots with whom I shared quarters on Guam. Another was also an Air Force Academy graduate, Capt. Jim "Genghis" Price of Mesquite, Nevada. Lt. Col. Tibbets got his call sign because of his grandfather; Capt. Price earned his after destroying a line of suspect buildings in Afghanistan with a "stick" of twenty-eight separate MK-82 500-pound gravity bombs, which he followed up by dropping cluster bombs on nearby cave entrances during Operation Anaconda in early 2002. This was when he was flying a B-52 Stratofortress, or BUFF ("Big Ugly Fat Fucker"), as pilots preferred to call that hall-of-fame bomber, which had gotten its debut in Vietnam.

Nuke Tibbets and Genghis Price were both inspired to join the Air Force because of their Army dads. That's right, it was less Tibbets's famous grandfather than his unfamous father who was the real influence on his life.

"My grandfather was the ultimate warrior," Tibbets began in a mild southern accent that had been disappearing over the years away from Alabama. "He was a gruff man of few words, whose real historic accomplishment was the B-29 unit he had organized and trained, which ended World War II. The fact that he personally flew the plane that dropped the first atomic bomb reflected his belief that the ultimate warrior is always in the front line. But it was a detail compared to his organizational accomplishment. For my grandfather," Nuke went on, "the mission was everything, which meant his family suffered. He divorced my grandmother and so wasn't around a lot when my dad was growing up. My dad had terrible eyesight and so couldn't be a pilot. He became a pharmacist in civilian life and rose to become a colonel in the Army Reserve, commanding a deployable MASH-like hospital unit. But my father gently encouraged me toward the Air Force. Good on him that he never forced it on me.

"Once I was in the Air Force, my grandfather rolled into my life and influenced me to be a bomber pilot. In his day, my grandfather wanted to fly bombers as they were taking the fight to the enemy, while pursuit aircraft were supporting that effort."

For Capt. Genghis Price it was simpler. His dad was an Army sergeant at Fort Carson, Colorado, close to the Air Force Academy, and all Genghis ever wanted to do was fly jets in combat. "It's a sappy story but it's true," he told me in a permanently eager voice.

Genghis was a practicing Mormon who had served on religious missions to Latin America and spoke fluent Spanish. "Macho" was never a word you would associate with either him or Nuke. Instead, what they exuded was a humble, introspective star quality. They had been handpicked to safeguard a plane so expensive that it qualified as a national asset, not to mention that they were also trained to drop nuclear weapons from the B-2's launcher assembly. When I asked Nuke what attributes he and others looked for when selecting members of his squadron, he told me: "People who are team players to such an extent that they are self-starters, who never want to be noticed or recognized."

Nuke and Genghis were of average size, with taut bodies and tensely ratcheted expressions. Genghis weighed only 126 pounds. In other words, their physiques matched the clarity of their quiet and technical personalities. They were different from both the A-10 and BUFF pilots whom I had befriended. The Warthog and B-52 guys were boisterous and hard-charging. Except for the squadron commander who was a lieutenant colonel, they tended to be captains, with the odd major or first lieutenant. But the B-2 pilots were older and calmer, with more majors than captains. Unlike attack and fighter jet pilots who specialized in very busy, short-duration flights, B-2 pilots had their patient personalities molded by fourteen-hour hauls from Whiteman direct to Kosovo, to use one example, with three aerial refuelings en route. This was before they could even enter the war zone. Nuke and Genghis did not have 9 gs available to them in order to avoid enemy fire like the pilots of fighter jets. They expected to get into a battlespace without being seen. Meticulous mission planning was what the B-2 was about.

I saw no nude pin-ups on their walls or on their computer screens; rather, what I saw were photos of wives and kids, even as I heard many references to community service and going to church. They rarely cursed, unlike almost everyone else I had met in frontline units throughout the military. And they were less transient: a B-2 pilot could spend five years deployed at Whiteman, whereas other combat Air Force pilots bounced around the country and the world every two years. It was a lifestyle that kept families together.

While the Air Force was run by aggressive, F-series fighter jocks (witness who the top generals were), B-2 guys were, in a deeper sense, the ultimate Air Force pilots. This Air Force mentality can be explained through a comparison with naval aviation. Whereas Marine pilots were primarily about CAS (close air support), and Navy aviators had the reputation of being screaming-off-the-carrier-deck daredevils, Air Force pilots had the reputation of being more operationally conservative. Navy aviators, alone in the ocean without having to bother about issues like noise restrictions, had fewer rules. Naval aviation was about what you could do with an airframe, the Air Force about what you couldn't. Begotten by the Big Army in 1947, the Air Force had its character molded by the Cold War SAC (Strategic Air Command), the core of our nuclear delivery system in the event of Armageddon. Because of its awesome strategic responsibilities, Air Force pilots were simply more by the book than their Navy brethren.

In fact, B-2 pilots had deeply internalized the characteristics of the Cold War that carried over into the twenty-first century. Being with them provided a palpable sense of the more terrifying, frighteningly complex conventional struggles that might lie ahead—beyond the dirty, low-tech counterinsurgencies in Iraq and Afghanistan. From Col. Robert Wheeler of Chicago, the commander of the operations group overseeing the 393rd, I learned about consequences of execution (COE). As he explained: "How do you take out a chemical-biological site of a rogue nation with surety, without inadvertently killing thousands of innocent civilians downwind? Well, the only certain way of avoiding collateral damage might be to obliterate the site in place."

If we had learned anything since the Berlin Wall fell, it was that nothing could be ruled out. The B-2 was developed in the 1980s "to combine the dime," as Col. Wheeler, or "Wheels," put it. It asymmetrically combined our technological and economic strengths to lure the Soviets into further wrecking their economy, by trying to counteract this stealthy nuclear bomber. But few back then thought that such an asset would be anything more than theoretical, especially after the Cold War ended. Then came three wars in which the B-2 was employed: Operation Allied Force (Kosovo), Operation Enduring Freedom (Afghanistan), and Operation Iraqi Freedom.

In particular, Kosovo in 1999 was a breakthrough war for the Air Force. Rather than multi-plane carpet bombing, you also had a few heavy bombers hitting multiple targets with the super-accuracy of fighter jets. No longer was air war about how many planes you needed in order to hit a big target, but about how many targets you could hit with a single plane. Kosovo also demonstrated how technology could enable limited wars. An asset like the B-2 had helped allow a president, Bill Clinton, with little appetite for casualties in a humanitarian intervention, to launch aircraft carrying eighty bombs each, with minimal risk to the pilots and without having to forward-deploy them to the war zone.

As for the present, Col. Wheeler noted, "The B-2 makes a statement. And that statement is, 'We Mean Business!' " he emphasized, banging on the table. Wheels was your classic, intense Air Force intellectual, with degrees in both engineering and strategic studies, experience in three wars, and a veteran of diplomatic postings in Europe. His insights came in hyperactive bursts while sipping from a quart-sized plastic coffee mug. "The deterrence piece of this airplane is bigger than the killing piece," he went on. "Any adversary knows that the B-2 can enter relatively unseen and prevent a WMD from being launched. Merely by having it, we affect decision-making in regional states, and encourage peer competitors to perhaps go another route in their national defense. It is a diplomatic and military instrument." For "regional states," read Iran and North Korea. For "peer competitors," read China and a resurgent, nationalistic Russia.

No plane was invisible to radar. Rather, it was a matter of reducing an airframe's signature so that you could "get iron past" a screen of overlapping, Soviet-designed double-digit surface-to-air missiles (SAMs), and single-digit legacy ones: the protective wall that, with variations, defined the aerial combat borders of Iran, North Korea, and the Chinese coast near Taiwan. A single B-2 had the ability to break down the doors of these countries through a severely reduced radar signature, and then drop the ordnance equivalent of an entire squadron of fighter jets. As the first plane to carry a Joint Direct Attack Munition (JDAM) into combat (in Kosovo), the B-2 could load up with several 5,000-pound-class bunker busters directed to targets by GPS tail kits.

Such a scenario was certainly within the realm of probability, as countries like Iran and North Korea put more and more of their critical facilities deep underground—in places that cruise missiles launched from offshore platforms like submarines lacked the kinetic energy to penetrate. If the United States ever had to attack Iran, you should expect to be reading a lot about the B-2. And if we never had to attack Iran, an asset like the B-2 would have been a hidden hand behind the muscular diplomacy that made it unnecessary.

North Korea hated the plane. The B-2, along with the F-22, was a large part of what would keep China from locking the U.S. out of the Taiwan Strait.

But the problem with such platforms, whose unit costs were staggering to contemplate, especially when measured against what $1.1 billion per plane—or $200 million per plane—could do if spent in other military spheres, was that if even one of these scenarios transpired, there might not be enough of them. As I've said, there were only twenty-one B-2s. And when you considered the odd malfunction, the scheduled maintenance checks ("phases"), and the planes needed regularly for training purposes, you really had about fifteen.

What had originally intrigued me about the B-2 was that, like the F-22, it was a fashionable plane to hate, because of the ugly fact of its price tag, combined with how unnecessary it seemed in current news cycles about Iraq and Afghanistan. One flaw of journalism is that because it is so consumed by the present, it cannot see the future, whose challenges may be entirely different. Spending time with B-2 pilots and their enlisted maintainers gave me an insight into what lay beyond such tasks as the need to secure Greater Baghdad.

Take Mike "Bo" Baumeister of Thousand Oaks, California, who retired as a chief master sergeant after twenty-six years in the Air Force and now worked as a civilian for "DOD [Department of Defense]," as he habitually called it. Bo was your typical good old boy, with a ball cap and generic country accent, who chewed Skoal and hunted deer and pigs beyond the base perimeter here at Andersen. "Why did you go to work for the government rather than for a private contractor and make real money?" I asked him. "I couldn't see leaving her," Bo replied, referring to the B-2. "And DOD offered me the chance to stay with the plane."

He explained further: "It's a pride thing. We're the B-2. We not only kick down your door, but we go in and out of your country without you even knowing it. We take out your head of state, your nuke and chembio plants, your SAM sites. . . . Follow us. We clear the path, we say to the other aerial platforms . . ."

The trend in technology was inexorable: the growing ability over the decades to hit ever smaller, more specific targets with less and less collateral damage. One could make a comparison with the aircraft carrier, whose gradual emergence as a strategic instrument of war was helped by the increasing capacity of jets to fly greater distances and refuel in the air. So, too, with heavy bombers, whose usefulness was being amplified by the electronic revolution in munitions. Taking out a specific individual, such as the head of a rogue state, would become increasingly possible as the years and decades rolled on. Of course, future generations of the Predator might trump heavy bombers such as the B-2. And yet, another trend in warfare was the exponential increase in operational complexity: of using a greater variety of related assets in one symphonic offensive.

I understood Bo's poignant infatuation with the plane. Indeed, it was endlessly fascinating merely to look at. Among soldiers and marines, there was a brotherhood of warriors. But with sailors and airmen, the relationship was triangulated by technology. An emotional bond existed with this class of ship or that type of airframe. The phenomenon was particularly noticeable with the B-2.

The B-2 was less a traditional aircraft than, as its official description

declared, a flying wing: a jagged gray-black boomerang with a small
bubble rising out of its center, where the pilot and mission commander
sat. Seen head-on, the bubble with its dark windshields looked like
nothing so much as the mask of Darth Vader, made more sinister by the
ever-so-slightly turned down beak design of the B-2's front tip. Then, as
you walked around the nose, the swept-backward angle of the wings
made them disappear on you, and the plane shrank in size so that it
looked like a small bat. That was deliberate: the very design helped reduce its radar signature. But as you continued walking around the back
of the plane, where the 172-foot wingspan became visually obvious, it
looked massive. It was at this rear angle where you most accurately *saw*
the plane, with its wingspan equal to that of a B-52, but with a fuselage
only the length of an F-15. The B-2's wings were longer than the distance covered by Orville Wright in his first flight at Kitty Hawk.

After another moment of observation, something else became obvious: the whole airframe had only two angles, one wing and the other.
Every object that normally protruded vertically from an airplane's
wings—the fuselage, the jet engines, the tail, and the various small
screws, rivets, tubes, and antennae—were embedded within the wings
themselves. The four engines were snugly implanted over the wings, in
a way that made the B-2 loud only when it was past you, but made it
quiet when the plane approached you on attack. The doors for the un-
dercarriage and the bomb bays had razor-sharp edges that were sucked
shut by pressure, making the exterior of the B-2 a seamlessly smooth
surface. The point was no bends, bumps, or ridges, however tiny; no angles from which radar could bounce off. The layers of composite were
filled with wire mesh so there was an electric current running from one
end of the plane to the other. Thus, when radar hit the airframe, it flew
across the wingspan rather than bounced off to send a signal. A whole
section of maintenance was dedicated to the plane's "skin care."

I was Spirit number 374, the 374th person to fly in the B-2 Spirit
since Northrop Grumman had rolled the plane out of the hangar in
1989. More people had been in space.* The twenty-one B-2s were al-

---

* As of June 2006 when I flew on the B-2, the number of people who had been in space was
   447.

most all named after states. The plane I flew in was the *Spirit of Georgia*. Inside the cockpit was the mean, definable, violent smell of metal. The pilot was Maj. Justin "Mulligan" Amann, a graduate of Purdue University's Air Force ROTC program. The mission commander was not on board, in order to make room for me. When the door closed, there was just enough room for a fold-out army cot on which the crew could take turns resting while on long flights to places like Kosovo and Afghanistan.

I attached the five buckles of my life-support harness to the ejection seat, and then connected the oxygen and communications gear to my helmet and face mask. Maj. Amann was already busy with the two laptops he had brought on board to supplement the dozen other liquid crystal displays. The laptops represented updates to the plane's computer system. As futuristic as the B-2 seemed, it really represented 1980s technology, just as most of the other planes and ships in the U.S. military arsenal represented technology from the 1960s and 1970s. This was a result of an acquisition and production process measured in years and decades. The upgrades were mainly in software and munitions, which had allowed for gee-whiz advances in targeting like GPS- and laser-guided "smart" bombs. Nevertheless, the two laptops, which brought a real-time battlespace and satellite e-mail to the cockpit, also meant an additional workload for the pilot.

The B-2, as I was to learn, was not about flying so much as about weapons programming, and coordination with other air and sea platforms. The rudders and elevons, as well as the "beaver" (the flap that functioned as a tail), all had their "trim" adjusted every second and minute by computers. The pilot no longer had this task. The B-2 truly did occupy the opposite end of the Air Force from the A-10.

As for coordination with other combat platforms, the naval ones were somewhat of a challenge. The more complex the communications and other technological protocols became, the more work was involved to achieve jointness, since the Navy and Air Force had different systems. It was like merging Apple and Microsoft, as one pilot told me.

The B-2 was an intellectual environment driven by multi-tasking. On each of Maj. Amann's knees was a strap-on flight board to hold the heavy manuals with their checklists to which he had to refer constantly.

Our flight call sign was Death 62. The other B-2 that would be flying alongside us was Death 72. While our plane's name was the *Spirit of
Georgia,* the maintainers had nicknamed it "The Dark Angel." Violence
was something for which nobody in the combat Air Force apologized.
Like the A-10 pilots, the crews of fast-attack subs, and top Army and
Marine platoons—to say nothing of the Special Operations community—the elite units of the military were about going to war, or "being
able to play," as the troops put it. As obvious as this sounds, it needs to
be emphasized, because it signifies an emotion that ran deep. One of the
maintainers, Master Sgt. Kelly Costo of Fremont, California, told me
that the most exhilarating moments of his professional life were helping
to load bombs aboard B-2s at Whiteman before the "heavies" left for
Kosovo and at Diego Garcia before they left for Afghanistan.

The flight itself, as I had expected, was not a thrill like a ride in a
fighter jet. We rose and turned at degrees no more dramatic than a commercial airliner. There was no *g*-force to speak of. After we reached
10,000 feet, Maj. Amann put the plane on autopilot, at a point at which
it rose to its cruising altitude of 32,000 feet with a ground speed of
450 miles per hour. We took our oxygen masks off, and he immediately
got busy programming two missiles and sixty-four separate 500-pound
JDAMs, which we later dropped over Saipan—virtually, of course. I
saw exactly what I would have had those bombs actually been released:
hexagons representing individual JDAMs disappearing in twos from the
computer screen. The more widespread and devastating the carnage, the
more bloodless the operation. Had any of them been nuclear warheads,
the screen display would have been the same.

It was a near perfect sky. Looking down on isolated bands of cumu-
lous clouds from 32,000 feet, I saw them as odd imperfections in the
stretched, glazed surface of the Philippine Sea. Sunlight so penetrated
the water that Saipan and Tinian looked backlit by the ocean. These islands were beautiful even as their historical resonances were ugly. Several times we flew over the old B-29 runways on Tinian, from where
Col. Paul Tibbets, Jr., in 1945 had flown the *Enola Gay* to bomb Hiroshima. At one point we unlocked the autopilot and I flew the plane for
ten minutes. It was similar to sailing on instruments, making constant

adjustments so that a vertical line stayed on, or close to, a dot on the screen. Truly, the art of flying was being lost.

What made this so easy was the world behind the plane: the maintainers. Deploying just four B-2s from Whiteman to Andersen required a maintenance crew of 155, in addition to 130 pieces of rolling stock—jammers, light carts, generators—anything on wheels and large enough so it had to be towed by a Ford truck. Then there were the massive pallets of equipment, including the 170 different chemicals used by the B-2, each of which required customized climate-controlled conditions and certified waste removal. The maintainers worked twelve-hour shifts, and filled up several buildings and hangars. To get the crew and equipment for the four B-2s to Guam had taken one C-17 Globemaster and four C-5 Galaxies, transport planes so monstrous in size that the C-130 Hercules seemed to disappear beside them.

The maintenance element for the B-2 dwarfed that of the A-10 by leaps and bounds. And that led me to a realization: forward-deploying such national assets was counterproductive. The only reason Guam made sense was that it was a U.S. territory, courtesy of the Spanish-American War and the blood of World War II marines. But in other cases, there was no point basing B-2s abroad if in the midst of a crisis we were denied permission by a host country to use them. Indeed, the continental United States was the place for the B-2, as well as for other top-of-the-line aircraft, in a future that would put a premium on airpower as a way to reduce our footprints on the ground—with all the unattractive political and cultural tensions they caused. And that meant the key task for the Air Force was to increase its capacity for air-to-air refueling.

Col. Wheeler made the point that conventional assets like the B-2 and fast-attack submarines were of a piece with the Predator, Special Forces A-teams, and Marine platoons. Forget the debate about having needed a larger footprint in Iraq after the initial invasion. As true as that might be, it was not what the next few decades would primarily be about; they would be about hitting specific targets with commando-style ground units that could, in turn, call in air and sea strikes from platforms that were either untouchable or unseen. For example, a war with a powerful rogue Middle Eastern state might see less of an emphasis on close air support with down-and-dirty platforms like the A-10 and the AC-130, and more emphasis on high-altitude "heavies" such as the B-2, as Special Operations teams were inserted for limited periods on the ground to identify targets for bunker buster and other high-impact bombs.

"We won't be able to mass troops like we used to," Col. Wheeler observed. "It's not just a matter of negative publicity from a global media, but of a profusion of competitors that will increasingly have the ability to hit such large formations with weapons of mass destruction. And that will be a chance we won't want to take. Think of bees," he continued. "Think of bees swarming together in a hive and then flying off again. That's the military formation of the twenty-first century. Lots of small, joint air-land-sea configurations that combine instantaneously for a big attack and then separate out just as fast."

Thus, many of the debates we were having were false—over conventional versus unconventional, and over money for Special Forces versus money for F-22s. The real issue was about mastering complexity: how to combine all or many of these assets in a single operation. It was not about what an A-team, or a submarine, or a Predator, or a B-2 bomber could do for you, but about how any one of these assets could leverage others.

But that raises another nagging issue. If the B-2 is necessary for both our force structure and our negotiating credibility, as Col. Wheeler believed, even though it cost over a billion dollars per plane, what a truly depressing fact that was about the price of empire!

As one former civilian defense official put it to me: "Look at the rate of return al-Qaeda got on 9/11. For an investment of just a few hundred thousand dollars, they forced us to spend billions. As necessary as the B-2 or F-22 might be, what's their rate of return? Twenty percent, perhaps? I'm not saying that we require a rate of return like al-Qaeda gets, but we'll need to narrow the difference if we're going to remain a great power."

ELEVEN

THE MORBID TYRANNY OUT OF ANTIQUITY

WITH U.S. FORCES, KOREA

Summer 2006

Since 2002, I had been covering deployments on several continents that had two overarching themes: fighting the Global War on Terrorism and positioning the U.S. military for the rise of China. It really was a global war—something that American troops in countries like Mali, Algeria, and the Philippines never tired of mentioning. Yet this new array of military commitments was layered atop old ones. The United States was in its fourth year of a war in Iraq. But it had been on a war footing in Korea for fifty-six years now. More than ten times as many Americans had been killed on the Korean Peninsula as in Mesopotamia. Whereas Americans hoped more or less to withdraw from Iraq within a few years, they still had 32,000 troops in South Korea over half a century after the armistice. Korea gave one a sense of historical perspective, as well as of America's imperial-like legacy. Furthermore, it provided a lesson in what could be accomplished with patience and dogged persistence.

Thus, I came to Korea.

I was struck by the somber, seaweed hue of the peninsula's lush and rugged landscape, and the hyperactive modernity of this economic powerhouse, which had become one of the most technologically precocious countries on earth. It wasn't always so. The drive from the airport at Inch'on to downtown Seoul went through the heart of a former urban war zone. South Korea's capital was taken and retaken four times in some of the most intense fighting of the Korean War.

It was a conflict that many people preferred to forget, even while it was being waged. However alluring the country might be with its dramatic mountainscapes and distinctive food, which, more than any other place on the Pacific Rim, bore an imprint of Inner Asia, the first thing that came to mind when recalling Korea from the American soldiers' viewpoint was the awful climate. One would suppose that as a peninsula, the climate would be moderated by the Yellow Sea and the Sea of Japan. But rather than warm weather issuing from those waters, in winter the winds came charging down from Siberia, and in summer the monsoon blew in from the Pacific Ocean; so winters were unbearably frigid, and summers hot and humid. The perennial dust blowing in from the Gobi Desert did not help matters. Ground troops sweated and froze accordingly, floundering in often horrific, nameless battles. Many hundreds of thousands of Korean lives were lost in combat between June 1950 and July 1953, in addition to 142,000 American casualties, of which over 33,000 were killed in action. Yet it was a military clash of "subtle and infuriating limitations, and ambiguous results," according to historian James L. Stokesbury.*

When communist North Korean troops crossed the 38th parallel and invaded South Korea, merely five years after the United States had defeated Japan and ended World War II, the American people were just as bewildered as when Saddam Hussein invaded Kuwait less than a year after the collapse of the Berlin Wall and the end of the Cold War.

What few fully grasped at the time was that by occupying Japan, America inherited strategic responsibility for the nearby Korean Peninsula; just as by ending Soviet domination of eastern Europe, America

---

* James L. Stokesbury, *A Short History of the Korean War* (New York: Morrow, 1988), p. 15. Much of the basic background about the Korean War comes from this book.

consequently enhanced its role in the adjacent Middle East, even as the Cold War status quo in the Arab world collapsed.

Following North Korea's invasion of South Korea in the early summer of 1950, it had taken only a few months for an American-dominated United Nations force to drive Communist troops back to the 38th parallel. Like the first Gulf War in 1991, which had ejected Iraqi forces from Kuwait, that initial phase of the Korean conflict restored the status quo ante. But subsequently, the Americans decided to push deep into North Korea, to solve the fundamental problem of the North Korean regime itself. The result was Communist China's entry into the war, which then dragged on for nearly three grinding, bloody years, until a cessation of hostilities back at the 38th parallel where it had begun.

As in Iraq, the Reserves had to be called up in significant numbers. A need arose to train an indigenous army, and to adapt to the tactics of guerrilla insurgents, even as the Pentagon brass grumbled that such a large indefinite commitment of troops to one place would undermine America's military posture everywhere else.

In Korea, the American public experienced a war that, at least from afar, appeared to be less about good and evil than about the abstractions of strategic positioning. And it did not much like or understand it. President Harry Truman left office an unpopular president. If people preferred to forget Iraq as though it were a bad dream, even before the bulk of American troops departed, it would not be the first time this happened in American history.

But there was another way to look at Korea. In 1953 many doubted that Asians were capable of mastering democracy and a free-market system. It would not be until 1992 that South Koreans elected a truly stable and democratic government. Given South Korea's economic transformation in the intervening decades, particularly under the dictatorship of Park Chung Hee in the 1960s and 1970s, the lesson might be that democracy should come last and not first in the transition from poverty and totalitarianism. Yes, that point could be argued. But a point that cannot be argued is this: a large reason South Korea eventually succeeded was *patience*—the patience of American policy makers and the American military, and their ability to persevere, decade after decade, in the Korean Peninsula. What old Korean men and women would always be grateful for was our "stick-to-itiveness," without which, in any case, we would have little hope of remaining a great power.[1]

—

In the heart of Seoul lay the Green Zone—that is, Yongsan Garrison ("Dragon Mountain"), a leafy, fortified Little America, guarded and surrounded by high walls. Inside these 630 acres, which most closely resembled the Panama Canal Zone before the Americans gave up control, were eight thousand American military and diplomatic personnel in manicured suburban homes, with their neatly clipped hedges and backyard barbecues. I drove by a high school, baseball and football fields, a driving range, a hospital, a massive commissary, a bowling alley, and restaurants.* South Post was the residential part of Yongsan; Main Post where U.S. Forces, Korea (USFK), and its attendant bureaucracies were located, in red-brick buildings that the Americans had inherited in 1945 from the former Japanese occupiers. USFK had another similarity with Iraq: Korea was so substantial a military commitment that it merited its own semi-autonomous subcommand of PACOM, just as Iraq, unofficially, merited its own four-star subcommand of CENTCOM.†

Alas, I arrived in Korea just as the Americans were to begin a troop drawdown. Having moved into Yongsan Garrison when Korea's future seemed highly uncertain, they now planned to give up this prime downtown real estate and relocate to Camp Humphreys in Pyongtaek, thirty miles south. The number of ground troops would drop to twenty thousand or less, and would essentially comprise a skeleton of logistical support shops able to add muscles and tendons in the form of a large invasion force, in the event that war ever did break out on the peninsula, though it wasn't clear how necessary a large invasion force would be.

---

* South Korea paid 40 percent of the stationing costs for American military personnel here, less than Germany and Japan paid for U.S. troops in their countries. If these troops were to come home as part of a withdrawal, the American taxpayer would have to pick up the tab for some of their living costs, unless the Army itself was downsized.

† In functional terms, the relationship between the four-star general in Baghdad and the one at CENTCOM headquarters in Tampa was somewhat comparable with that of the four-star commander in Seoul and the one at PACOM in Honolulu. Of course, Korea had further levels of complexity: the American four-star was also the head of the U.N. command, and of the combined command that comprised the forces of the United States and South Korea. This was all a legacy of the Korean War, in which the U.S. and its allies fought officially as a U.N. force.

Integrated with the American military to an unprecedented extent, with the most Americanized officer corps in the world, the South Korean Army had literally a half century longer than the Iraqi Army to perfect itself. It was a first-tier Asian military at the same level of sophistication, technologically and operationally, as Singapore's. Thus, it would be able to shoulder many burdens in wartime. South Korea's special forces units were becoming so interoperable with the U.S. Air Force that their forward air controllers on the ground were trained to call in close air support from American A-10s and to laser-guide B-2 pilots from Whiteman to high-value targets.

The ability of the United States to draw down land forces did not in any way indicate a lessening of responsibility for the American military here. Indeed, North Korea presented the U.S. and Pacific Rim countries with unique security challenges that made it, perhaps, every bit as pivotal in terms of how the twenty-first century would unfold as the rise of China and the actions of al-Qaeda. While the Communist regime in Pyongyang was a legacy of the Cold War, at the same time its collapse could become the catalytic event that set the outlines for a new Asian military century.

Perhaps no regime in the early twenty-first century bore as close a resemblance to the morbid, crushing tyrannies of antiquity, as described in the Old Testament and in Herodotus, as that of North Korea. The worldview of Kim Il Sung, the founder of the Communist state, was something like a mix of Lenin's "fight-talk, fight-talk" dictum and the view expressed in Hitler's *Mein Kampf* that an organism that does not always fight dies.* *Juche,* the regime's ruling philosophy of self-reliance, described as "Dear Leader Absolutism," warped the Confucian ethos into a means for controlling an entire population.† For decades after the emergence of the North Korean state in the mid-twentieth cen-

---

* This and succeeding paragraphs of background information regarding the nature of the regime, the force structure on the Korea Peninsula, and likely responses to a meltdown of North Korea rely heavily on the writing and thinking of both Army Col. David S. Maxwell, a Special Forces officer and Korean area expert, and Stephen Bradner, a special advisor to the United Nations Command and USFK in Korea.

† "Dear Leader Absolutism" was a term coined by Hwang Jang Yop, who defected from the North in 1997.

tury, the regime operated like a combination of a crime family and a religious cult, undergirded by layers of myth and fabrication. In this storybook universe, it was Kim and his guerrilla forces alone who had expelled the Japanese in 1945. It was said that Kim Jong Il, the son and successor of Kim Il Sung, was born on Paektu-san, the highest mountain in Korea, on the Chinese border, where a deity descended from heaven. The American military acronym for North Korea said it all: KFR, the Kim Family Regime.

It was a regime that Americans misunderstood because of their own myths. Kim Il Sung was not simply a dreary Stalinist tyrant. As North Korean defectors will tell you, he was also a charismatic anti-Japanese guerrilla leader with stores of popular legitimacy, very much in the mold of Enver Hoxha, the Stalinist tyrant of Albania who earlier had led his countrymen in a successful insurgency against the Nazis, with relatively little help from the Allies. Nor was Kim Jong Il the childish psychopath of the film *Team America: World Police.* Expertly tutored by his father, he had consolidated power largely on his own and manipulated the Chinese, Americans, and South Koreans in the 1990s into subsidizing the Communist regime. One thing Kim Jong Il was not was impulsive. North Korea had the equivalent of think tanks that concentrated on military responses to attacks from the U.S. and South Korea, attacks that themselves would be reactions to crises initiated by Pyongyang.

"The regime constitutes an extremely rational bunch of killers," said Andrei Lankov, professor of history at Seoul's Kookmin University. Lankov, who grew up in the Soviet Union and spoke fluent Korean, told me that the Kim Family Regime was unusual in this critical sense: even in Stalinist systems such as the former East Germany and Leonid Brezhnev's U.S.S.R., the children of top party officials rarely followed in their parents' footsteps. In fact, quite a few became writers and avant-garde artists, helped along in their careers by their parents' privileges and social connections. But the top officials of the KFR begot top officials of the KFR. The regime was biologically self-perpetuating. Nor was there a particular interest in liberalization or contacts with South Korea. The KFR saw how West German *Ost-Politik* had helped destroy the former East Germany.

And so, seventeen years after the crumbling of the Berlin Wall and the end of subsidies from the East Bloc, North Korea plodded on, resilient and relentless. Kim Jong Il *had been* a playboy, but he had evolved into a remarkable operator in his own right. In Lankov's view, under different circumstances Kim Jong Il might have become the successful Hollywood film producer that his propaganda machine claimed he was. Helping his succession had been his father's ability to link the regime in the mind of its subjects to the Joseon dynasty, which had ruled the Korean Peninsula for five hundred years, thus justifying the KFR's system of primogeniture.

And yet Kim Jong Il's talents were slipping. It wasn't so much the post-9/11 reality that he might not have properly taken into account, in which the United States saw provocations like missile tests in a wholly different light, but the post-Iraq reality, in which an administration in Washington, humbled by events, was particularly unlikely to be impulsive and thus careful not to play into the KFR's hands.

Eras don't end neatly and all at once. And as North Korea demonstrated, that also went for the Cold War. On the border dividing the two Koreas, amidst the cry of egrets and Manchurian cranes, I saw South Korean soldiers standing frozen in tae kwon do–ready positions, their fists and forearms clenched, staring into the faces of their North Korean counterparts. Each side picked its tallest, most intimidating soldiers for the task. The South had raised a 328-foot flagpole; the North responded with a 525-foot pole, then hoisted a flag atop it whose dry weight was 595 pounds. The North built a two-story building in the Joint Security Area at Panmunjom, so the South built a three-story one. The North then added another story to its building. "The land of one-upmanship," is how one U.S. Army sergeant described the demilitarized zone (DMZ). The two sides once held a meeting in Panmunjom that went on for eleven hours. Because there was no formal agreement when to take a restroom break, neither side budged. It became known as the "Battle of the Bladders."

Childish and yet illuminating, for beneath our civilized pretensions, the behavior on the DMZ demonstrated how deep down human beings were still chest-thumping silverbacks (or testosterone-charged adolescents) playing King of the Hill. Although the formalized hatred on display in the DMZ would be consigned to history on some foreseeable morrow, as for war itself there could be no end.

When you looked at other divided-country scenarios in the twentieth century—Vietnam, Germany, Yemen—it seemed apparent that however long the division persisted, the forces of unity ultimately triumphed. But the historical record also indicated that unification did not happen through a calibrated political process in which the interests of all sides were respected. Rather, it tended to happen through a fast-moving cataclysm of events that, despite decades of war gaming, caught experts by surprise. And the weaker the North Korean regime became, the more dangerous the overall situation: totalitarian regimes close to demise were apt to be panicky and, therefore, irresponsible.

Given that the North's 1.2 million-man army—the fifth largest in the world—was increasingly being deployed *forward,* to the border with South Korea, the Korean Peninsula loomed for the U.S. military, at least theoretically, as the next horrendous land nightmare out there following Iraq.* As the saying went among American soldiers, "There is no peacetime in the ROK [Republic of Korea, pronounced 'rock']." One merely had to notice the Patriot missile batteries, the reinforced-concrete hangars, and the blast barriers at Osan and Kunsan air bases south of Seoul, as fortified as any bases in Iraq, to know that. I remember one marine in Okinawa telling me that North Korea's was not some third-rate, Middle Eastern conventional army that would disintegrate like Iraq's. Those "brainwashed Asians," as he put it crudely, "would stand and fight." Ominously, uniformed Americans here referred to the 1950–53 fighting as "the first Korean War," as if there might be a second.

North Korea boasted 100,000 well-trained special operations forces. With one of the world's largest biological and chemical arsenals, the North Korean People's Army was trained to operate in a chemical environment, and to deploy chemical weapons in order to create opportunities for field maneuver. Furthermore, the experience of de-Baathification

---

* Whereas in 1980, 40 percent of North Korean combat forces were deployed south of Pyongyang along the demilitarized zone, by 2003 over 70 percent were.

in Iraq suggested that the collapse of a governing infrastructure in Pyongyang, combined with the unconventional guerrilla mentality of the Kim Family Regime's armed forces—the legacy of Kim Il Sung's own guerrilla experience—could result in widespread lawlessness, as well as mass migration within and out of North Korea. The myths and *Juche* philosophy of the regime would increase the potential for an insurgency. This was to say nothing of the need to gain immediate control over nuclear and other weapons of mass destruction (WMD) facilities.

Kim Jong Il's compulsion to demonstrate his missile prowess was a sign of his weakness. Contrary to popular perception in the United States, Kim didn't stay up at night worrying about what the Americans might do to him; it wasn't North Korea's weakness relative to the United States that preoccupied him. Rather, if he did stay up late worrying, it was about China. He knew the Chinese had always had a greater interest in North Korea's geography—with its additional outlets to the sea close to Russia—than they had in the long-term survival of his regime. (Like us, even as they wanted the regime to survive, the Chinese had plans for the northern half of the Korean Peninsula that did not include the "Dear Leader.") One of Kim's main goals in so aggressively displaying North Korea's missile capacity was to compel the United States to deal directly with him, thereby making his otherwise weakening state seem stronger. And the stronger Pyongyang appeared to be, the better off it was in its crucial dealings with Beijing, which were what really mattered to Kim.

Even as the pros and cons of various diplomatic strategies toward the Korean Peninsula were discussed, middle- and upper-middle-level American officers based in South Korea and Japan were beyond that. They were planning for an unconventional meltdown of the North that, within days or hours even, might present the "world"—that is, substantially the U.S. military—with its greatest stabilization operation since the end of World War II. "It could be the mother of all humanitarian relief operations," Army Special Forces Col. David Maxwell of Springfield, Massachusetts, told me. On one day, a semi-starving population of twenty-three million people would be Kim Jong Il's responsibility; on the next it could be that of U.S. Forces, Korea, and PACOM.

More likely, it would be a drawn-out process. Robert Collins, a retired Army master sergeant, now the chief civilian area expert for the American military here, outlined for me seven phases of collapse in the North. Phase One: resource depletions. Phase Two: the failure to maintain infrastructure around the country because of resource depletions. Phase Three: the rise of independent fiefdoms and widespread corruption to circumvent a failing central government. Phase Four: such tendencies reached a point whereby the KFR had to attempt to suppress them. Phase Five: resistance against the central government. Phase Six: the regime fractured. Phase Seven: the formation of new national leadership. The regime had probably reached Phase Four in the mid-1990s, but was saved by subsidies from China and South Korea, as well as by famine aid from the United States. It had now gone back to Phase Three.

The Kim Family Regime had learned a powerful lesson about survival from the fall of the Ceauşescu Family Regime in Romania: take utter and complete control of the military. And so it had. The KFR now ruled through the army. Only individual North Korean soldiers had defected to the South, not units—not even squads. That would have indicated soldiers were talking to one another and were no longer afraid of exposure by comrades. One defector from the North's special operations forces told me that everybody in the ranks was afraid to discuss politics with one another.

Nevertheless, the North Korean People's Army was simply too big to be kept well fed, so the regime concentrated on bribing its elite units. This defector, a scout swimmer, also told me that while his men lived well, the extreme poverty of the conventional troops would make their loyalty in a difficult war problematic. Would they fight for the KFR if there was an unforeseen rebellion? Again, the Romanian lesson was that it depended on the contextual peculiarities of the event. When workers revolted in 1987 in Braşov, the Romanian military crushed them, but when ethnic Hungarians did two years later in Timişoara, the military deserted the regime.

Col. Maxwell, the chief of staff of Special Operations Forces in South Korea, had thought hard over the years about the tactical and operational aspects of an unraveling North Korean state. "The regime in

Pyongyang could collapse without necessarily its army corps and brigades collapsing," he told me. "So we might have to mount a relief operation at the same that we'd be conducting combat ops. If there is anybody in the U.N. who thinks it will just be a matter of feeding people, they're smoking dope."

Maxwell spoke from experience. He had been the commander of the 1st Battalion of the 1st Special Forces Group when it had landed on Basilan in the southern Philippines in early 2002, a mission that combined unconventional warfare—humanitarian assistance, in this case—with counterinsurgency against Jemaah Islamiyah and the Abu Sayyaf Group. "The situation in the North could become so messy and ambiguous," he went on, "that the collapse of the chain of command of the KFR could be more dangerous than the preservation of it, particularly when one considers control over WMD."

He indicated that such a relief operation would necessitate contacts with ex-regime generals and various factions of the former North Korean military, who would be vying for control in different regions and who could form the basis of an insurgency if not brought under the coalition's operational command structure. The Chinese would certainly be in the best position to do this, but the role of U.S. Army Special Forces in this effort could be substantial. Green Berets and OGAs (other governmental agencies, especially the CIA) would be among the *first in,* very much like in Afghanistan in 2001, in order to prevent a debacle of the sort that occurred in Iraq, with even deadlier consequences.

But the U.S. could not insert troops into a dissolved North Korea unilaterally. It would likely be a four-power intervention force, officially sanctioned by the United Nations: the U.S., South Korea, China, and Russia. Japan would be kept out, though all parties would gladly accept Japanese money for the endeavor.

Let's take these other powers one at a time. Because of their proximity to the Korean Peninsula and anti-Japanese feeling here resulting from a brutal occupation from 1910 to 1945, the Japanese, of all the parties, had the most to fear from a reunified Korea, even as Korean hatred of the Japanese made participation of Japanese troops in an intervention force unlikely. Japan had occupied not only Korea but China too, and had defeated Russia on land and at sea in the early twentieth century. Thus, Japan bore the brunt of widespread hostility in a volatile strategic environment. While this could make it all the more necessary, from the Japanese standpoint, to put boots on the ground in a collapsed North Korea, China and South Korea would fight tooth and nail to prevent that from happening. Because the Japanese had so far failed over the decades to confront their own brutal behavior during World War II, nobody in the region yet trusted them, and thus they would likely be dependent on U.S. diplomatic and military support.

Whereas Japan's strategic position would be weakened dramatically by a collapsed North Korean state, China might eventually benefit. China was already positioning itself for a reunified Korean Peninsula, to some extent under the control of South Korea. China was South Korea's biggest trading partner. Driving along the Yellow Sea all I saw at South Korean ports were Chinese ships. China harbored thousands of North Korean defectors that it wanted to send back, in order to build a favorable political base for China's gradual economic takeover of the Tumen River region—where China, Russia, and North Korea came together, with good port facilities on the Pacific. De facto control of a future Tumen Prosperity Sphere would bolster China's economic strength, helping it to do fiscal battle with the U.S. and Japan. Expect China to sanction the coalition, provided its own troops could, at the least, carve out a buffer zone in the part of North Korea near the border with Manchuria, where China was already developing massive infrastructure projects like roads and ports. In other words, China was already on third base in regard to a Greater Korea.

Russia's weakness in the Far East, as demonstrated by its failure to prevent the creeping demographic conquest of its eastern territories by ethnic Chinese, meant that it would be that much more truculent in guarding its interests on the Korean Peninsula. The fact that North Korea was a Soviet creation was but one example of how Russia did, in fact, have a historical legacy here. It might be less trouble for the other powers to allow some Russian troops into Korea rather than to keep them out.

South Korea would bear the brunt of the economic and social disruption in returning the peninsula to normalcy following the collapse of the North. Its interests were paramount. Though no one would say it out loud, there was little interest in the region in a reunified Korea, unless it happened gradually over years and decades. What was really preferred was a sort of South Korean protectorate in parts of the North, officially under an international trusteeship, that would keep the two Koreas functionally separate for a significant period. This would allow everyone to reposition himself for a truly unified Korean state, without the attendant chaos.

The early implementation of a stable polity in the North, following the Communist regime's collapse, could likely fall to PACOM and U.S. Forces, Korea. But while the U.S. military would probably have operational responsibility, it might not have the desired control. It would, in effect, have to lead a coalition (of, in some cases, mutually suspicious states) that deployed fast and furiously to stabilize the North, as well as deliver humanitarian assistance. A successful relief operation in North Korea in the weeks following the regime's collapse might determine the difference between anarchy and prosperity on the peninsula for years to come.

But what if the opposite occurred? What if rather than simply unraveling, North Korea actually launched a surprise attack on South Korea? Maxwell and others were busy filling in the details of that tactical battlefield as well.

Merely driving through Seoul, one of the world's great and congested mega-cities, made it clear that a conventional infantry attack on South Korea's capital was something that not even Hitler would have contemplated. With that reality in mind, think of North Korea's People's Army as a mass of artillery supported by a scheme of maneuver. Its 13,000 artillery pieces and multiple rocket launchers could fire over 300,000 shells per hour on the South Korean capital, in a low-grade demonstration of "shock and awe," which, because of its very indiscriminateness, would cause widespread havoc in Greater Seoul, where close to half of South Korea's 48.5 million people lived. The havoc would be amplified by infiltrating North Korean special operations forces, who might sabotage water plants and train and bus terminals. As for its maneuvering infantry, all roads led to Uijongbu, north of Seoul, from where the North Korean People's Army would cross over the Han River and bypass Seoul from the east. One objective would be fuel stations to keep their vehicles moving before the South Koreans and the Americans could mobilize properly.

But this strategy could never succeed. For one thing, while A-10s, F-16s, and other aerial platforms would take out enemy missile batteries and kill many North Korean troops inside South Korea, submarine-launched missiles and B-2 Spirit bombers from Guam and Whiteman Air Force Base in Missouri would destroy strategic targets inside North Korea, both above and below ground. For another thing, the South Korean Army would quickly occupy the transport hubs, while unleashing their own divisions and special operations forces. Such an invasion would have to be the act of a regime in the middle and later phases of disintegration. Its lone hope would be that given the hourly carnage, in the time between the first artillery barrage on Seoul and the beginning of a robust military response by South Korea and the United States, some political factions inside South Korea, abetted by the United Nations and elements of the global media, would cry out for diplomacy as an alternative to violence.

The violence would be horrific. Iraq and Afghanistan would be clean by comparison. A South Korea filled with North Korean troops would constitute a target-rich environment in urbanized areas where the good guys and bad guys would always be close to each other. "Gnarly chaos" is how one F-16 Viper pilot described it: "the ultimate fog of war." The battlefield would be made more confusing by the serious language barrier that still existed after fifty years between American pilots and South Korean joint tactical air controllers, who would have to guide the Americans to many of their targets. Both A-10 and F-16 pilots complained to me that this weak link in the bilateral military relationship would drive up the incidences of friendly fire and collateral civilian deaths—on which the media would then concentrate. As part of a deal to halt the bloodbath, members of the KFR might be able to negotiate their own post-regime survival.

It wasn't just that a land invasion of Greater Seoul was impossible, and that even the scenario just described was far-fetched; it was that the real worry was less of infantry units storming across the border than of refugees doing so. North Korea's collapse terrified South Korea much more than its missile program.

Yet there was a conventional military option for North Korea that American officers and senior NCOs, as well as some civilians with whom I spoke, truly worried about. Start with the fact that it really wasn't a matter of A-10s, F-16s, or B-2s, but of a combined American–South Korean military machine that would not only respond speedily to a North Korean artillery barrage, but would then in short order march much of the way to the Yalu River on the North Korean border with China, thus finally putting an end to the Korean War. Following an artillery barrage on the South, China would not necessarily oppose this plan; we could give Beijing the guarantees it needed regarding postwar access to the peninsula, especially control over a Yalu River buffer zone.

Obviously, the KFR knew all of this. Remember, it was deliberate and calculating, not impulsive, provided, of course, that it was not in one of Collins's final phases of collapse.

Therefore, middle and upper-middle levels of the American military were worried less about an indiscriminate artillery attack on the South than a very discriminate one. For example, take the missile launches that occurred during my visit. My sources feared that the Bush administration actually might have been foolish enough to respond militarily. As they explained it, don't think that before Kim Jong Il even fueled those missiles he hadn't already calibrated a response strategy were they to be destroyed by the United States, since to have them destroyed, without a military response of its own, would have unraveled the regime's mythology of omnipotence and control.

The KFR's response to such a provocation would have to be linked to one of its primary strategic goals: splitting the alliance between South Korea and the United States. How would it do that? After the U.S. had destroyed the missiles, or had responded militarily in a very targeted fashion to some other specific challenge—resulting in the embarrassment of the Kim Family Regime—the North would launch, say, an intensive five- or ten-minute artillery barrage on the heart of Seoul, killing Americans and South Koreans in the vicinity of Yongsan. Then it simply would stop. And after the shellfire halted, the proverbial question among American officers in a quandary would arise: What now, lieutenant?

Politically speaking, we would be trumped. South Koreans, encouraged by their leftist movement—the upshot of both an intrusively large American troop presence and decades of manipulation by the North—would instantly blame the U.S. for the targeted strike against North Korea that led to the carnage in their capital. The United Nations and the global media would subtly blame Washington for the crisis and highlight the argument for talks. With that, the KFR could have an injection of new life, with more aid forthcoming.

That's why, short of a march toward the Yalu, some officers and NCOs with whom I spoke favored economic warfare against the North. Do not help the regime through food aid. Its population had been semi-starving for decades. Its forests were denuded. People were eating tree barks. Stop prolonging the agony. Help the KFR collapse.

One problem with this strategy was that in the latter stages of collapse, the likelihood of the more far-fetched military options improved—conventional and unconventional. Another problem was that it wasn't we but the Chinese who were really keeping the regime alive, though they did not necessarily exert foreign policy control over Pyongyang: the KFR, bent on its own survival, made a very bad puppet. In fact, China was in the process of gaining operational control over anything in the North of strategic economic and military value: mines, railways, and so on.

In other words, the Korean Peninsula was arguably the most dangerous place on earth; hard landings were easier to describe than soft ones. And a soft landing would more likely be orchestrated by Beijing than by Washington, even as the Chinese might not mind saddling the Americans with the short-term military responsibility of stabilizing a collapsed North.

But a landing there would be.

As I've indicated, a reunified Korea would have an instant, undisputed enemy: Japan. Any Korean politician would be able to stand up in parliament and get political mileage out of an anti-Japanese tirade. The Japanese knew this, and it was fueling their remilitarization, particularly in regard to their navy, with the latest, quiet diesel submarines and Aegis destroyers. While I was in Korea, in addition to the missile launches, there was a saber-rattling contest with Japan over disputed islets that South Koreans called Dokdo and the Japanese Takeshima, in what the Koreans referred to as the East Sea and the Japanese the Sea of Japan. Both sides sent survey ships to the area. Another option for Kim Jong Il, therefore, would be to leave South Korea alone and attack Japan instead, thereby playing on pan-Korean anti-Japanese nationalism.

Here it is useful to review Korean history. While in the medieval era the Koreans fought wars against Chinese dynasties like the Sui and Tang, later on, following the coming to power of Korea's own Joseon dynasty in 1392, Japan gradually matched China as Korea's principal adversary. There were repeated Japanese violations of the peninsula, culminating in an orgy of rape and murder at the end of the sixteenth century, and a savage occupation at the beginning of the twentieth, which ended only with the Soviet and American conquests, though it wasn't altogether black and white. South Koreans had trouble admitting that Japanese colonialism in the early twentieth century nearly doubled the life expectancy of the average Korean.

Japan's main consolation, according to Syung Je Park of the Asia Strategy Institute in Seoul, was that a Greater Korea might serve as a balance against an even more significant threat to Japan: a rising China. But the situation looked to be far more subtle than that. This anti-Japanese Greater Korea could also be a linchpin in China's twenty-first-century Asian economic prosperity sphere, a more benign version of Imperial Japan's Co-Prosperity Sphere of the 1930s and 1940s. Korean businessmen would certainly resist Chinese economic domination; but this would be tempered by anti-Japanese feeling and some lingering anti-Americanism in Korea, as the generation that remembered the sacrifices of American soldiers during the Korean War faded entirely. As in Germany, America will have made Korea a free society through a large troop presence, one that a younger, ahistorical generation might remember only negatively. But what would not fade from local memory was how the United States had its occupation of the Philippines supported by Japan, in return for American acceptance of the brutal Japanese occupation of Korea following the Russo-Japanese War of 1904–05. Such were the wages of imperialism, even when, as in the case of America and South Korea, it led to good results.

Greater Korea's relationship with China might ultimately be determined by how America itself decided to act: specifically, the degree to which the United States could get Japan to recognize its war guilt. If the U.S. had a military alliance with Japan without Japan publicly coming to terms with its past, psychologically it would push Greater Korea's population toward China. Henceforth, China and its implicit ally, Greater Korea, would have a tense relationship with Japan and its allies the U.S. and India, though, because of its own manifold business interests in China, America could only balance against China delicately.

Perhaps the wisest thing the U.S. could do was to keep ten thousand troops or so on the Korean Peninsula even after the KFR collapsed and the northern half of the peninsula was stabilized. At least this was the opinion of South Korean Army Col. Chung Kyung Yung of Seoul's National Defense University. Such a contingent, he told me, would serve as a political statement that the U.S. was not abandoning Korea to a militarily resurgent Japan. The best way to secure peace and prosperity in Asia, Col. Chung emphasized, was not to have an initially fragile Greater Korea without U.S. troops become a bone of contention between China and Japan. Moreover, because the United States was the farthest away of all these powers, it should be perceived as the least dangerous—the one power without territorial ambitions.[2]

The problem with that idea was that it might run counter to what was doable in South Korean politics. It is true that South Korean anti-Americanism was exaggerated, mainly the product of a sixties-style student movement that had come to fruition a decade after the ones in America and Europe, partly because the end of war and middle-class prosperity had also come later here. This was still a country where the few statues of foreigners included American Generals Douglas MacArthur and James Van Fleet, the latter the father of the South Korean armed forces. Protestantism was practically the dominant religion, the result of late-nineteenth-century American missionary activity. (When and if North Korea collapsed, expect Christian evangelicism to replace the Communist regime's *Juche* ethos of self-reliance. Pyongyang was once the "Jerusalem of Asia" because of its missionary associations a century ago.) Yet, despite such comforting legacies, South Koreans had, by and large, convinced themselves to be nearly as worried about the Americans as they were about the Chinese, just as they had convinced themselves to be as afraid of the Japanese as of the North Koreans. In truth, many South Koreans had an interest in the perpetuation of the Kim Family Regime, for its collapse would usher in a period of economic sacrifice here that nobody was prepared for. A long-standing commitment by the American military had allowed South Korea to evolve into a status quo, materialistic society. Thus, few here wanted to rock the boat.

While Washington was keen on a free and democratic Korean Peninsula, Beijing, with its infrastructure investments, was laying the groundwork for a Tibet-like buffer state in much of the North, to be ruled indirectly through its ethnic Korean cronies, once the Kim Family Regime unraveled. This buffer would be less oppressive than the morbid, crushing tyranny that it would replace, even as Beijing would bear the cost of it. Therefore, from the point of view of the average South Korean, the Chinese might offer a better deal. The more Washington thought narrowly in terms of a democratic Korean Peninsula, the more Beijing had the potential to lock us out of it. Ultimately, victory here would go to the side with the most indirect and nuanced strategy.

The logic of our policy on the Korean Peninsula was dependent upon the willingness of South Koreans to make some measure of sacrifice for the sake of freedom in the North. But sacrifice is not a word that voters in free and prosperous societies anywhere tend to like. Indeed, if voters in Western-style democracies were good at anything, it was rationalizing their own selfishness. It seemed that the authoritarian Chinese might have understood the voters of this free and democratic society better than we did.

Our whole military strategy worldwide was bent on nurturing such free societies. But once these societies were on their feet, rather than be on our side, they would more likely become states that we would, well, just have to put up with. We were right in our mission, so long as we recognized its tragic contradictions.

———

Before leaving Korea, I heard an American general exhort his troops to be proud of the sacrifices that they and their predecessors in uniform had made for the Korean people, whether or not young South Koreans appreciated it. Some days later, on July 4, 2006, there was a toast at the Special Forces Association picnic at Yongsan Garrison for the members who were "absent"—those who had been killed, or might still be missing in action (MIA) in North Korea and Vietnam. And some days after that, I went on a long road trip to the mountainous southern end of the peninsula with an old friend from the Philippines, Master Sgt. Mark Lopez of Yuba City, California.* To pass the time, I asked him, if he had the choice, when would he have most liked to be born? His answer was swift: "Right before the Great Depression, so that I could enlist as a combat pilot and fight in World War II and Korea, and still be young enough to fight in Vietnam." Mark and so many others I knew saw these three wars as equally sanctified—not as one good war, one stalemate, and one bad war.

On all of these occasions, it struck me how the military had historical memories that the public did not. To wit, my own generation saw Korea as a blur and Vietnam as a cause. But for those like Mark, those two Asian conflicts were, well, wars, like World War II—with heroic mythologies no less tragic and glorious.

Korea brought to mind Gen. Douglas MacArthur's amphibious landing at Inch'on, the U.S. 1st Cavalry Division's and South Korean 1st Infantry Division's initial capture of Pyongyang, the 1st Marine Division's brave retreat in the snow from the Chosin Reservoir following heavy fighting with seven Chinese divisions (one of the proudest moments in Marine history), the U.S. Navy's unrelenting artillery support of ROK infantry landings on the southern Korean coast, and the B-29 pilots who bombed behind enemy lines: it was in Korea where the new U.S. Air Force made its bones.

As for Vietnam, because so many of their dads had fought there, the uniformed Americans I knew were also on intimate terms with that conflict. Thus, they saw it in all its gray shades: with its tactical successes and tactical failures, with its Marine combined action platoons and Green Beret infiltrations that worked, and its Big Army ones that didn't; with its Big Army generals who succeeded like Creighton Abrams, and

* See *Imperial Grunts,* Chapter 4, for a profile of Lopez.

its Army generals who failed like William Westmoreland; with its moments of glory like Hue, and its moments of disgrace like My Lai; and
above all, with its heroes, like the Son Tay Raiders, who had attempted
to free American POWs in 1970, and the "Misty" forward air controllers and "Sandy" search-and-rescue pilots, who risked their lives for
untold hours over North Vietnam, identifying targets and prowling for
downed American pilots. It was because these soldiers knew their history that they did not get discouraged easily. Thus, they were armed
with stores of patience for the bad times.

Master Sgt. Lopez was one of a half-dozen NCOs from the Army's
1st Special Forces Group who were embedded with South Korean special forces detachments on one-man missions. In a quiet bar in Seoul
one night, I discussed with these Americans the perennial subject of
host-country NCOs, the quality of which they had been working all
their professional lives to improve. As good as South Korean NCOs
were compared to those of other foreign armies, everyone at the table
agreed that Korean noncoms were not up to American standards. It was
cultural, Mark insisted. Married to a local—like most of the guys at the
table—he loved and respected the ingenuity of Koreans, who, he admitted, were in many ways superior to Americans. "But Koreans are also
hierarchical," he said, "and so their NCOs are too subservient to their
officers."

Americans were definitely not hierarchical, everyone chimed in. We
were still a fluid, middle-class society born of a frontier ethos where respect was based on work done, not on social position or who your parents happened to be. I looked around the room and thought that these
men were as good an example of that ideal as any you could find.

I had met many like them since 9/11. For despite their uniforms and
short haircuts that were supposed to have robbed them of their individ-
uality, the American troops whom I met I remember only as individuals. Of course, I might have had the same impression writing about coal
miners with pickaxes and shovels instead of rifles, or about construction
workers, or cod fishermen, all of whom dressed in veritable uniforms
and had their characters invigorated by dangerous physical labor.
While the troops looked alike to outsiders, after a few days with them

their personalities achieved vivid proportions, without the need of affectation.

I wanted to continue traveling in their company, but the more experiences one accumulated of a certain kind, the more that memory began to edit them into oblivion. If I continued my restless life with the military, I knew that these individuals would start running together into composites. My travels had reached the point of diminishing returns.

Individuals these troops were. Yet the best of them shared a common trait that had nothing to do with following orders, or thinking literally about the task at hand, or some such thing. It was their metaphysical direction. The best of them groped toward an indefinable frontier. In his "Invocation" to *The Year of Decision: 1846,* Bernard DeVoto cites a passage from Henry David Thoreau: "Eastward I go only by force; but westward I go free . . . I must walk toward Oregon, and not toward Europe."[3]

This should not be confused with nativism, or anything connected to America's current tensions with Europe, or even a hankering for Asia. Instead, Thoreau and DeVoto refer to a spirit of pioneering ambition that invigorated the best military units I knew, whatever the foreign policy or administration of the moment. It is a spirit that provided for a healthy enthusiasm among those taking part in deployments in Iraq or Afghanistan, Kosovo or Indonesia, and so many other places. It is a spirit that had nothing to do with conquest.

THE NON-WARRIOR DEMOCRACY

I f a glimpse of the future is possible, it must come from an intimacy with the present, further clarified by the great works of the past. Rereading, upon a halt in my travels, *The Art of Warfare* by the fourth century B.C. Chinese court minister Sun-Tzu and *On War* by the early-nineteenth-century Prussian general Karl von Clausewitz, I was struck by something straightaway—something that has little to do with the specific ideas of the two men, but is everywhere in the background of their thoughts. It is something that the many months I spent with the combat arms community alerted me to.

Both Sun-Tzu and Clausewitz *believe*—in their states, their sovereigns, their homelands. Because they *believe,* both are willing to *fight.* That is so clear that they never need to state it.

Sun-Tzu is concerned with war on the highest strategic level; Clausewitz more on the operational level. Sun-Tzu affirms that the greatest warrior is one who calculates so well that he never needs to fight. For Clausewitz, war takes precedence only after other forms of politics have failed. In sum, both men have internalized the fact that war is so awful that it constitutes a last resort. Both are opponents of militarism. But there is never the slightest doubt that each would fight if necessary, and that each man could live only with a policy of such vigor that it would never, at any moment, fail to communicate a warrior spirit.

Sun-Tzu respects only a leader "who plans and calculates like a hungry man," who sanctions every manner of deceit provided it is neces-

sary to gain strategic advantage, who is never swayed by public opinion, and "who advances without any thought of winning personal fame
and withdraws in spite of certain punishment," if he judges it to be in the
interest of his army and his state.[1] Clausewitz is no less committed. "In
affairs so dangerous as war," he writes, "false ideas proceeding from
kindness of heart are precisely the worst." He adds: "The fact that
slaughter is a horrifying spectacle must make us take war more seriously, but not provide an excuse for gradually blunting our swords in
the name of humanity. Sooner or later someone will come along with a
sharp sword and hack off our arms."

The logic of both men is grounded in patriotic commitment. According to Clausewitz, an army's national feeling is among "the chief moral
powers" in war. Each man, to quote Theodore Roosevelt, has actually
been in the arena. He "knows great enthusiasms, the great devotions";
he has spent "himself in a worthy cause . . . so that his place shall never
be with those cold and timid souls who know neither victory nor defeat."*

Sun-Tzu was likely a court minister during the chaos of the Warring
States 2,300 years ago, prior to the relative stability of Han rule.[†]
Clausewitz was a veteran of the Napoleonic Wars, who served with both
the Prussian and Russian armies against the French. While each man
seeks to avoid war, each is a warrior. What stands out in *The Art of Warfare* and *On War,* more so than the incisiveness of the analysis, is the
character of the writers themselves. Because knowing something ab-
stractly is different from knowing it firsthand, I could grasp this vividly
only after living beside junior officers and senior NCOs, whose logic
also flowed from their patriotic commitment.

Patriotism, in the famously quoted phrase of Samuel Johnson, is the
last refuge of the scoundrel.[‡] Yet such a truth is misused by those who
have little loyalty to any place, and who therefore lack any accountabil-
ity, since it is easy to be in favor of this cause, or against that cause, if
one has no down-to-earth stake in the outcome. While some patriots

---

* Speech delivered April 23, 1910, see p. 299.
† Possibly Sun-Tzu never existed at all. His book may represent the accumulated wisdom of
  many people.
‡ Johnson was actually referring to a specific group of patriots.

certainly are scoundrels, the vast majority are more trustworthy than those who are not.

Patriotism, as I learned from one soldier and marine, one sailor and airman, after another, overlaps with moral hardiness. I can best illustrate moral hardiness and its opposite by describing two characters of Joseph Conrad, whose writings, like those of Sun-Tzu and Clausewitz, took on a richer meaning following my travels with the military.

Captain MacWhirr is the protagonist in Conrad's short story "Typhoon" (1902). The son of a Belfast grocer, he is a man of few words and little imagination, a man so taciturn that his chief mate says of him: "There are feelings that this man simply hasn't got. . . . You might just as well try to make a bedpost understand." As Captain MacWhirr's steamer, *Nan-Shan,* sets out to the coast of China to return Chinese coolies home, a great storm is brewing in the Formosa Channel, recorded by the dramatic drop of his barometer. But what would terrify most other men he accepts matter-of-factly.

A few hours later, his ship is in chaos. The wind alone has such a "disintegrating" force, Conrad writes, that it "isolates" every man on board from every other. The mates panic, the coolies riot as the *Nan-Shan* nearly splits apart. As for MacWhirr, rather than sail miles off course to get around the storm, he quietly decides to plow straight into it, like a platoon leader charging straight into an ambush. "Facing it— always facing it," he mumbles, "that's the way to get through." So it is that this ordinary, very extraordinary man saves the ship because, as Conrad mightily suggests, he not only believes, but also believes deeply in his moral duty to the shipping company and to the men under him. Once the storm is past, rather than sleep, or remove his boots even, he makes sure that every coolie gets his proper wages.

MacWhirr is not clever. He is not even minimally well spoken. But his abiding faith results in an iron certainty about himself, for which words are quite beside the point.

MacWhirr is not the type to be afraid, whether of a typhoon or, for that matter, months upon months of god-awful headlines. During the worst of times in Iraq, one officer after another, commissioned and non-commissioned, communicated to me a fierce conviction. Take the otherwise quiet, MacWhirr-like Sgt. Maj. Dennis Zavodsky of Mapleton,

Oregon, who at a Thanksgiving service in Mosul remarked that the Pilgrims during the first winter in the New World experienced a casualty rate that would render any combat unit ineffective. "This country isn't a quitter," he said. "It doesn't withdraw. It doesn't give in." Stubbornness, inspired by faith, was the rule among those I was privileged to be with.

I do not mean religious faith per se, since quite a few of those I met despised "the Bible thumpers." I mean simply the moral stamina of a MacWhirr—something that has a tendency to go hand in hand with the bumps and bruises of a dangerous, working-class existence.

Yet the moment I left these combat units I encountered the Martin Decouds of this world, the brilliant sneerers who analyzed everything into oblivion.

Martin Decoud is a character in the novel *Nostromo* (1904), about an imaginary Latin American country, Costaguana, in the throes of upheaval. Decoud has studied law in Paris, dabbles in literature, writes political commentary, and all in all, as Conrad explains, is an "idle boulevardier." Decoud becomes heroic only when he is faced with a political crisis that matters to his own welfare. But when he finds himself alone on an island off Costaguana, he gives in to despair, even though he has been told he will be rescued. The "brilliant" journalist Decoud, the "spoiled darling" of his family, as Conrad writes, "was not fit to grapple with himself single-handed." Whereas Captain MacWhirr could assume the breathtaking loneliness of command in the midst of a nighttime typhoon that silences all human voices, Decoud, also faced with disintegrative natural forces, breaks down. Despite Decoud's virtuoso conversation and commentary, as Conrad tells us, in a crisis it turns out he "believed in nothing."

Alas, in the unpredictable fog and Clausewitzian "friction" of war, to believe—to believe in something—is more important than to be blessed by mere logic, or the ability for talented argument.

———

"Faith is the great strategic factor that unbelieving faculties and bureaucracies ignore," writes retired Army Lt. Col. Ralph Peters (Ret.) in an essay, "The Counterrevolution in Military Affairs."[2] This idea is not new. The signal flaw of the upper classes, in Dostoevsky's words, is that they "want to base justice on reason alone," not on any deeper belief system, absent which everything can be rationalized, so the will of a society to fight and survive withers away.[3]

Peters fears that Islamic revolutionaries believe in themselves more than we believe in ourselves. Terrorists do not fear the Pentagon's much touted "network-centric warfare," he writes, because they have mastered it for a fraction of a cent on the dollar, "achieving greater relative effects with the Internet, cellphones, and cheap airline tickets" than have all of our military technologies. He notes that our trillion-dollar arsenal cannot produce an instrument of war as effective as the suicide bomber—"the breakthrough weapon of our time."

Kipling understood this. In the poem "Arithmetic on the Frontier," Kipling writes that as the hillsides of eastern Afghanistan teem with "home-bred" troops brought from England at "vast expense of time and steam," the odds remain, nevertheless, "on the cheaper man"—the native fighter, that is. The suicide bomber is Kipling's "cheaper man" incarnate. This breakthrough weapon is a product of fanatical belief—of a different sort than Captain MacWhirr's, but of belief nonetheless.

Take jihad, which places more emphasis on the "mystical dimension" of sacrifice than on any tactical or strategic objective. Jihad is an act of individual exultation rather than of collective action, observes the French academic and scholar of Islam Olivier Roy. As Roy explains, it is "an affair between the believer and God and not between the believer and his enemy. There is no obligation to obtain a result. Hence the demonstrative, even exhibitionist, aspects of the attacks."*

The suicide bomber is the distilled essence of jihad, the result of an age when the electronic media provide an unprecedented platform for exhibitionism. Clausewitz's rules of war do not apply in this case, for he conceived of nothing like the modern media, whose members tend to be as avowedly secular as suicide bombers are devout. Without a stabilizing belief system, the global media's spiritual void has been partially filled by a resentment against the United States—the embodiment of unruly modernization and raw political and military power that the global citizens of the media detest. And so it is that the video camera—

---

* Olivier Roy, *The Failure of Political Islam*, trans. Carol Volk (Cambridge, Mass.: Harvard University Press, 1994), pp. 65–67, 157. Roy draws, in part, on the work of Jean-Paul Charnay, *L'Islam et la guerre* (Paris: Fayard, 1986).

"that insatiable accomplice of the terrorist" in Peters's words—becomes the "cheap negation" of American military technology.

Even as we narrow our own view of warfare's acceptable parameters, our enemies amplify the concept of total war, which is about targeting tens, or hundreds, or occasionally thousands of civilians, in order to undermine the morale of millions. The killing of three thousand civilians on September 11, 2001, might have temporarily awakened a warrior spirit in American democracy, but such a spirit is hard to sustain in the crucible of conflict. In Iraq, a country of twenty-six million people in which over a million American troops have passed through, killing a few Americans and three dozen or so Iraqis daily in suicide bombings is enough to demoralize a home front seven thousand miles away. A non-warrior democracy with a very limited appetite for casualties is a good thing, in terms of putting brakes on a directionless war strategy. All I am saying is that we as a people, as we grow increasingly prosperous, will find it harder to wage war.

Stark religious faith, in concert with a generally irreligious global media, makes for a cheap and efficient weapon of war. Of course, nationalism is another form of faith. Nationalism, of a kind that is going out of fashion among sectors of the American elite, could also defeat us.

Here is where someone like Ralph Peters comes completely in line with someone of impeccable credentials from the academic establishment: Paul Bracken, Yale University professor of political science, and defense consultant to both Democratic and Republican administrations. Bracken's book *Fire in the East: The Rise of Asian Military Power and the Second Nuclear Age* has, as one of its major themes, the ascent of blood-and-soil nationalism. In discussing the acquisition of nuclear technology by China, Iran, India, Pakistan, and other powers on the Asian continent, Bracken writes:

> The link to nationalism makes the second nuclear age even harder for the West to comprehend. Nationalism is not viewed kindly in the West these days. It is seen as nonsensical, a throwback, and, it is hoped, a dying force in the world. The notion that the Chinese or Indians could conduct foreign policy on the assumption of their own

national superiority goes against nearly every important trend in American and West European thought.[4]

Bracken next observes that successful nuclear tests in places like India and Pakistan "set off public euphoria—literally, people danced in the streets." It was an "emotional embrace of a technology Westerners have been taught to loathe and abhor." Americans forget, perhaps at their peril, how in the 1950s the atomic bomb "was an important source of American pride," in Bracken's words. Henceforth, "no one should be surprised that Asian countries today feel the same way." The Yale professor adds, again, completely in line with the iconoclastic Peters: "In focusing on whether the West can keep its lead in technology, the United States is asking the wrong question. It overlooks the military advantages that accrue to societies with a less fastidious approach to violence."[5]

In such a world, the real threat to our national security may be our own lack of faith in ourselves, which, in turn, leads to an overdependence on technology by our military establishment. How to kill at no risk to our troops is only in our eyes a sign of strength; in those of our enemy it is a sign of weakness, cowardice even.

Never-say-die religious faith, accompanied by old-fashioned nationalism, is alive in America, to such a degree that I have found it a match for the most fanatical suicide bombers. But with some exceptions, it is confined to our finest combat infantry units, and to specific sections of the country and socioeconomic strata from which these "warriors" (as they like to call themselves) hail. It is not characteristic of a country that in many ways is going in the opposite direction, because of irreversible economic and social forces. This is not the 1950s when Americans took a certain relief in possessing "the bomb."

Faith, which is about struggle and having confidence precisely when the odds are the worst, is receding among a social and economic class that is increasingly motivated by universal values—that is, caring for the suffering of famine victims abroad as much as for hurricane victims at home. Universal values are not the opposite of faith, but they should never be confused with it. You may care to the point of tears about suffering humankind without having the will to actually fight (let alone inconvenience yourself) for your concerns. Thus, if accompanied by a loss of faith, universal values pose an existential challenge to national security.

The loss of a warrior mentality and the rise of universal values is a feature of all stable, Western-style middle-class democracies. Witness our situation. The Reserve is desperate for officers. Yet there is little urge among our elites to volunteer, and thus our military takes on more of a regional caste. The British Army may have been drawn from the dregs of society, but it was officered by the country's political class. Not so ours, which has little to do with the business of soldiering, and is socially disconnected from what guards us in our sleep. Nine Princeton graduates in the class of 2006 entered the military, compared to four hundred in 1956, when there was a draft. Other Ivy League schools had no one enter the military in 2006. Only one member of the Stanford graduating class had a parent in the military.[6] Nor do our top schools encourage recruitment; in fact, they often actively discourage it. Many people, especially academics and intellectuals, have a visceral distrust of units like Special Forces. They are more comfortable with regular citizen armies that seem to better represent democracy. But other than a professional warrior class or a draft, what is available to a democracy whose upper stratum has less and less of a commitment to military values?

As for the combat arms community itself, warrior consciousness will further intensify, even as the identities of each of the four armed services become less distinct. This is an exceedingly slow process, more noticeable at the top levels of command than elsewhere. But rather than Army green, Air Force blue, or Navy khaki, for example, the trend could be toward purple—the color of *jointness*. This is not to say that the services are losing their individual cultures, only that operations both big and small are more and more integrated affairs.

As each year goes by, the interaction between the services deepens. The Air Force, with its once cushy, corporate way of existence, is becoming a bit more hardened and austere like the Army, as the Big Army becomes more small unit–oriented like the Marine Corps. The Big Navy, with its new emphasis on small ships to meet the demands of littoral combat, is becoming more unconventional and powered down, also like the Marines. Without a draft (or a revitalized Reserve and National Guard that ties the military closer to civilian society), in the decades ahead American troops, at least in frontline units, may become less soldiers, marines, sailors, and airmen, and more and more *purple warriors:* a guild practically, in which the profession of combat arms is passed down from father to son. It was striking how many troops I met whose parents and other relatives had also been in the service, especially among the units whose members face the highest level of personal risk.

At the 2006 Stanford commencement ceremony, a Marine general whose son was the lone graduating student from a military family said he was struck by how many of the other parents had never even met a member of the military before he introduced himself.[7]

A citizen army is composed of conscripts from all classes and parts of the country in roughly equal amounts. But a volunteer military is necessarily dominated by those regions with an old-fashioned fighting ethos. I refer to the South and the adjacent Bible Belts of the southern Midwest and Great Plains. Marine and Army infantry units, in particular Army Special Forces A-teams, manifested a proclivity for volunteers from the states of the former Confederacy, as well as Irish and Hispanics from poorer, more culturally conservative sections of coastal cities. In sum, the American military has become, in some respects, a higher-quality version of what it was on the eve of World War II.

The Greatest Generation may have come from all walks of life and all regions of the country, but when it got to boot camp its trainers were professional soldiers, often with southern accents, intent on doing their thirty years. But the southern soldier of today is different from back then. Take Army Special Forces Maj. Robert E. Lee, Jr., of Mobile, Alabama, whom I met in the Philippines in 2003. Maj. Lee named his son "Stonewall." But Maj. Lee also worked as a church-based volunteer in a poor African-American section of Wichita, Kansas. "It was my first real exposure to blacks, I mean not from afar," he told me. "It was a year of learning, day after day, that folks are just folks." He was not unusual. It is a commonplace among observers of the American military that race relations in the barracks are significantly better than in the society at large.

Yet even such an encouraging evolution constitutes another sign of the emergence of a separate caste. I found that it wasn't just in war zones where soldiers bond with one another, but at bases within the United States, too, where troops and their families live separately from close-by civilian communities, and the short duty rotation makes it hard for the inhabitants of the base to develop ties outside it. Spending months upon months with American troops, I entered a social world where friendships stretched across units and racial lines more than across military-civilian ones, and home-front references were to forts rather than to states.

Commonly, liberal democratic societies have been defended by conservative military establishments, whose members may lack the sensitivities and social graces of the cosmopolitan classes whom they protect. Such a traditional American military, very much rooted in the old nation-state, now has a thankless task. When one considers that much of what it does abroad is guard sea-lanes and train troops of fledgling democracies, it helps provide the security armature for an emerging global civilization that, the more that civilization evolves—with its own mass media, nongovernmental organizations, and professional class— the less credit and sympathy it grants to the American troops who at times risk and give their lives for it.

The military historian James L. Stokesbury writes that middle-class democracies fight two kinds of wars well: little wars, fought by professional warriors, which garner little media attention and which consequently the public does not bother about; and big wars, in which the whole country, in spite of itself, may occasionally get caught up in a patriotic fervor. The small footprint deployments I have covered in recent years are a variation of these little wars, as are the many discreet intelligence operations and raids that various branches of the national security apparatus continue to carry out around the globe.

The problem, as Stokesbury explains, arises not with the little or big wars, but with the "middle-sized" ones, of which the public is very much aware, thanks now to the twenty-four-hour news cycle, but is nevertheless confused as to its goals. These middle-sized wars are very bloody affairs, in which we are nevertheless forced to place a high value on the individual because of our universal values, even as the enemy does not.[8] Abu Ghraib, which showed America at its worst, does not register in terms of barbarity compared to what the enemy was doing on a daily basis in Iraq at the same time. In big, good-versus-evil wars, the home front feels itself a part of the fighting machine. In little and middle-sized wars, it does not. But in little wars, it doesn't matter that the public doesn't feel itself at war, because it is largely unknowing about it in the first place. It is the middle-sized war that creates the worst sort of combination for a non-warrior democracy, one in which the public is keenly knowledgeable of the worst details, yet has no context in which to assimilate them, and is otherwise unaffected.

Stokesbury's example of a middle-sized war is Korea, but his point also applies to Vietnam and Iraq. The so-called Powell Doctrine, in which then-Chairman of the Joint Chiefs Gen. Colin Powell advised that the United States should not get involved in a war without overwhelming force, a near certainty of victory, and a clear exit strategy, may seem overly timid to many. But if one views the Powell Doctrine as a way to avoid middle-sized wars (or little wars that through miscalculations can become middle-sized ones), it makes sense for the needs of a non-warrior democracy.

In these wars, the lack of a broad-based warrior mentality is clearly a disadvantage. The problem, though, is that it often isn't clear what will become a middle-sized war and what won't. The Powell Doctrine was used as an argument not to get involved in Bosnia and Kosovo in the 1990s. But we inserted troops anyway and they did not turn out to be middle-sized wars. The gradual stabilization of the former Yugoslavia and the expansion of NATO to the Black Sea indicate that the Balkan interventions of 1995 and 1999 were in the nation's interest. Few if any of the neoconservatives, realists, and liberals who supported the invasion of Iraq expected it to be a middle-sized war that would go on for years. Simply never to get involved anywhere, except in the smallest deployments, or in a bigger one without the absolute certainty of a clean victory, is itself an indication of defeat and retreat from the world. Alas, the Powell Doctrine is not perfect.

Great Britain employed others to help it fight Napoleon, and it maintained an elite navy rather than a vast and financially debilitating national army. But it's not that we haven't tried to do this. All our training missions around the world are designed to bring indigenous forces up to the level where they can fight on their own. Moreover, PACOM officials are obsessed with military multilateralism. Even President Bush attempted to build a military coalition of major nations for invading Iraq, before he did so with the help of mainly Great Britain. And Iraq was the exception. The American way of war is, by and large, by coalitions. As for sea power, for over six decades we've been the successor to the Royal Navy. Yet in coming decades we will likely have no choice but to gradually cede some of that oceanic space to the rising Indian and Chinese navies.

The warrior spirit of our illiberal adversaries means that deterrence also requires a credible, land-based conventional force structure: it's that or appeasement if we want to avoid middle-sized wars and still be taken seriously. This brings me to Frederick Kagan, an analyst at the American Enterprise Institute in Washington, and author of "A Strategy for Heroes: What's Wrong with the 2006 Quadrennial Defense Review."*

Kagan believes that troop numbers really do matter, and while they may not be able to solve the problem of suicide bombers, they can solve a lot of other problems that will allow us to prosper. For example, he notes that even as airpower becomes increasingly effective, we should not expect it to obviate the need for large numbers of conventional ground troops in future crises—something Iraq has demonstrated. Here he seems to be in disagreement with those like Air Force Col. Robert Wheeler, operations commander for the B-2 squadron on Guam, who told me that the massing of troops will become less and less feasible as time goes on.

"Wise commanders," Kagan writes, "design plans that can be executed by ordinary soldiers." Yet Pentagon planners, he complains, with their focus on light and lethal small-footprint strategies, are wedded to a concept that "only heroes" can make work. Of course, light and lethal

---

* *The Weekly Standard,* Feb. 20, 2006. The fact that *The Weekly Standard* published this and the Peters article is not surprising. Non-establishment journals with modest budgets often have been the venues for path-breaking ideas, and as neoconservatives take an especial interest in military matters, it follows that *The Weekly Standard* would be strong on this general subject—and open-minded. Peters, for example, is not a neoconservative.

small-footprint strategies are what I have spent much of my time covering. And I found that they worked quite well, in terms of their low risk and reasonable degree of success, particularly in relation to their costs, since expensive hardware is not needed so much as basics like language and diplomatic skills. Small footprints are about little wars, which, unlike middle-sized ones, are to our advantage.

Still, Kagan has a point. After all, he isn't referring to most of the operations that I reported on, in which, for the most part, American troops have been invited into various countries not to stabilize dictatorships, as in the past, but to help stabilize and professionalize the militaries of new democracies along Western lines. Rather, he is referring to contingencies for middle- and big-sized wars, for another way to avoid such wars is to plan perfectly for them. Instead, he finds a Pentagon strategy that only heroes can make work—if your definition of heroes is the kind of marines and Green Berets that I kept running into, whose main worry was that they would not get to fight in Iraq or Afghanistan.

As much as I respect the troops whom I profile, I also realize that the armed services constitute a vast world in which the majority of enlistees, as well as of reservists and national guardsmen, have joined for complex social and economic reasons that often have little to do with wanting to see combat. Defense strategy must accept this reality. The members of our social and economic elite that avoid military service, and encourage their children to do likewise, are not the only problem. Just as the American public has a limited appetite for grand causes and conflicts, so do the troops themselves, outside of the best units. Thus, there needs to be enough of a strategic reserve of manpower so that even in times of conflict, units will not be overdeployed and overworked indefinitely.

Kagan's other point is that by putting so much emphasis on Special Operations–type activities, the Quadrennial Defense Review of 2006, which generally reflects the thinking of former Secretary of Defense Donald Rumsfeld, commits a classic error—that of seeing the future as a continuation of the present, while at the same time not taking into account the mistakes of the present.

To wit, the future will be about much more than counterinsurgency against the likes of al-Qaeda. As Iraq has demonstrated, in the years ahead the Pentagon may require many ordinary soldiers in the field. The festering problems of Iran and North Korea, and the rise of China's military power to accompany its economic weight, all point to the need for a large, well-funded conventional military, as well as for a much better, more linguistically adroit unconventional one than we have now. (As I've written in an earlier chapter, the debate over conventional versus unconventional is a false one. Both are necessary, and in any case the distinction between them is eroding.)

Kagan is not saying that we will fight Iran, North Korea, Russia, and China, or even any one of them, or any combination of them. But he is saying that we must be prepared for these and other contingencies. Optimism is not the Pentagon's job. Donald Rumsfeld thought in terms of worst-case scenarios for the original invasion of Iraq, and got the best possible result; but because he thought in terms of best-case scenarios for the ensuing occupation, he got the worst possible result.

Colin S. Gray, an advisor to British and American governments for a quarter century on defense policy, writes that when it comes to optimism and pessimism, "optimism is apt to kill with greater certainty." Nothing is more dangerous, he says, than "a policy that amounts to an investment of hope either that humankind has forsworn most forms of warfare, or, more likely, that someone else will be on call to bear the security burden."[9] Gray, whose book *Another Bloody Century* offers a thorough, nonpolemical analysis of the forms of twenty-first-century military conflict, is, like Kagan, very impressed with the health and persistence of interstate rivalries. Such rivalries, he concludes, have the probability in the next few decades of overshadowing the danger of al-Qaeda–style insurgencies. An example he cites may be the slow-motion emergence of an anti-American, Sino-Russian continental axis in Asia, to which illiberal regimes will overtly gravitate, and terrorist groups covertly so. In such a future, while we hope to defend ourselves, *pace* Wheeler's vision, through air-land-sea combinations that fuse together for sudden strikes without having to risk large numbers of ground troops, we will still need large numbers of ground troops available.

In this reckoning, the United States military will not only have to get better, and even more light and lethal, but also bigger and more robust in many ways. The only way for the defense establishment to avoid tragedy is to think tragically, for we will be up against adversaries who have not had their fighting spirits as debilitated as ours by globalization. Though everyone will be affected by technological and economic integration, those who are less so will have the psychological advantage when it comes to war.

———

Despite globalization, national militaries will not diminish in importance, at least for some decades. To the contrary, in some cases, they could grow in significance compared to other forms of human organizations. The "technologies of wealth and war have always been closely connected," Bracken warns. To a significant degree since the early 1990s, "missile and bomb tests . . . biological warfare programs, and . . . chemical weapons" have been "the products of a prosperous, liberalizing Asia."

Indeed, the political-military map of Eurasia—one-third of the earth's landmass—is changing radically. Europe is increasingly less a serious military power. Its own peoples see their respective militaries not as defenders of their homelands but as civil servants in uniforms. A revitalized, more expeditionary NATO can certainly mitigate this situation. But the overall trend will more likely see Europe devote itself to peacekeeping and disaster details. And while Europe slowly recedes as a purely military factor, a chain of Asian countries, from Israel to North Korea—including Syria, Iran, Pakistan, India, and China—have assembled nuclear and/or chemical stockpiles, aided by ballistic missile delivery systems in more and more cases.

The key element in judging the future of national militaries will be the civilian-military relationship in each particular country. In Europe, as I've noted, civilians take little pride in their standing armies. In America, they do. In this respect, Iraq has not been like Vietnam. While Americans may have turned against the Iraq war, they have not turned against the troops there, and, if anything, in recent years have grown more appreciative of them. Precisely because they are so socially disconnected from the military, many members of the elite hold the military in awe. Though our own elite may want no part of military life, and show no warrior spirit when a military situation becomes difficult, nevertheless, openly mocking the idea of military service is by and large not socially acceptable. The upshot: America has a first-class, professional military that is respected, even as it is not reflective of society.

Though the American military in qualitative terms (though not in manpower terms) gets better and better, increasingly restrictive rules of engagement, coupled with the ascent of Asian militaries, could make it increasingly weaker in relative terms. Whereas Asian militaries, particularly in the case of China and India, used to be characterized by mass conscript armies of peasants who could withdraw into the countryside, so one vast country did not in any real operational sense threaten its neighbors, homegrown communications technologies, including digital phones, satellites, and so on, have created real civilian-military industrial complexes across the Asian landmass.[10]

These countries are not weighed down by the kind of imperial responsibilities that burden America—the legacy of World War II, Korea, and beyond. While Army Special Forces and the Marines, for relatively small outlays of money, experiment at the unconventional edges of the battlefield, the Air Force and Navy patrol vast air and sea spaces at significant cost to the American taxpayer. A country like China can build an empire of sorts for less money than the U.S. spends merely to keep its. As we have seen in Korea, the more established an empire is, the harder and more expensive it is to maintain.

Americans like to believe that the advance of democracy the world over will make them more secure. They may be right. But it is also worth considering that the United States is a status quo power, like every other in history, meaning its power depends on the current situation in world affairs, and as that situation changes, whether because of the advance of democracy or its retreat, its power is threatened.

Take China. Many analysts posit that if China remains repressive it will be a threat, whereas if China embraces democracy it will be a friend. Obviously, China's future will see a mixture of both trends. Even so, a repressive China could face internal problems that could actually diminish its expansionist tendencies, while an increasingly free China, rather than be benign, could exhibit a kind of nationalist dynamism that will make it more of a challenge to the United States. My point is only that an age of democracy will give free rein to an array of vibrant new forces that make it unlikely America's global role will be as dominant as it is now.

That could turn out to be a good thing, not just for the outer world but for individual Americans, too. For example, Great Britain is no longer the world power it was, but the average Briton certainly lives better than his forebears of an imperial age. It is not a question of whether we will fade away as a great power over the decades and centuries, but how, at what pace, and at what price we will do so.

Our current imperial-like situation is quite real, in terms of a military presence around the globe that bears similarities to the frustrations and challenges of other empires, during other times in history, when empires took a much different form. With the possible exception of Iraq, these deployments have been something in which Americans can take genuine pride. Yet, there is no contradiction in acknowledging this pride, and also acknowledging that an American empire of sorts is not the natural order of things to come. There is no contradiction in being frankly impressed with the troops and their accomplishments in places as diverse as Colombia, Mali, and the Strait of Malacca, and accepting the fact that such tasks have an end point. There may be nothing healthier for running an empire-of-sorts than to look forward to its own obsolescence. That way there is a goal, rather than an enjoyment of power for its own sake.

The goal to which I refer is not world government, or anything of the sort—a tyranny of the worst kind because there will always be arguments about how to organize society and improve it. Still, the overarching objective of the American military's imperial-like deployments should be, as I wrote near the beginning of this odyssey, to provide a security armature for an emerging global civilization, which, in turn, nurtures a loose set of international arrangements that have arisen organically among responsible and like-minded states. Winston Churchill saw in the United States a worthy successor to the British Empire, one that would carry on Britain's liberalizing mission. We cannot rest until something emerges that is just as estimable and concrete as what Churchill saw.[11]

But that something remains elusive, especially at a time when globalization is having the ironic effect of encouraging both nationalism and the acquisition of nuclear arsenals from the Mediterranean to the Pacific. Our tensions with a responsible regime like China's, and even with irresponsible ones like Iran's and North Korea's, will hopefully be solved at the negotiating table. But the power that American diplomats will wield in these cases is the result not just of our economic weight, but also of the American military being deployed where it is, and the armaments and manpower it brings to bear.

Let me end with an observation by Air Force Col. Robert Wheeler, a combat pilot I met with the B-2 squadron on Guam whose résumé I will reprise because it is the kind that solid, middle-of-the-road citizens trust. He is a midwesterner with an engineering degree from the University of Wisconsin, whose post-graduate degrees include a master of arts in strategic studies from the Naval War College. He participated in several wars over the course of three administrations, Democratic and Republican, and was the senior advisor to the U.S. Mission for the Vienna-based Organization for Security and Cooperation in Europe, a job less military than diplomatic.

Wheeler told me that "decadence" is the essential condition of "a society which believes it has evolved to the point where it will never have to go to war" since, by eliminating war as a possibility, "it has nothing left to fight and sacrifice for, and thus no longer wants to make a difference." In such a situation, historical memory becomes lost, while pleasure and convenience take over as values in and of themselves. While a society should certainly never want to go to war, it should nevertheless feel the need to always be prepared for it; for to *believe* is to be willing—when necessary—to *fight*.

The United States is far from being a decadent country. We have enormous reserves of good character, in and out of the military. Americans are still willing to fight the necessary fight, so long as their leaders can speak plainly about situations that almost invariably pair limited goals with uncertain costs. Certainly, no one can blame the American public for becoming disenchanted with a war that has gone on for so long and that has been so badly handled. The question is, in what direction is our morale headed, as well as the morale of our current and future adversaries? Argue the question as we may, one thing is clear: we're fated to find out.

ACKNOWLEDGMENTS

The Atlantic Monthly continues to sustain me and run excerpts from my books. For that I am grateful to its owner, David G. Bradley, and the editorial guidance he has brought to the magazine in the person of James Bennet. I thank Cullen Murphy and Robert Messenger for their help with the manuscript, as well as Benjamin Healy, Justine Isola, Yvonne Rolzhausen, Elizabeth Shelburne, and Scott Stossel. More help came from my literary agents, Carl D. Brandt and Marianne Merola. The editorial team of Kate Medina and Robin Rolewicz at Random House was once again a distinct pleasure to work with. Thanks also go to copy editor Charlotte Gross.

The John M. Olin, Smith Richardson, and Earhart foundations were generous in their support. In particular, I want to thank James Piereson of the Olin Foundation for his encouragement of my work for two decades. Assistance also came from the Foreign Policy Research Institute in Philadelphia, specifically Harvey Sicherman, Alan Luxenberg, and Michael Noonan.

The following persons were instrumental in getting me access to people and situations that form the core of this book: Navy Capt. Matt Brown, Army Lt. Col. Ken Comer, Marine Maj. Tim Keefe, Air Force Senior Master Sgt. Charles Ramey, Navy Lt. Comdr. Jason Salata, Army Maj. Holly Silkman, and Army Lt. Col. John Silkman

Heartfelt thanks go to the crew of the USS *Benfold* during its fall and winter 2004–05 deployment to the western Pacific; to the crew of the

USS *Houston* during its spring 2005 journey from Hawaii to Guam; to the Army's 172nd Stryker Brigade Combat Team (especially the 4th Battalion of the 23rd Infantry Regiment) during its 2005–06 deployment to Iraq; to the Air Force's 25th Fighter Squadron out of Osan Air Base, South Korea; and to the 393rd Bomb Squadron out of Whiteman Air Force Base, Missouri, during its 2006 deployment to Guam.

I am also grateful to Army Maj. Romero Alonso, Navy Senior Chief Jon Annis, Navy Lt. Chuck Bell, Navy Comdr. Jeff Bender, Navy Lt. Dave Benham, Army Lt. Col. Bill Bigelow, Army Capt. Michael Blankartz, Army Maj. Don Bridgers, Navy Lt. Rob Briggs, Army Col. Bob Brown, Army Lt. Gen. John M. Brown III, Air Force Tech. Sgt. Michael Canfield, Army Lt. Col. Kevin Clark, Army Gen. John Craddock, Navy Lt. Comdr. Jeff Davis, Air Force Lt. Gen. David Deptula, Army Col. Jack Dibrell, Air Force Col. Daniel Doty, Air Force Capt. Daniel Dubois, Army Lt. Col. Scott Eaddy, Army Capt. Paul Edwards, Army Maj. Gen. Karl Eikenberry, Air Force Capt. Giovanni Estrada, Navy Adm. William Fallon, Navy Adm. Thomas B. Fargo, Air Force Tech. Sgt. James Fisher, Army Lt. Col. (Reserve) Roman Fontes, Army Maj. Kirk Gohlke, Navy Capt. Curry Graham, Marine Lt. Gen. Wallace Gregson, Army Chief Warrant Officer III Bill Gunter, Marine Gen. Michael Hagee, Air Force Master Sgt. John Hancock, Army Chief Warrant Officer IV John Haywood, Army Brig. Gen. James Hirai, Ship's Master Richard Horne, Navy Comdr. Brian Howes, Air Force Col. Alan Hunt, Navy Lt. Comdr. Bill Irwin, Air Force Capt. Victoria Keegan, Ship's Master Ken Kujala, Air Force Maj. Gen. Dennis Larson, Army 2nd Lt. Michelle Lunato, Marine Capt. Dan McSweeney, Air Force 1st Lt. Justin McVay, Army Lt. Col. Dave Markowsky, Marine Staff Sgt. Jonathan Moor, Navy Vice Adm. John Morgan, Air Force Gen. T. Michael Moseley, Army Maj. Glen Nunez, Army Chief Warrant Officer III Wilkie Pietri, Air Force Maj. Joe Puskar, Air Force Maj. Glen Roberts, Army Col. Michael Shields, Navy Capt. John Singley, Air Force Lt. Col. Jay Steuck, Marine Lt. Eric Tausch, Army Lt. Col. Scott Taylor, Army Capt. Troy Terrebonne, Army Col. Rick Thomas, Marine Chief Warrant Officer V Richard Thompson, Army Capt. Victor Torres, Air Force Gen. Charles Wald, Air Force Master Sgt. Roy Watson, Army

Maj. Tom Weaver, Navy Comdr. Clayton Wilcox, and Army Col. Tony Williams.

Another delight was traveling for six weeks with a television crew from 3BM in London, sponsored by WETA, the public television station in Washington, D.C. The companionship of Paul Lang, Vaughn Matthews, Paul Paragon, and Tim Pritchard was enthralling. For that I am grateful to Jeff Bieber, Phil Craig, and David Wilson.

Others who helped were Grenville Byford, Charles Canterbury, Tom Clements, George Cooper, Tim Dougherty, Milton Drucker, Dennis Fujii, Adam Garfinkle, Hitman Gurung, Laura D. Lucas, Kevin Lulloff, James Moriarity, Mohan Prasai, Thomas G. Reich, Satish Jung Shahi, Prem Singh, William Slape, Patricia Stigliani, James P. Thomas, Mike Vickers, and W. J. Wesley.

I completed this book while teaching at the United States Naval Academy, a deeply rewarding experience, for which I thank the Annapolis graduating class of 1960, which has sponsored my visiting professorship, and my colleagues of the political science department for their friendship and help.

Elizabeth Lockyer is the finest assistant one could hope for. I am continually blessed by my wife, Maria Cabral, and my son, Michael.

GLOSSARY

ADCAP: advanced capability.

Aegis system: U.S. Navy total weapons system that has multi-function radar capable of automatically detecting and tracking more than one hundred targets and launching guided missiles simultaneously at one hundred nautical miles.

AK-47: lightweight and compact Russian assault rifle that fires 7.62mm cartridges. One of the first assault rifles (1947), it is reliable and easy to use in the field. Also called Kalashnikov, after its designer.

Alaska barrier: twelve-foot-high reinforced concrete barrier.

ANZAC: Australian and New Zealand Army Corps.

AOR: area of responsibility. Geographical area for which a military unit has authority.

AT: anti-tank weapon.

A-team: a U.S. Army Special Forces team that operates in a remote, often hostile area with little or no supervision.

A-10 Thunderbolt: a versatile U.S. Air Force ground attack aircraft nicknamed "Warthog" because it hovers low to the ground. Highly survivable, it is used to provide close air support.

AWACS: Airborne Warning and Control System.

baffles: 120-degree cone-shaped blind spot in the water off a boat created by propeller-made white water and where sonar technicians can hear only the noise of the propeller.

battlespace: battlefield and the airspace over it.

BDU: bomb demonstration unit, or practice bomb.

Beretta: 9mm lightweight semiautomatic pistol that has been the standard U.S. Army sidearm since 1983.

berthing: living quarters for enlisted men on a vessel.

BIAP: Baghdad International Airport.

big deck carrier: a warship with a large open deck on which conventional fixed-wing aircraft can be launched and landed.

blast barrier: specially formulated reinforced-concrete barrier.

blue on blue: friendly fire.

blue utilities: Navy blue shirt or jacket.

blue water: deep water.

BMC: bosun's mate chief.

boom: projection (spar or outrigger) connecting the tail and main support structure of an airplane.

boomer: ballistic missile submarine.

bosun: deck crew chief.

Bravo: weapons specialist on a Special Forces A-team.

brevity code: code words.

B-2 Spirit: U.S. multi-role stealth bomber able to deliver conventional and nuclear weapons. Its unique design allows it to penetrate enemy airspace without being detected.

BUB: battle update brief.

BUFF: "Big Ugly Fat Fucker"—the B-52 Stratofortress, a heavy bomber first used in the Vietnam War.

CamelBak: small backpack filled with drinking water.

CAS: close air support.

CENTCOM: Central Command.

C-4: a very powerful plastic explosive that is easy to hide and difficult to detect.

chaff: material such as thin narrow metallic strips of various lengths and frequency responses launched into the air to reflect radar waves and confuse enemy radar-guided missiles so that they will lock on to it instead of real targets.

chai: Arabic word for tea.

Charlie: engineer on a Special Forces A-team.

CIC: combat information center. A bank of computer terminals.

CIWS: Close-In Weapons System. A fast-reaction gun system consisting of radars, computers, and multiple rapid-fire guns placed on a rotating gun mount on U.S. ships and submarines.

CJSOTF: Combined Joint Special Operations Task Force. Task force made up of Special Operations forces of the United States and another country or other countries.

COB: chief of the boat. A senior enlisted man on a U.S. submarine who assists and advises the commanding officer and executive officer on order and discipline of the crew.

Cobra Gold: Pacific Command's biggest annual military exercise, held in Thailand.

COE: consequences of execution.

Comrel: community relations exercise.

concertina wire: coiled barbed wire along the tops of fences and walls for deterrence.

C-130: a four-engine U.S. Air Force troop and cargo transport aircraft that can airdrop into a combat zone.

conning officer: naval officer who is responsible for navigation.

CSAR: combat search and rescue.

CSL: cooperative security location. An austere forward operating base.

CSO: combat systems officer.

DCU: desert camouflage uniform.

deconflict: the separation of friendly aircraft in an attack so that they do not interfere with or fire at one another.

defilade: protection from hostile observation and fire provided by a hill, ridge, bank, or other natural barrier.

degaussing: see magnetic silencing.

Delta barrier: retractable barrier at entrances and exits that can withstand being crashed into.

Delta Force: the elite U.S. Army outfit of Special Operations Command.

desertification: the process by which an area becomes a desert.

DMPI: desired mean point of impact.

DMZ: demilitarized zone.

DOD: Department of Defense.

Dragonov: Russian-made sniper rifle.

draw: a drainageway having a shallow bed.

EAB: emergency air breather. A sock-like mask with a filter and tube that snaps into one of the oxygen manifolds on a submarine.

18 Delta: U.S. Army Special Forces medic.

elevon: a control surface on an airplane that functions as an elevator and an aileron (the movable flap on the wing that controls the plane's roll and banking).

ESM: electronic surveillance measure such as monitoring enemy radar.

EUCOM: European Command.

FAC: forward air controller. An officer at a forward ground or air position who controls aircraft in close air support of ground troops.

fairlead: a device such as a pulley, hook, or ring to guide a ship's line, rope, or cable around something, keep something out of the way, or prevent vibration or chafing.

FBCB2: Force Battle Command for Brigade and Battalion. The computer system on a Stryker.

FCS: fire control system—killing or intercepting an incoming missile from a rogue state.

FOB: forward operating or operations base. In Special Operations, a base established in a friendly territory to extend command and control of communications, or to provide support for training and tactical operations.

Force Recon: Force Reconnaissance. Elite Marine unit.

forward operating or **operations base:** see FOB.

full bell: full speed.

GPS: global positioning system. Navigational system that uses satellite signals to fix the location of a radio receiver.

Green Zone: see IZ.

grunt: noncommissioned or enlisted combat infantryman.

GWOT: Global War on Terrorism.

Harpoon Launcher: ship-to-ship missile launched from a canister.

haversack: shoulder bag similar to a knapsack.

havildar: noncommissioned officer in the army of British India equivalent to a sergeant.

Hellfire missile: Helicopter-launched fire-and-forget. U.S. air-to-ground laser-guided missile used by helicopters against heavily armored vehicles from greater distances than were possible before.

HESCO baskets: large wire-mesh baskets that are filled with sandbags to create barriers.

high-and-tight: a buzz cut.

HIT: human intelligence team.

HUD: heads-up display—information a pilot sees on his computer screen.

Humvee: U.S. Army all-purpose four-wheel-drive vehicle.

IED: improvised explosive device, such as a roadside bomb.

IMT: individual movement tactics—that is, buddy teams advancing in tandem despite live fire so no one accidentally gets hit.

indigs: indigenous troops in a given country.

IP: Iraqi police.

IZ: International Zone in Baghdad, the nerve center of the U.S. military occupation. Also called Green Zone.

JCET: Joint Combined Exercise for Training.

JDAM: Joint Direct Attack Munition. A massive GPS-guided air-to-ground bomb.

jingle truck: a four-wheel-drive truck built for rugged terrain, usually adorned with colorful stickers and chimes, and garishly painted.

JPAC: Joint POW/MIA Accounting Command, for locating MIAs, etc.

JSOTF: Joint Special Operations Task Force. It is composed of Special Operations units from more than one service to carry out a specific special operation or special operations in support of a campaign.

JTAC: joint terminal attack controller. Directs action of combat aircraft engaged in close air support and other offensive air operations.

JUSMAG: Joint United States Military Assistance Group. Provides military training and security assistance to other countries.

Kalashnikov: see AK-47.

KC-10 Extender: tanker and cargo aircraft that provides increased mobility for U.S. forces in air-to-air refueling.

Kevlar: strong, lightweight fiber used for protective apparel, including helmets. It is flexible and comfortable.

KFR: Kim Family Regime (North Korea).

KISS: keep it simple, stupid.

k-loader: truck that carries cargo to and from the cargo ramp of a plane or dock.

kukri: short curved knife with a broad blade used by Gurkhas.

kurta: loose shirt falling above or below the knee that is worn in Nepal and neighboring countries by men and women.

LAW: 66mm light anti-tank weapon.

layer depth: depth at which submarines operate, several hundred feet below the surface layer, where cooler temperatures and greater water pressure optimize the movement of sound waves.

LCC: last place of cover and concealment.

leatherneck: marine, from the protective leather collar that was once part of the uniform.

LED: light-emitting diode. A semiconductor diode that emits light when current is conducted through it. It is used in electronic equipment to display readings.

LFE: large force exercise.

log officer: logistics officer.

magnetic silencing: a process of reducing a boat's magnetic field by running electronic coils, permanent magnets, or electric currents through it so that it cannot be threatened by magnetic mines. Also called degaussing.

MA1: first class chief master-at-arms.

Makarov pistol: 9mm service sidearm of the Soviet Union during the Cold War that is compact and easy to use and maintain.

MARFORPAC: Marine Forces, Pacific.

MBITR: multi-band inter-team radio.

MEB: Marine Expeditionary Brigade. Consists of a reinforced infantry regiment, aircraft group, and service support. Larger than MEU.

MEDCAP: medical civic action program. Free medical care for local people in the area where it is set up.

MEF: Marine Expeditionary Force. Largest unit of marines sent overseas, about forty thousand.

MEU: Marine Expeditionary Unit. Smaller configuration in which marines usually deploy. .

M-4: light, compact 5.56mm assault rifle used by some U.S. Army and Special Operations units. It can be operated in close quarters.

mil: sight setting in a pilot's display.

MOD: maximum operating depth of a submarine.

MOG: maximum on ground space (for aircraft).

M1A1: Abrams tank—the main U.S. Army battle tank. Provides mobile fire for armored divisions. Also used by the Marines.

MOUT: military operations in urban terrain.

MPS: maritime pre-positioning ship. Ship with a civilian crew that has pre-positioned equipment and a month's supplies to support three MEBs.

MRE: meal ready to eat.

M-16: U.S. Army 5.56mm assault rifle, lightweight and easy to use.

MWR: Morale, Welfare, and Recreation.

NCO: noncommissioned officer.

NGO: nongovernmental organization.

NORTHCOM: Northern Command.

OEF: see Operation Enduring Freedom.

officer of the deck: naval officer given charge of a vessel by the commanding officer for an assigned period.

OGA: other government agency.

OIF: see Operation Iraqi Freedom.

OL: operating location.

Operation Enduring Freedom: U.S. military response, primarily in Afghanistan, to September 11, 2001, attacks.

Operation Iraqi Freedom–1: U.S. invasion of Iraq in 2003.

Operation Iraqi Freedom–2: U.S. military operations in Iraq since 2004.

OPSEC: operations security.

PACAF: Pacific Air Forces.

PACOM: Pacific Command.

pallet: a flat platform on an aircraft used to facilitate loading and unloading.

pelican hook: hinged hook, like a pelican's bill, that opens and closes, and is used on a ship to grasp and release.

perisher: related to periscope use.

pillbox: a small, low concrete emplacement for machine guns and anti-tank weapons.

pirogue: a canoe made by hollowing out and shaping a large log.

PMI: primary marksmanship instructor.

pop: of an airplane, steep emergence from low altitude and roll out to the other side of a barrier to hit the enemy by surprise.

Predator: small, unmanned aerial vehicle, operated by remote control, that can be in the air up to twenty-four hours. It is sometimes armed with laser-guided anti-tank missiles to kill targeted individuals.

p-way: passageway on a vessel.

QMC: quartermaster chief.

QRF: quick reaction force.

quartermaster chief: a petty officer responsible for a ship's helm and its navigating apparatus.

rack: U.S. Navy term for bunk.

RAMOD: of a submarine, to reach and maintain ordered depth.

Red Flag: principal large force exercise of the U.S. Air Force.

rhino: prison wagon retrofitted with heavy armor for use in Baghdad.

ROE: rules of engagement.

ROK: Republic of Korea (South Korea).

ropeyarns: running errands on a ship.

RPG: rocket-propelled grenade.

RTN: Royal Thai Navy.

SAC: Strategic Air Command. U.S. Air Force command responsible for U.S. bombers and the ballistic missile nuclear arsenal during the Cold War (1946–92).

Sahel: a belt of savannah and scrub south of the Sahara Desert.

SAM: Soviet-made surface-to-air missile. See SA-2.

SARNEG: search-and-rescue number encryption grid. It enables a downed pilot to send his GPS coordinates in code without giving away his location.

SA-2: the most widely used surface-to-air defense missile. It was developed by the Soviet Union in 1959.

savannah: a plain of coarse grasslands and scattered trees in a tropical or subtropical area of seasonal rainfall.

SAW: squad automatic weapon. A lightweight, portable machine gun.

screw: propeller on a submarine.

Seabee: member of a Navy construction battalion who builds land facilities in combat zones.

SEAL: commando team of the U.S. Navy. Acronym for "sea, air, land."

SF: Special Forces. Highly trained branch of the U.S. Army that specializes in unconventional warfare. Popularly called Green Berets, though they don't often refer to themselves as such.

shack: to bomb.

side boy: enlisted seaman who stands at the gangway as a sign of respect to a visitor entering or leaving a vessel.

SM: standard missile.

smart: equipped with its own electronic guidance system so it can fine-tune.

SOCOM: Special Operations Command.

SOF: Special Operations Forces.

Special Forces: see SF.

SSBN: sub-surface ballistic nuclear submarine.

SSN: sub-surface nuclear submarine.

Stryker: U.S. Army eight-wheeled light-armored vehicle with an MK-19 grenade launcher and a .50-caliber machine gun that can transport eleven soldiers at sixty miles an hour for 330 miles without refueling.

STS: Sonar Technician Submarines.

TAO: tactical actions officer.

TBS: The Basic School. The Marines' officer school in Quantico, Virginia.

TCP: traffic control point.

TDA: target designation area.

tender: ship that services another vessel.

thermocline: layer in the ocean or other large body of water where the temperature decreases rapidly with depth.

thermoluminescent dosimetry: measurement of radiation levels in the body using a heated crystal that emits light.

TIC: troops in contact.

TM: Torpedoman.

TOC: tactical operations center. Command post where staff direct combat and support operations.

topi: originally from India, a lightweight, insulated, brimmed helmet made of pith of cork, worn as a sunhat.

triple-A: anti-aircraft artillery.

TTFACORB: targets, threats, friendlies, artillery, clearance, ordnance, restrictions, battle damage.

UAV: unmanned aerial vehicle.

Un-Rep: in the U.S. Navy, an underway replenishment—the Navy equivalent of air-to-air refueling.

USAID: United States Agency for International Development.

USARAK: U.S. Army, Alaska.

USFK: U.S. Forces, Korea.

USNS: U.S. Naval Ship. Designation for U.S. Navy ships with crews of both sailors and civilian merchant seamen.

VETCAP: veterinary civil action program. Free veterinary care for livestock and pets in the area where it is set up.

VLS: vertical launch system. A missile-firing system used aboard submarines and surface ships that enables them to carry more missiles than they would otherwise.

wadi: in arid regions of Southwest Asia, a streambed that is dry except during the rainy season.

Warthog: see A-10 Thunderbolt.

wattle: pole interwoven with thin branches or twigs and thatch, used in building huts.

weaps: weapons officer.

wet transmission checks: checks on the circuitry of torpedoes while they are in tubes pressurized with seawater.

WMD: weapons of mass destruction.

XO: executive officer, second-in-command.

zeriba: in Africa, an enclosure made of thornbushes for protection.

zero: to adjust a firearm so that it will be in range of a target.

ZULU time: military time, numbered in hours to twenty-four and expressed in four digits—for example, 2300 is 11 p.m. Equivalent to Greenwich mean time not adjusted to daylight saving.

NOTES

PROLOGUE—THE BETTER THEY FOUGHT, THE BETTER RELIEF WORKERS THEY BECAME

1. Robert D. Kaplan, *Imperial Grunts: The American Military on the Ground* (New York: Random House, 2005).
2. Samuel H. Preston and Emily Buzzell, "Service in Iraq: Just How Risky?" *The Washington Post,* Aug. 26, 2006.
3. Gen. Charles C. Krulak, "Cultivating Intuitive Decisionmaking," *Marine Corps Gazette,* May 1999.
4. Fernando Pessoa, *The Book of Disquiet,* trans. Margaret Jull Costa (1982; New York: Serpent's Tail, 1991).
5. Everett Carl Dolman, *The Warrior State: How Military Organization Structures Politics* (New York: Palgrave Macmillan, 2004), p. 160.
6. Leon Uris, *Battle Cry* (New York: Putnam, 1953), p. 3.

CHAPTER 1—AMERICA'S AFRICAN RIFLES

1. Tacitus, *The Annals of Imperial Rome,* trans. Michael Grant (London: Penguin, 1956), ch. 15.
2. Herodotus, *The Histories,* trans. Aubrey de Selincourt (Middlesex, Eng.: Penguin, 1954), 2: 32.
3. Douglas Porch, *The Conquest of the Sahara* (New York: Knopf, 1984), p. 65.
4. See Zachary Karabell's review of *The Sword and the Cross* by Fergus Fleming, *Los Angeles Times Book Review,* May 30, 2004.
5. See Adam M. Smith, "At Last unto the Breach: The Logic of a U.S. Military Command in West Africa," *Orbis,* Spring 2004.

6. See Craig S. Smith, "U.S. Training African Forces to Uproot Terrorists," *The New York Times,* May 11, 2004; and Brian Love, "Libyans Find al-Qaeda-linked Militant Camp," Reuters, July 5, 2004.

7. See Olivier Roy, *The Failure of Political Islam* (Cambridge, Mass.: Harvard University Press, 1994), pp. 31–35.

8. National Intelligence Council, *Global Trends: 2015* (Washington, D.C.: U.S. Government Printing Office, 2002). See also A. Smith, "At Last unto the Breach."

9. See Lt. Col. Dave Grossman, *On Killing: The Psychological Cost of Learning to Kill in War and Society* (Boston: Little, Brown, 1995), esp. p. 256.

10. Richard Tregaskis, *Guadalcanal Diary* (New York: Random House, 1943); Bing West, *The Village* (New York: Pocket Books, 1972); and Harold G. Moore and Joseph L. Galloway, *We Were Soldiers Once . . . and Young: Ia Drang, the Battle That Changed the War in Vietnam* (New York: Random House, 1992).

11. Robert Sherrod, *Tarawa: The Story of a Battle* (New York: Duell, Sloan and Pearce, 1944), pp. 83, 109.

12. Ibid., pp. 147–51.

13. Malcolm Cowley, Introduction to *The Portable Faulkner* (New York: Viking, 1946).

CHAPTER 2—ALASKA TO THAILAND: THE ORGANIZING PRINCIPLE OF THE EARTH'S SURFACE

1. See Franklin Walker's Foreword to Jack London, *The Call of the Wild* (New York: New American Library, 1960).

2. Robert W. Service, "The Shooting of Dan McGrew," in *Songs of a Sourdough* (New York: Putnam, 1907).

3. Jack London, "Eight Factors of Literary Success" (1917); reprinted in *The Portable Jack London,* ed. Earle Labor (New York: Penguin, 1994).

4. Josef Joffe, "Hubs, Spokes, and Public Goods," *The National Interest,* Fall 2002.

5. Henry Kissinger, *Diplomacy* (New York: Simon & Schuster, 1994), pp. 122, 125, 127–28.

6. Ralph Peters, *New Glory: Expanding America's Global Supremacy* (New York: Sentinel, 2005), p. 267.

7. Hendrik Van Loon, *The Fall of the Dutch Republic* (Boston: Houghton Mifflin, 1924), p. 5; Otto Hintze, *The Historical Essays* (New York: Oxford University Press, 1975), pp. 213–15; Everett Carl Dolman, *The Warrior State: How Military Organization Structures Politics* (New York: Palgrave Macmillan, 2004), pp. 9, 85.

8. Eric Grove, *The Future of Sea Power* (Annapolis, Md.: Naval Institute Press, 1990), p. 187.

9. H. P. Willmott, *Sea Warfare: Weapons, Tactics and Strategy* (New York: Hippocrene, 1981), pp. 68–69.

10. Ibid., p. 87.

11. Grove, *Future of Sea Power,* pp. 47, 138, 139.

12. See John Henderson and Benjamin Reilly, "Dragon in Paradise: China's Rising Star in Oceania," *The National Interest,* Summer 2003.

13. See R. R. Keene, "Guam, 'Wake Up and Die, Marine!' " *Leatherneck,* July 2004.

14. William Manchester, *Goodbye, Darkness: A Memoir of the Pacific War* (Boston: Little, Brown, 1979), pp. 385–86.

15. Victor Davis Hanson, *Ripples of Battle: How Wars of the Past Still Determine How We Fight, How We Live, and How We Think* (New York: Doubleday, 2003), pp. 31–32.

16. Manchester, *Goodbye, Darkness,* pp. 359–60.

17. See Robert Burns, "Pentagon to Close 35 Percent of Overseas Bases: 'Forward Operating Sites' to Replace Cold War–Era Bases," Associated Press, Sept. 23, 2004.

18. See Robert D. Kaplan, *Imperial Grunts: The American Military on the Ground* (New York: Random House, 2005), ch. 4.

CHAPTER 3—A CIVILIZATION UNTO ITSELF,
SWISHING THROUGH THE CRUSHING VOID

1. Owen Harries, "Harry Lee's Story," *The National Interest,* June 1999. See, too, Lee's memoir: Lee Kuan Yew, *The Singapore Story* (New York: Harper-Collins, 1998) and its updated edition, *From Third World to First: The Singapore Story, 1965–2000* (New York: HarperCollins, 2000).

2. Maria A. Ressa, *Seeds of Terror: An Eyewitness Account of al-Qaeda's Newest Center in Southeast Asia* (New York: Free Press, 2003), p. 150.

3. Back jacket flap, Lee Kuan Yew, *The Singapore Story* (Singapore: Singapore Press Holdings, 1998).

4. *Lord Jim* (1900); *Nostromo: A Tale of the Seaboard* (1904).

5. Michael Vlahos, "Culture's Mask: War and Change After Iraq," Johns Hopkins University, Applied Physics Laboratory, Laurel, Md., 2004.

6. Quoted in *The Green Wave and the Navy: The History of the USS* Benfold (Wentachee, Wash.: Redrosebush, 1999), p. 262.

7. From brochure prepared by Charles R. Anderson of the U.S. Army Center of Military History.

8. See James D. Hornfischer, *The Last Stand of the Tin Can Sailors: The Extraordinary World War II Story of the U.S. Navy's Finest Hour* (New York: Bantam, 2004).

CHAPTER 4—GEEKS WITH TATTOOS:
THE MOST DRIVEN MEN I HAVE EVER KNOWN

1. See Robert D. Kaplan, *Imperial Grunts: The American Military on the Ground* (New York: Random House, 2005), ch. 8.
2. Jack Spencer, "Congress Should Restore Funding to Refuel Attack Submarines," Heritage Foundation, Mar. 30, 2005.
3. Sherry Sontag and Christopher Drew, with Annette Lawrence Drew, *Blind Man's Bluff: The Untold Story of American Submarine Espionage* (New York: PublicAffairs, 1998), pp. xv, xviii, 37–38, 251.
4. Ibid., p. 379; Spencer, "Congress Should Restore Funding."
5. David Lague, "China Beefs Up Undersea Force," *The Wall Street Journal, Asia,* Nov. 29, 2004.
6. Jules Verne, *Twenty Thousand Leagues Under the Sea,* trans. William Butcher (1870; New York: Oxford University Press, 1998), p. 68.
7. Ibid., p. 161, and Butcher's Introduction, p. xxii, in which he refers to the interpretation of Verne by the French scholar Roland Barthes.
8. Jack London, *The Sea Wolf* (1904; New York: Bantam, 1960), p. 68.
9. Ibid., p. 17.

CHAPTER 5—NATO'S RAGGED SOUTHERN EDGE

1. Richard F. Burton, *Wanderings in West Africa* (1863; Mineola, N.Y.: Dover, 1991), pp. 135–36.
2. See William Langewiesche, *Sahara Unveiled: A Journey Across the Desert* (New York: Pantheon, 1996), pp. 129–31.
3. Alistair Horne, *A Savage War of Peace: Algeria, 1954–1962* (London: Macmillan, 1977), p. 44.

CHAPTER 6—THE GURKHA STANDARD

1. Samuel Johnson, *A Journey to the Western Islands of Scotland* (1775; Edinburgh: Canongate, 1996), p. 81.
2. Robert Gersony, "Sowing the Wind: History and Dynamics of the Maoist Revolt in Nepal's Rapti Hills," submitted to Mercy Corps International in 2003, pp. 71–72. See, too, Thomas A. Marks, "Insurgency in Nepal," U.S. Army War College, Carlisle Barracks, Pa., 2003.
3. See Robert D. Kaplan, *Imperial Grunts: The American Military on the Ground* (New York: Random House, 2005).
4. For some of the material in these paragraphs, see Byron Farwell, *The Gurkhas* (New York: Norton, 1984, 1990), pp. 12, 14, 28–29, 77–78.

5. A. E. Housman, "Epitaph on an Army of Mercenaries," 1914.

6. See, too, John Masters, *Bugles and a Tiger* (New York: Viking, 1956).

7. Farwell, *The Gurkhas,* pp. 52, 58, 84.

8. See Kaplan, *Imperial Grunts,* ch. 3.

9. J. P. Cross, *The Call of Nepal* (Kathmandu: Bibliotheca Himalayica, 1996), p. 14.

10. J. P. Cross, *Jungle Warfare* (Dehra Dun, India: English Book Depot, 1992), p. 42.

CHAPTER 7—TRIBAL MAFIAS

1. See Robert D. Kaplan, *Imperial Grunts: The American Military on the Ground* (New York: Random House, 2005), ch. 8.

2. Samuel Huntington, *Political Order in Changing Societies* (New Haven, Conn.: Yale University Press, 1968).

3. William Manchester, *Goodbye, Darkness: A Memoir of the Pacific War* (Boston: Little, Brown, 1979), pp. 374, 391–95.

4. Brig. Gen. James E. Shelton (Ret.), *The Beast Was Out There: The 28th Infantry Black Lions and the Battle of Ong Thanh, Vietnam, October 1967* (Chicago: Cantigny Military History Series, 2002), p. 217.

5. LexisNexis as of June 25, 2005. See, too, *The American Enterprise,* September 2005, p. 13.

CHAPTER 8—A DEPENDABLE BLUE-COLLAR PLANE

1. John J. Tkacik, Jr., and Dana Dillon, "China's Quest for Asia," *Policy Review,* December 2005/January 2006.

2. Ibid.

3. Robert D. Kaplan, *Imperial Grunts: The American Military on the Ground* (New York: Random House, 2005), ch. 5.

4. Colin S. Gray, *Another Bloody Century: Future Warfare* (London: Weidenfeld & Nicolson, 2005), pp. 119, 46; Everett Carl Dolman, *The Warrior State: How Military Organization Structures Politics* (New York: Palgrave Macmillan, 2004), p. 37.

5. See Kaplan, *Imperial Grunts,* ch. 2.

6. Tkacik and Dillon, "China's Quest for Asia."

CHAPTER 9—TIMBUKTU, SOVIET STONEHENGE, AND GNARLY-ASS JUNGLE

1. See Robert D. Kaplan, *Imperial Grunts: The American Military on the Ground* (New York: Random House, 2005), "Prologue: Injun Country."

2. Ibid., ch. 4.

3. Ibid.

4. Ibid.

5. Ibid., ch. 2.

CHAPTER 11—THE MORBID TYRANNY OUT OF ANTIQUITY

1. Robert Killebrew, "A Different Model for Iraq: Forget the Vietnam Analogies; Korea's a Better Model," *The Washington Post,* Apr. 9, 2006.

2. Peter Beck, director, North East Asia Project, International Crisis Group, interview, July 3, 2006, Seoul.

3. Bernard DeVoto, *The Year of Decision: 1846* (Boston: Little, Brown, 1943).

AFTERWORD—THE NON-WARRIOR DEMOCRACY

1. See *The Book of War,* comprising Sun-Tzu's *The Art of Warfare,* trans. Roger T. Ames (1993), and Karl von Clausewitz's *On War,* trans. O. J. Matthijs Jolles (1943) (New York: Modern Library, 2000). See, too, Robert D. Kaplan, *Warrior Politics: Why Leadership Demands a Pagan Ethos* (New York: Random House, 2001), ch. 4.

2. Ralph Peters, "The Counterrevolution in Military Affairs," *The Weekly Standard,* Feb. 6, 2006.

3. Fyodor Dostoevsky, *The Brothers Karamazov,* trans. Constance Garnett (1879–80; New York: Modern Library, 1996).

4. Paul Bracken, *Fire in the East: The Rise of Asian Military Power and the Second Nuclear Age* (New York: HarperCollins, 1999), p. 111.

5. Ibid., pp. 112, 136, 138.

6. Marine Maj. Gen. Michael R. Lehnert recited these and other statistics in a speech before the San Diego Chamber of Commerce, June 26, 2006.

7. Ibid.

8. James L. Stokesbury, *A Short History of the Korean War* (New York: Morrow, 1988), p. 157.

9. Colin S. Gray, *Another Bloody Century: Future Warfare* (London: Weidenfeld & Nicolson, 2005), p. 34.

10. Bracken, *Fire in the East,* pp. 26–29.

11. Robert D. Kaplan, "Supremacy by Stealth," *The Atlantic Monthly,* July/August 2003.

INDEX

ALSO BY ROBERT D. KAPLAN

IMPERIAL GRUNTS

On the Ground with the American Military, from Mongolia to the Philippines to Iraq and Beyond

Plunging deep into the midst of some of the hottest conflicts on the globe, Robert D. Kaplan takes us through mud and jungle, desert and dirt to the men and women on the ground who are leading the charge against threats to American security. These soldiers, fighting in thick Colombian jungles or on dusty Afghani plains, are the forefront of the new American foreign policy, a policy being implemented one soldier at a time. As Kaplan brings us inside their thoughts, feelings, and operations, these modern grunts provide insight and understanding into the War on Terror, bringing the war, which sometimes seems so distant, vividly to life.

Military History/Current Affairs/978-1-4000-3457-4

ALSO AVAILABLE

The Coming Anarchy, 978-0-375-70759-9
Eastward to Tartary, 978-0-375-70576-2
An Empire Wilderness, 978-0-679-77687-1
The Ends of the Earth, 978-0-679-75123-6
Mediterranean Winter, 978-0-375-71433-7
Soldiers of God, 978-1-4000-3025-5
Surrender or Starve, 978-1-4000-3452-9
Warrior Politics, 978-0-375-72627-9

VINTAGE BOOKS
Available at your local bookstore, or
visit www.randomhouse.com